MW00330905

# For every kind of computer user, there is a SYBEX book.

All computer users learn in their own way. Some need straightforward and methodical explanations. Others are just too busy for this approach. But no matter what camp you fall into, SYBEX has a book that can help you get the most out of your computer and computer software while learning at your own pace.

Beginners generally want to start at the beginning. The **ABC's** series, with its step-by-step lessons in plain language, helps you build basic skills quickly. For a more personal approach, there are the **Murphy's Laws** and **Guided Tour** series. Or you might try our **Quick & Easy** series, the friendly, full-color guide, with **Quick & Easy References**, the companion pocket references to the **Quick & Easy** series. If you learn best by doing rather than reading, find out about the **Hands-On Live!** series, our new interactive multimedia training software. For hardware novices, there's the **Your First** series.

The **Mastering** and **Understanding** series will tell you everything you need to know about a subject. They're perfect for intermediate and advanced computer users, yet they don't make the mistake of leaving beginners behind. Add one of our **Instant References** and you'll have more than enough help when you have a question about your computer software. You may even want to check into our **Secrets & Solutions** series.

SYBEX even offers special titles on subjects that don't neatly fit a category—like our **Pushbutton Guides**, our books about the Internet, our books about the latest computer games, and a wide range of books for Macintosh computers and software.

SYBEX books are written by authors who are experts in their subjects. In fact, many make their living as professionals, consultants, or teachers in the field of computer software. And their manuscripts are thoroughly reviewed by our technical and editorial staff for accuracy and ease-of-use.

So when you want answers about computers or any popular software package, just help yourself to SYBEX.

## For a complete catalog of our publications, please write:

SYBEX Inc.
2021 Challenger Drive
Alameda, CA 94501
Tel: (510) 523-8233/(800) 227-2346 Telex: 336311
Fax: (510) 523-2373

SYBEX is committed to using natural resources wisely to preserve and improve our environment. As a leader in the computer book publishing industry, we are aware that over 40% of America's solid waste is paper. This is why we have been printing the text of books like this one on recycled paper since 1982.

This year our use of recycled paper will result in the saving of more than 15,300 trees. We will lower air pollution effluents by 54,000 pounds, save 6,300,000 gallons of water, and reduce landfill by 2,700 cubic yards.

In choosing a SYBEX book you are not only making a choice for the best in skills and information, you are also choosing to enhance the quality of life for all of us.

# TALK TO SYBEX ONLINE.

# The
# COMPACT GUIDE to
# LOTUS® SMARTSUITE®

## SANDRA E. EDDY

SYBEX®   San Francisco ▪ Paris ▪ Düsseldorf ▪ Soest

Acquisitions Editors: Joanne Cuthbertson, Kristine Plachy
Developmental Editors: Sarah Wadsworth, Richard Mills
Editors: Michelle Nance, Michelle Khazai
Technical Editor: Adebisi Oladipupo
Book Designer: Suzanne Albertson
Production Artists: Suzanne Albertson, Lucie Zivny
Screen Graphics: Aldo Bermudez, John Corrigan, Frank Seidel
Desktop Publishing Specialist: Alissa Feinberg
Production Assistants: Emily Smith, Kristin Amlie, Kate Westrich
Indexer: Matthew Spence
Cover Designer and Illustrator: Joanna Kim Gladden

Screen reproductions produced with Collage Plus.

Collage Plus is a trademark of Inner Media Inc.

SYBEX is a registered trademark of SYBEX Inc.

SmartSuite is a registered trademark of Lotus Development Corporation.

Library of Congress Card Number: 94-65380
ISBN: 0-7821-1484-9

Manufactured in the United States of America
10 9 8 7 6 5 4 3 2

*For Andy, who got me into this*

# Acknowledgments

Writing a computer book is not a lonely pursuit. Although the author may be working in an ivory tower in some remote spot, there is friendly support from the editors and the production team from the first chapter to the last appendix and beyond. In this section, I'd like to thank all the people whose efforts have been so important.

I especially thank the people at SYBEX for all their help and encouragement. Special thanks go to Developmental Editor Sarah Wadsworth and Editor Michelle Nance. Thanks also to Suzanne Albertson, Kristin Amlie, Aldo Bermudez, John Corrigan, Alissa Feinberg, Frank Seidel, Emily Smith, and Lucie Zivny.

For accuracy and attention in reviewing every page and figure, a special thank you to the Technical Editor, Adebisi Oladipupo.

For their continued encouragement, my family and friends—you know who you are.

For their special and continuing contributions—Indy, Toni, and Bart. In memory of Ciera, Flash, and other Comstock friends.

Sandra E. Eddy

73510,3154 (CompuServe)

# Contents
## at a Glance

# Contents

# Introduction

Welcome to *The Compact Guide to Lotus SmartSuite*, a comprehensive guide to the powerful Lotus SmartSuite package and its individual components: 1-2-3, Ami Pro, Approach, Freelance Graphics, and Organizer. Whether you are using one, two, or all five SmartSuite applications, this book will help to answer most of your questions—from how to start and use one of the five award-winning SmartSuite applications individually to how to work with two or more applications to accomplish a task.

The primary advantage of SmartSuite is that the diverse applications work together so well. For example, you can create an Organizer address book and import some or all of its data into a form letter designed in Approach or Ami Pro to create a mailing to go out to all your friends or clients. You can create an Approach database using data you've compiled with 1-2-3. When you prepare a Freelance Graphics presentation, you can write its outline in Ami Pro, import 1-2-3 ranges or charts or Approach data to build your case, and then top it all off with a logo you created in Ami Pro. You can then import parts of your presentation into an Ami Pro report.

1-2-3, Ami Pro, Approach, and Freelance Graphics all provide you with *SmartMasters*, templates that help you get started with any project. For example, in 1-2-3 you can find SmartMasters for time sheets, invoices, home budgets, and complete sets of financial statements. The Freelance Graphics SmartMasters include over 100 professionally designed backgrounds for presentations and 11 different page designs you can use as a basis for your own projects. You'll never have to stare at a blank computer screen again!

All five SmartSuite applications also have *SmartIcons*, toolbar buttons that allow you to perform common tasks. As you jump from application to application, you'll find many SmartIcons that look and behave the same throughout SmartSuite. For example, to open any file—regardless of the SmartSuite application—click on the Open SmartIcon; to print, click on the Print SmartIcon. Before you read another word, take a look at the colorful SmartIcons poster bound inside the back cover of this book. It illustrates and describes 150 of the most common SmartIcons. Put it up on your wall immediately!

The *SmartCenter* feature allows you to start any SmartSuite application (or any application that you wish to add to the SmartCenter) by clicking on an icon palette that's always on your computer screen.

You've never gotten as much Help support as you'll get in SmartSuite. Each SmartSuite application provides its own full-featured Help facility. You can run tutorials in 1-2-3, Ami Pro, Approach, and Freelance Graphics. When viewing any dialog box, you can click on the question-mark icon or press F1 to get Help about that dialog box. In any SmartSuite application, just place the mouse pointer on a SmartIcon and you'll see a "bubble" with a description of what that icon does. Clicking on the SuiteAnswers icon on the SmartCenter icon palette tells you how to use one SmartSuite application with another. You can even view movies that show you how to use common SmartSuite functions.

# Who Should Read This Book

This book is designed for people who are familiar with Windows but may be new to one or more of the SmartSuite applications. If you are a SmartSuite or Windows novice, be sure to review Chapters 1, 2, and 3, where you'll learn the basics.

Although this book assumes that you have some knowledge of Windows, you can always refer to Appendix B for information about the Windows features that will help you run SmartSuite applications more efficiently.

# How to Use This Book

This book is a combination reference and tutorial. Throughout the book, you'll find useful tables, illustrations, sets of procedures to guide you through SmartSuite applications. You'll also find these special features:

**Working Together Sidebars**     teach you how to use a particular Smart-Suite feature or supplementary Lotus application, or how to get two applications to work together to complete a task.

**Notes**     emphasize important information about a topic.

**Tips**     provide shortcuts and easy-to-use methods for performing functions.

**Warnings**     inform you about potential problems and pitfalls.

**Pushbutton Poster**     illustrates and describes 150 of SmartSuite's SmartIcons in full color.

You can use this book along with your SmartSuite manuals and SmartSuite Help to get a comprehensive picture of SmartSuite features and functions. The book is arranged in the following six parts.

**Part One: Organizing Your Business with Lotus SmartSuite**   Part One introduces you to each SmartSuite application and to the Working Together Bonus Pack. It provides information about the elements of application windows and teaches you the basics of working with the applications. It also covers launching multiple SmartSuite applications, viewing two applications at the same time, and moving between applications.

**Part Two: Mastering Finances with 1-2-3**   Part Two introduces spreadsheets and teaches you how to plan and create them. It also provides information about editing and formatting spreadsheets in 1-2-3—from an individual cell to the entire spreadsheet.

**Part Three: Processing Words with Ami Pro**   Part Three teaches you to work with the Ami Pro word processor, create a document, and use the thesaurus and the grammar checker. You'll learn to format text, select print options, and create and modify a picture.

**Part Four: Organizing Information with Approach**   Part Four introduces databases and teaches you how to plan and create them using Approach. You'll learn how to design a form, define fields and field types, and create a report.

**Part Five: Presenting Information with Freelance Graphics**   Part Five teaches you to plan, create, and edit a presentation with Freelance Graphics. You'll learn how to import and add tables and charts, insert symbols and pictures on a presentation page, run and edit screen shows, and add special effects to a screen show.

**Part Six: Managing Time with Organizer**  Part Six covers using the Organizer Calendar, To Do, Address, Notepad, Anniversary, and Calls sections, and shows you how to select print options.

**Appendices**  There are four appendices that provide detailed information about installing SmartSuite, using Windows, customizing your environment in all five SmartSuite applications, and using SmartSuite shortcut keys and key combinations.

# Conventions Used in This Book

This book provides the following keyboard and text conventions.

## Keyboard Conventions

Windows applications such as 1-2-3, Ami Pro, Approach, Freelance Graphics, and Organizer support both the mouse and the keyboard. This book follows these keyboard conventions:

**Key Combinations**  Press a *key combination* (pressing two or three keys simultaneously) as a shortcut to execute commands or perform actions. In this book, key combinations are shown as two or three keys, each separated by a plus sign (+); an example would be Ctrl+P. Many, but not all, commands have key combinations.

To execute a key combination, press and hold down the first key, then press the next key or keys.

**Issuing Menu Commands**  You can also issue commands by pressing the underlined keys in menus and commands. (See Appendix B for information about using underlined letters within dialog boxes.) To select a menu, press the Alt key. Then press the underlined letter for the menu that you want.

In this book, the menu-command selections are represented by this combination of text and symbol: File ➤ Open. This sequence tells you to choose File from the menu bar; then select the Open command from the displayed File menu.

Occasionally, you'll see a sequence consisting of a menu, a command, and a subcommand. For example, if you see Tools ➤ Macros ➤ Playback, you'll choose Tools from the menu bar, choose the Macros command, which opens a cascading menu, and then choose the Playback command.

## Text Conventions

In this book, *italicized* text represents both variables (for example, a file name or value to be typed) and new terms.

This font

```
=123 Main Street
123 Main Street
```

indicates statements that you type or emulate when creating your own statements.

**Boldfaced** text generally indicates text that you should key in.

# *Organizing Your Business with Lotus SmartSuite*

Part One introduces you to Lotus SmartSuite, its individual applications, and how they work together. In this part, you'll learn about features common to all SmartSuite applications—how to start and exit an application; how to view, edit, and format files; and how to get help. You'll discover how you can use the Windows Clipboard, Dynamic Data Exchange (DDE), and Object Linking and Embedding (OLE) to transfer information among SmartSuite and other Windows applications.

Table I.1 illustrates SmartIcons for SmartSuite and other related applications.

# SmartSuite and Related Applications SmartIcons

| SMARTICON | DESCRIPTION |
|-----------|-------------|
| **SmartSuite and Related Applications SmartIcons** | |
| | Opens 1-2-3 |
| | Opens Ami Pro |
| | Opens Approach |
| | Opens Freelance Graphics |
| | Opens Organizer |
| | Opens Dialog Editor |
| | Opens Improv, if installed |
| | Opens Notes, if installed |
| | Opens cc:Mail, if installed |

# What Is SmartSuite?

# SmartSuite
### CHAPTER I

Lotus SmartSuite provides all the applications that you need to run your business or department efficiently. The Smart-Suite applications are the 1-2-3 spreadsheet program, Ami Pro word processor, Approach relational database, Freelance Graphics presentation software, and Organizer personal information manager (PIM). Designed to work together, elements and options in each of these applications look and function almost identically. This means that once you have learned one application, you are well on your way to becoming familiar with the others. Each SmartSuite application has a similar set of menu commands and dialog boxes and a complete help facility.

## What Can I Do with SmartSuite?

SmartSuite applications are designed so that you can transfer information from one application to another quickly and easily. And because SmartSuite runs under Windows, you can also import to and export from other Windows applications. If you are part of a network or mail group and if you have either cc:Mail or Lotus Notes installed on your computer system, you can send and receive mail from within any SmartSuite application.

SmartSuite applications are sophisticated and extensive, yet easy to use. Each application is based on the Windows *graphical user interface* (GUI, pronounced "gooey"), a display format that allows you to select commands, choose functions, and even start other Windows applications by double-clicking on the application's icon with your mouse. However, if you do not have a mouse or do not wish to use it, you can still access every command and function by pressing keys on your keyboard.

All the SmartSuite applications fit together so well that if you are more comfortable working with one of them, you can often launch other applications and create other types of files from that application. For example, if you create a 1-2-3 spreadsheet, you can copy all or part of it into an Ami Pro document while remaining in either 1-2-3 or Ami Pro. Or you can copy a report from Approach or from a 1-2-3 chart into a Freelance Graphics presentation.

## SmartSuite Features

These are some of the SmartSuite features:

- *SmartCenter*—a control center for launching SmartSuite and other Windows applications
- true WYSIWYG ("what you see is what you get"). The printed page looks just like the contents of your screen.
- a spell checker with a main dictionary and user dictionary
- *SmartIcons*—customizable tool bar buttons that reduce the steps necessary to perform a task
- an active status bar with which you can see your current settings and even the current date and time
- automatic save, in which the current file is automatically saved every few minutes
- recognition of other spreadsheet, word processor, database, presentation, and graphic file formats for easy export and import
- *SmartMasters*—templates for creating SmartSuite files

## The SmartSuite Components

Let's look a little more closely at the SmartSuite applications and the major features that each offers.

## Starting Your Favorite
## Applications with the Lotus SmartCenter

It's easy to start any SmartSuite or Windows application by using the Lotus SmartCenter, a palette containing icons representing all the SmartSuite applications. Just click on a button to launch an application. The starting Lotus SmartCenter icon palette, which is always conveniently on top of your desktop, looks like this:

From left to right, these are the default SmartCenter icons:

**SmartCenter menu**    Click on this icon to display a menu from which you can change the position of the icon palette, hide or display bubble icon descriptions, customize the icon palette, and close the SmartCenter.

**SuiteAnswers**    Click on this icon to display the SuiteAnswers Help menu. Here you can view Help Cards, which provide descriptions and how-to's about SmartSuite features and functions; select a ScreenCam movie from the Movie Guide; take a Guided Tour of SmartCenter and/or SmartSuite features; or view an animated copyright and version window.

**1-2-3**    Click on this icon to start 1-2-3.

**Freelance Graphics**    Click on this icon to start Freelance Graphics.

**Ami Pro**    Click on this icon to start Ami Pro.

**Organizer**    Click on this icon to start Organizer.

**Approach**    Click on this icon to start Approach.

**WORKING TOGETHER**
▲

If you installed SmartCenter when you installed SmartSuite, the Welcome to Lotus SmartSuite dialog box appears automatically when you start Windows. Click on OK to start SmartCenter. To close SmartCenter, click on the SmartCenter menu icon on the icon palette, and click on Exit. To start SmartCenter again, double-click on the SmartCenter icon in the Lotus Applications Window, and click on OK. Note that you'll learn how to turn off the SmartCenter Welcome dialog box later in this section.

Once you have started SmartCenter, you can change the position of the icon palette, which by default is in the upper-right corner of your desktop. Simply click on the SmartCenter menu icon on the icon palette and choose Float Icons in Window. Then drag the icon palette by its title bar to its new position.

To place the icon palette back in the upper-right corner of the desktop, click on the SmartCenter menu icon and choose Anchor Icons to Top of Screen. Note that you can still move the icon palette by moving the mouse pointer to the black area below the control menu button, pressing and holding down the left mouse button, and dragging.

By default, when you move the mouse pointer to an icon on the icon palette, SmartCenter displays a bubble description of the icon. To turn off this description, click on the SmartCenter menu icon, and choose Hide Icon Descriptions. To redisplay the descriptions, click on the SmartCenter menu icon and choose Show Icon Descriptions.

You can customize the SmartCenter in several ways: you can change the position of an icon, add the name of an application icon to the SmartCenter menu; add, remove, and/or change an application; and specify startup, window, and icon preferences.

To change the position of an icon on the icon palette, point to the icon, press Ctrl, and drag the icon over the icon in the desired position. When you release the mouse button, the icon moves into its new position, pushing all the remaining icons to its right.

SmartSuite

**WORKING TOGETHER** ▲

To add an application to the SmartCenter menu, follow these steps:

1. Click on the SmartCenter menu icon.

2. Choose Customize SmartCenter. SmartCenter displays the Customize Lotus SmartCenter dialog box.

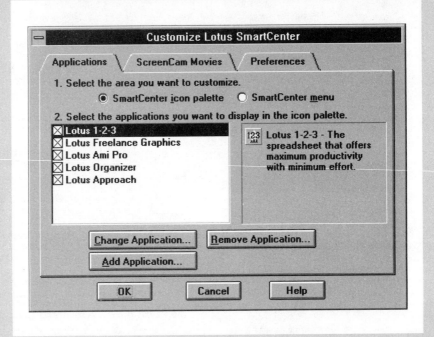

3. Click on the SmartCenter Menu option button.

4. Check the check box of the application to be added to the menu and click on OK. SmartCenter closes the dialog box and adds the selected application to the SmartCenter menu.

To remove the application from the SmartCenter menu, click on the SmartCenter menu icon, choose Customize SmartCenter, check the SmartCenter Menu option button, clear the check box, and click on OK. SmartCenter displays the Customize Lotus SmartCenter dialog box.

To add an application to the icon palette, follow these steps:

1. Click on the SmartCenter menu icon.
2. Choose Customize SmartCenter.
3. In the Customize Lotus SmartCenter dialog box, click on the Add Application button. The Add Application dialog box appears.

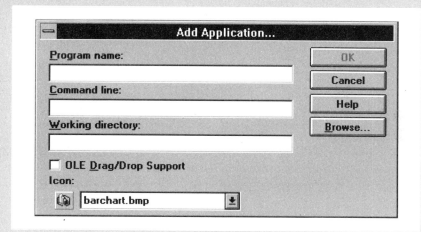

4. Click on the Browse button to find the executable file for the application to be added. The Browse for Command Line dialog box appears.

9

**WORKING TOGETHER**
▲

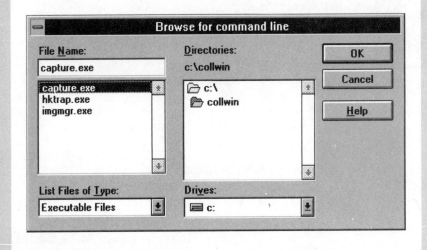

5. Find the desired executable file. You may have to select a subdirectory from the Directories scroll box and a drive from the Drives drop-down list box. Click on OK.

6. When you return to the Add Application dialog box, type the application name in the Program Name text box. (This text becomes the bubble description for the new icon.)

7. Open the Icon drop-down list box and click on the icon that best reminds you of the application.

8. Click on OK. SmartCenter closes the dialog box and adds the icon to the icon palette.

To remove the icon from the icon palette, click on the SmartCenter menu icon, choose Customize SmartCenter, clear the check box, and click on OK.

To change an application, click on the SmartCenter menu icon, choose Customize SmartCenter, and click on the Change Application button.

WORKING
TOGETHER
▲

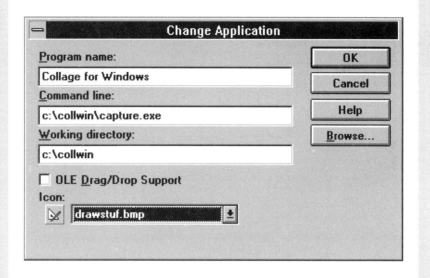

**SmartSuite**

In the Change Application dialog box, edit the contents of the text boxes, or choose a new icon from the Icon drop-down list box. When you have finished, click on OK twice.

You can specify a new path for your ScreenCam movies. For example, if you wish to store all your movies in a subdirectory called \movies, create the new directory in Windows File Manager, and follow these steps:

1. Click on the SmartCenter menu icon.

2. Choose Customize SmartCenter.

3. In the Customize Lotus SmartCenter dialog box, click on the ScreenCam Movies tab and click on the Add Location button. The Add Application dialog box appears.

4. Find the new directory so that its name is highlighted in the Directory scroll box.

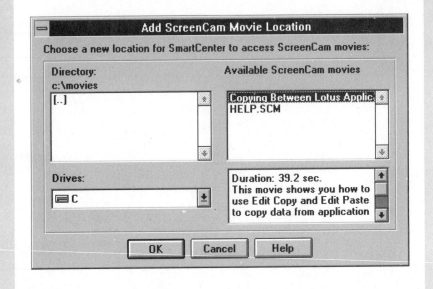

**Add ScreenCam Movie Location**

Choose a new location for SmartCenter to access ScreenCam movies:

Directory:
c:\movies

[..]

Available ScreenCam movies

Copying Between Lotus Applic.
HELP.SCM

Drives:

▭ C

Duration: 39.2 sec.
This movie shows you how to
use Edit Copy and Edit Paste
to copy data from application

OK      Cancel      Help

**5.** Click on OK twice. SmartCenter closes the dialog box and defines the new path.

SmartCenter enables you to customize your version of SmartCenter. Just click on the SmartCenter menu icon, choose Customize SmartCenter, click on the Preferences tab, and check or clear check boxes.

These are the checkboxes in the Preferences section of the Customize Lotus SmartCenter dialog box:

**Load SmartCenter at Windows Startup**    Check this check box to automatically start SmartCenter when you start Windows. If this check box is clear, you can start SmartCenter by double-clicking on its icon in the Lotus Applications window.

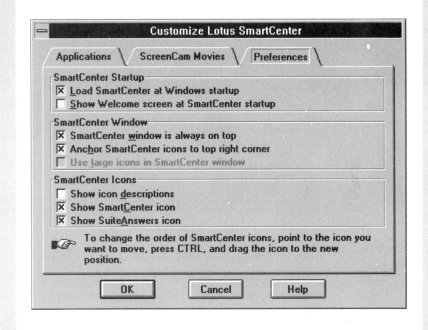

### Show Welcome Screen at SmartCenter Startup

Check this check box to display the Welcome screen when SmartCenter starts. If this check box is clear, the SmartCenter icon palette automatically appears when SmartCenter starts.

### SmartCenter Window Is Always on Top

Check this check box to always display SmartCenter dialog boxes and windows on top of all other windows—even if they are active. If this check box is clear, the active window is displayed in front of SmartCenter dialog boxes and windows.

**Anchor SmartCenter Icons to Top Right Corner**
Check this check box to display the icon palette in the top right corner of the desktop, but you can drag it from that position. If this check box is clear, the icon palette has a full title bar and can be sized. To temporarily switch between anchored and floating icon palettes, choose Float Icons in Window and Anchor Icons to Top of Screen, respectively, from the SmartCenter menu.

**Use Large Icons in SmartCenter Window**     Check this check box to display a larger version of the icon palette. This check box is dimmed unless the icons are floating (that is, not anchored to the upper-right corner). If this check box is clear, the icon palette is a smaller size.

**Show Icon Descriptions**     Check this check box to display bubble descriptions when you move the mouse pointer to an icon on the icon palette. If this check box is clear, no bubble description appears. To temporarily switch between displayed and hidden bubble descriptions, choose Show Icon Descriptions and Hide Icon Descriptions, respectively, from the SmartCenter menu.

**Show SmartCenter Icon**     Check this check box to display the SmartCenter icon on the icon palette. If this check box is clear, SmartCenter removes the icon from the palette after you respond to a prompt. Then, to open the SmartCenter menu, either click the right mouse button or open the Control menu and choose from the SmartCenter cascading menu.

**Show SuiteAnswers Icon**     Check this check box to display the SuiteAnswers icon on the icon palette. If this check box is clear, SmartCenter removes the icon from the palette and SuiteAnswers are not available.

# 1-2-3

Lotus 1-2-3 is a spreadsheet program that allows you to organize and graph information on your computer desktop. Some 1-2-3 features are

- more than 200 built-in math, engineering, financial, and statistical functions

- in-cell editing, alignment, and formatting

- shortcut menus associated with the active object. Just click your right mouse button to display a menu from which you can select commonly used commands.

- easily displayed dialog boxes associated with the active object. Just double-click your left mouse button to display the relevant dialog box.

- three-dimensional worksheets with which you can organize an entire category of spreadsheets (for example, this year's actual expenses and next year's budget). Tabbed worksheet pages, which you can name and which help you quickly move from one spreadsheet in a file to another.

- palettes of 256 colors, 64 fill patterns, 8 edge/data line styles, and 16 designer frames to help you custom-format your spreadsheets.

- multiple currency formats so that you can use many international currencies in your spreadsheets.

- intelligent charting, automatic charts with titles, legends, and data.

- 19 types of easy-to-edit charts.

- the Version Manager, which allows several users to set up what-if scenarios related to alternate values and formulas. View the Version Manager index to see a master list of scenarios.

- a variety of database queries which can evaluate data from within 1-2-3, Approach, or other popular database programs.

- Lotus Maps, an integrated mapping tool which allows you to link worksheet data to a map.

For information about 1-2-3, see Chapters 4–7.

## Ami Pro

Ami Pro is a full-featured word processor that enables you to create any type of document—from a one-page memo or letter to a large manual with headers, footers, footnotes, a table of contents, and index.

Some Ami Pro features are

- a thesaurus and grammar checker with rules that you can set for several levels of checking
- an easy-to-use mail merge
- character, paragraph, and document formatting
- multiple column formatting
- styles
- outlining
- frames

For information about Ami Pro, see Chapters 8–10.

## Approach

Approach is a relational database that allows you to plan, design, create, and manage your information. Approach allows you to work with data using forms, reports, form letters, and mailing labels.

Some Approach features are

- SmartMasters, predesigned database templates
- free-form and easily edited reports, forms, form letters, and mailing labels
- Report Assistant, PowerClick reporting, and Quick Click features which allow you to automate report creation
- Four environments in which you can work: Browse, Design, Find, and Preview
- built-in forms
- self-contained mail merge facility

■ the InfoBox, a dialog box in which you can change almost every characteristic of an object

■ Named styles, in which you can save InfoBox characteristics and apply them to other objects

■ Avery label support

■ joined database files so that you can use information from several databases

■ comprehensive sort and retrieve capabilities

■ point and click data entry

■ shortcut menus associated with the active object. Just click your right mouse button to display a menu from which you can select commonly used commands.

For information about Approach, see Chapters 11–14.

## Freelance Graphics

Freelance Graphics enables you to create business presentations complete with slides, overheads, handouts, and speaker notes. You can enhance your presentation by using graphics, charts, and text from other SmartSuite or Windows applications or by generating them from within Freelance Graphics. Some Freelance Graphics features are

■ 65 SmartMasters design sets, which guide you through the creation process. Select the look and page layout, then start filling in each page.

■ Galleries of charts, tables, organization charts, symbols, and maps.

■ Smart Charting, which aids in laying out charts.

■ Outliner, which lays out a presentation as an outline and converts the outline to a series of presentation pages.

■ Page Sorter, which allows you to see all presentation pages on your desktop.

■ Screen Shows with transitional effects and on-screen drawing, to which you can add sound and animation.

For information about Freelance Graphics, see Chapters 15 and 16.

**WORKING TOGETHER** ▲

## Using Lotus ScreenCam

You can record both sounds (if you have a sound card, microphone, and sound software installed) and activities on the computer screen using Lotus ScreenCam. You can then distribute those files to train users, demonstrate applications, or respond to colleagues. For example, you can illustrate how to edit an Ami Pro document, open a 1-2-3 file, embed a ScreenCam demo in a Freelance Graphics presentation, or show the changes that you would like in another Windows application document.

The Lotus ScreenCam window contains these controls:

| | |
|---|---|
| Play | Plays the current movie or sound file |
| Rew | Rewinds the current movie or sound file |
| FF | Fast-forwards the current movie or sound file |
| Exit | Closes Lotus ScreenCam |
| Vol | Controls the volume of sound |
| Rec | Records a movie or sound file |
| Clear | Clears the current movie so that you can record a new one. (To delete a movie, start File Manager, press Del, and respond to any prompts.) |

**WORKING TOGETHER** ▲

| | |
|---|---|
| Mic | Records a sound file |
| Both | Records a movie with sound |
| Cam | Records a movie without sound |

Before creating a movie, plan it carefully. Keep in mind that a long movie takes a great deal of computer or disk space. Before recording, turn off your Windows wallpaper to save computer memory. Because a Lotus ScreenCam movie shows every movement of the mouse, know ahead of time the directions in which you'll move the mouse; don't record extraneous movements, plan to move the mouse in a straight line, and move it more slowly than you usually do.

To create a movie, follow these steps:

1. Start Lotus ScreenCam.
2. Click on either the Mic, Both, or Cam button to indicate whether you will record sound, a movie with sound, or a movie without sound.
3. Click on the Rec button. Lotus ScreenCam places a Stop box in the lower-right corner of the current window. Before moving the mouse pointer or recording a sound, wait for the stopwatch cursor to change to an arrow.
4. Record mouse movement and/or sound. When you have completed recording, click on the Stop button.

To show a movie or hear a sound file, click on the Play button.

To save a movie or sound file, choose one of these options:

- Choose File ➤ Save or press Ctrl+S to save a new ScreenCam movie (*.scm).
- Choose File ➤ Save As to save a movie as a ScreenCam movie (*.scm), in a different directory or drive, or under a new name.

**WORKING TOGETHER**

▲

- Choose <u>F</u>ile ➤ <u>E</u>xport to save a stand-alone movie (*.exe) that a user can run without having Lotus ScreenCam installed.
- Choose <u>F</u>ile ➤ <u>E</u>xport to save a sound file (*.wav).

To embed a Lotus ScreenCam movie in a Windows application with the <u>E</u>dit ➤ Insert <u>O</u>bject or <u>I</u>nsert ➤ <u>O</u>bject command, follow these steps:

1. Open the application in which you wish to embed the movie.
2. Choose <u>E</u>dit ➤ Insert <u>O</u>bject or <u>I</u>nsert ➤ <u>O</u>bject. The application opens a dialog box from which you can select an object.
3. Double-click on Lotus ScreenCam.
4. Choose <u>F</u>ile ➤ <u>R</u>ead (or press Ctrl+O) to open an existing movie file, choose <u>F</u>ile ➤ <u>I</u>mport to import a stand-alone movie, or create a new movie and save it.
5. Choose <u>F</u>ile ➤ <u>U</u>pdate or press Ctrl+S to embed the Lotus ScreenCam logo in the application at the insertion point.
6. Either click on the Exit button or choose <u>F</u>ile ➤ E<u>x</u>it to close Lotus ScreenCam and return to the application.

You can also embed a movie in a Windows application by choosing <u>E</u>dit ➤ Paste <u>S</u>pecial. For instructions, see "Embed a Movie in Another Document" in the Lotus ScreenCam Help facility.

To show the embedded movie, double-click on the Lotus ScreenCam icon.

## Organizer

Organizer, your own personal information manager (PIM), tracks your work and schedule, automates your address book, keeps notes, reminds you of anniversaries and birthdays, displays your to-do list, and monitors your telephone calls.

Organizer's pages are divided into tabbed sections, each representing a different information category. Click on a tab, and the application displays the opening "page" of that section.

Organizer allows you to do the following:

- Schedule appointments and set alarms that remind you of the time.
- Type to-do lists that appear on your Calendar until you remove them.
- Keep an up-to-date address book and anniversary list. You can import names and addresses from Approach or other database programs.
- Print any section on pages that are compatible with almost any label or personal organizer binder.
- Add or customize sections within the Organizer notebook.
- Import text and graphics into the Notepad section.
- Keep a chart of your activities or projects.
- Track your telephone calls—both incoming and outgoing.

For information about Organizer, see Chapters 17 and 18.

# Working Together with SmartSuite Applications

One of the major advantages of working with Windows applications such as SmartSuite is that it's easy to exchange data among open applications, as shown in Figure 1.1. There are three ways to transfer data:

- copying, moving, and pasting data using the Windows Clipboard
- using Dynamic Data Exchange (DDE)
- using Object Linking and Embedding (OLE)

## Copying, Moving, and Pasting Data

Windows applications allow you to easily transfer data and objects from one application to another. You can select data or an object in the source application and either place a copy or move the selection to the target application. Then, if you wish to edit a copied or moved selection, you have two choices: edit the selection in all its locations, or edit in one place and copy or move it all over again. You'll learn about copying and moving selections in Chapter 3.

SmartSuite

**FIGURE I.I**

Exchanging data
among applications

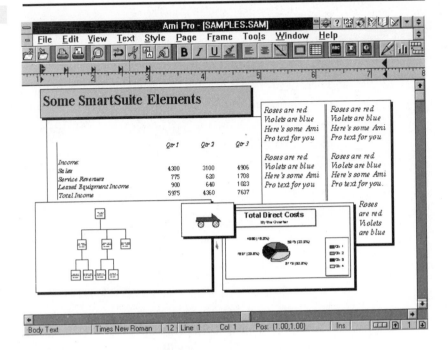

## Exchanging Data Using DDE

Windows' Dynamic Data Exchange (DDE) feature allows you to exchange
data among two or more active Windows applications and to edit in just one
place. If you have linked applications by choosing a Link or Paste Link command from the Edit menu, when you change an object or information in one
application, it automatically changes in all other linked applications.

## Linking and Embedding with OLE

Windows' Object Linking and Embedding (OLE) is another link feature by
which you can use an object created within one Windows application in
other Windows applications. When you wish to edit the object, you don't
have to leave the *client application*, in which it is embedded; you can call up
the *server application*, the application in which the object was created, from
within the client.

**WORKING TOGETHER**

# How to Link an Object

Linking uses either Dynamic Data Exchange (DDE) or Object Linking and Embedding (OLE); both the *client* (the application using the object) and *server* (the application providing the object) must support DDE OLE. When you link to an object in another application, you can allow the client to choose the type of link format (for example, Windows Metafile, Bitmap, and Text), or you can specify the format.

To update a linked object, edit it in its original application. Then, depending on the type of link, the object is automatically updated or you must manually update it. The type of link that you have is dependent on the client and server applications involved in the link.

To link to an object and let the client define the format, follow these steps:

1. Start both the client and server applications and keep them running throughout the link process. Although OLE does not require this, DDE does. (You can minimize the server application once you have copied the selected object, and you can minimize the client application before you need to make the link.)

2. In the server application, open the file containing the object that you wish to use in the client application. If you haven't saved the file, save it; linking requires named, saved files.

3. Select the object.

4. Choose Edit ➤ Copy, click on the Copy SmartIcon, or press Ctrl+C. This copies the object to the Clipboard.

5. In the client application, open the file in which you'll place the object. If you are starting with a new file, save it; linking requires named, saved files.

6. In the newly opened file, move the insertion point to the desired location of the object.

**SmartSuite**

**WORKING TOGETHER** ▲

**7.** Choose Edit ➤ Paste Link. (If the Paste Link command is dimmed, you may need to save the client or server file.) The application creates the link.

To link to an object and define the link format yourself, follow steps 1–7 above. Then complete steps 8 and 9 listed below:

**8.** Choose Edit ➤ Paste Special to open the Paste Special dialog box.

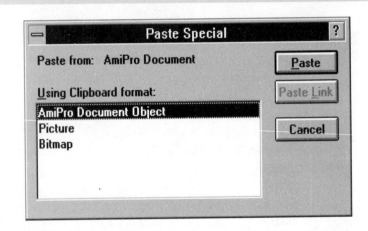

**9.** In the Paste Special dialog box, select a Clipboard format, and click on Paste Link.

For general information about links, DDE, and OLE, see "Understanding Links" in the Ami Pro Help facility.

To manually update a linked object after you have edited it in the server application, choose Edit ➤ Link Options or Edit ➤ Links, click on Update or Update All, and click on Close.

**WORKING TOGETHER** ▲

# How to Embed an Object

Embedding, an Object Linking and Embedding (OLE) feature, enables you to edit an object, or even create a new object, while remaining in the current application. Both the application in which you work on the object and the current application must support object embedding and must run under Windows.

After embedding an object, you can select it (usually by double-clicking on it) for editing. When the originating application opens, edit the object, and then exit, thus returning to the application in which the object is embedded.

To embed an object, follow these steps:

1. In the current file, move the insertion point to the location where the object will be embedded.

2. Choose Edit ➤ Insert Object/Insert Object (1-2-3 or Freelance Graphics), Edit ➤ Insert ➤ New Object (Ami Pro), or Objects ➤ Insert Object (Approach). The Insert Object dialog box appears.

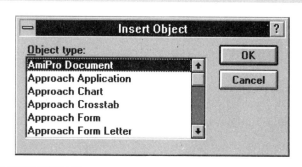

3. Select the desired object, and either click on OK or press ↵. The selected application opens.

**SmartSuite**

**WORKING TOGETHER**
▲

**4.** Either create or open the object.

**5.** Choose File ➤ Update in the application in which the object is now located. The object is inserted at the insertion point in the original application.

**6.** Choose File ➤ Exit & Return to close the application in which you created or edited the object.

To edit the embedded object, double-click on it. The application in which you created it opens. After editing, choose File ➤ Update, and File ➤ Exit & Return.

## Working Together Bonus Pack

The Working Together Bonus Pack contains a set of macros that integrate Ami Pro with other SmartSuite and Lotus Windows applications. For example, with the Bonus Pack, you can

- launch other Lotus Windows applications, including SmartSuite.

- horizontally or vertically tile two Lotus Windows applications on your desktop.

- calculate monthly mortgage payments, estimate college fund needs, and compute your potential savings and investment growth. The Bonus Pack provides many other calculators and enables you to build your own.

- accumulate ranges of data and copy them to an Ami Pro document.

- collect and copy slides from a Freelance Graphics presentation to an Ami Pro document. You can also build an automated screen show from a Freelance Graphics presentation.

- use your Organizer address book to create a mail merge or label file.

**WORKING TOGETHER**

# SmartSuite Macros

Ami Pro installation provides not only program files but also macro files that can help you run SmartSuite applications more efficiently and have a little fun, too. In addition, the Working Together Bonus Pack, also included with SmartSuite, provides many more macros. The following list describes each macro file.

**_AUTORUN.SMM**     Enables you to define the macros that run automatically when you start Ami Pro (Working Together)

**123COPY.SMM**     Runs Collect & Copy to collect and copy parts of a 1-2-3 for Windows spreadsheet to an Ami Pro document (Working Together)

**123STYLE.SMM**     Styles a 1-2-3 for Windows spreadsheet using the styles in an Ami Pro document (Working Together)

**123W.SMM**     Launches 1-2-3 for Windows from within Ami Pro

**ACODES.SMM**     Inserts the ACodes menu on the menu bar so that you can look up geographical and time information about a selected area.

**AMIMENUS.SMM**     Adds a command to or deletes a command from an Ami Pro menu

**APPROACH.SMM**     Starts Approach

**AUTOCAL.SMM**     Automates monthly calendar creation when you select the _cal-mon.sty style

**BUILD.SMM**     Constructs a calculator (Working Together)

**CCMAIL.SMM**     Launches cc:Mail if you have access to the application from your computer system

**SmartSuite**

**WORKING TOGETHER**

**CHARMAP.SMM**   Launches Windows Character Map so that you can insert a special character into the current document

**CHGFONT.SMM**   Changes style sheet fonts

**CHKDATE.SMM**   Displays the creation date and size of a selected file

**CLEANSCR.SMM**   Displays the parts of the screen that Clean Screen hides or reveals when you choose <u>V</u>iew ➤ Show Clean Scree<u>n</u>.

**CLOSEALL.SMM**   Closes all open documents after you respond to the save prompt

**CNTRFRAM.SMM**   Centers the selected frame between the left and right margins

**COLLECT.SMM**   Enables you to add or change personal information that some automatic style sheets use to fill in documents

**CONVERT.SMM**   Converts a selected batch of files to the Ami Pro format

**COPYRITE.SMM**   Inserts the copyright symbol at the insertion point

**CROSSREF.SMM**   Places cross-references in files in a master document

**DATAMAN.SMM**   Adds the <u>C</u>ard File menu to Ami Pro so that you can create or edit a Paradox-format card file from within Ami Pro.

**DOCONLIN.SMM**   Starts SmarText, if installed, from within Ami Pro (Working Together)

**WORKING TOGETHER** ▲

**DOS.SMM**    Displays a DOS window from within Windows. Type **Exit** to return to Ami Pro.

**EDITMAC.SMM**    Displays a macro so that you can edit it from within Ami Pro

**FIND.SMM**    Finds a text string in a document

**FINDFILE.SMM**    Finds files, which are in a specified directory and which contain specified text. If the files are *SAM files, you can open them.

**FIT2SCRN.SMM**    Adjusts the Custom view percentage so that the current document fits the screen

**FLW.SMM**    Starts Freelance Graphics from within Ami Pro

**FLWCOPY.SMM**    Runs Collect & Copy to collect and copy parts of a Freelance Graphics presentation file to an Ami Pro document (Working Together)

**FLWCURVE.SMM**    Curves text in an Ami Pro document using a Freelance Graphics option (Working Together)

**FLWHAND.SMM**    Creates Ami Pro handouts for a Freelance Graphics presentation (Working Together)

**FLWORG.SMM**    Creates an organization chart in Ami Pro using Freelance Graphics (Working Together)

**FLWSHOW.SMM**    Prepares a Freelance Graphics screen show from an Ami Pro outline (Working Together)

**FONTDN.SMM**    Decreases the point size of the selected text

**FONTUP.SMM**    Increases the point size of the selected text

SmartSuite

**WORKING TOGETHER** ▲

**FRAMGLOS.SMM**    Adds a command to the Frame menu so that you can save frames in a glossary file, allowing you to easily find and use them at a later time

**FREPLACE.SMM**    Finds a search string and replaces with a replace string in a group of files

**FSPELL.SMM**    Runs the spell checker for a group of files

**GAME.SMM**    Starts the MacroMindBlaster game, which is similar to Master Mind

**HPCLIP.SMM**    Adjusts certain Hewlett-Packard LaserJet or compatible printer settings to correct problems when printing opaque frames over text or reverse text

**IMPRCOPY.SMM**    Runs Collect & Copy to collect and copy parts of an Improv worksheet to an Ami Pro document (Working Together)

**INDEXALL.SMM**    Marks all occurrences of a word for an index

**KEYWORD.SMM**    Finds files in a specific directory and limited by wildcards for file names and/or extensions (if you wish), using descriptions and keywords document information

**LOTUSPAL.SMM**    Runs Lotus Application Manager, which is the predecessor to Lotus SmartCenter (Working Together)

**LOTUSTIL.SMM**    Tiles Lotus applications horizontally or vertically (Working Together)

**MAKELABL.SMM**    Saves merge label and document options for custom labels

**MARKMENU.SMM**    Adds the Bookmarks menu to the menu bar so that you can add a bookmark

**WORKING TOGETHER** ▲

**MASTRODOC.SMM**    Allows you to view the files making up a master document

**MENULITE.SMM**    Displays short or long menus

**NEWNOW.SMM**    Opens a new document

**NOTES.SMM**    Starts Lotus Notes, if you can access the application from your computer system

**OLDKEYS.SMM**    Uses the Ami Pro 2.0 shortcut keys rather than those for Ami Pro 3.0

**OPENDOCS.SMM**    Opens as many as nine documents at once in a full or minimized screen

**ORGANIZE.SMM**    Starts Lotus Organizer from within Ami Pro

**ORGCAL.SMM**    Creates a calendar using Organizer data (Working Together)

**PRINTNOW.SMM**    Prints the current document using the printing defaults (without opening the Print dialog box)

**PRNBATCH.SMM**    Prints several selected documents, using options that you specify, now or at a specified time

**PRNPAGES.SMM**    Enables you to print selected pages in the current document

**PRNSHADE.SMM**    Prints the selected text in the current document

**QK_MAIL.SMM**    Adds the Send Mail command to the File menu

**QKCOLLG.SMM**    Runs the college savings calculator (Working Together)

SmartSuite

**WORKING TOGETHER**
▲

**QKDEPREC.SMM**     Runs the depreciation table calculator (Working Together)

**QKDUCTS.SMM**     Runs the rectangular duct calculator (Working Together)

**QKFUNCT.SMM**     Runs the @function calculator (Working Together)

**QKGEOM.SMM**     Calculates the sine, cosine, and tangent of an angle (Working Together)

**QKHOUSE.SMM**     Runs the mortgage payment calculator (Working Together)

**QKPERC.SMM**     Runs the percentage calculator for specified numbers (Working Together)

**QKPOWER.SMM**     Calculates a number raised to a power (Working Together)

**QKQUAD.SMM**     Runs the quadratic equation calculator (Working Together)

**QKROOT.SMM**     Calculates the root of a number (Working Together)

**QKSAVE.SMM**     Runs the savings growth calculator (Working Together)

**QKSEND.SMM**     Creates a Lotus Mail message in Ami Pro (Working Together)

**QKSTAT.SMM**     Calculates the sum, average, maximum, or minimum for specified numbers (Working Together)

**QKTABLE.SMM**     Runs the loan payment calculator (Working Together)

**QKTEMP.SMM**     Runs the temperature converter calculator (Working Together)

**QKTERM.SMM**    Runs the investment growth calculator (Working Together)

**QKTREND.SMM**    Calculates the trend (percentage increase or decrease) of a particular data item in a group (Working Together)

**QS_FIRST.SMM**    Starts the tutorial

**REGMARK.SMM**    Inserts a registered trademark symbol at the insertion point

**SAVEINFO.SMM**    Displays the Doc Info dialog box when saving a document

**SAVSHADE.SMM**    Saves selected text to a new file

**SKAUTO.SMM**    Runs the SwitchKit (a WordPerfect converter) automatically

**SKDATA1.SMM**    Contains data for the SwitchKit

**SKDATA2.SMM**    Contains data for the SwitchKit

**SKEXIT.SMM**    Exits the macro for the SWITCH.SMM file

**SMARTEXT.SMM**    Starts Lotus SmarText, if it is installed on your computer system

**SMARTFLD.SMM**    Enables you to build an automated style sheet

**SMARTPIC.SMM**    Starts Lotus SmartPics Sampler, if it is installed on your computer system

**SMARTYPE.SMM**    Converts certain characters (such as " and —) to typeset characters

**SPECIALF.SMM**    Installs the Ami Pro special features menu item on the Tools menu

**SWITCH.SMM**    Runs the SwitchKit

**WORKING TOGETHER** ▲

**TILEHORZ.SMM**     Tiles open documents horizontally on the desktop

**TM.SMM**     Inserts the trademark symbol at the insertion point

**TOA.SMM**     Runs the Table of Authorities application for legal documents

**TOAGEN.SMM**     Generates a Table of Authorities

**TOALONG.SMM**     Marks selected text as a Table of Authorities long entry

**TOAREMOV.SMM**     Removes a Table of Authorities mark from the selection

**TOASHORT.SMM**     Marks selected text as a Table of Authorities short entry

**TYPECHAR.SMM**     Adds the Chars menu to the menu bar so that you can select ANSI characters for insertion at the insertion point

**WELCOME.SMM**     Displays the Ami Pro Welcome dialog box

**WINAPPS.SMM**     Adds the WinApps menu to the menu bar so that you can go to another active application, define a password, or view a selected part of the window

**WINFILE.SMM**     Opens the Windows File Manager window from within Ami Pro

**WORDCNT.SMM**     Displays the number of words, number of pages, file size, and the last save date for the current file

**WORKGRUP.SMM**     Opens the Build Workgroup dialog box so that you can build a group of related documents that you can open at once

**WORKING TOGETHER**
▲

# Automatically Loading and Running Multiple Macros

Ami Pro's Working Together Bonus Pack provides a macro that automatically loads and runs other macros. After running _AUTORUN.SMM, the specified macros run when you start Ami Pro. Note that Ami Pro must be running for the specified macros to keep running. To define macros to be automatically loaded, follow these steps:

**1.** Choose Tools ➤ Macros ➤ Playback or click on the appropriate SmartIcon in the Bonus Pack SmartIcons set. Ami Pro displays the Play Macro dialog box.

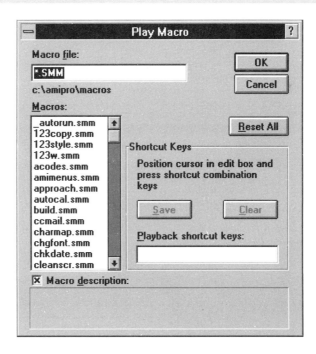

**WORKING TOGETHER**
▲

**2.** Choose _AUTORUN.SMM and click on OK. Ami Pro displays the Autorun Macro dialog box, in which macros are displayed alphabetically by macro name.

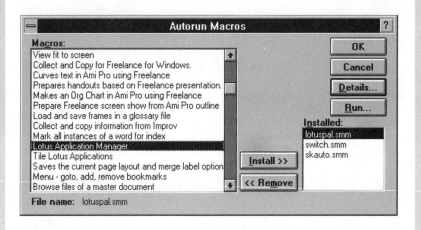

**3.** Select a macro from the Macros scroll box and click on Install. Repeat this for as many macros as you wish to automatically run. Note that autoloading several macros can affect the speed at which Ami Pro launches.

**4.** If you want more information about a macro, click on Details. Ami Pro opens GOODIES.SAM, which lists and describes each macro.

**5.** To remove a macro from the Installed list, select it and click on Remove.

**6.** To see a demonstration of the macro, select it and click on Run.

**7.** After completing the selection process, click on OK. Starting with the next time you launch Ami Pro, the selected macro runs every time you start Ami Pro.

2

# Getting Acquainted with SmartSuite

T he best way to learn how an application works is not by reading a manual and applying the information that you have read at a later date, but by starting to use the application right away.

One of the biggest advantages of working with Windows applications is that after learning how to use one application, you know many features common to all. In this chapter, you'll learn about starting and exiting applications; opening, editing, saving, and printing files; and more. As you read this chapter, try using each feature. Before you start, however, you'll have to start Windows, if you haven't already done so.

## Starting Windows

After turning on your computer, if Windows is not running, type **win** at the DOS prompt (which probably looks something like C:\), and then press ↵. Windows displays a series of screens ending with the Program Manager window. To learn about some of the other ways to start Windows, see Appendix B.

## Starting a SmartSuite Application

After starting Windows, start one of the SmartSuite applications—preferably the one with which you'll be working most often—by moving the mouse pointer to the icon representing the application and *double-clicking* (pressing the left mouse button twice). You can also start a SmartSuite application by clicking on its icon in the SmartCenter icon palette. Once you start an application, you'll see an application window such as the 1-2-3 window shown in Figure 2.1.

**FIGURE 2.1**

An opening 1-2-3 application window with typical Windows elements: title bar, menu bar, tool bar, work area, and status bar

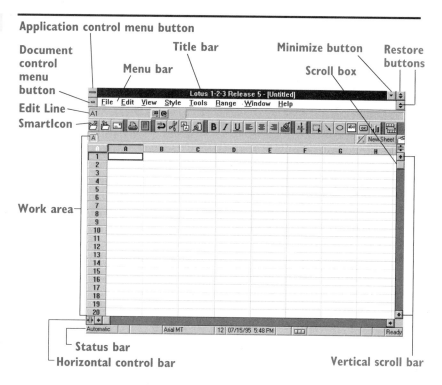

Application control menu button

Document control menu button

Title bar

Minimize button

Restore buttons

Menu bar

Scroll box

Edit Line

SmartIcon

Work area

Status bar

Horizontal control bar

Vertical scroll bar

TIP

If you use Organizer every day immediately after you start Windows, put its icon in the StartUp program group in the Program Manager window. Then, after starting Windows, you'll have the Organizer application window on your desktop. After you first install Windows, the Startup group is empty. Copy or move icons representing applications that you want to start automatically after Windows starts. Select Organizer, a screen saver, or any other often-used Windows application. For more Windows information, see Appendix B.

Before you learn about the elements of a typical application window, let's open LESSON8.WK4, a spreadsheet from the \123r5w\sample\tutorial subdirectory, which is installed during a complete 1-2-3 installation. With an open file in the application window, you'll be able to see how all the pieces of the window work.

**WORKING
TOGETHER**
▲

# Playing the MacroMindBlaster Game

In a set of applications as complete as SmartSuite, if you search long and hard enough, novelties will pop up. Perhaps the most unique part of SmartSuite is Ami Pro's MacroMindBlaster game, which is a close relative of Master Mind. To play MacroMindBlaster (and to practice your mouse pointing and clicking skills), follow these steps:

1. Choose Tools ➤ Macros ➤ Playback. Ami Pro displays the Play Macro dialog box.

2. Double-click on game.smm. Ami Pro displays the Mind Blaster dialog box.

3. Click on a pattern of black "pegs," and click on the Guess ? button. The game displays how many guesses are right.

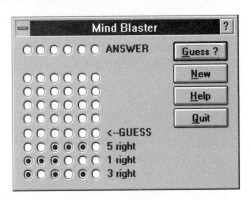

4. Based on your analysis of the number of previous right choices, click on the next pattern of black "pegs," and click on the Guess ? button.

5. Repeat step 4 until you win or run out of rows.

6. When you have finished playing, click on the Quit button.

# Opening a File

Opening a 1-2-3 file is very similar to opening a file in any other SmartSuite or Windows application. The process involves opening a *dialog box*, a small window in which you select or change application settings or specify how you want to perform an action.

The Open File dialog box shown in Figure 2.2 is an example of a common Windows dialog box. You'll find similar dialog boxes in the other SmartSuite applications. In fact, as you read through this chapter, you'll notice that the Save As dialog box is almost identical to the Open File dialog box. You'll learn more about the elements of Windows dialog boxes in a following section and in Appendix B. To find out about the options in this type of dialog box, see the "About the Save As Dialog Box" section later in this chapter.

To open a 1-2-3 file, follow the steps below. (Before opening the file, if the Welcome diaolg box is displayed, click on Cancel to close it.)

1. Either press the shortcut key combination Ctrl+O or choose File ➤ Open. 1-2-3 displays the Open File dialog box (Figure 2.2).

2. The LESSON8.WK4 spreadsheet is located in the 123R5W \ SAMPLE \ TUTORIAL subdirectory. To display the list of files in \TUTORIAL, double-click on the icon next to the word *tutorial* in the Directories scroll box.

3. Double-click on LESSON8.WK4. 1-2-3 opens the file (see Figure 2.3).

**If the file that you wish to open is one of the last few on which you have worked (the number of files listed depends on the SmartSuite application you are using), you can select it from the bottom of the open File menu. Either double-click on the file name or type the underlined number preceding the file name.**

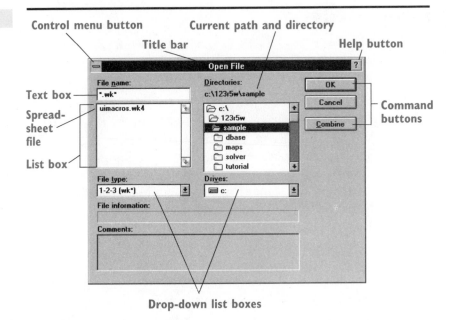

Control menu button

Current path and directory

Title bar

Help button

Text box

Spread-sheet file

List box

Command buttons

Drop-down list boxes

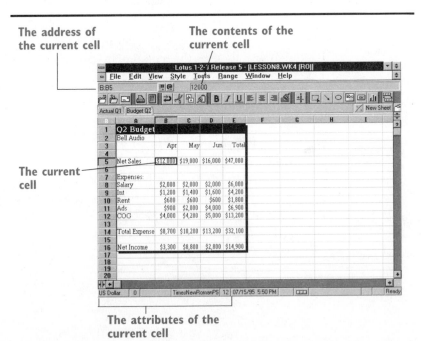

## FIGURE 2.3

The LESSON8.WK4 spreadsheet shows a small budget for Bell Audio's second quarter.

The address of the current cell

The contents of the current cell

The current cell

The attributes of the current cell

# The Elements of the Application Window

Much of the application window is similar to most Windows applications, but a few elements are unique to each SmartSuite application. Let's look more closely at the 1-2-3 window. For additional information about Windows application windows, see Appendix B.

At the top of the application window is the Control Panel, consisting of the title bar, the menu bar, and the edit line. The *title bar* (Figure 2.4), along the very top of the window, displays the name of the application, the current file, or both. Before you open a file, the title bar simply shows the name of the Windows application—in this case, Lotus 1-2-3. Once you open a file, its name is added to the title bar. The title bar sometimes provides useful information; whenever you open a menu, the title bar shows a short description of the menu or command. For more information about how menus work, see the following section.

**FIGURE 2.4**

The Lotus 1-2-3 title bar. Notice the name of the application and the name of the current file. Other SmartSuite title bars look just the same.

Application control menu button

Application name    File name

Lotus 1-2-3 Release 5 - [LESSON8.WK4 (RO)]

Minimize button
Restore button

The title bar also contains small buttons at each end: the Application Control Menu button, the Minimize button, and either the Maximize button or the Restore button. For more information about what these title bar buttons do, see Appendix B.

## Using the Menu Bar

Immediately below the title bar is the *menu bar* (Figure 2.5), which displays the menus from which you can select commands. Menu commands begin an action, open a dialog box, or open a *cascading menu*, branching off to the right.

**FIGURE 2.5**

The 1-2-3 menu bar contains eight menus from which you can select commands.

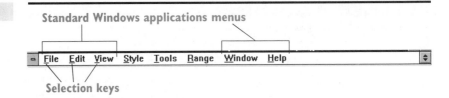

The standard 1-2-3 menus are File (where you opened LESSON8.WK4), Edit, View, Style, Tools, Window, and Help. (The Range menu appears on this particular menu bar, but is replaced by other menus in other sections of 1-2-3.) Some menus—File, Edit, Window, and Help—are common to most Windows applications; some—View, Style, and Tools—appear with most other Smart-Suite applications, and the rest are unique to 1-2-3.

Underneath the menu bar is the *edit line* (Figure 2.6), which is unique to 1-2-3 and which will be explained in Chapter 3.

**FIGURE 2.6**

The 1-2-3 edit line, which is a unique part of the 1-2-3 application window

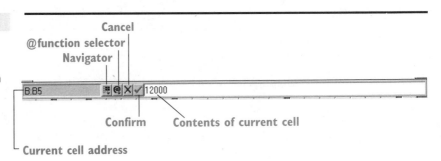

## Using SmartIcons

Under the edit line are the *SmartIcons*, a series of toolbar buttons. When you click on a SmartIcon, you tell the application to do something (such as open, save, or print a file) that would otherwise take a couple of steps using menus, commands, and dialog boxes. The display of SmartIcons varies depending on the current SmartSuite application and your situation within that application.

The way buttons are positioned indicates their relationship. For example, the left-most two buttons (Open and Save) on the 1-2-3 application window are

SmartSuite

closely related because they help in file management, but the third button (Send Mail) is not related to the fourth (Print).

 **TIP** Move the mouse pointer over any SmartIcon in any Smart-Suite application to view a short description of it in the title bar. Some applications also allow you to click with the right mouse button to view a description in a "bubble."

Now let's take a brief look at a few SmartIcons. As you read, try clicking on SmartIcons to see what happens. (If you open a dialog box, either click on the Cancel button or press Esc to close it without taking any action.)

For every SmartIcon, there is a counterpart menu command and quite often a shortcut key or key combination. Table 2.1 illustrates and describes some of the most common SmartSuite SmartIcons. (You won't see all of them on your starting 1-2-3 application window.) For information about SmartIcons used for specific applications, see the charts at the beginning of each part. To learn how to customize SmartIcons, see Appendix C.

**TABLE 2.1:** Common SmartSuite SmartIcons

| SMARTICON | DESCRIPTION | EQUIVALENT COMMAND | SHORTCUT KEYS |
|---|---|---|---|
| | Opens an existing file | File ➤ Open | Ctrl+O |
| | Saves the current file | File ➤ Save | Ctrl+S |
| | Prints the current file using the options in the Print dialog box | File ➤ Print | Ctrl+P |
| | Closes this window | File ➤ Close | N/A |
| | Exits this application | File ➤ Exit | Alt+F4 |

**TABLE 2.1:**   Common SmartSuite SmartIcons (continued)

| SMARTICON | DESCRIPTION | EQUIVALENT COMMAND | SHORTCUT KEYS |
|---|---|---|---|
| | Undoes the last action, if allowed | Edit ➤ Undo | Ctrl+Z |
| | Cuts the selection and places it in the Clipboard | Edit ➤ Cut | Ctrl+X or Shift+Del |
| | Copies the selection to the Clipboard | Edit ➤ Copy | Ctrl+C or Ctrl+Ins |
| | Pastes the contents of the Clipboard into the file at the current cursor location. (Other buttons with the glue bottle graphic also perform pasting actions.) | Edit ➤ Paste | Ctrl+V or Shift+Ins |
| **B** | Applies or removes boldface from the selection | Style ➤ Font & Attributes | Ctrl+B |
| *I* | Applies or removes italics from the selection | Style ➤ Font & Attributes | Ctrl+I |

## The Work Area

The largest part of the window is the work area, in which you work on your files. If you have been testing features and functions as you read this chapter, you have already seen changes to the contents of the work area, including open dialog boxes and menus.

## The Status Bar

At the bottom of the window, the active status bar (Figure 2.7) shows you a variety of information and allows you to perform certain actions. For example, if you click on the button that looks like three squares, you display a list of SmartIcons:

If you choose Working Together from the list, you can start other SmartSuite applications from the current application. As you learn about each Smart-Suite application, you'll find out about its unique status bar.

**FIGURE 2.7**

The 1-2-3 active status bar provides information about the application and allows you to take some actions.

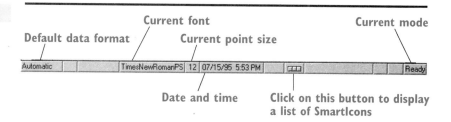

## Selecting a Command

Now that you have learned some application window basics, the next step is to find out the details. Let's open a menu from the menu bar and select a command. The 1-2-3 Tools menu (Figure 2.8) provides tools that allow you to create a chart, map, picture, or database; spell check your text; audit a spreadsheet; customize your SmartIcons and user setup; and so on.

Choose Tools ➤ User Setup to display the User Setup dialog box (Figure 2.9), which allows you to customize 1-2-3 options so that they match your working style. If you're using a mouse, click on the word Tools and when the menu opens, click on User Setup. To open a menu using the keyboard, press Alt, the

**FIGURE 2.8**

From the open <u>T</u>ools menu, you can create a chart, map, picture, or database, and check your spelling and customize your personal settings for an application.

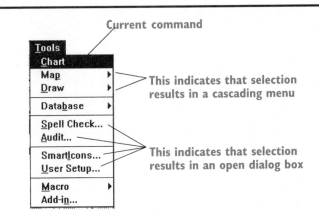

underlined selection letter on the menu (**T** for <u>T</u>ools), and the selection letter on the command (**U** for <u>U</u>ser Setup). For information about Windows menu and command syntax, see Appendix B.

## Selecting Options in Dialog Boxes

Most dialog boxes, such as the User Setup dialog box, contain a variety of boxes and buttons with which you instruct the active application. For example, you can click in the <u>B</u>eep on Error check box to turn off the sound that indicates to all your colleagues that you have made a mistake. Or to change the directory in which you store worksheets, type a path in the <u>W</u>orksheet directory text box. You can even open another dialog box by clicking on either <u>I</u>nternational or <u>R</u>ecalculation. When you finish selecting options and typing values, click on the OK command button (or press ↵). To close a dialog box or menu without taking any action, click on the Cancel command button (or press Esc). If you need more information about how Windows dialog boxes work, see Appendix B. To learn how to customize SmartSuite applications, see Appendix C.

## Selecting Commands from Shortcut Menus

As you learn more about SmartSuite applications, you'll find that usually there are many ways to do a job. For example, you can copy a selection to the

**FIGURE 2.9**

The User Setup dialog box, from which you can customize options that personalize your application

Check box

Text/list boxes

Text boxes

Help button

Command buttons

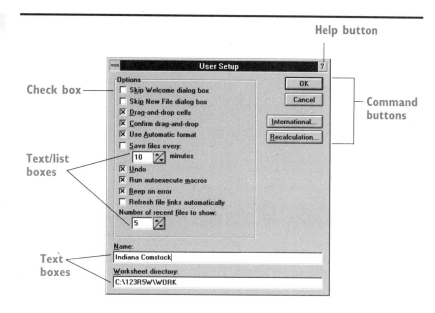

Clipboard by clicking on the Copy SmartIcon, by choosing Edit ➤ Copy, or by pressing either Ctrl+C or Ctrl+Ins. If you are working on an item, the quickest way to copy it is by clicking on the right mouse button to reveal a shortcut menu (Figure 2.10), which contains the most common 1-2-3 commands. Then select Copy (by pressing either the left or right mouse button).

**FIGURE 2.10**

A shortcut menu next to the active cell

Current cell

Unavailable commands

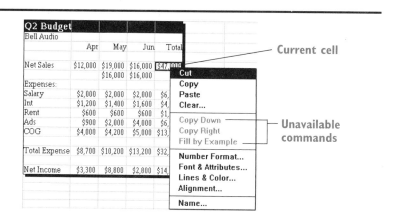

**NOTE** The only way to reveal a shortcut menu is to click on the right mouse button; therefore, there's no need for underlined selection letters.

In the following sections, you'll learn some of the details of using the mouse and the keyboard to open menus, select commands, and specify options.

# Using the Mouse

Although you can move around the current window and the active application using either the mouse or the keyboard, it's easier for a novice to use the mouse (after learning how to move the mouse around the mouse pad and click the mouse buttons). In contrast, using the keyboard requires knowledge of the application; selection letters on menus and commands provide clues for getting around, but you have to know the application to know its shortcut keys. In addition, the only way to use some objects, such as SmartIcons, is to click a mouse button. However, as you find out about each SmartSuite application, you'll discover that using shortcut keys is the fastest way to perform an action. So you'll probably issue commands using both the mouse and the keyboard.

The mouse pointer changes shape depending on its location in the window and the action that you are taking. Table 2.2 shows many types of mouse pointers and provides a description of each.

**TABLE 2.2:** Common SmartSuite Mouse Pointers

| MOUSE POINTER | DESCRIPTION |
|---|---|
| ⌖ | Points to objects (menus, buttons, boxes, windows, icons, and so on) on the screen so that you can select them. This is the default mouse pointer. |
| ⧗ | Indicates that the application is working and you must wait until performing another action. |

**TABLE 2.2:** Common SmartSuite Mouse Pointers (continued)

| MOUSE POINTER | DESCRIPTION |
|---|---|
| | Adjusts the width of a column. |
| | Adjusts the height of a row. |
| | Adjusts the height of a window. |
| | Adjusts the width of a window. |
| | Adjusts both the height and width of a window. |
| | Moves or sizes a window using the Control menu. |
| | Marks the insertion point for text or data entry. |
| | Defines a range for selection. |
| | Shows that you are ready to drag a selection. |
| | Shows that you have started to drag a selection. |
| | Shows that you have started to drag a copy of a selection. |
| | Marks the starting position of a new chart. |
| | Marks the starting position of a new picture. |
| | Marks a selection of objects. |
| | Marks help text that when clicked on either displays terminology or a description or jumps to a related help topic. |
| | Magnifies the clicked-on window. |

SmartSuite

There are four basic ways in which you can use the mouse:

**Point**   Move the mouse around the mouse pad or table top until the mouse pointer is located at the desired position on the screen.

**Click**   Press and release the mouse button once.

**Double-click**   Rapidly press and release the mouse button twice.

**Drag**   Press and hold down the mouse button while moving the mouse around the mouse pad.

## Using the Keyboard

If you have more experience with the keyboard than with the mouse, or if you don't have a mouse, you can execute commands by using just the keyboard. You can activate commands by pressing shortcut keys, which are single keys or *key combinations* (pressing two or three keys simultaneously). In this book, key combinations are shown as a series of keys, each separated by a plus sign (+). For example, the key combination used to print a file in any SmartSuite application is Ctrl+P. Table 2.3 lists some common SmartSuite shortcut keys and key combinations used to execute commands and perform other actions.

**TABLE 2.3:**   SmartSuite Shortcut Keys and Key Combinations - Commands and Actions

| SHORTCUT KEY OR KEY COMBINATION | DESCRIPTION |
| --- | --- |
| Alt | Activates the menu bar |
| Alt+↑ | Opens and closes a drop-down list box |
| Alt+↓ | Opens and closes a drop-down list box |
| Alt+- | Opens the Control menu for the current window |
| Alt+spacebar | Opens the Control menu |
| Alt+Esc | Cycles through all active Windows applications |
| Alt+F4 | Closes a window or application |

**TABLE 2.3:** SmartSuite Shortcut Keys and Key Combinations - Commands and Actions (continued)

| SHORTCUT KEY OR KEY COMBINATION | DESCRIPTION |
| --- | --- |
| Alt+F4 | Closes a dialog box without taking any actions |
| Ctrl+Esc | Opens the Windows Task List from which you can select an active application |
| Ctrl+F4 | Closes the current window |
| Ctrl+O | Opens the Open File dialog box |
| Ctrl+P | Opens the Print dialog box from which you can print all or part of the current file |
| Ctrl+S | Saves the current file |
| ↵ | Signals the completion of filling in the dialog box, then closes the dialog box |
| Esc | Closes the dialog box without taking any actions |
| F1 | Displays the help contents window |
| F10 | Activates the menu bar |

# Moving around a File

You can use either the mouse or the keyboard to move around any SmartSuite file. Some SmartSuite applications offer other means of navigation; you'll learn about those methods in later chapters.

## Scrolling around the Work Area Using the Mouse

There are two ways to use the mouse to move around a file.

- Move the mouse pointer around the work area currently displayed in the active window.

- Press, hold down, and drag the mouse pointer in the vertical and horizontal scroll bars (Figure 2.11) to display other parts of the file.

**NOTE** If your file is small enough to fit within the work area, the scroll bars will either be dimmed (which indicates that they are unavailable) or you won't be able to use them. For example, in Freelance Graphics, if you try to use the scroll bar for a one-page presentation, the application beeps at you.

**FIGURE 2.11**

Use the arrows, the scroll box, and the area within the horizontal scroll bar to move around a file.

Scroll bar arrow

Scroll bar arrow

Scroll box

Except for the position in which they are displayed, vertical and horizontal scroll bars look exactly the same. Use the vertical scroll bar to move through a file from top to bottom, and use the horizontal scroll bar to move from side to side.

A scroll bar consists of arrows, the area within the scroll bar and between the arrows, and the *scroll box* (the small box within the scroll bar). You can use any part of a scroll bar to scroll through a file.

**Scroll bar arrows** Move horizontally or vertically through a file by moving the mouse pointer to the arrows at either end of a horizontal or vertical scroll bar and pressing and holding down the left mouse button on the scroll bar arrows. As your file scrolls side to side or up and down the desktop, the scroll box also moves to indicate the part of the file currently in the work area. If you click once on a scroll bar arrow, the file moves a small distance (for example, one row or column in 1-2-3).

**Within the scroll bar** The area within the scroll bar represents the entire length or width of your file. If you click on any part of this area other than the scroll box, you'll see the next or previous screen of the file. For example, in 1-2-3, if you are currently viewing columns J–Q, if you click to the left of the scroll box, you'll see columns A–I. Then if you click to the right of the scroll box, once again you'll see J–Q. Again, click to the right and R–Y are displayed.

**Scroll box**    Drag the scroll box (which is also called the *thumb*) to a new position on the scroll bar. When you release the left mouse button, you'll move to a comparable position in the file. For example, if you move the scroll box to the middle of the scroll bar, you'll see the middle of the file.

## Scrolling around the Work Area Using the Keyboard

When you are typing, you'll find that you can move around a file more quickly with the keyboard than with the mouse. After you learn the basics of an application, you'll find that you memorize and use certain command key-strokes. Table 2.4 lists the keys and key combinations with which you can scroll around SmartSuite files.

**TABLE 2.4:**    SmartSuite Shortcut Keys and Key Combinations—Navigation

| SHORTCUT KEY OR KEY COMBINATION | DESCRIPTION |
| --- | --- |
| ↑ | Moves up to the previous item in a group |
| ↓ | Moves down to the next item in a group |
| ← | Moves up to the previous item in a group |
| → | Moves down to the next item in a group |
| Ctrl+← | Moves the cursor to the left of the previous word (label); moves to the beginning of the value (values) |
| Ctrl+→ | Moves the cursor to the left of the next word (label); moves to the end of the value (values) |
| Ctrl+Home | Moves the cursor to the first cell in the current file (the first cell in the first spreadsheet in the file) |

**TABLE 2.4:** SmartSuite Shortcut Keys and Key Combinations—Navigation (continued)

| SHORTCUT KEY OR KEY COMBINATION | DESCRIPTION |
| --- | --- |
| Ctrl+PgDn | Moves the cursor to the first cell in the prior worksheet in the file |
| Ctrl+PgUp | Moves the cursor to the first cell in the next worksheet in the file |
| End | Moves the cursor to the end of the entry |
| End+Ctrl+Home | Moves the cursor to the bottom-right corner of the active area in the current file |
| End+Ctrl+PgDn | Moves the cursor to the next worksheet with a cell that contains data and is next to an empty cell in the same cell position as the current position |
| End+Ctrl+PgUp | Moves the cursor to the prior worksheet with a cell that contains data and is next to an empty cell in the same cell position as the current position |
| Home | Moves the cursor to the beginning of the entry |
| Shift+Tab | Moves to the previous option, from right to left and from bottom to top order |
| Tab | Moves to the next option, from left to right and from top to bottom order |

# Checking Spelling

After you have created a 1-2-3, Ami Pro, or Freelance Graphics file and spent some time editing it, you should check its spelling and the occurrence of duplicate words. These SmartSuite applications have two dictionaries—the language (main) dictionary and the user dictionary into which you add your own words, such as unique technical terms, product and company names, and so on. You can check just one part of a file by selecting it; otherwise, the spell checker evaluates the entire file. To set spell checker options and run the spell checker, choose Tools ➤ Spell Check (for 1-2-3 and Approach) or Tools ➤ Spell Check (Ami Pro and Freelance Graphics). The Spell Check dialog box (Figure 2.12) appears. (To run the spell checker without setting options, click on the Spell Check SmartIcon.)

**FIGURE 2.12**

The opening Spell Check dialog box for 1-2-3 allows you to set spell check options.

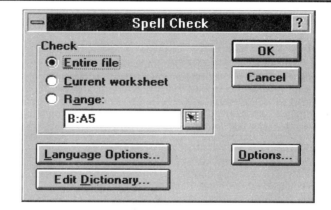

The starting Spell Check dialog boxes for 1-2-3, Ami Pro, Approach, and Freelance Graphics contain several common options:

**Language Options**    Click on this button to display the Language Options dialog box (Figure 2.13) in which you can change the path where the dictionaries are located. If you change to an invalid path, you'll see a message to that effect. You can also select a dictionary for a particular language by opening the Language drop-down list box and selecting from the list.

**Edit Dictionary**    Click on this button to display the Edit Dictionary dialog box (Figure 2.14), which allows you to view and add words to the list in the user dictionary. You can also add words as you run the spell checker, as you will see shortly.

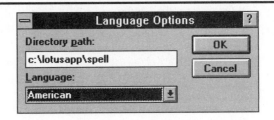

**FIGURE 2.13**

The 1-2-3 Language
Options dialog box lets
you change the path in
which the dictionaries
are located and select a
dictionary for a
particular language.

**FIGURE 2.14**

The 1-2-3 Edit
Dictionary dialog box
lets you view and add
words to the list
of words in your
user dictionary.

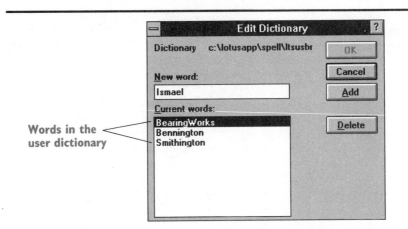

Words in the
user dictionary

**Options**   Click on this button to display the Options dialog box (Figure 2.15), which contains five check boxes to be checked or cleared:

- Check for <u>R</u>epeated Words determines whether the spell checker checks for repeat words.

- Check Words with <u>N</u>umbers determines whether the spell checker checks for words including numbers (for example, Address1).

- Check Words with <u>I</u>nitial Caps determines whether the spell checker checks for words starting with uppercase characters (that is, proper nouns such as surnames and company names).

**FIGURE 2.15**

The Options dialog box provides check boxes, which you can use to refine the spell check process.

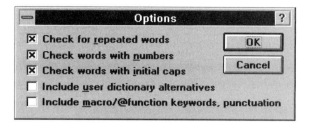

■ Include <u>U</u>ser Dictionary Alternatives determines whether the spell checker includes words from the user dictionary in the list of alternate spellings.

■ Include <u>M</u>acro/@Function Keywords, Punctuation (only in 1-2-3) determines whether the spell checker uses a dictionary of keywords and functions when checking words.

When you have set spell checker options, click on OK to start the spell checker. When it encounters its first unknown word, another Spell Check dialog box (Figure 2.16) appears.

**FIGURE 2.16**

The main 1-2-3 Spell Check dialog box allows you to control the spell checker as it reviews your file.

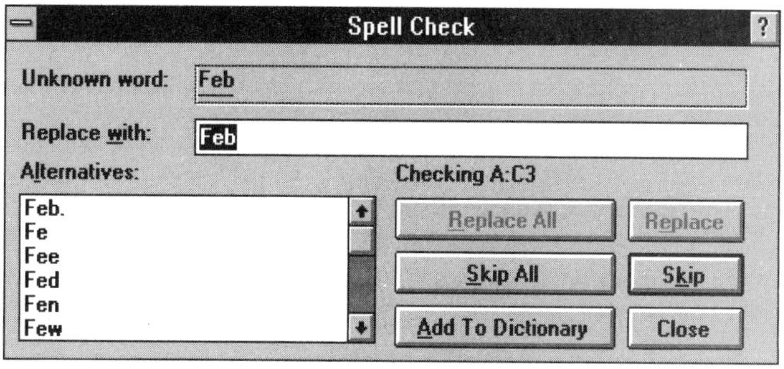

**Spell Check**

Unknown word: Feb

Replace with: Feb

Alternatives:      Checking A:C3

Feb.
Fe
Fee
Fed
Fen
Few

Replace All    Replace
Skip All    Skip
Add To Dictionary    Close

The options in this dialog box are as follows:

| | |
|---|---|
| Unknown Word (in 1-2-3), Unnamed (in Freelance Graphics) | Displays a word that is not in the language or user dictionary. |
| Replace With | Contains the first word in the Alternatives box. |
| Alternatives | Lists suggested replacement words. |
| Replace All | Replaces all occurrences of the unknown word with the word in the Replace With text box. |
| Replace | Replaces this occurrence of the unknown word with the word in the Replace With text box. |
| Skip All | Skips all occurrences of the unknown word in the rest of this file. |
| Skip | Skips this occurrence of the unknown word. |
| Add to Dictionary | Adds the unknown word to the user dictionary. |

When the spell checker has completed its work, it displays an information box:

Click on OK to return to your file.

## Saving a File

Once you have put a certain amount of work into a file, you'll want to save it so that you don't have to reconstruct it later. You can save a file any time—

even before you type your first character—using the commands listed below:

File ➤ Save (or press Ctrl+S)
: If you are saving the file for the first time, displays the Save As dialog box (Figure 2.17). If you are saving the file after that, this command just saves the file using its original name.

File ➤ Save As
: Displays the Save As dialog box so that you can save this file using a different name, location, or save option. Use this command to create a backup file.

Tools ➤ User Setup
: Displays the User Setup dialog box (shown above in Figure 2.9) in which you can define options for automatically saving your files every few minutes as you are working on them.

You'll learn how to use each of these save commands in the sections below.

**FIGURE 2.17**

The 1-2-3 Save As dialog box lets you name a file and provide other information about it.

Suggested file name

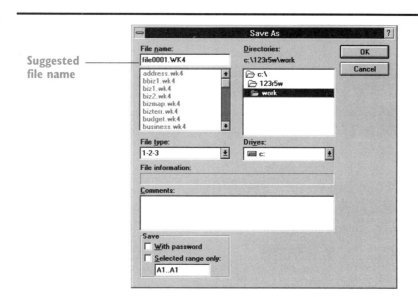

SmartSuite

## About the Save As Dialog Box

There are several ways to save a file:

- Choose File ➤ Save
- Press Ctrl+S

- Click on the Save SmartIcon
- Choose File ➤ Save As
- Turn on the automatic save feature

If you save a file by choosing File ➤ Save, pressing Ctrl+S, or clicking on the Save SmartIcon, and if you have saved this file before, your application will save the file using its current name and location. If the file you are saving has never been saved before, the Save As dialog box appears. Regardless of whether this file has been saved before, if you choose File ➤ Save As, the application displays the Save As dialog box. This dialog box may look complex when you first see it, but it is in fact easy to use.

**The Save As dialog box is a typical Windows dialog box. It closely resembles the Open dialog box (used when you opened the current file).**

These are the parts the SmartSuite Save As dialog boxes have in common:

**File Name**    This text/list box lists all the files in the current directory, to ensure that the name you give a file is unique. If you decide to select a duplicate name, the application asks you whether you want to replace the current file with this file, create a backup file, or cancel the save. To learn about valid file names, see the next section of this chapter.

**File Type** (in Ami Pro, **List Files of Type**)    When you open this drop-down list box, you can see the file types to which you can save this file. For example, in 1-2-3, you have the choice of saving files in four 1-2-3 formats and in text format.

**SmartSuite**

**D**irectories    This box displays the path to the current directory and shows you the current directory structure. For example, in Figure 2.17 you can see the c:\, or root directory; the main 1-2-3 subdirectory (123r5w); and the current subdirectory, *sample*, which is illustrated by a shaded open file folder icon.

**NOTE**    **A computer's directory structure is like an upside-down tree. The root directory, at the top, is the trunk from which all the branches, or subdirectories, come. (To see a better picture of your computer system's directory structure, open File Manager and look at the Directory pane, on the left side of the File Manager window.) Alignment in the <u>D</u>irectories box shows how far a subdirectory is from the root directory, which is aligned against the left border of the box. Immediately underneath and to the right of the root directory icon is the 123r5w icon, and under that (and further to the right) is the sample icon. Notice that these three icons illustrate the path. \123r5w is a subdirectory of the root directory, and \sample is a subdirectory of 123r5w.**

**Dri<u>v</u>es**    This drop-down list box displays the name of the current drive. When you open the list box, you'll see the other drives on your computer system. For example, c: represents the hard drive, and a: and b: indicate floppy disk drives for many (but not all) computer systems.

The Save As dialog box also provides other options that are related to the specific type of application. For example, in Figure 2.17, notice the Save group, which is applicable to 1-2-3 only.

**TIP** One of the most important reasons to save a file is to create a backup copy of the file. The best way to back up a file is to save it to disk and store the disk in a location away from your computer—in another room or even in another building. To back up a file, insert a disk in the appropriate disk drive and choose File ➤ Save As. In the Save As dialog box, type or select the file name in the File Name text/list box, open the Drives drop-down list box, and select the identifier for the disk drive. Then either click on OK or press ↵. After saving, make sure that before you save or open your next file, you change the disk identifier to the hard drive, if necessary.

## Naming a File

When you save a file that is unnamed, the Save As dialog box highlights the File Name text box and sometimes suggests a name (for example, in 1-2-3 the suggested name is file000n.wk4, where n represents a unique number, which is increased by 1 if you have selected the previously suggested file name).

If you wish to assign another file name, follow these naming rules: Select a file name from one to eight characters in length, and select valid characters (A–Z, 0–9, underscores, and hyphens, but no spaces). When a SmartSuite application saves a file, it automatically adds a period (.) and the appropriate extension to the file name. Table 2.5 lists SmartSuite extensions and the applications to which they are related.

**TABLE 2.5:** SmartSuite File Extensions

| EXTENSION | APPLICATION |
| --- | --- |
| .WK4 | 1-2-3 |
| .SAM | Ami Pro |
| .APR | Approach |
| .PRE | Freelance Graphics |
| .OR2 | Organizer |

## Setting Up the Automatic Save Feature

Anyone with much computer experience can tell you at least one horror story about losing a file when the power went out. To prevent losing too much of your valuable time, take advantage of the automatic save features in 1-2-3, Ami Pro, and Freelance Graphics. Simply choose Tools ➤ User Setup. In the User Setup dialog box, check the Save Files Every check box and select a value from 1 to 99 minutes between saves. The default is 10 minutes. Then click on OK or press ↵.

When the automatic save feature is turned on, the current application counts the minutes since the last save, either automatic or manual. Since this count goes on in the background, you can continue your work. When the count equals the specified number of minutes, the application is ready to save your file. The next time you pause (perhaps to look up a number or to think of the next word), the application quickly saves the file. Then the count begins again.

# Printing a File

Once you have previewed and edited your file, you can print it. SmartSuite applications provide several ways to print a file:

- Click on the Print SmartIcon in either the Print Preview window or the application window.
- Choose File ➤ Print.
- Press Ctrl+P.

Whatever the method you use, the Print dialog box (Figure 2.18) appears. Each SmartSuite Print dialog box provides a combination of common options and application-specific options. Application-specific printing options are covered in Chapters 6, 9, 14, 15, and 17.

These are some of the common options in SmartSuite Print dialog boxes:

**Number of Copies** or **Copies**    In this text/list box, select the number of copies of the file to be printed.

## FIGURE 2.18

1-2-3's Print dialog box has several options that are common to any Windows application Print dialog box and several that are application specific.

The default printer

Click on this button to change page layout settings

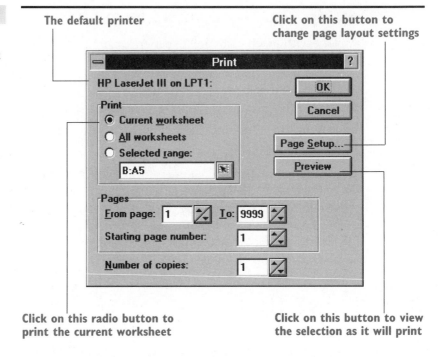

Click on this radio button to print the current worksheet

Click on this button to view the selection as it will print

**From Page, From Page,** or **From**    In this text/list box, select the starting page number.

**To**    In this text/list box, select the number of the last page to be printed.

**Current Worksheet, Current Form, Current Page Only,** or **Current Page**    Click in this button to print only the page in which the insertion point is located.

**All Worksheets** or **All**    Click in this button to print the entire file.

**Page Setup, Page Setup,** or **Setup**    To change the default page settings, click on this button. When the Page Setup dialog box appears, select from its options and either click on OK or press ↵.

# Deleting Files

In general, Windows applications do not provide commands for deleting files. Instead, most applications take advantage of the file maintenance capabilities of the Windows File Manager program.

  Before deleting a file, make sure that you no longer need it. Unless you back up the file before removing it (a very good idea), a deleted file is gone forever!

If you are running Windows as you installed it, you will open File Manager from Program Manager. From within a SmartSuite application, either press Alt+Esc or Ctrl+Esc. Pressing Alt+Esc allows you to cycle through all the active applications until you reach Program Manager. Pressing Ctrl+Esc opens the Task List (Figure 2.19) from which you can select Program Manager by double-clicking on its line. If you are running very few applications, pressing Alt+Esc is your best choice. However, if several applications are active, choosing from the Task List is more efficient. In either case, once the Program Manager window is on your desktop, delete a file by following these steps:

1. Open File Manager by double-clicking on its icon.

2. In the Tree pane on the left side of the File Manager window (Figure 2.20), click on the icon that represents the directory in which the file to be deleted is located.

**FIGURE 2.19**

You can go to an active application by selecting it from the Windows Task List.

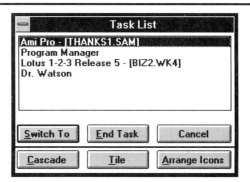

## FIGURE 2.20

The File Manager Window has two panes: the Tree pane on the left side and the Directory pane on the right.

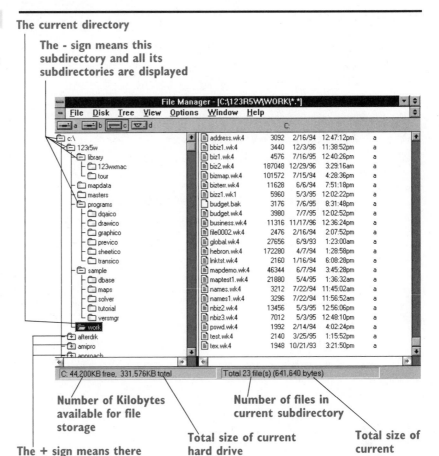

The current directory

The - sign means this subdirectory and all its subdirectories are displayed

Number of Kilobytes available for file storage

Number of files in current subdirectory

Total size of current hard drive

Total size of current subdirectory

The + sign means there are subdirectories to be displayed

**3.** On the right side of the File Manager window in the Directory pane, find the name of the file to be deleted and select it.

**4.** Delete the files by choosing File ➤ Delete or by pressing the Del key. Depending on your File Manager attributes, Windows displays one or two dialog boxes to which you must respond.

**5.** Close File Manager and return to your work by pressing either Ctrl+Esc or Alt+Esc.

To learn more about using File Manager and other Windows features, see Appendix B.

# Getting Help

Once you have found out how to get help in one Windows application, you will know how most Windows Help facilities work. If you have a question about a SmartSuite feature, element, or procedure, you can get help in several ways:

- To get general help about an application, from an application window click on Help on the menu bar; a menu (Figure 2.21) opens from which you can choose.
- To open a Help Contents window (Figure 2.22), press F1.
- To get Windows help, press F1 from an active Help window. To return to the application, click on Back.
-  To get information about using a dialog box, click on the question mark button at the upper-right corner or press F1.
- To display SmartCenter information, display Help Cards, take the Guided Tour, or use the Movie Guide, click on the SmartAnswers icon on the SmartCenter icon palette.

---

**FIGURE 2.21**

The open 1-2-3
Help menu.

| Help |
| :--- |
| **Contents** |
| Search... |
| Using Help |
| Keyboard |
| How Do I? |
| For Upgraders |
| Tutorial |
| About 1-2-3... |

FIGURE 2.22

Open the 1-2-3 Help
Contents window by
choosing Help ➤
Contents or by
pressing F1 from an
application window.

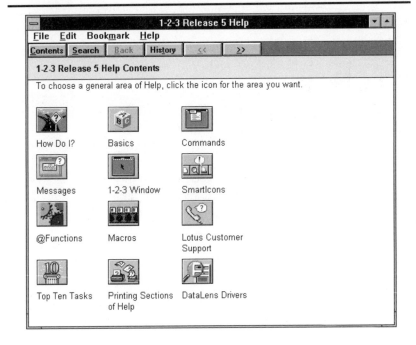

There are eight commands available in the 1-2-3 Help Contents window:

**Contents**    Provides icons representing help topics. Click on an icon to see a list of topics.

**Search**    Opens a dialog box (Figure 2.23) that lists topics and functions about which you can learn more. Simply select a topic and click on the Show Topics button. When the Help facility displays one or more related topics, select one and click on the Go To button. At this point, you will see one or more screens of helpful information.

**Using Help**    Opens a window that explains how the Help facility works.

**Keyboard**    Lists help topics on keys and key combinations.

**How Do I?**    Provides a list of tasks from which you can choose.

**For Upgraders**    Lists information about upgrading from a prior release of the application.

**FIGURE 2.23**

Use the Search dialog box to find help topics that can help you to accomplish a task.

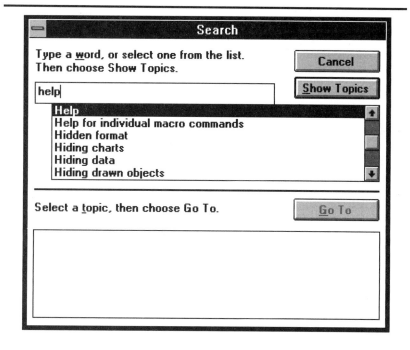

Tutorial   Starts the tutorial for this application. To view the tutorial, select it and follow the instructions in the tutorial window. To return to the application using the mouse, click on Exit. To return to the application using the keyboard, tab through the topics until Exit is highlighted, then press ↵.

About *application*   Provides copyright information about the application.

# Launching One SmartSuite Application from within Another

When you are running one SmartSuite application, it's easy to start another and move between the two. In fact, your computer's memory is the only limit to the number of applications you can run at the same time. To launch a

SmartSuite application, either click on the appropriate icon on the Smart-Center icon palette or display the Working Together SmartIcons and click on the appropriate SmartIcon.

There are two ways to display a particular set of SmartIcons:

- Click on the SmartIcon button on the status bar, and select the Working Together SmartIcon set. Click on the appropriate SmartIcon.

- Click repeatedly on the Next SmartIcon button until you see the appropriate SmartSuite SmartIcon. Then click on the appropriate SmartIcon.

The Part One opening pages list the SmartIcons with which you can start other SmartSuite and related Lotus applications.

# Viewing Two Applications Simultaneously

Windows provides two commands—Cascade and Tile—that allow you to display multiple windows on your desktop. (However, keep in mind that the more windows you display, the less of each window's content you will see.)

When you choose Window ➤ Tile or click on the Tile button, windows are arranged so that they look like a tile floor or wall; each window is partially displayed, but you can see all four borders (Figure 2.24). Tiling windows allows you to get a better look at their contents than cascading them does.

When you choose Window ➤ Cascade or click on the Cascade button, all windows cascade down the desktop so that you can see each title bar (Figure 2.25), but probably not much more.

The location from which you execute Tile or Cascade causes different results:

- If you choose Window ➤ Tile or Window ➤ Cascade in an application window, multiple windows from within the application (for example, multiple files or spreadsheets) are tiled or cascaded.

- If you choose Window ➤ Tile (or press Shift+F4) or Window ➤ Cascade (or press Shift+F5) in the Program Manager window, multiple restored group windows (for example, Main and Applications) are tiled or cascaded.

**FIGURE 2.24**

These 1-2-3, Approach, and Program Manager windows were tiled from the Task List.

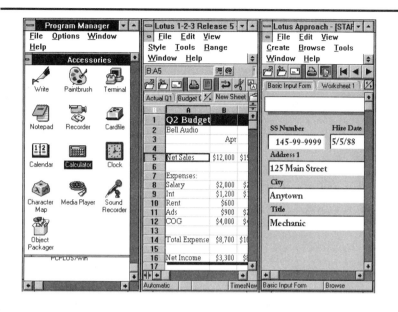

**FIGURE 2.25**

Cascading 1-2-3, Approach, and Program Manager windows

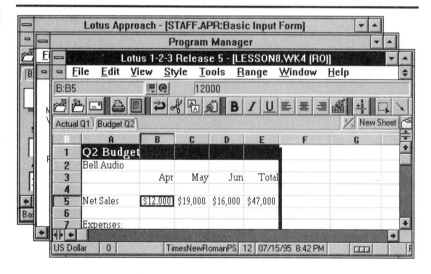

■ If you click on the <u>T</u>ile or <u>W</u>indow button at the bottom of the Task List (press Ctrl+Esc), multiple restored application windows (for example, active Ami Pro and 1-2-3 windows) are tiled or cascaded.

So, to tile or cascade your active application windows, open the Task List and click on either the Tile or Cascade button. You'll notice that all your application windows—perhaps more than you had hoped—appear on your desktop in their new order. If you have tiled your application windows, all you have to do to display only the desired applications is to drag their borders so that you cover the unwanted application windows. You can also drag the windows around by their title bars to reposition them and to change their dimensions.

## Moving between Applications

The way that you move between open applications differs, depending on how you have arranged the application windows on your desktop. Here are some suggestions:

- If you have tiled your applications, click anywhere in the desired application window to make it active.

**WORKING TOGETHER**

### Tiling and Cascading Windows Using Windows and Ami Pro

Windows provides several ways to arrange windows on the desktop:

- Choose the Program Manager's Window ➤ Cascade command (or press Shift+F5) to cascade all the restored or maximized windows, including windows displayed in the Program Manager and the active application windows.

- Choose the Program Manager's Window ➤ Tile command (or press Shift+F4) to tile all the restored or maximized windows, including windows displayed in the Program Manager and the active application windows.

**WORKING TOGETHER** ▲

- Press Ctrl+Esc to open the Task List. Click on <u>C</u>ascade to cascade Program Manager and restored and maximized active applications on the desktop.
- Press Ctrl+Esc to open the Task List. Click on <u>T</u>ile to tile Program Manager and restored and maximized active applications on the desktop.

Ami Pro provides a way in which you can tile two Lotus Windows application windows:

**1.** Choose Too<u>l</u>s ➤ <u>M</u>acros ➤ <u>P</u>layback or click on the appropriate SmartIcon in the Bonus Pack SmartIcons set. Ami Pro displays the Play Macro dialog box.

SmartSuite

**WORKING TOGETHER**
▲

**2.** Choose LOTUSTIL.SMM and click on OK. Ami Pro displays the Lotus Application Tiler dialog box.

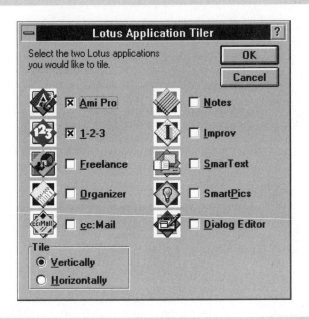

**NOTE**

**If you have two applications in adjacent positions, you can use drag and drop to move objects from one application to another. Simply move the mouse pointer to an object, press and hold down the left mouse button, and drag the object to its new application window.**

■ If you have cascaded your application windows, to move to a particular application, click on its title bar to make it active and then maximize it, if needed. To make active another application window, choose Window ➤ Cascade, click on the desired title bar, and maximize again. Repeat these steps, if needed.

**WORKING TOGETHER** ▲

**3.** Click on <u>V</u>ertically (the default) or <u>H</u>orizontally to tile the two applications vertically or horizontally, respectively.

**4.** Click on OK. Lotus tiles the applications.

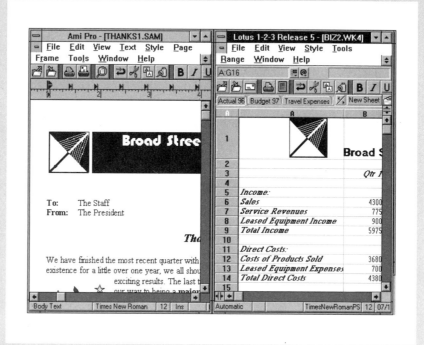

■ You can start applications and minimize each of them. When you need to move from one application to another, simply minimize the application with which you have been working and either restore or maximize the application with which you want to work (Figure 2.26).

■ If you have several applications running in either restored or maximized windows (that is, untiled or uncascaded), press Alt+Esc to cycle through each application in turn. When you have arrived at the desired application, start working. Pressing Alt+Esc works better when you have few open applications; you don't waste time by displaying each application.

**FIGURE 2.26**

Approach and Ami Pro
minimized windows.

**The current Ami Pro file**

■ If you have several applications running in either restored or maximized windows, press Ctrl+Esc to open the Task List. Then double-click on the desired application on the list. Pressing Ctrl+Esc works better when you have a long list of open applications; you can select from the list rather than cycling through applications one at a time.

## Exiting an Application

Exiting an application is the same whether it is the only active application or one of several; Windows is intelligent enough to realize that other open applications should continue running.

To exit an active SmartSuite application, choose File ➤ Exit, type the key combination Alt+F4, or double-click on the Application Control Menu button. The application will prompt you to save any unsaved work before you actually end the work session.

## Exiting Windows

To exit Windows, follow the same steps you just learned: choose File ➤ Exit, type Alt+F4, or double-click on the Application Control Menu button. Windows prompts you to verify that you want to end your Windows session.

3

# Editing in SmartSuite Applications

**O**nce you have created a file, whether it's a 1-2-3 spreadsheet, an Ami Pro document, an Approach database, a Freelance Graphics presentation, or even an Organizer calendar entry, you can edit it to change its content or look or enhance it to improve its appearance.

In this chapter, you'll learn some of the basic editing and enhancement capabilities of SmartSuite applications. Then as you read about and learn to use each application in future chapters, you'll find out the particulars of editing and enhancing a file in a specific application.

# Magnifying and Reducing Your File in the Application Window

*Zooming* the information displayed on the computer screen helps you to see things in two ways: magnified (Figure 3.1) or reduced (Figure 3.2). If you zoom in to magnify the information, you can see the details of a file (for example, a piece of clip art in a document or presentation or a particular number in a spreadsheet). If you zoom out to reduce the information, you'll see how the information looks on your desktop (for example, how the text fits using the margins that you have specified and how the headers compare with the body text).

The way in which you zoom varies with the SmartSuite application you are using, but all SmartSuite applications except Organizer allow you to choose a command from the View menu to magnify, reduce, or change the view in another way. In addition, any SmartIcon that looks like a magnifying glass changes the view. For example, in addition to Zoom In and Zoom Out, Freelance Graphics provides three more zoom commands and one SmartIcon, while 1-2-3 has one additional zoom command and three SmartIcons. Table 3.1 provides a list of all SmartSuite zoom commands.

**FIGURE 3.1**

A magnified application window

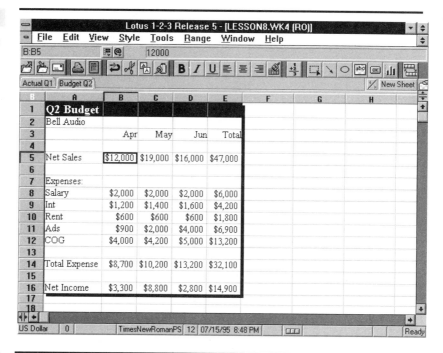

**FIGURE 3.2**

A reduced application window. The asterisks indicate that the numbers normally displayed in a cell won't fit anymore.

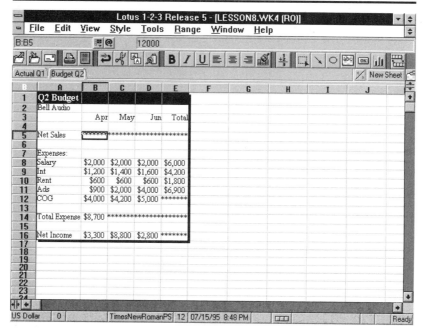

TABLE 3.1: SmartSuite Zoom Commands

| MENU COMMAND | DESCRIPTION | SHORTCUT KEY |
|---|---|---|
| *Application: 1-2-3* | | |
| View ➤ Zoom In | Displays the cells in a spreadsheet in an increased size | N/A |
| View ➤ Zoom Out | Displays the cells in a spreadsheet in a reduced size | N/A |
| View ➤ Custom | Displays a page in a size that you select (from 10% to 400%) | N/A |
| *Application: Ami Pro* | | |
| View ➤ Full Page | Displays a complete page on the desktop | If you are in custom view, Ctrl+D; otherwise N/A |
| View ➤ Custom | Displays a page in a size that you select (from 10% to 400%) | If you are in full page view, Ctrl+D; otherwise N/A |
| View ➤ Standard | Displays a page in a size that other Windows applications use as a default | N/A |
| View ➤ Enlarged | Displays a page in a magnified size | N/A |
| View ➤ Facing Pages | Displays two side-by-side pages | N/A |
| *Application: Approach* | | |
| View ➤ Zoom In | Displays a form, page of mailing labels, report, or form letter in a magnified size | N/A |

**TABLE 3.1:** SmartSuite Zoom Commands (continued)

| MENU COMMAND | DESCRIPTION | SHORTCUT KEY |
|---|---|---|
| Application: **Approach (continued)** | | |
| <u>V</u>iew ➤ <u>A</u>ctual Size | Displays a form, page of mailing labels, report, or form letter in its actual size | Ctrl+I |
| <u>V</u>iew ➤ Zoom <u>O</u>ut | Displays a form, page of mailing labels, report, or form letter in a reduced size | N/A |
| Application: **Freelance Graphics** | | |
| <u>V</u>iew ➤ <u>F</u>ull Page | Displays a full page after zooming in or zooming out | N/A |
| <u>V</u>iew ➤ Zoom <u>I</u>n | Displays a page in an enlarged size | N/A |
| <u>V</u>iew ➤ Zoom <u>O</u>ut | Displays a page in a reduced view | N/A |
| <u>V</u>iew ➤ <u>L</u>ast | Returns to the previously selected view | N/A |

**SmartSuite**

# An Introduction to Editing

In most cases, you can expect a newly-created file to be around for a long time. However, you'll probably have to modify its look and contents throughout its lifetime. For example, you might create a 1-2-3 spreadsheet or Approach database to be used as the basis for your inventory or payroll systems and their weekly, yearly, and annual reports. You could put your business plan on Ami Pro, 1-2-3, and even Freelance Graphics and let it evolve as your business and business conditions change. In fact, every time you use Organizer, you might add, delete, or change items on your To-Do or anniversary lists and modify entries in your address book.

## Making a Selection

Before you edit a file, you'll have to identify the area of the file on which the editing command will act. As you work, you can select blocks of varying size—from a single character all the way to the entire file—so that you can copy, move, delete, or change the look of the selection.

## Using the Mouse to Select

As you have already learned, using the mouse when you first learn an application is easier than using the keyboard. Using a mouse allows you to set the boundaries of a selection without having to learn keystrokes for each type of selection.

To select with the mouse, move the mouse pointer to a starting position (that is, a corner, character, line, row, or column). Then press and hold down the left mouse button and drag the mouse pointer toward the other end of your selection. As you move the mouse, your selection is highlighted. If you are working in monochrome, the highlight is in reverse video. If you are working in color, the highlight is either the complementary color of the original (for example, blue becomes red and yellow becomes green) or black. When you move the mouse to the end of the selection, release the mouse button. The list below lists mouse shortcuts for selecting particular items in a file.

| TO SELECT THIS: | MOVE THE MOUSE POINTER HERE: |
|---|---|
| One or more characters in an Approach database | Click on the Text icon and drag from the first to last character. |
| A word or number in a 1-2-3 spreadsheet | Any character in the word or number and click the left mouse button. |
| A word in an Ami Pro document | To the word and double-click the left mouse button. |
| A word in an Approach database | Click on the Text icon and double-click the word. |
| A field in an Approach database | To the field and click. |

| TO SELECT THIS: | MOVE THE MOUSE POINTER HERE: |
| --- | --- |
| An object | To the object and click. |
| Several objects | To the first object and click, press the Shift key, and drag around objects to be added. |
| A element of a chart | To the element and click. |
| An entire chart | To an empty area in the chart and click. |
| Several words in an Ami Pro document | To the first word, double-click the left mouse button, and drag to the end of the last word in the range. |
| A row in a 1-2-3 spreadsheet | The left side of the row and click the left mouse button. |
| Several contiguous rows in a 1-2-3 spreadsheet | The left side of the row and click the left mouse button. Then either: |

- continue to hold the left mouse button down and drag the mouse up or down from the point at which you first clicked, or
- press the Shift key and either click on rows to be added to the selection or click at the row on the other end of the selection.

| TO SELECT THIS: | MOVE THE MOUSE POINTER HERE: |
| --- | --- |
| Several noncontiguous rows in a 1-2-3 spreadsheet | The left side of the row and click the left mouse button. Then press the Ctrl key and click on rows to be added to the selection. |
| A column in a 1-2-3 spreadsheet | The top of the column and click the left mouse button. |
| Several contiguous columns in a 1-2-3 spreadsheet | The top of the column and click the left mouse button. Then either: |

- continue to hold the left mouse button down and drag the mouse to the left or to the right from the point at which you first clicked, or
- press the Shift key and either click on columns to be added to the selection or click on the column on the other end of the selection.

| TO SELECT THIS: | MOVE THE MOUSE POINTER HERE: |
| --- | --- |
| Several noncontiguous columns in a 1-2-3 spreadsheet | The top of the column and click the left mouse button. Then press the Ctrl key and click on columns to be added to the selection. |
| A sentence in an Ami Pro document | To the sentence, press the Ctrl key, and click the left mouse button. |
| Several sentences in an Ami Pro document | To the first sentence, press the Ctrl key, click the left mouse button, and drag to the end of the last sentence in the range. |
| A paragraph in an Ami Pro document | To the paragraph, press Ctrl, and double-click the left mouse button. |
| Several paragraphs in an Ami Pro document | To the first paragraph, double-click the left mouse button, and drag to the end of the last word in the range. |
| A page in a Freelance Graphics presentation | To the page and click with the left mouse button. |
| Several pages in a Freelance Graphics presentation in Page Layout view | To the next page in the selection, press the Shift key, and click on the page. Then repeat to add more pages to the selection. |
| Several pages in a Freelance Graphics presentation in Page Sorter view | To the first page in the selection and drag the selection box around all the pages to be selected. |
| An entire 1-2-3 spreadsheet | The selection button (above row 1 and to the left of column A) and click the left mouse button. |

To remove the highlight from the current selection, just move the mouse pointer off the selection and click the left mouse button. To remove the highlight from parts of the selection, continue to hold down the left mouse button and move the mouse back toward the start of the selection.

## Using the Keyboard to Select

For every mouse selection action, there is a keyboard method. Table 3.2 lists the keys and key combinations that you can use to select characters for later editing.

You can always change the dimensions of the selection by pressing selection keys. For example, to remove the last line or row from a selection in 1-2-3, press ↑, or to remove the last character from a word selection, press ←. You can also remove larger blocks from a selection by pressing the reverse of the last key or key combination you used. For example, if you pressed Shift+PgDn to select a screenful of characters, reverse the selection by pressing Shift+PgUp.

Making a selection usually means that you're going to do something with it. You can copy or move the selection to another part of the current file or even to a file in another Windows application. Or you can keep the selection in its location and change the way it looks: you can apply boldface to it or increase its size. Let's find out more about your choices in handling a selection.

**TABLE 3.2:**  SmartSuite Keyboard Selection Shortcuts

| SHORTCUT KEY OR KEY COMBINATION | DESCRIPTION |
| --- | --- |
| ← | Selects or reduces the selection of the prior character or cell in 1-2-3 |
| → | Selects or reduces the selection of the next character or cell in 1-2-3 |
| ↑ | Selects or reduces the selection of the character or cell above the current cursor location in 1-2-3 |
| ↓ | Selects or reduces the selection of the character or cell below the current cursor location in 1-2-3 |
| Ctrl+Shift+← | Selects the word to the left in Approach |
| Ctrl+Shift+RA | Selects the word to the right in Approach |

**TABLE 3.2:** SmartSuite Keyboard Selection Shortcuts (continued)

| SHORTCUT KEY OR KEY COMBINATION | DESCRIPTION |
| --- | --- |
| F4 | Selects all the objects on a page in Freelance Graphics |
| Shift+← | Extends or reduces the selection to the left of the current cursor location |
| Shift+→ | Extends or reduces the selection to the right of the current cursor location |
| Shift+↓ | Extends or reduces the selection below the current cursor location |
| Shift+↑ | Extends or reduces the selection above the current cursor location |
| Shift+Home | Extends or reduces the selection from the current cursor location to the top of the file in 1-2-3 |
| Shift+Home | Selects characters to the beginning of a line in Freelance Graphics. |
| Shift+Ctrl+Home | Extends or reduces the selection from the current cursor location to the top of the file in Ami Pro |
| Shift+End | Extends or reduces the selection from the current cursor location to the bottom of the file in 1-2-3 |
| Shift+End | Selects characters to the end of a line in Freelance Graphics. |
| Shift+Ctrl+End | Extends or reduces the selection from the current cursor location to the bottom of the file in Ami Pro |
| Shift+PgUp | Extends or reduces the selection from the current cursor location up one screen toward the top of the file |
| Shift+PgDn | Extends or reduces the selection from the current cursor location down one screen toward the bottom of the file |

## About the Windows Clipboard

The *Clipboard*, an application that runs under Windows, is a temporary
storage facility that almost any Windows application can use to copy or
move (cut) selected characters or graphics. You can use the Clipboard
to copy or cut a selection within one Windows application or among
several Windows applications.

The Clipboard holds only one selection at a time. Every time you copy or cut
a selection, the last contents of the Clipboard are replaced with the new selection. If you exit the active application but stay in Windows, the contents of
the Clipboard remain. However, once you exit Windows, the Clipboard is
emptied (unless you have saved the contents to a file). Because of the differences in formatting options from one Windows application to another, a
pasted item may not look exactly same as it did in the source application.

Clipboard
Viewer

Through the *Clipboard Viewer* (Figure 3.3), you can see the contents of the
Clipboard, and you can manipulate its contents. For example, you can choose
File ➤ Save As to save its contents to a file, or you can open a Clipboard
.CLP file to insert its contents back into the Clipboard.

**FIGURE 3.3**

The Clipboard Viewer
with an open File
menu and a stored
selection behind it

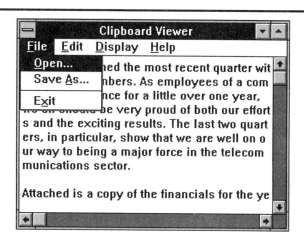

There are two ways to open the Clipboard Viewer:

- Press Ctrl+Esc to open the Windows Task List (Figure 3.4), double-click on the Program Manager line, and double-click on the Clipboard Viewer icon, which by default is in the Main program group.

- Press Alt+Esc to cycle through all your Windows active windows. When the Program Manager window appears, double-click on the Clipboard Viewer icon.

Table 3.3 presents shortcut keys and key combinations related to using the Windows Clipboard. To learn more about the Clipboard, see your Windows manuals.

**FIGURE 3.4**

The Windows Task List dialog box, from which you can choose an active application, such as the Program Manager

Click on Switch To or press ↵ to display Program Manager

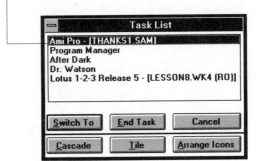

## Copying and Pasting a Selection

Once you have made a selection, you can copy or move it to another location in the current file or in another file altogether. To leave a copy of the selection in its current location and to place a copy in another location, follow these steps:

 **1.** Choose Edit ➤ Copy, press Ctrl+C or Ctrl+Ins, or click on the Copy SmartIcon to copy the selection to the Clipboard.

TABLE 3.3: Windows Clipboard Keys and Key Combinations

| SHORTCUT KEY OR KEY COMBINATION | DESCRIPTION |
| --- | --- |
| Alt+PrtSc | Copies the active window into the Clipboard |
| Ctrl+C | Copies a selection from a Windows application into the Clipboard |
| Ctrl+Ins | Copies a selection from a Windows application into the Clipboard |
| Ctrl+V | Pastes the contents of the Clipboard into a Windows application |
| Ctrl+X | Removes a selection from a Windows application into the Clipboard |
| Del | Clears the contents of the Clipboard once you confirm the deletion |
| Print Screen (PrtSc) | Copies the current screen into the Clipboard |
| Shift+Del | Removes a selection from a Windows application into the Clipboard |
| Shift+Ins | Pastes the contents of the Clipboard into a Windows application |

**2.** Move the cursor to the location at which you wish to insert the selection. You can move the cursor within the current file or to a file in this or another Windows application.

**3.** Choose Edit ➤ Paste, press Ctrl+V or Shift+Ins, or click on the Paste SmartIcon to insert the selection from the Clipboard to its new location. Remember that the selection also remains in its original location.

Once a selection is in the Clipboard, you can paste it as often as you desire in any location in a Windows application file. Simply move the cursor to the place at which you want to insert the selection and choose Edit ➤ Paste.

## Cutting and Pasting a Selection

With one important difference, cutting and pasting a selection is the same as copying and pasting. While copying leaves the selection in its original location, cutting removes the selection from its original location. To cut a selection, follow these steps:

1. Choose Edit ➤ Cut, press Ctrl+X or Shift+Del, or click on the Cut SmartIcon to cut (move) the selection to the Clipboard.

2. Move the cursor to the location at which you wish to insert the selection. You can move the cursor within the current file or to a file in this or another Windows application.

3. Choose Edit ➤ Paste, press Ctrl+V or Shift+Ins, or click on the Paste SmartIcon to insert the selection from the Clipboard to its new location. Remember that the selection is no longer in its original location.

## Moving a Selection Using Drag and Drop

Many Windows applications, including those in the SmartSuite, allow you to use a shortcut cut-and-paste method, *drag and drop,* to move a selection. As you might guess, drag and drop involves dragging a selection and then dropping it in its new location either within the window or from window to window. To drag and drop a selection in 1-2-3, follow these steps:

1. Move the mouse pointer to the edge of your selection. When the mouse pointer changes from an arrow to a miniature hand, you are ready to drag.

2. Press and hold down the left mouse button. The hand closes to indicate that it is holding the selection and the application adds a dashed border to show the current location in which the selection would be dropped.

3. Drag the selection to its new location.

4. When you reach the new location, release the left mouse button. The mouse pointer changes back to an arrow.

**TIP** To cut a selection without replacing the contents of the Clipboard, press the Del key. To move a selection without replacing the contents of the Clipboard, drag and drop the selection.

## Undoing an Action

As you edit a file, you'll take some actions that you might think are irreversible. Fortunately, you can correct many mistakes immediately after you make them by choosing Edit ➤ Undo, pressing Ctrl+Z, or clicking on the Undo SmartIcon.

You can't undo all actions. For example, you can't undo printing, saving to disk, or recalculating, and you can't undo an undo. If the Undo command can't undo an action, it will be dimmed, and therefore unavailable, on the Edit menu.

# Changing the Look of the Contents of a File

You can change the appearance of the characters in a selection. In SmartSuite applications, you can change the design or size of the characters, and you can enhance a selection with boldface, italics, underlines, and so on.

## About Fonts

One way of emphasizing a selection (such as spreadsheet and document headings or specific rows or columns in a database) is to change its *font*, the design that applies to an entire set of characters. For example, as you read this book, notice that the heading text and body text differ, not only in size but also in design. Headings, which are generally short pieces of text that draw your attention, are usually unembellished and simple. Body text, which can go on for page after page, is meant to be readable. It's easy to differentiate between headings and body text because of their different fonts and sizes.

An important font factor is whether it is proportional or monospace (or non-proportional). *Proportional* fonts use different widths for each letter, and *monospace* fonts use the same widths, regardless of the character. For example, the letter I needs less space than the letter M. A proportional font will reserve much less space for a narrow letter than for a wide one. However, a monospace font assigns the same width to every character. For this reason, monospace fonts are very useful in tables in which you want to align characters from one row to the next. In general, body text is proportional because proportional text is much easier to read.

## About Point Size

As you compare headings and body text in this book, notice that headings and body text differ in size as well as font. In general, the larger a character is, the more you notice it. The height of a character (from the top of a letter such as h to the bottom of a letter like q) is measured in *points*, with one point being $\frac{1}{72}$ of an inch. The available point size for SmartSuite applications starts at 6 or 8, which is about $\frac{1}{9}$ or $\frac{1}{12}$ of an inch tall, and increases to 72, which is about one inch tall.

## Changing the Font and Point Size

A SmartSuite file starts out with a default font and point size. For example, when you start Ami Pro, the default font is Times New Roman, which is an easy-to-read font, and the point size is 12, which is a comfortable size for text. However, when you start Freelance Graphics, the default font is Arial MT but the default point size is much larger—titles are 53.8 points and subtitles are 36.9.

There are two ways to change font and point size in SmartSuite applications—by using the menu bar and using the status bar. Using a menu command to change the font and point size allows you to change other character attributes (such as changing color or adding underlines) at the same time. On the other hand, using the status bar is often faster. Approach provides another choice — the Info box, a small dialog box that you can open by clicking on a Smart-Icon, selecting a menu command, or double-clicking on the object to be changed.

## Changing Font and Point Size with the Menu Bar

To change text formats for a selection in any SmartSuite application, choose from the menus and commands shown in Table 3.4.

After choosing a menu command, the active SmartSuite application displays a dialog box (Figure 3.5) in which you can select font, point size, and other text options.

Options in a typical Font dialog box include the following:

**Face**    A text/list box from which you can choose a font. If you don't see the name of the font on the list, either type it in the text box or scroll down the list until you find it and click on it.

**FIGURE 3.5**

The 1-2-3 Font dialog box provides options that are common to all SmartSuite applications, but contains some unique options as well.

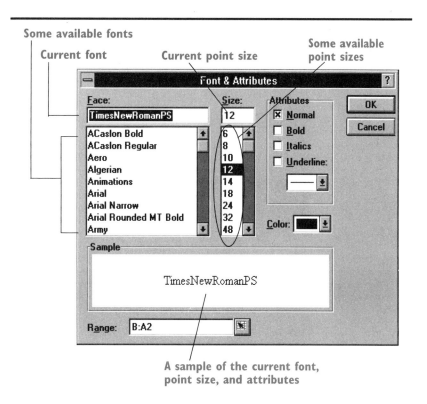

Some available fonts

Current font

Current point size

Some available point sizes

A sample of the current font, point size, and attributes

**TABLE 3.4:** SmartSuite Font and Point Size Menu Commands

| APPLICATION | COMMAND |
| --- | --- |
| 1-2-3 | Style ➤ Font & Attributes |
| Ami Pro | Text ➤ Font |
| Approach | Object ➤ Style & Properties (or press Ctrl+E or click on the Style & Properties SmartIcon) |
| Freelance Graphics | Text ➤ Font |
| Organizer | Edit ➤ Layouts (or press Ctrl+Y); Click on Styles; Click on Font |

**Size**    A text/list box from which you can choose a point size. If you don't see the point size on the list, either type it in the text box or scroll down the list until you find it and click on it. Point sizes vary by the application.

**Attributes**    A group in which you can check or clear a check box. You can select from character emphasis options, such as Normal, Bold, Italics, and Underline. Options vary by the application. In most Windows applications, you can also press Ctrl+N, Ctrl+B, Ctrl+I, and Ctrl+U, respectively, to apply or remeove character emphasis.

**Color**    A drop-down list box, which reveals a palette from which you can choose a color for the selected text.

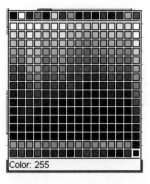

**Sample**    A box in which you can see a sample of the current settings for your selection.

If you have a long list of fonts from which to choose, you can select a font in the Font dialog box and see how it looks before clicking on OK and closing the dialog box.

### Changing Font and Point Size from the Status Bar

To change the font or point size or both without further emphasizing the selected characters, all you have to do is select from the status bar (Figure 3.6).

Simply click on the name of the current font or point size to open a list of choices. Once you click on a choice, the application changes the characters in the selection and closes the list.

The 1-2-3 status bar with the point list displayed. Every SmartSuite application except Organizer provides the same point list.

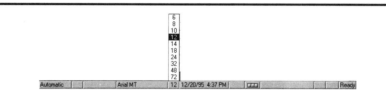

## Enhancing a File

You can change the appearance of a selection without changing the font and point size by applying any combination of boldface, italics, underline, and so on. Either open the Font dialog box as you did to change a font (see Table 3.4), or click on a SmartIcon. Keep in mind that for most SmartSuite applications, you can use the Font dialog box to emphasize a selection and to also change the font and point size at the same time.

You can also press shortcut keys to enhance a selection. Table 3.5 presents shortcut key combinations for applying and removing emphasis from a selection. These key combinations apply to all SmartSuite applications except Approach and Organizer.

**TABLE 3.5:** Character Emphasis Shortcut Key Combinations

| KEY COMBINATION | ACTION |
| --- | --- |
| Ctrl+B | Applies or removes boldface |
| Ctrl+I | Applies or removes italics |
| Ctrl+N | Removes boldface, italics, and underlines and returns to normal text, the default |
| Ctrl+U | Applies or removes underlines |

**WORKING TOGETHER**

## Curving Text

Using the FLWCURVE.SMM macro, you can apply one of a group of curves to Ami Pro text. To curve text, follow these steps:

1. Choose Tools ➤ Macros ➤ Playback or click on the appropriate SmartIcon in the Bonus Pack SmartIcons set. Ami Pro displays the Play Macro dialog box.

2. Choose FLWCURVE.SMM and click on OK. Ami Pro displays the Curved Text dialog box.

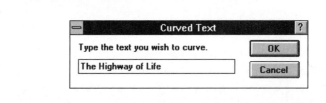

3. Type the text that you wish to curve in the text box. (If you have selected text in your document, it appears in the text box.) Then either click on OK or press ↵. The macro starts Freelance Graphics unless it is already active.

**4.** Select the shape of the curve from the scroll box in the next version of the Curved Text dialog box.

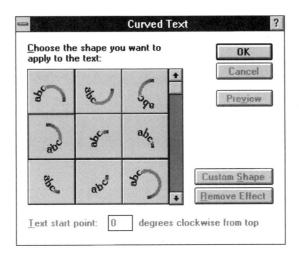

**5.** For some selected shapes, you can type the degree at which you want the first character in the text to appear in the Text Start Point text box. This text box is not always available.

**6.** If you have selected text and a shape that has been converted to lines or polygons, you can click on the Custom Shape button to apply the shape to the selected text. This button is not always available.

**7.** Click on Remove Effect to convert the curved text to a straight line. This button is not always available.

**8.** To preview certain images, click on Preview. This button is not always available.

**9.** Click on OK. Freelance Graphics applies the curve to the selected text.

# An Overview of Finding and Replacing

When you edit a file, automating your actions whenever possible is the way to go. For example, if you need to change the same name or value throughout a file, why manually change the text page by page when you can issue a single command?

Simply choose a find or search command to open a dialog box (Figure 3.7). Then type the *search string*, the text for which you are searching. If you wish to replace the search string, also type a replace string. Then either click on a command key to start the search and optional replace process. You'll find out more about find and replace commands as you learn about each SmartSuite application. Table 3.6 summarizes SmartSuite search and replace commands.

**FIGURE 3.7**

Use the Find & Replace dialog box to search for strings of text.

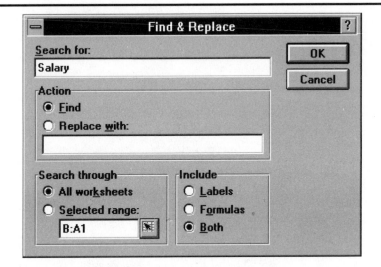

**TABLE 3.6:** SmartSuite Search and Replace Menu Commands and Shortcut Keys

| APPLICATION | SHORTCUT KEYS | COMMAND |
|---|---|---|
| 1-2-3 | N/A | Edit ➤ Find & Replace |
| Ami Pro | Ctrl+F | Edit ➤ Find & Replace |
| Approach | Ctrl+F | Browse ➤ Find |
| Organizer | Ctrl+F | Edit ➤ Find |

# PART TWO

# Mastering Finances
# with 1-2-3

In Part Two you'll learn how to use 1-2-3 spreadsheets to organize, calculate, track, and chart your income and expenses. You'll discover how to build a spreadsheet—from titles and labels to the formulas and @functions that are the backbone of electronic spreadsheets. You'll also discover how to enhance and format your spreadsheets and how to create multiple spreadsheets within a single file. After you've learned the basics, you'll learn to perform "what-if" analysis with 1-2-3's Version Manager using your data and that of your colleagues. Finally, you'll learn how to show off your data with a wide variety of charts.

Table II.1 illustrates and describes many 1-2-3 SmartIcons.

# 1-2-3 SmartIcons

| SMARTICON | DESCRIPTION |
|-----------|-------------|
| **Common 1-2-3 SmartIcons** | |

Opens an existing file. [File ➤ Open] *Shortcut:* Ctrl+O

Saves the current file. [File ➤ Save] *Shortcut:* Ctrl+S

Sends data using electronic mail. [File ➤ Send Mail]

Prints the current file using the options in the Print dialog box. [File ➤ Print] *Shortcut:* Ctrl+P

Displays all or part of a spreadsheet as it will print. [File ➤ Print Preview]

Undoes the last action, if allowed. [Edit ➤ Undo] *Shortcut:* Ctrl+Z

Cuts the selection and places it in the Clipboard. [Edit ➤ Cut] *Shortcut:* Ctrl+X or Shift+Del

Copies the selection to the Clipboard. [Edit ➤ Copy] *Shortcut:* Ctrl+C or Ctrl+Ins

Pastes the contents of the Clipboard into the file at the current cursor location. [Edit ➤ Paste] *Shortcut:* Ctrl+V or Shift+Ins

Applies or removes boldface from the selection. [Style ➤ Font & Attributes] *Shortcut:* Ctrl+B

Applies or removes italics from the selection. [Style ➤ Font & Attributes] *Shortcut:* Ctrl+I

Adds or removes an underline from the selection. [Style ➤ Font & Attributes] *Shortcut:* Ctrl+U

**Common 1-2-3 SmartIcons (continued)**

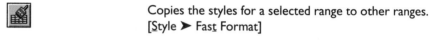 Aligns the selection to the left margin of the cell. [Style ➤ Alignment]

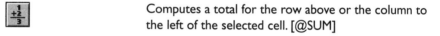 Centers the selection between the left and right margins of the cell [Style ➤ Alignment]

 Aligns the selection to the right margin of the cell. [Style ➤ Alignment]

 Copies the styles for a selected range to other ranges. [Style ➤ Fast Format]

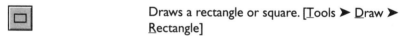 Computes a total for the row above or the column to the left of the selected cell. [@SUM]

 Selects a group of objects.

Draws an arrow in the direction that you drag. [Tools ➤ Draw ➤ Arrow]

Draws a rectangle or square. [Tools ➤ Draw ➤ Rectangle]

Draws an ellipse or circle. [Tools ➤ Draw ➤ Ellipse]

Draws a text box in which you can type characters. [Tools ➤ Draw ➤ Text]

Draws a macro button, which you can click to run a macro. [Tools ➤ Draw ➤ Button]

Draws a graph. [Tools ➤ Chart]

Displays the next set of SmartIcons. [Tools ➤ SmartIcons]

# 1-2-3 SmartIcons

| SMARTICON | DESCRIPTION |
|-----------|-------------|
| | **Common 1-2-3 SmartIcons (continued)** |

Deletes the selection permanently. [Edit ➤ Delete]
*Shortcut:* Ctrl+– or Del

Deletes the styles from a selection. [Edit ➤ Clear;
then select Styles Only]

Pastes the contents of the selected cell into the cell at
the insertion point. [Edit ➤ Paste Special; then select
Cell Contents Only]

Pastes the style of the selected cell into the cell at the
insertion point. [Edit ➤ Paste Special; then select
Styles Only]

Pastes a 1-2-3 file, DDE link, or OLE link at the
insertion point. [Edit ➤ Paste Link]

Pastes a formula as a value into the cell at the
insertion point. [Edit ➤ Paste Special; then select
Formulas as Values]

Fills in the selected cells with the next item following
the first selected cell (for example, if the first cell
contains *January,* 1-2-3 fills the following cells with
*February, March, April,* and so on). [Range ➤ Fill by
Example]

Copies the first column in the spreadsheet to a range.
[Edit ➤ Copy Right]

Copies the top row in the spreadsheet to a range.
[Edit ➤ Copy Down]

**Common 1-2-3 SmartIcons (continued)**

 Inserts a row at the insertion point. [Edit ➤ Insert; then select Row] *Shortcut:* Ctrl++ (on the numeric keypad)

 Inserts a column at the insertion point. [Edit ➤ Insert; then select Column] *Shortcut:* Ctrl++ (on the numeric keypad)

 Deletes selected rows from the spreadsheet. [Edit ➤ Delete; then select Row] *Shortcut:* Ctrl+– (on numeric keypad)

 Deletes selected columns from the spreadsheet. [Edit ➤ Delete; then select Column] *Shortcut:* Ctrl+– (on numeric keypad)

 Deletes the selected worksheet. [Edit ➤ Delete; then select Sheet] *Shortcut:* Ctrl+– (on numeric keypad)

 Aligns the selection with both the left and right borders. [Style ➤ Alignment; then select Evenly Spaced]

 Opens the Gallery dialog box so that you can choose a style for the selection. [Style ➤ Gallery]

 Opens the Fonts & Attributes dialog box so that you can change the font, attributes, or both for the selection. [Style ➤ Font & Attributes]

 Opens the Lines & Color dialog box so that you can change interior or border patterns, colors, and attributes. [Style ➤ Lines & Color]

# 1-2-3 SmartIcons

| SMARTICON | DESCRIPTION |
|-----------|-------------|
| | **Common 1-2-3 SmartIcons (continued)** |
| | Widens the column to fit the longest entry. [Style ➤ Column Width; then select Fit Widest Entry] |
| | Copies the styles of one selection to another without using the Clipboard. |
| | Opens the Version Manager dialog box so that you can work with or create versions and scenarios. [Range ➤ Version] |
| | Magnifies the size of the cells displayed on the desktop. [View ➤ Zoom In] |
| | Reduces the size of the cells displayed on the desktop. [View ➤ Zoom Out] |
| | Displays the spreadsheet at the default size set in the Set View Preferences dialog box. [View ➤ Set View Preferences] |
| | Opens the Audit dialog box so that you can produce a report on the logic or relationships of the formulas in the current file. [Tools ➤ Audit] |
| | Runs the spell checker on the current selection or file. [Tools ➤ Spell Check] |
| | Opens the SmartIcons dialog box so that you can edit icons, change the size or location of icons, and save or delete icon sets. **Warning**: If you delete an icon set, there is no prompt for confirmation; the deletion is permanent. [Tools ➤ SmartIcons] |
| | Opens the Name dialog box so that you can create or delete range names. [Range ➤ Name] |

Inserts a range into a worksheet. [Edit ➤ Insert] *Shortcut:* Ctrl++ (numeric keypad)

Deletes a selected range from a worksheet. [Edit ➤ Delete] *Shortcut:* Ctrl+− (numeric keypad)

Opens the Page Setup dialog box so that you can define page attributes. [File ➤ Page Setup]

Selects the range of data to be printed. [File ➤ Print; then choose a Selected Range] *Shortcut:* Ctrl+P

Specifies orientation as portrait mode. [File ➤ Page Setup; then choose Portrait]

Specifies orientation as landscape mode. [File ➤ Page Setup; then choose Landscape]

Sizes printed output using data as the guide. [File ➤ Page Setup; then choose Fit All to Page from Size group]

Inserts a rowwise page break. [Style ➤ Page Break; then choose Row]

Inserts a columnwise page break. [Style ➤ Page Break; then choose Column]

Recalculates the worksheet. [Tools ➤ User Setup; then click on Recalculation] *Shortcut:* F9 (only in Ready mode)

Highlights all the cells that have formulas. [Tools ➤ Audit; then choose All Formulas]

# 1-2-3 SmartIcons

| SMARTICON | DESCRIPTION |
|---|---|
| | **Common 1-2-3 SmartIcons (continued)** |
| | Highlights all the cells that have links to other 1-2-3 files. [Tools ➤ Audit; then choose File Links] |
| | Highlights all the cells that have DDE links. [Tools ➤ Audit; then choose DDE Links] |
| | Goes to the first cell in the next range of cells. [Edit ➤ Go To; then choose Range from Type of Item] *Shortcut:* F5 |
| | Goes to the first cell in the previous range of cells. [Edit ➤ Go To; then choose Range from Type of Item] *Shortcut:* F5 |
| | Goes to the top left cell in the worksheet. [Edit ➤ Go To; then choose Range from Type of Item] *Shortcut:* Home |
| | Inserts an object from another application in the worksheet. [Edit ➤ Insert Object] |
| | Starts Ami Pro. |
| | Starts Freelance Graphics. |
| | Starts Lotus Organizer. |
| | Starts Lotus Improv, if it is installed. |
| | Starts Lotus Notes, if it is installed. |
| | Starts cc:Mail, if it is installed. |

# 4

# Planning and Creating Your First Spreadsheet

In this chapter, you'll create a spreadsheet from scratch. As you work, you'll learn about spreadsheets in general. You'll find out about the elements of the 1-2-3 application window and a 1-2-3 spreadsheet, the type of data that you can put in a spreadsheet, how to use formulas, and some of the most common 1-2-3 @functions. Remember that you can learn the basics of opening and saving files by reviewing Chapter 2.

# Introducing 1-2-3

To control your company's finances, a spreadsheet program is invaluable. Using a 1-2-3 spreadsheet or worksheet, you can do all of the following:

- Perform statistical analyses on your sales and expenses by region, division, office location, product, cost center, or individual employee.

- Calculate and graph how much you spent on office supplies or computers last year and budget for this year.

- Analyze demographic information for your region to determine the location of your next plant or decide how to target your advertising budget.

- Track your inventory, accounts receivable, accounts payable, and wages paid.

## Reading and Writing Common File Formats

1-2-3 reads the WK* files compatible with other 1-2-3 releases and reads Smartmaster (.WT4), Shared (.NS4), Text (.PRN, .CSV, .DAT, .OUT, and .ASC), Symphony (.WR*), Excel (.XLS, .XLT, and .XLW), ANSI Metafiles (.CGM), 1-2-3 PIC (.PIC), dBASE (.DBF), and Paradox (.DB) formats. 1-2-3 writes to 1-2-3 (.WK1, .WK3, and .WK4), SmartMaster (.WT4), Shared (.NS4), Text (.TXT), Excel Workbook (.XLW), Excel Worksheet (.XLS), dBASE (.DBF), and Paradox (.DB) formats. In addition, many other spreadsheet programs (such as Excel and Quattro Pro) support 1-2-3's .WK* format. So you won't have any problems sharing files with users of other spreadsheet programs.

# What Is a Spreadsheet?

Before computers, accountants and bookkeepers kept track of income, expenses, and other financial information by using worksheet paper, which is made up of grids of rows and columns. The *rows* run horizontally and the *columns* run vertically. Where a row and column meet is a *cell*, which holds one piece of information.

Rows, columns, and cells form the body of an electronic spreadsheet or worksheet. To help you find your way around when the cells contain numbers and other characters, 1-2-3 labels columns and rows. At the top border of a spreadsheet are column labels: A–Z, then AA, AB, and so on (all the way to IV, for a total of 256 columns). On the left border of a spreadsheet are row labels: 1–8192. You can have up to 256 spreadsheets in one 1-2-3 file, which means that you can hold a great deal of information in a single file.

# Planning a Spreadsheet

To be fully effective, a spreadsheet requires careful planning. You should make sure that you provide only the appropriate data—superfluous information clutters the spreadsheet. In the beginning, it's a good idea to sketch out your spreadsheet on paper before you create it. As you become more familiar with 1-2-3, you'll be able to design spreadsheets right in the program, adjusting labels and formats "on the fly." Here are some useful guidelines to help you plan your spreadsheet:

■ Make your first spreadsheet small enough so that it fits on your computer desktop. In this way, you can learn about moving around and the effect of formulas and formats.

■ Provide label names that are as short as possible, yet understandable. When planning your spreadsheet, think of the other people who will use or view it.

■ When naming a spreadsheet, use a name that helps you to identify it in its directory, particularly if you plan to use it only occasionally.

Once you have a spreadsheet plan on paper, you can simply start entering the title and labels. But before that, start 1-2-3 so that you can learn about the 1-2-3 application window.

# Viewing the 1-2-3 Window

The 1-2-3 application window (Figure 4.1) contains many of the elements that you found out about in Chapter 2. Because you are now working with a spreadsheet application, its window includes unique elements to help make your job easier. In this section, you'll find out about the edit line, special 1-2-3 SmartIcons, the worksheet window and its tabs and buttons, and the 1-2-3 status bar.

**FIGURE 4.1**

The 1-2-3 application window provides many helpful elements to help you create and edit spreadsheets.

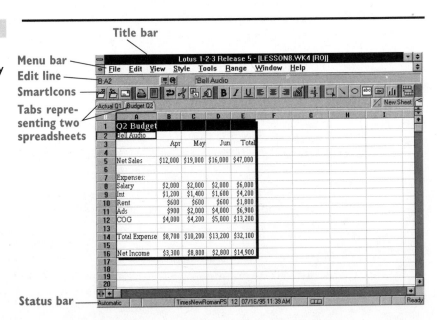

## The Edit Line

The *edit line* (Figure 4.2) shows information about the current selection and provides tools with which you can edit it. If there is a blank spreadsheet on your desktop, A1 appears on the left side of the edit line. This tells you that the *cell pointer* highlights column A, row 1. When you start typing labels, data, and formulas into the spreadsheet, the edit line shows the contents of the current cell, which contains the cell pointer. If you have more than one spreadsheet in the current file, the cell identifier is preceded by the spreadsheet identifier (for example, A) followed by a colon.

**FIGURE 4.2**

The 1-2-3 edit line

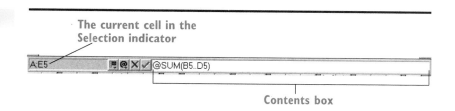

The current cell in the Selection indicator

A:E5    @SUM(B5..D5)

Contents box

The edit line contains these components:

**Selection indicator**   Displays the worksheet letter (if there are multiple worksheets in this file), the cell or range address, or the object name.

**Navigator**   Goes to and/or selects any named range. You can select a named range to insert in a formula, @function (explained later in this chapter), or text box.

**@function selector**   Displays a menu with common @functions and allows you to see a complete list of all @functions. If you select List All, 1-2-3 displays the @Function List dialog box, in which you can insert an @function or customize the @function menu.

**Cancel button**   Cancels the entry on the edit line.

**Confirm button**   Completes the entry on the edit line.

**Contents box**   Contains the information, formulas, or @functions that you type for this cell.

## 1-2-3 SmartIcons

The pages starting Part Two (the beginning of the 1-2-3 section) show many of the common SmartIcons for 1-2-3. To learn how SmartIcons work, see Chapter 2. When you start 1-2-3 for the first time, the Default Sheet SmartIcons appear. From then on, the SmartIcons set with which you end a 1-2-3 session are those that appear when you start a new session.

## The Worksheet Window

The Worksheet window (Figure 4.3) contains the spreadsheet itself—with letters A–H (column names) across the top and the numbers 1–20 (row names) going down the left side. Each set of numbers or characters, labels, or formulas will occupy a cell, which is the intersection of a row and a column.

**FIGURE 4.3**

The 1-2-3 worksheet window, in which you enter labels, values, formulas, and do other work

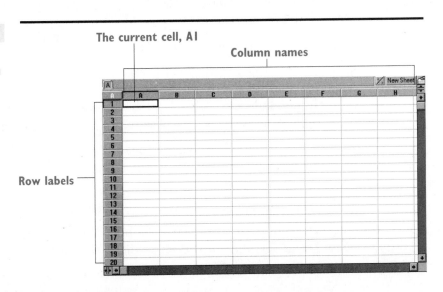

The current cell, A1

Column names

Row labels

Each cell in a spreadsheet has a unique *cell address*, the combination of row and column labels. For example, the cell in the top left corner of the work area, in column A and row 1, is known as A1. Notice on your desktop that A1 is surrounded by a dark border and both A and 1 appear to be pressed in. As you move the cell pointer, notice that the highlight moves, other labels are pressed in, and the contents of the edit line change.

The top of the spreadsheet contains the items shown below, which aid you in using multiple spreadsheets within a single file.

Click on a tab (from A to IV) to reveal the desired spreadsheet:

Click on an arrow to move to the previous or next spreadsheet in a set:

Click on this button to create a new spreadsheet within the same file:

Click on this button to display or hide all the items in this area:

Drag this object to split the window horizontally so that you can work in two areas of the spreadsheet. (Notice a similar object at the bottom left corner of the spreadsheet area. Drag this object to split the window vertically.)

## The 1-2-3 Status Bar

The 1-2-3 status bar (Figure 4.4) allows you to change formats, specify the number of decimal places for certain number formats, name a user-defined style, select a font, specify a point size, check the date and time or the row height and column width of the selected cell, display a set of SmartIcons, check for possible circular references, and find out the current mode.

**Format selector**     Click on this button to reveal a list of formats (Figure 4.5) for number and text values.

The 1-2-3 status bar consists of buttons with which you can change formats and enhancements and check your current status.

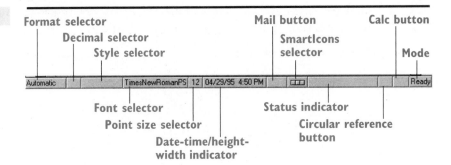

The list of 1-2-3 formats for number and text values

**Decimal selector**    If the current cell contains a number, click on this button to provide a list of decimal places, from 0–15.

**Style selector**    If you have defined any custom styles by choosing <u>S</u>tyle ➤ Named <u>S</u>tyle, click on this button to show a list of choices.

**Font selector**    Click on this button to reveal a list of the installed fonts (Figure 4.6).

**Point-size selector**    Click on this button to display a list of point sizes (6, 8, 10, 12, 14, 18, 24, 32, 48, and 72) for the selected cell.

**Date-time/height-width indicator**    Click on this button to either display the computer system date and time or the row height and column width of the selected cell.

**Mail button**    If you have cc:Mail or Notes and you see an envelope on this button, click to read your mail.

**SmartIcons selector**    Click on this button to display a list of Smart-Icons (Figure 4.7). (The highlighted list item is the current SmartIcons set.) Click on Hide SmartIcons to remove all SmartIcons from the desktop.

**Status indicator**    This area indicates the status of the cell, pane, or worksheet. Table 4.1 lists the 1-2-3 status indicators. For information about applying or removing security, see the *Lotus 1-2-3 User's Guide*.

**TABLE 4.1:**  1-2-3 Status Indicators

| INDICATOR | DESCRIPTION |
| --- | --- |
| Cmd | 1-2-3 is executing a command. |
| Group | This file is in Group mode. |
| Pr | This spreadsheet or cell is protected. |
| U | This spreadsheet or cell is unprotected. |
| Zoom | You are viewing this spreadsheet or *pane* (a small window within the application window) on the full screen. |

FIGURE 4.6

A list of some of the
fonts installed on one
computer system

**TIP**

If you want to modify a selection in many ways (e.g., change the font, increase or decrease font size, enhance other text attributes, and even alter the color), the most efficient way is to choose Style ➤ Font & Attributes. Then, in the Font & Attributes dialog box, you can make all your changes and, as a bonus, see how the selection looks before either making other changes or clicking on OK.

**FIGURE 4.7**

The 1-2-3 SmartIcons
sets from which you
can choose

**Circular-reference button**     Click on this button to go to a *circular reference*, a formula that uses itself to solve itself. Although the result may not be in error, you should be aware that a circular reference exists in your worksheet and check your results.

**Calc button**     Click on this button to manually recalculate the formulas in this worksheet. To select automatic or manual recalculation, choose Tools ➤ User Setup, click on Recalculation, select either Automatic or Manual, and either click on OK or press ↵ twice.

**Mode**     This area shows the current mode as listed in Table 4.2.

# Creating Your First Spreadsheet

After planning a spreadsheet, the next step is to start entering information—titles, labels, data, and formulas. In this section, you'll enter a title, row labels, and column labels.

## Entering Titles and Labels

All you have to do to enter any sort of information in a spreadsheet is to start typing. You can either type in the cell itself, or double-click in the contents

**TABLE 4.2:**

| MODE | DESCRIPTION |
|------|-------------|
| Edit | You are editing the contents of a cell, you are typing or editing text in a text box, or 1-2-3 senses that your last entry is in error. |
| Error | You are reading a 1-2-3 error message. |
| Files | 1-2-3 Classic is displaying a list of files. |
| Label | You are typing a label. |
| Menu | You have opened a menu or a dialog box. |
| Point | You are specifying a range. |
| Ready | 1-2-3 is ready for you to perform an action. This is the default mode. |
| Value | You are typing a value. |
| Wait | You are waiting for 1-2-3 to complete an action. |

box of the edit line and start typing there. Whether you start typing in a cell or activate the contents box, 1-2-3 changes the edit line by adding the Cancel and Confirm buttons. If you type in a cell, 1-2-3 places the *insertion point,* the vertical bar that shows you the location of the next character to be typed, in the cell itself. As you type, 1-2-3 also adds the characters in the contents box. If you type in the edit line, 1-2-3 places the insertion point in the contents box and changes the background color of the contents box.

When you type the first character for a cell, 1-2-3 recognizes whether you are entering a title or label, formula, or value. If the first character in a cell is alphabetic, 1-2-3 understands that you are typing a title or label. A mathematical sign, such as a plus or minus sign, indicates that you have started to enter a formula. If you type a number, 1-2-3 automatically recognizes that you are typing a value.

When you finish typing the last character, press ↵. This signals that this entry is complete and that you are ready to perform your next action.

When you type a series of alphabetic or numeric characters that extend beyond the borders of the current cell, 1-2-3 treats labels and values differently, sometimes depending on the contents of adjacent cells:

- When you press ↵ after typing a label that extends over several empty cells, 1-2-3 displays the entire label in its original cell, adjacent cells, and in the edit line.

- When you press ↵ after typing a label that extends over several cells, some of which are filled, 1-2-3 displays as much of the label as it can until a filled cell is encountered.

- When you press ↵ after typing a number that extends over several cells, 1-2-3 automatically converts the value so that it fits within the cell. However, the value in the edit line remains as originally typed. (For example, if you type 123212321232123, that value remains in the edit line, but the contents of the cell change to 1.2E+14.)

If you type values or labels for a series of adjacent cells, you can use shortcut keys to avoid typing extra keystrokes. For example, if you are filling in several cells in a column, you can press ↵ and ↓ to move to the next cell. However, if you type ↓, 1-2-3 realizes that you have finished working in the current cell and implicitly presses ↵ for you. Other keys that perform the same action are →, ←, ↑, Home, and End.

 1-2-3 enables you to automatically enter certain labels, such as months, years, and quarters. Just type the first label, select the *range* of cells to be filled in, and click on the Fill by Example SmartIcon. Table 4.3 lists the values that 1-2-3 automatically fills in.

 **You can fill in the first two cells in a range and have 1-2-3 fill in the remaining cells.**

To create your first spreadsheet, follow these steps:

1. Highlight cell B1. (If the cell pointer is not close to the upper- left corner of the spreadsheet, press Home and then press → to go to B1.)

2. Type the title **Broad Street Telecommunications** (Figure 4.8). Note how the title appears in both the edit line and in the spreadsheet.

**TABLE 4.3:** 1-2-3 Sequence Item Names

| SEQUENTIAL ITEM | EXAMPLES |
|---|---|
| Integers | 1, 2, 3, 4, 5,… |
| | 1994, 1995, 1996,… |
| Letters | A, B, C, D, E,… |
| | x, y, z, a, b,… |
| Letters and Integers | A1, A2, A3, A4, A5,… |
| | Part 1, Part 2, Part 3, Part 4, Part 5,… |
| Months | Jan, Feb, Mar, Apr, May,… |
| | January, February, March, April,… |
| Days | Mon, Tue, Wed, Thu, Fri,… |
| | mon, tue, wed, thu, fri,… |
| | Monday, Tuesday, Wednesday,… |
| Quarters | Q1, Q2, Q3, Q4, Q1,… |
| | Qtr 1, Qtr 2, Qtr 3, Qtr 4… |

**FIGURE 4.8**

The top of a new spreadsheet with the company name appearing in the edit

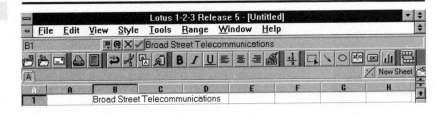

**3.** Press ↵. 1-2-3 adds a single quote before the title and removes the Cancel and Confirm buttons from the edit line.

**4.** Move the cell pointer to A5 and start typing row labels:

| CELL | LABEL |
|---|---|
| A5 | Income: |
| A6 | Sales |

| CELL | LABEL |
|------|-------|
| A7 | Service Revenues |
| A8 | Leased Equipment Income |
| A9 | Total Income |
| A11 | Direct Costs: |
| A12 | Costs of Products Sold |
| A13 | Leased Equipment Expenses |
| A14 | Total Direct Costs |
| A16 | Net Income |

**5.** Move the cell pointer to cell B3, type **Qtr 1** (i.e., the first quarter), and press ⏎.

**6.** Enter the remaining column labels by selecting B3–E3 and clicking on the Fill by Example SmartIcon. 1-2-3 fills in **Qtr 2**, **Qtr 3**, and **Qtr 4**. Clicking on this button is equivalent to choosing <u>R</u>ange ➤ Fill by <u>E</u>xample.

**7.** In cell F3, type **Total** and press ⏎. Figure 4.9 shows your spreadsheet with titles and labels.

## Adjusting Column Width

When the contents of cells in one column appear to run into the contents of cells in the next column (such as columns A and B as they now appear in the sample spreadsheet), you can adjust column widths so that the contents of each row are separated from adjacent rows. You can drag a column border by using the mouse, clicking on the Best Fit SmartIcon, or choosing <u>S</u>tyle ➤ <u>C</u>olumn Width to change the width of selected columns. You can also permanently change the default width of all columns in new spreadsheets. (Existing spreadsheets are not affected by this change in the column width default.)

**NOTE** As a default, a 1-2-3 column is eight valid characters followed by one space. Valid characters are numbers, spaces, decimal points, commas, dollar signs, and percent signs.

# 1-2-3

## CHAPTER 4

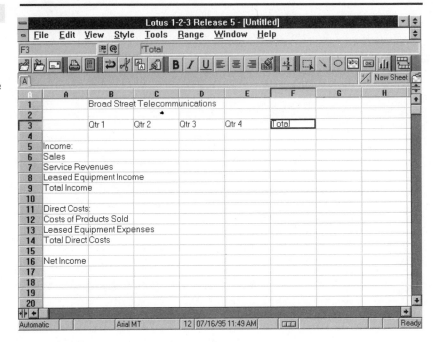

**FIGURE 4.9**

The sample spreadsheet with titles and labels. Notice that although you typed the title in cell B1, it appears to be located in B1, C1, and D1.

If the information typed or calculated for a cell is longer than can be shown given the cell's dimensions, 1-2-3 displays a series of asterisks in the cell, depending on the cell's format type. If the value takes up almost the entire width of the cell and is currency, +/-, percent, or any date or time format, asterisks appear. Other formats, especially those that don't use as much space, do not change to asterisks. Asterisks do not change the underlying value; they just act as placeholders for values that are too long to display on screen.

## Using the Mouse to Adjust Column Width

To widen a selected column to the width of the cell containing the most characters, move the mouse pointer to the line that separates that column from the next column and double-click. For example, if you wish to adjust column A to its longest value, place the mouse pointer between A and B. When the pointer changes to a double-pointed arrow, double-click.

You can also use the mouse to drag the column to a new width. Notice that as you drag the border between two columns, 1-2-3 displays its current width in the selection indicator in the edit line.

### Using a SmartIcon to Adjust Column Width

 To adjust column width using a SmartIcon, select one or more columns and click on the Best Fit SmartIcon.

### Using a Menu Command to Adjust Column Width

To use a menu command to adjust a column's width to fit its longest value, select the cell with the longest value and choose Style ➤ Column Width. When 1-2-3 opens the Column Width dialog box (Figure 4.10), click on Fit Widest Entry, and either click on OK or press ↵.

You can also set a column value for the selected column. Once again, choose Style ➤ Column Width. In the Column Width dialog box, select or type a value in the Set Width to *n* Characters list/text box, where *n* represents a value from 1 to 240.

Figure 4.11 shows the sample spreadsheet with column A adjusted to fit the widest label.

**FIGURE 4.10**

In the Column Width dialog box, you can change the width of the selected column.

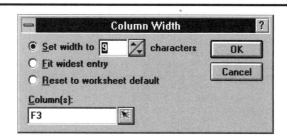

### FIGURE 4.11

Our sample
spreadsheet with
column A adjusted to
fit the longest label

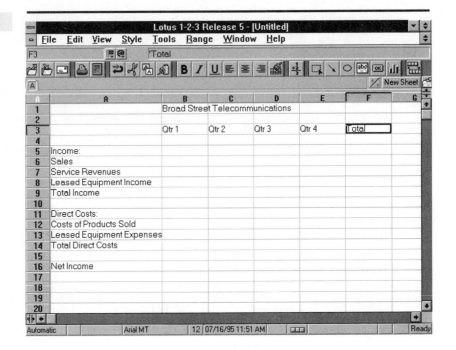

> **NOTE**
>
>
>
> In selected 1-2-3 dialog boxes, you'll find text boxes with
> range selector arrows on the right sides. To select a range,
> click on the range selector. 1-2-3 returns you to the
> spreadsheet in which you select a range and then redisplays
> the dialog box.

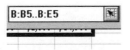

## Setting a New Default Column Width

To permanently change the column width for all new spreadsheets only (until
you change this option again), choose Style ➤ Worksheet Defaults. In the
Worksheet Defaults dialog box (Figure 4.12), either type or select a value in
the Column Width list/text box.

**FIGURE 4.12**

The Worksheet Default dialog box, in which you can change worksheet defaults.

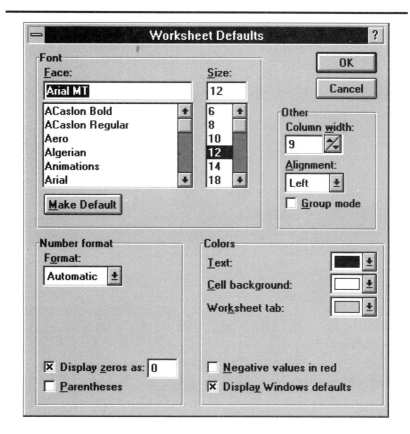

## Adjusting Row Height

Changing row height works almost the same as changing column width. You can use either a mouse shortcut or a menu command (but not a SmartIcon, as you can when adjusting column width).

**NOTE** You **cannot** permanently change the height of all rows in new spreadsheets as you can for column width.

### Using the Mouse to Adjust Row Height

To adjust the height of a row, you can drag the row boundary. Notice that as you drag the border between two rows, 1-2-3 displays its current height in the selection indicator in the edit line. The default row height is 14 points.

### Using a Menu Command to Adjust Row Height

To adjust row height using a menu command, select a row and choose Style ➤ Row Height. When 1-2-3 opens the Row Height dialog box (Figure 4.13), you can have 1-2-3 find the largest font in the row or you can select a point value for the row height. Either click on Fit Largest Font or select or type a value in the Set Height to *n* Points list/text box, where *n* represents a value from 1 to 240. Then either click on OK or press ↵.

**FIGURE 4.13**

The Row Height dialog box, in which you can specify the numeric width or adjust the fit for the largest font

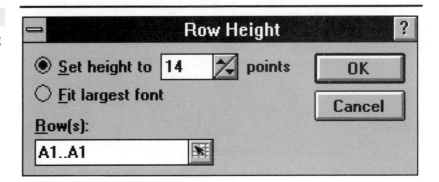

## Moving around in a Spreadsheet

You learned all about general SmartSuite navigation keys in Table 2.4. 1-2-3 has additional navigation keys and key combinations, shown in Table 4.4.

**TABLE 4.4:** 1-2-3 Navigation Keys and Key Combinations

| KEY OR KEY COMBINATION | DOES THIS: |
| --- | --- |
| End+Ctrl+PgDn | Moves the cursor to the next worksheet with a cell that contains data and is next to an empty cell in the same cell position as the current one |
| End+Ctrl+PgUp | Moves the cursor to the prior worksheet with a cell that contains data and is next to an empty cell in the same cell position as the current one |
| Home | Moves to cell A1 |
| PgUp | Moves up one screen |
| PgDn | Moves down one screen |
| Ctrl+← | Moves left one screen |
| Ctrl+→ | Moves right one screen |
| End, ↑ | Moves up to the next cell adjacent to an empty cell or to the top of the spreadsheet, staying in the same column |
| End, ↓ | Moves down to the next cell adjacent to an empty cell or to the bottom of the spreadsheet, staying in the same column |
| End, ← | Moves left to the prior cell adjacent to an empty cell or to the first column (that is, A), staying in the same row |
| End, → | Moves right to the next cell adjacent to an empty cell or to the last column (that is, IV), staying in the same row |
| End, Home | Moves to the lower-right corner of the spreadsheet in the last row or column that contains data |

1-2-3

# 5

# Entering Formulas and Data

In the last chapter, you built the "skeleton" of a spreadsheet. You added a title and column and row labels. In this chapter, you'll find out how to add the actual data—either by typing it in or by computing it. You'll learn about 1-2-3 data formats before you start creating your first formulas. Finally, you'll discover how to put a formula together, including how to use @*functions*, 1-2-3's built-in formulas.

# Entering Data

The main purpose for a spreadsheet's existence is to store data. Then, once you have information to work with, you can perform mathematical and statistical calculations and edit, graph, and analyze it.

## Manually Entering Data

You'll enter most information manually, one cell at a time. However, as you learned when you entered month labels, there are ways to automatically enter values. Enter data just as you enter labels and titles. For example, for our sample spreadsheet, enter the following data, making sure to skip the cells in which results of calculations will be stored:

| ROW LABEL | B | C | D | E |
|---|---|---|---|---|
| Sales | 4300 | 3100 | 4906 | 5400 |
| Service Revenues | 775 | 620 | 1708 | 2110 |
| Leased Equipment Income | 900 | 640 | 1023 | 1263 |
| Costs of Products Sold | 3680 | 2630 | 4220 | 4650 |
| Leased Equipment Expenses | 700 | 500 | 800 | 950 |

If you type a value in the wrong cell, the easiest way to move it to its proper cell location is to use drag and drop. Click on the cell that currently holds the value, and move the mouse pointer to one of the cell borders. When the mouse pointer changes to an open hand, press and hold down the left mouse button. When the mouse pointer changes to a closed hand, drag the cell contents to the desired location.

Figure 5.1 shows the sample spreadsheet with income and expense data entered.

**FIGURE 5.1**

Our sample spreadsheet with several rows of data entered

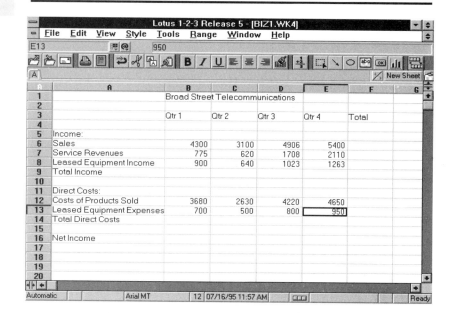

## Automatically Entering Data in Ranges of Cells

In the previous chapter, you learned how to fill in column labels with the Fill by Example SmartIcon or the Range ➤ Fill by Example command. An alternate way of automatically filling cells is by choosing Range ➤ Fill. When 1-2-3 opens the Fill dialog box (Figure 5.2), you have several ways to manipulate the fill values. For example, you can't use the Range ➤ Fill by Example command to fill in a series of payroll dates (i.e., every Friday); 1-2-3 places sequential dates in the cell (e.g., 26-Nov-96, 27-Nov-96, 28-Nov-96, and so on).

**FIGURE 5.2**

The Fill dialog box, from which you can select values to fill a selected range of cells

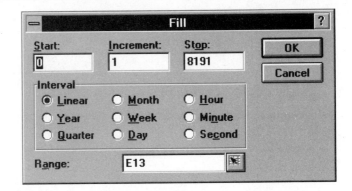

However, if you choose <u>R</u>ange ➤ <u>F</u>ill, fill in the date for the starting Friday in the <u>S</u>tart text box, accept the default Increment of 1, and either click on OK or press ↵, then 1-2-3 fills in the appropriate dates (e.g., 26-Nov-96, 03-Dec-96, 10-Dec-96, and so on).

**TIP** Fill in the same value in selected cells by choosing <u>R</u>ange ➤ <u>F</u>ill. In the Fill dialog box, type the value to be placed in all cells in the <u>S</u>tart text box. In the <u>I</u>ncrement box, type 0, and either click on OK or press ↵. 1-2-3 closes the dialog box and fills all the selected cells with the same value.

# Types of Data

1-2-3 recognizes several types of data formats: fixed, scientific, currency, comma, general, +/–, percent, text, hidden, automatic, label, and several date and time formats. In this section, you'll learn how each of them works.

## Applying Data Formats

For selected cells, you can apply data formats from the status bar or the menu bar:

- Click on the Format selector (Figure 5.3) on the left side of the status bar and select a format. You can revert to the original cell format by selecting Reset from the bottom of the list.

- Choose <u>S</u>tyle ➤ <u>N</u>umber Format to open the Number Format dialog box (Figure 5.4).

1-2-3

**FIGURE 5.3**

The Format selector, from which you can choose the appropriate format for the contents of the current cell

**FIGURE 5.4**

The Number Format dialog box

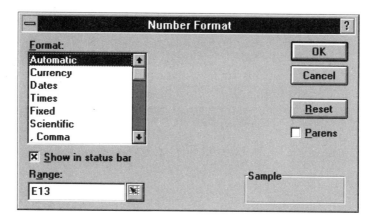

In the Number Format dialog box, you can select from these options:

| | |
|---|---|
| Format | Select a number or text format from this scroll list. |
| Parens | Check or clear this check box to indicate whether negative numbers are displayed within parentheses for certain number formats. |
| Show in Status Bar | Check or clear this check box to display or hide the selected format in the Number Format list in the status bar. |
| Range | Click on the range selector on the right side of this text box to select a range of cells. |
| Modify Symbol | When you select a currency format, you can click on this button to change the currency symbol. |
| Decimal Places | In this text/list box, either type or select the number of decimal places (from 1 to 15) for particular types of number formats. |
| Reset | Click on this button to revert to the original number or text format. |

 **In most cases, the value remains in the contents box of the edit line as originally entered.**

You can change number and text format defaults for the current spreadsheet by selecting Style ➤ Worksheet Defaults. In the Worksheet Defaults dialog box, select from the Format drop-down list box, and then either click on OK or press ↵.

## Automatic Format

Automatic format is the default 1-2-3 format. After you type data into a cell having Automatic format, 1-2-3 analyzes the characters in order to change the data format to one of the other data formats.

**WORKING TOGETHER** ▲

# Converting Fahrenheit to Celsius

Ami Pro's Working Together Bonus Pack provides a temperature converter. Use this calculator to convert from Fahrenheit to Celsius or from Celsius to Fahrenheit. To convert the value of a temperature, follow these steps:

1. Choose Tools ➤ Macros ➤ Playback or click on the appropriate SmartIcon in the Bonus Pack SmartIcons set. Ami Pro displays the Play Macro dialog box.

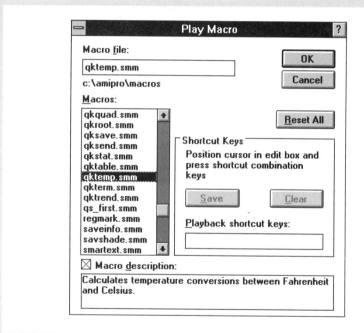

2. Choose QKTEMP.SMM and click on OK. Ami Pro displays the QuickTemp dialog box.

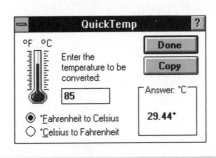

**WORKING TOGETHER**

**3.** Select Fahrenheit to Celsius or Celsius to Fahrenheit.

**4.** View the answer in the Answer box, and click on Done.

| IF 1-2-3 FINDS: | THE NEW DATA FORMAT IS: |
|---|---|
| A comma embedded in a number | , Comma |
| The default currency symbol preceding a number | US Dollar (or another currency format if you have changed the default) |
| A percent sign following a number | Percentage |
| *dd-Mon-yy*, *dd-Mon*, or *mm/dd/yy* (see the Date format for the syntax) | Date |
| *hh-mm*, *hh-mm-ss*, *hh-mm AM*, *or hh-mm PM* (see the Time format for the syntax) | Time |
| *nE+n* (where *n* represents a number with one or more digits) | Scientific |

Automatic is the default format for 1-2-3 spreadsheets. To change to no default, choose Tools ➤ User Setup, clear the Use Automatic Format check box, and either click on OK or press ↵.

**WORKING TOGETHER**

# Calculating Mortgage Payments

To calculate monthly mortgage payments and the total dollars spent over the life of a mortgage, depending on house price, interest rate, and length of the mortgage, follow these steps:

1. Choose Tools ➤ Macros ➤ Playback or click on the appropriate SmartIcon in the Bonus Pack SmartIcons set. Ami Pro displays the Play Macro dialog box.

2. Choose QKHOUSE.SMM. Ami Pro displays the Calculate Mortgage Payment dialog box (shown filled in).

*This estimate was especially prepared for*
*Jane Sanders by*
*Acme Mortgages, Unlimited*

| | Years of Mortgage |
|---|---|
| | 25 |
| **Mortgage Amount** | |
| Mortgage Amount | $150,000.00 |
| **Estimated Monthly Cost of Home** | |
| Estimated Interest Rate % | 6.000% |
| Estimated Loan Discount Points | |
| Payment Principal & Interest | $966.45 |
| Estimated Homeowner's Insurance | |
| Estimated Property Taxes | |
| Private Mortgage Insurance (PMI) | |
| **Estimated Gross Monthly House Payment** | $966.45 |

3. Fill in the Price of House, Number of Years, and Interest Rate text boxes, either pressing Tab or clicking to get to the next text box. The macro fills in the Payments box. (You can change values; the macro changes the values in the Payments box immediately.)

4. To close the dialog box without further action, either click on Done or press ↵.

5. To produce a report, click on Report.

WORKING
TOGETHER
▲

6. If desired, fill in the Default Information dialog box and click on OK; otherwise, click on Cancel.

7. If desired, fill in the Optional Information dialog box. The macro displays the report, which uses the _mortgag.sty mortgage calculation form style sheet.

WORKING
TOGETHER
▲

# Calculating a College Savings Plan

To calculate monthly mortgage payments and the total dollars spent over the life of a mortgage, follow these steps:

1. Choose Tools ➤ Macros ➤ Playback or click on the appropriate SmartIcon in the Bonus Pack SmartIcons set. Ami Pro displays the Play Macro dialog box.

2. Choose QKCOLLG.SMM. Ami Pro displays the The College Fund dialog box (shown filled in).

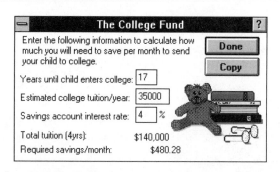

3. Fill in the Years Until Child Enters College, Estimated College Tuition/Year, and Savings Account Interest Rate text boxes, either pressing Tab or clicking to get to the next text box. The macro fills in the Total Tuition and Required Savings/Month areas as you type. (You can change values; the macro changes the values immediately.)

4. To copy an image of the dialog box for later insertion in a document, press Alt+PrtSc (Print Screen).

5. To close the dialog box without further action, either click on Done or press ↵.

6. To copy the Required Savings/Month to the Clipboard and close the dialog box, click on Copy.

7. Either choose Edit ➤ Paste, click on the Paste SmartIcon, or press Ctrl+V to paste the contents of the Clipboard in the current document at the insertion point.

## Date Format

1-2-3 provides five date formats: *dd-Mon-yy*, *dd-Mon*, *Mon-yy*, *mm/dd/yy*, and *mm/dd*, where

- *dd* is a two-digit day
- *Mon* is a three-character month
- *yy* is the two-digit year
- *mm* is a two-digit month

Enter any number, select a date format, and 1-2-3 converts the number to that format.

If the current cell is formatted as Automatic, you can enter a date in any of these formats: *dd-Mon-yy*, *dd-Mon*, or *mm/dd/yy*, and 1-2-3 automatically applies the appropriate date format. If you enter a date using the *mm/dd* format, 1-2-3 interprets the value as a formula that divides *mm* by *dd*.

**WORKING TOGETHER** ▲

# Calculating Savings

The Working Together Bonus Pack has two macros that enable you to calculate savings. You can estimate accumulated savings over time using the QKSAVE.SMM macro. You can find out how long it will take for you to accumulate a certain amount of money using the QKTERM.SMM macro.

You can estimate total accumulated savings by entering the interest rate, savings per month, and the number of months, and letting the macro run. To calculate savings, follow these steps:

1. Choose Tools ➤ Macros ➤ Playback or click on the appropriate SmartIcon in the Bonus Pack SmartIcons set. Ami Pro displays the Play Macro dialog box.

2. Choose QKSAVE.SMM. Ami Pro displays the Calculate Savings Account dialog box (shown filled in).

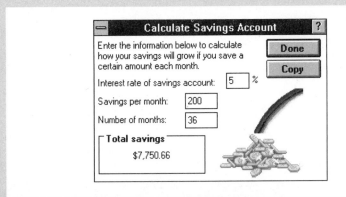

3. Fill in the Interest Rate of Savings Account, Savings Per Month, and Number of Months text boxes, either pressing Tab or clicking to get to the next text box. The macro fills in the Total Savings box as you type. (You can change values; the macro changes the values immediately.)

**WORKING TOGETHER**

4. To copy an image of the dialog box for later insertion in a document, press Alt+PrtSc (Print Screen).

5. To close the dialog box without further action, either click on Done or press ↵.

6. To copy the Required Savings/Month to the Clipboard and close the dialog box, click on Copy.

7. Either choose Edit ➤ Paste, click on the Paste SmartIcon, or press Ctrl+V to paste the contents of the Clipboard in the current document at the insertion point.

You can estimate how long it will take you to save a specific amount by entering the interest rate, savings per year, the amount you wish to accumulate, and letting the macro run. To calculate accumulated savings, follow these steps:

1. Choose Tools ➤ Macros ➤ Playback or click on the appropriate SmartIcon in the Bonus Pack SmartIcons set. Ami Pro displays the Play Macro dialog box.

2. Choose QKTERM.SMM. Ami Pro displays the Determine Investment Growth dialog box (shown filled in).

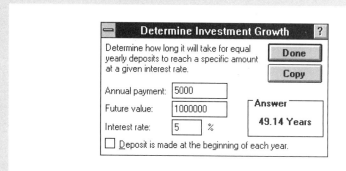

3. Fill in the Annual Payment, Future Value, and Interest Rate text boxes, either pressing Tab or clicking to get to the next text box. The macro fills in the Answer box as you type. (You can change values; the macro changes the values immediately.)

**WORKING TOGETHER**

4. Check the <u>D</u>eposit Is Made at the Beginning of Each Year check box if you wish to get the full effect of interest rates based on early deposit.

5. To copy an image of the dialog box for later insertion in a document, press Alt+PrtSc (Print Screen).

6. To close the dialog box without further action, either click on Done or press ↵.

7. To copy the contents of the Answer box to the Clipboard and close the dialog box, click on Copy.

8. Either choose <u>E</u>dit ➤ <u>P</u>aste, click on the Paste SmartIcon, or press Ctrl+V to paste the contents of the Clipboard in the current document at the insertion point.

## Time Format

1-2-3 provides four time formats—two for 12-hour (AM | PM) and two for 24-hour military: *hh-mm-ss* AM | PM, *hh-mm* AM | PM, *hh-mm-ss* military, and *hh/mm* military, where

- *hh* represents the hour
- *mm* represents minutes
- *ss* represents seconds
- AM is the period from one minute after midnight until noon
- PM is the period from one minute after noon until midnight

Enter any number, select a time format, and 1-2-3 converts the number to that format.

If the current cell is formatted as Automatic, you can enter a time in any of these formats: *hh-mm, hh-mm-ss, hh-mm* AM, *or hh-mm* PM and 1-2-3 automatically applies the appropriate time format. If you type an hour between 13 and 24, 1-2-3 formats the time based on the 24-hour clock. If you type a number greater than 24, 1-2-3 interprets it as a label rather than a time.

## Scientific Format

Scientific format displays positive or negative numbers as exponents, with up to 15 decimal points. Simply type a number and apply Scientific format. For example, when formatting with two decimal places,

| IF YOU TYPE: | 1-2-3 CONVERTS TO: |
|---|---|
| 0.1 | 1.00E–01 |
| 99999.90 | 1.00E+05 |
| –4.3 | –4.30E+00 |

If the current cell is formatted as Automatic, you can type an exponent (i.e., $nE+n$, where $n$ represents a number with one or more digits), and 1-2-3 automatically converts the format to Scientific.

## Currency Format

Currency format displays numbers preceded by a currency symbol, with embedded thousands separators, and with up to 15 decimal points. Negative numbers are surrounded by parentheses. Simply type a number and apply Currency format. For example, when formatting with two decimal places,

| IF YOU TYPE: | 1-2-3 CONVERTS TO: |
|---|---|
| 0.1 | $0.10 |
| 99999.9 | $99,999.90 |
| –4.3 | ($4.30) |

If the current cell is formatted as Automatic, you can type a dollar sign (or your selected currency symbol) and a series of numbers, and 1-2-3 converts the format to Currency. The US Dollar is the default currency format. You can also select British Pound, Canadian Dollar, Japanese Yen, or Mexican Peso from the Number Format list from the status bar. In the Number Format dialog box, you can select from a total of 44 currency formats (including those in the Number Format list).

# Calculating and Building a Loan Payment Table

To calculate and create a loan payment table for a range of loan amounts over a specified number of years, follow these steps:

1. Choose Tools ➤ Macros ➤ Playback or click on the appropriate SmartIcon in the Bonus Pack SmartIcons set. Ami Pro displays the Play Macro dialog box.

2. Choose QKTABLE.SMM. Ami Pro displays the Calculate Loan Payment Table dialog box (shown filled in).

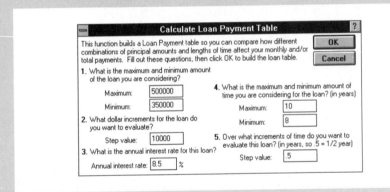

3. Answer question 1 by filling in the Maximum and Minimum amounts of the loan.

4. Answer question 2 by specifying the value of the steps between the minimum and maximum values (so that the table will start at the minimum amount, add the step value for the next amount, and repeat adding the step value to the previous amount until reaching the maximum value).

5. Answer question 3 by filling in the annual interest rate.

6. Answer question 4 by filling in the Maximum and Minimum years over which the loan will run.

**WORKING TOGETHER**

7. Answer question 5 by specifying the value of the steps between the minimum and maximum time period (so that the table will start at the minimum time, add the step value for the next time period, and repeat adding the step value to the previous time until reaching the maximum time).

8. Click on OK. The macro builds a loan payment table based on the _loanpay.sty style sheet.

| Loan Payment Table | | | | |
|---|---|---|---|---|
| Loan Assumptions: | | | | |
| Interest Rate: | 8.50% | | | |
| Max. Amount: | 500,000.00 | | | |
| Min. Amount: | 350,000.00 | | | |
| Max. Time: | 10 years | | | |
| Min. Time: | 8 years | | | |
| | | | | |
| | | Years | | |
| 8.00 | 8.50 | 9.00 | 9.50 | 10.00 |
| 350,000.00 | 5,037.25 | 4,830.57 | 4,647.77 | 4,485.09 | 4,339.50 |
| 483,575.52 | 492,717.67 | 501,959.53 | 511,300.49 | 520,739.89 |
| 360,000.00 | 5,181.17 | 4,968.58 | 4,780.57 | 4,613.24 | 4,463.48 |
| 497,391.96 | 506,795.32 | 516,301.23 | 525,909.07 | 535,618.18 |
| 370,000.00 | 5,325.09 | 5,106.60 | 4,913.36 | 4,741.38 | 4,587.47 |
| 511,208.41 | 520,872.97 | 530,642.93 | 540,517.66 | 550,496.46 |

## , Comma Format

, Comma format displays numbers with embedded thousands separators and with up to 15 decimal points. Negative numbers are surrounded by parentheses. Simply type a number and apply , Comma format. The only difference between this format and Currency format is the lack of a currency symbol. For example, when formatting with four decimal places,

| IF YOU TYPE: | 1-2-3 CONVERTS TO: |
|---|---|
| 0.10003 | 0.10003 |
| 99999.9009 | 99,999.9009 |
| –49786.3023 | (49,786.3023) |

## WORKING TOGETHER
▲

# Calculating and Building a Depreciation Table

To calculate and create a depreciation table for an asset, follow these steps:

1. Choose Tools ➤ Macros ➤ Playback or click on the appropriate SmartIcon in the Bonus Pack SmartIcons set. Ami Pro displays the Play Macro dialog box.

2. Choose QKDEPREC.SMM. Ami Pro displays the QuickDepreciation dialog box (shown filled in).

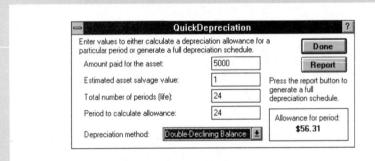

3. Fill in the dollar value paid for the asset, its estimated salvage value, its estimated life (in periods), and the periods over which to calculate the depreciation allowance.

4. Select a method of depreciation: Double-Declining Balance, Sum-of-Years' Digits, or Straight-Line.

5. To close the dialog box at any time, click on Done.

6. To generate a report, click on Report. The macro closes the dialog box and generates the report.

| Depreciation Schedule | | |
|---|---:|---:|
| Period | Depreciation | Net Book Value |
| 1 | 416.67 | 4,583.33 |
| 2 | 381.94 | 4,201.39 |
| 3 | 350.12 | 3,851.27 |
| 4 | 320.94 | 3,530.33 |
| 5 | 294.19 | 3,236.14 |
| 6 | 269.68 | 2,966.46 |
| 7 | 247.21 | 2,719.26 |
| 8 | 226.6 | 2,492.65 |
| 9 | 207.72 | 2,284.93 |
| 10 | 190.41 | 2,094.52 |
| 11 | 174.54 | 1,919.98 |
| 12 | 160 | 1,759.98 |

If the current cell is formatted as Automatic, you can type a number including a comma, and 1-2-3 converts the format to , Comma.

## Percent Format

Percent format displays a number as a percentage, with a percentage sign suffix, without thousands separators, and with up to 15 decimal places. Negative numbers are preceded by a minus sign. Simply type a number and apply Percent format. For example, when using four decimal places,

| IF YOU TYPE: | 1-2-3 CONVERTS TO: |
|---|---|
| 0.1 | 10% |
| 99999.90 | 9999990% |
| −49786.3023 | −4978630.2300% |

**WORKING TOGETHER** ▲

# Calculating Statistics for Selected Data

You can compute statistics for a list of data and either view the statistics in a dialog box or paste the results into an Ami Pro document at the insertion point. To compute statistics, follow these steps:

1. Select a list of data in an Ami Pro document.

2. Choose Tools ➤ Macros ➤ Playback or click on the appropriate SmartIcon in the Bonus Pack SmartIcons set. Ami Pro displays the Play Macro dialog box.

3. Choose QKSTAT.SMM and click on OK. Ami Pro displays the QuickStats dialog box with displayed statistics for the selection next to the appropriate option button. (To close the dialog box after checking the results, click on Done.)

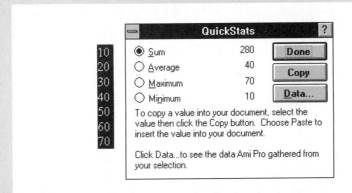

4. To edit the data, click on the Data button. In the Data dialog box, edit the list, or add a new list item by pressing Ctrl+M. Then click on OK. When you return to the QuickStats dialog box, the macro changes the displayed statistics to reflect your editing. (To close the dialog box at any time without copying one result into the Clipboard, click on Done.)

Types of Data

1-2-3

**WORKING TOGETHER**
▲

...o that you can insert it in
...ge, Maximum, or Minimum.

...e dialog box and returns to

...ation in which you wish to in-

...the Paste SmartIcon, or
...lipboard are inserted at the

If ... you can type a number with a
p... ...ormat to Percent.

## Fixed

F... ... decimal places and no thousands
s... ...mbers preceded by a minus sign,
a... ...ample, when using two decimal
... ...s to:

| | |
|---|---|
| 0.1 | 0.10 |
| −4.3 | −4.30 |

**153**

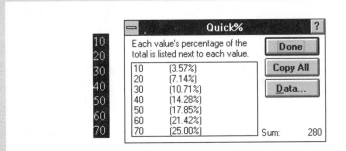

WORKING
TOGETHER
▲

# Calculating Percentages for Selected Data

You can compute percentages for a list of data and either view the statistics in a dialog box or paste the results into an Ami Pro document at the insertion point. To compute percentages, follow these steps:

1. Select a list of data in an Ami Pro document.

2. Choose Tools ➤ Macros ➤ Playback or click on the appropriate SmartIcon in the Bonus Pack SmartIcons set. Ami Pro displays the Play Macro dialog box.

3. Choose QKPERC.SMM and click on OK. Ami Pro displays the Quick% dialog box with displayed percentages for the selection. (To close the dialog box after checking the results, click on Done.)

4. To edit the data, click on the Data button. In the Data dialog box, edit the list, or add a new list item by pressing Ctrl+M. Then, click on OK. When you return to the Quick% dialog box, the macro changes the displayed percentages to reflect your editing. (To close the dialog box at any time without copying one result into the Clipboard, click on Done.)

**WORKING TOGETHER**

5. To copy a result into the Clipboard so that you can insert it in your document, click on Copy All. The dialog box closes and you return to your document.

6. Move the insertion point to the location in which you wish to insert the copied values and percentages.

7. Either choose Edit ➤ Paste, click on the Paste SmartIcon, or press Ctrl+V. The contents of the Clipboard are inserted at the insertion point.

## General Format

General format displays numbers as entered, but without thousands separators, leading zeroes, and trailing zeroes. Negative numbers are preceded by a minus sign. For example,

| IF YOU TYPE: | 1-2-3 CONVERTS TO: |
|---|---|
| 99999.9 | 99999.9 |
| 0.1 | 0.1 |
| −4.3 | −4.3 |

## +/− Format

+/− format displays a series of plus signs, minus signs, or a single period representing an integer value of a number. Positive values are represented by plus signs, negative values are represented by minus signs, and values between −1 and +1 are represented by a period. For example,

| IF YOU TYPE: | 1-2-3 CONVERTS TO: |
|---|---|
| 0.1 | . |
| 9 | +++++++++ |
| −4.3 | ──── |

WORKING TOGETHER

▲

# Calculating Percentage Trends for Selected Data

You can compute the percentage of growth from one item to another in a list of data. You can either view the statistics in a dialog box or paste the results into an Ami Pro document at the insertion point. To compute percentage trends, follow these steps:

1. Select a list of data in an Ami Pro document.

2. Choose Tools ➤ Macros ➤ Playback or click on the appropriate SmartIcon in the Bonus Pack SmartIcons set. Ami Pro displays the Play Macro dialog box.

3. Choose QKTREND.SMM and click on OK. Ami Pro displays the QuickTrend dialog box with displayed percentages for the selection. (To close the dialog box after checking the results, click on Done.)

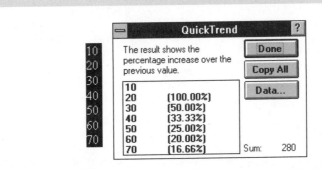

4. To edit the data, click on the Data button. In the Data dialog box, edit the list, or add a new list item by pressing Ctrl+M. Then click on OK. When you return to the QuickTrend dialog box, the macro changes the displayed percentages to reflect your editing. (To close the dialog box at any time without copying one result into the Clipboard, click on Done.)

**WORKING TOGETHER** ▲

5. To copy a result into the Clipboard so that you can insert it in your document, click on Copy All. The dialog box closes and you return to your document.

6. Move the insertion point to the location in which you wish to insert the copied values and percentages.

7. Either choose Edit ➤ Paste, click on the Paste SmartIcon, or press Ctrl+V. The contents of the Clipboard are inserted at the insertion point.

## Text Format

Text format displays numbers and formulas as they are entered. Use this format to display a formula rather than the result of the formula.

## Hidden Format

Hidden format hides the contents of the cell, but the value, title, label, or formula remains in the contents box of the edit line.

## Label Format

Label format displays text as a label and numbers using the General format.

# Entering Formulas

Up to this point, you have used 1-2-3 just to store numbers and text. Remember that one of the most important reasons for using a spreadsheet program is to manipulate numbers. There are three types of 1-2-3 formulas: numeric, logical, and text. A *numeric formula* computes numbers using the arithmetic operators +, −, *, /, and ^. Table 5.1 describes each arithmetic operator.

**TABLE 5.1:** 1-2-3 Arithmetic Operators

| OPERATOR | MATHEMATICAL OPERATION PERFORMED |
|---|---|
| + | Addition |
| − | Subtraction |
| * | Multiplication |
| / | Division |
| ^ | Exponentiation |

A *logical formula* determines whether a condition is true or false using these logical operators: =, <, >, <=, >=, <>, #AND#, #NOT#, and #OR#. Logical operators are described below:

| OPERATOR | LOGICAL OPERATION PERFORMED |
|---|---|
| = | Tests value A against value B and returns True (1) if they are equal or False (0) if they are not equal |
| <> | Tests value A against value B and returns True (1) if they are not equal or False (0) if they are equal |
| < | Tests value A against value B and returns True (1) if A is less than B; otherwise, 1-2-3 returns False (0) |
| <= | Tests value A against value B and returns True (1) if A is less than or equal to B; otherwise, 1-2-3 returns False (0) |
| > | Tests value A against value B and returns True (1) if A is greater than B; otherwise, 1-2-3 returns False (0) |
| >= | Tests value A against value B and returns True (1) if A is greater than or equal to B; otherwise, 1-2-3 returns False (0) |
| #AND# | Tests two combined values with these results: |

■ if value A is False *and* value B is False, 1-2-3 returns False (0)

■ if value A is False *and* value B is True, 1-2-3 returns False (0)

■ if value A is True *and* value B is False, 1-2-3 returns False (0)

■ if value A is True *and* value B is True, 1-2-3 returns True (1)

#NOT#     Reverses a value so that if value A is False (0), 1-2-3 returns True (1), and if value A is True (1), 1-2-3 returns False (0)

#OR#     Tests two separate values with these results:

■ if value A is False *or* value B is False, 1-2-3 returns False (0)

■ if value A is False *or* value B is True, 1-2-3 returns True (1)

■ if value A is True *or* value B is False, 1-2-3 returns True (1)

■ if value A is True *or* value B is True, 1-2-3 returns True (1)

A *text formula* uses text and the text operator & to display combined text strings. For example, you can combine the strings "John "&"Doe" in a cell. (The space after *John* ensures that the first and last names are properly separated.)

Operators determine the order in which a formula is processed. Table 5.2 lists the order of precedence for 1-2-3.

The simplest way to enter a formula is to build it one step at a time using combinations of names of cells, mathematical and logical operators, strings, or numbers. Suppose you have the value *22.5* stored in cell F16. To add 22.5 to a formula, you could type **22.5** or **F16**. When you refer to a cell name, it's easier to change values in your spreadsheets and to keep track of those values. So in most cases, it's preferable to use the cell name within formulas.

To write a very simple formula using just cells and operators, highlight the cell in which the results will appear. Type a mathematical operator (typically, the plus sign), which tells 1-2-3 that you are about to enter a formula. Then click on a cell to add it to the formula. Type another mathematical operator, click on another cell to add it to the formula, and so on. When you have completed the formula, press ↵ or click on the Confirm button in the edit line.

For our sample spreadsheet, follow these steps:

1. Click in cell B9 (in which the total will appear).

2. Type **+**.

3. Click on cell B6.

**TABLE 5.2:** 1-2-3 Order of Precedence

| ORDER | OPERATOR | DESCRIPTION |
|-------|----------|-------------|
| First | () | Values in parentheses |
| Second | − | Negative values |
|  | + | Positive values |
| Third | * | Multiplication |
|  | / | Division |
| Fourth | + | Addition |
|  | − | Subtraction |
| Fifth | = | Equal to |
|  | <> | Not equal to |
|  | < | Less than |
|  | > | Greater than |
|  | <= | Less than or equal to |
|  | >= | Greater than or equal to |
| Sixth | NOT | Reverses the values being compared |
| Seventh | AND | Both values being compared are true |
|  | OR | One value being compared is true |

4. Type +.

5. Click on cell B7.

6. Type +.

7. Click on cell B8.

8. Press ↵ or click on the Confirm button. 1-2-3 completes the formula in the contents box of the edit line. It also adds the contents of cells B6, B7, and B8, placing the total in B9.

Using the preceding steps, add cells B12 and B13, placing the results in cell B14. Figure 5.5 shows the sample spreadsheet with the results of the preceding steps and the addition of cells B12 and B13.

**FIGURE 5.5**

The sample spreadsheet with totals in cells B9 and B14 and a completed formula in the contents box

The formula in the current cell

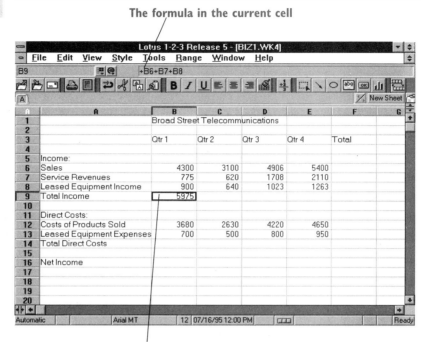

The results of computing the formula in this cell

## Automatically Copying Formulas

There is no need to repeat the preceding steps to copy a formula that is made up of the same cell-mathematical operator combination and that will occur in the same row or column in a spreadsheet. You can use the Copy Down or Copy Right commands or SmartIcons to copy a formula and have 1-2-3 adjust its contents to reflect its new column or row location.

 To copy a formula from the column above the currently selected cell, either click on the Copy Down SmartIcon, choose Copy Down from the shortcut menu (make your selection and click the right mouse button), or choose Edit ➤ Copy Down.

 To copy a formula from the row to the left of the currently selected cell, either click on the Copy Right SmartIcon, choose Copy Right from the shortcut menu, or choose Edit ➤ Copy Right.

NOTE  To see other Copy SmartIcons, see the part opening pages immediately preceding Chapter 4.

To copy formulas in our sample spreadsheet, follow these steps:

1. Highlight cell B9 and drag to cell E9.

2. Press down the right mouse button.

3. Choose Copy Right. 1-2-3 copies the formula in cell B9 to cells C9, D9, and E9 and edits the copied formulas so that they reflect the cells that they are to add.

Using the preceding steps, copy the formula from B14 into C14, D14, and E14. Then compute the Net Income for cell B16 using this formula: +B9–B14. Copy the formula to cells C16, D16, and E16. At this point, the spreadsheet should look like Figure 5.6.

## Relative Cell References and Absolute Cell References

You could copy formulas using the preceding steps because you were using *relative cell references*, the default. 1-2-3 found the cells to which the formulas referred by comparing their position relative to the cells holding the formulas. When you copy the formulas to other cells in the same row or column, the relative cells remain in the same position. For example, the ranges B6..B8, C6..C8, D6..D8, and E6..E8 (the two periods between B6 and E6 indicate that you are selecting a range) are in the same position relative to cells B9, C9, D9, and E9, respectively.

*Absolute cell references* do not change when you copy a formula to another cell. For example, if you calculate interest always using the same interest rate, you don't need to use a relative cell reference. To define an absolute cell reference, use the dollar sign prefix. If the interest rate is stored in cell E16, build a series of formulas in this way: +E15*$E16, +F15*$E16, +G15*$E16, and so on. When you copy a formula with an absolute cell reference, although other parts of the formula may change to reflect relative cell references, the absolute cell reference remains the same.

**FIGURE 5.6**

The sample spreadsheet with up-to-date data and results.

The formula in the current cell

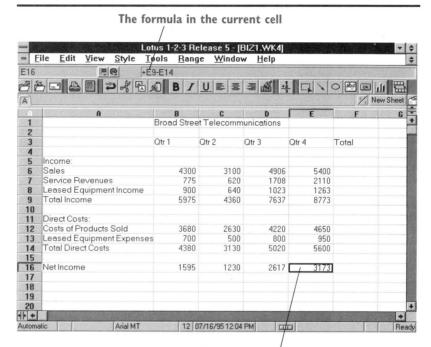

The results of the formula in this cell

## Introducing @Functions

Rather than build a formula step by step, you can use *@functions*, which are predefined formulas that automatically perform common mathematical, statistical, or business calculations. Probably the most common @function is @SUM, which computes the totals for a list. For our sample spreadsheet, you'll compute the totals in the Total column using these steps:

**1.** Move the mouse pointer to cell F6 and click the left mouse button.

**2.** Click on the @function selector in the edit line.

**3.** From the list, click on SUM. 1-2-3 displays @SUM(list) in F6.

**4.** Click in B6 and drag across to E6. Notice that 1-2-3 replaces *list* with B6..E6.

**5.** Either click on the Confirm button or press ↵. 1-2-3 sums cells B6, C6, D6, and E6, and places the results in F6 (Figure 5.7).

You can compute the sums for rows and columns at the same time by highlighting a range of cells and clicking on the Sum SmartIcon. 1-2-3 builds a set of @SUM formulas to total the contents of the cells above and to the left of the current range. To compute totals for the year in our sample spreadsheet, follow these steps:

**1.** Highlight cell F7 and drag to cell F9.

**2.** Click on the Sum SmartIcon. 1-2-3 creates @SUM formulas that calculate the sum of the quarters for each Income row of our sample spreadsheet. Figure 5.8 shows our sample spreadsheet after the sum of the quarters for the income rows.

You'll find out about other common @functions at the end of this chapter.

**FIGURE 5.7**

The sample spreadsheet with its first column F total

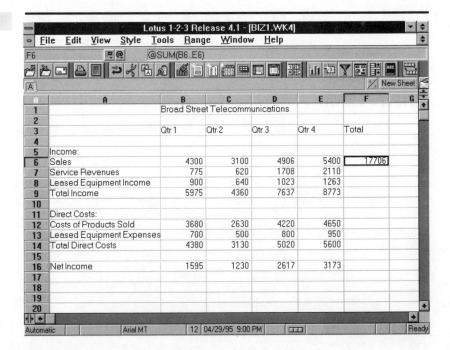

FIGURE 5.8

The sample
spreadsheet after the
income rows have
been totaled

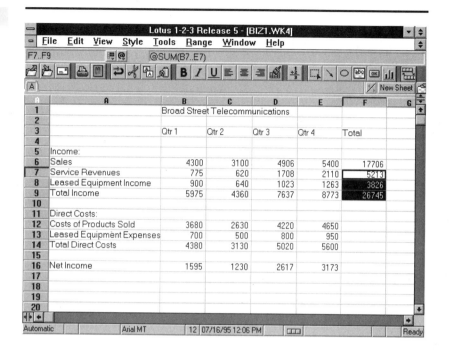

## Defining Ranges

Although you have already worked with ranges (for example, cells F7 to F9 in the preceding steps) and Range commands (Fill and Fill by Example) earlier in this chapter, you have not had a formal introduction. Simply put, a *range* is a group of connected cells. A range can be a single cell, one column of cells, one row of cells, or a block of cells consisting of several rows by several columns. For example, one of the ranges that you have worked with in this chapter are three cells in a column; another is four cells in a row. You can create ranges that extend the full length or width of a spreadsheet.

## Naming Ranges

If you use the same range often, you can name that range, allowing you to create formulas more easily and quickly than by pointing to cells one at a time. To name a range, select Range ➤ Name. In the Name dialog box (Figure 5.9), type the name in the Name text box and click on Add to add the name to the list.

**WORKING TOGETHER**
▲

# Returning the Value of an @Function

You can test and solve formulas and @functions before inserting them in a 1-2-3 spreadsheet. To run the @function macro, follow these steps:

**1.** Choose Tools ➤ Macros ➤ Playback or click on the appropriate SmartIcon in the Bonus Pack SmartIcons set. Ami Pro displays the Play Macro dialog box.

**2.** Choose QKFUNCT.SMM and click on OK. Ami Pro displays the Solve @Function dialog box.

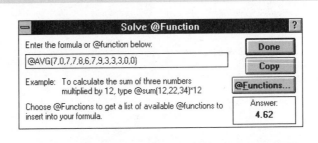

**3.** To insert an @function in the Enter the Formula or @Function Below text box, click on @Functions. The More @Functions dialog box appears.

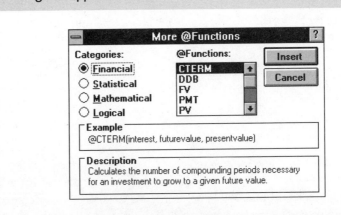

**WORKING TOGETHER**

4. Select a category, select an @function, and click on Insert. (Notice the brief description of the selected @function at the bottom of the dialog box.) The macro closes the dialog box and inserts the @function (and its arguments and syntax) in the Solve @Function dialog box.

5. Edit the formula, inserting your values. As you edit, the macro displays the current answer in the Answer box.

6. To close the dialog box at any time, click on Done.

7. To copy a result into the Clipboard so that you can insert it in your document, click on Copy. The dialog box closes and you return to your document.

8. Move the insertion point to the location in which you wish to insert the copied values and percentages.

9. Either choose Edit ➤ Paste, click on the Paste SmartIcon, or press Ctrl+V. The contents of the Clipboard are inserted at the insertion point.

**FIGURE 5.9**

The Name dialog box, in which you can name a range of cells

The current range name

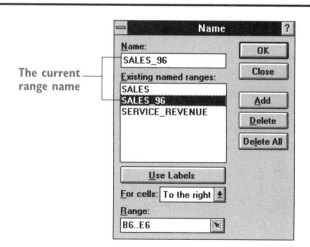

Either click on OK or press ↵. After you name ranges, you'll notice that 1-2-3 changes formulas containing those ranges. For example, if a formula previously referred to B6..E6 and you named that range SALES_96, 1-2-3 automatically replaces B6..E6 with SALES_96.

When naming ranges, note that range names can have up to 15 characters, starting with an alphabetic character.

 **WARNING** Don't use spaces, 1-2-3 @function names, key names, cell address names, or any characters that 1-2-3 reserves for mathematical or logical operations. Don't use any of these characters in range names: . ; , ! + ~ - * / & > < @ # {.

You can delete range names using the Name dialog box. To delete a single range name, select it from the <u>E</u>xisting Named Ranges list box, click on the Delete button, and either click on OK or press ↵. To delete all the range names for this file, click on De<u>l</u>ete All, and either click on OK or press ↵.

You can name a particular cell immediately to the right or immediately below a label by following these steps:

1. Select the label that you wish to refer to a cell.

2. Choose <u>R</u>ange ➤ <u>N</u>ame.

3. In the Name dialog box, click on the <u>U</u>se Labels button.

4. From the <u>F</u>or Cells drop-down list box, select the direction that indicates the location of the cell to be named. You can select To the Right or To the Left to refer to directions through rows, or Above or Below to refer to directions through columns.

5. Either click on OK or press ↵.

**NOTE** Before moving on to the following section, in the sample spreadsheet, name the range B13..E13 LEASED_EXPS.

## Inserting Named Ranges in Formulas

 When you wish to use a named range in a formula, 1-2-3 provides some short-cuts. You have already used the @function selector to write a simple formula. Now you'll use the @function selector and the navigator to write a more complex formula. To write a formula using an @function and the navigator, follow these steps:

1. Click on the cell in which you wish to insert the formula. For the sample spreadsheet, click on F13.

2. Click on the @function selector. 1-2-3 displays the list of common @functions.

3. Select SUM. 1-2-3 inserts the formula @SUM(list) in the current cell. Notice that list is highlighted.

4. Click on the navigator. 1-2-3 displays a list of all the named ranges (Figure 5.10) for this file.

5. Click on a range name, such as LEASED_EXPS. 1-2-3 replaces list with the name of the range.

**FIGURE 5.10**

The open navigator list of all the named ranges for this file

**Ranges for this spreadsheet** ———

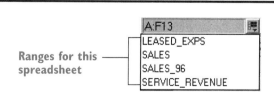

6. Either click on the Confirm button or press ↵ to indicate that the formula is complete. 1-2-3 calculates the formula and places the results in the current cell.

Figure 5.11 shows the sample spreadsheet completely filled in. Notice in the Contents box that the highlighted cell contains a formula that subtracts the contents of one cell from another.

# Building Formulas with Common 1-2-3 @Functions

In the preceding sections in this chapter, you learned about creating formulas using the @SUM @function. In this section, you'll learn about a few of the common 1-2-3 @functions and how to use them in formulas. Finally, you'll find out about how to get information about any of the more than 200 1-2-3 @functions.

**FIGURE 5.11**

The sample spreadsheet with all formulas entered and results in place

A formula that subtracts one value from another

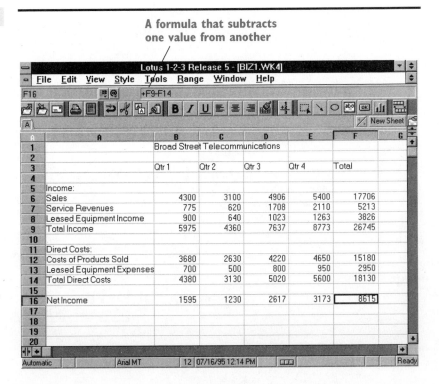

**WORKING TOGETHER** ▲

# Calculating Mathematical Equations

You can calculate four types of mathematical equations using a Working Together Bonus Pack macro. For example, to calculate the sine, cosine, and tangent for an angle, follow these steps:

1. Choose Tools ➤ Macros ➤ Playback or click on the appropriate SmartIcon in the Bonus Pack SmartIcons set. Ami Pro displays the Play Macro dialog box.

2. Choose QKGEOM.SMM and click on OK. Ami Pro displays the QuickGeometry dialog box.

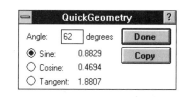

3. Type the degrees for the angle in the Angle text box.

4. To close the dialog box at any time, click on Done.

5. To copy a result into the Clipboard so that you can insert it in your document, click on the sine, cosine, or tangent option button and click on Copy. The dialog box closes and you return to your document.

6. Move the insertion point to the location in which you wish to insert the copied value.

7. Either choose Edit ➤ Paste, click on the Paste SmartIcon, or press Ctrl+V. The contents of the Clipboard are inserted at the insertion point.

**WORKING TOGETHER** ▲

These are other Working Together Bonus Pack mathematical calculators:

| | |
|---|---|
| QKQUAD.SMM | calculates a quadratic equation |
| QKPOWER.SMM | calculates a number raised to a power |
| QKROOT.SMM | calculates the root of a number |

## Computing an Average

The @AVG function computes the average of a list of values:

`@AVG(E6..E11)`

adds the contents of E6, E7, E8, E9, E10, and E11 and then divides by six, the number of cells. If a cell contains a label, 1-2-3 does not add or count it.

## Identifying Maximum and Minimum Values

Use @MAX and @MIN to identify the maximum and minimum values in a list:

`@MAX(E6..E11)`

finds the highest value in the cells E6, E7, E8, E9, E10, and E11 and

`@MIN(E6..E11)`

finds the lowest value in the list E6, E7, E8, E9, E10, and E11.

## Returning the Date and Time

You can display the date or time by using date and time functions such as @DATE, @TIME, @TODAY, or @NOW. If you are setting up a new spreadsheet, you can insert a particular date by using @DATE:

`@DATE(96;8;27)`

returns 35304, which you can convert to a date format by selecting a date format from the status line.

@TIME works in exactly the same way:

`@TIME(12;12;12)`

returns 0.5084722. Select a time format to convert the value to a time.

Using @NOW, you can stamp today's date and time into a spreadsheet:

`@NOW`

returns a number representing the date and time to which your computer system has been set. 1-2-3 returns a number representing both today's date and time, which you can use in calculations. However, because 1-2-3 does not provide a combination date/time format, you can see either the date or time, but not both, in the selected format.

## Rounding Values

The @ROUND function rounds a number to a specified number of places:

`@ROUND(956.453964599;2)`

looks like 956.45 as displayed in a cell, and

`@ROUND(956.453964599;-2)`

looks like 1000. In the formula, the 2 and −2 following the semicolon control the rounding. A positive number rounds the digits to the right of the decimal point, and a negative number rounds to the left of the decimal point.

You can round a value by referring to the cell in which it is located:

`@ROUND(B9,-3)`

rounds the integer portion of the contents of cell B9 to three one-hundredths.

## Testing for Conditions

One of the most important and most used spreadsheet functions is @IF. Use @IF to compare two values; if the first value is true, 1-2-3 returns a particular value, and if the second value is true, 1-2-3 returns another value:

`@IF(C9>=500;FEE=0;FEE=10)`

computes a fee for a checking account. If the balance is greater than or equal to $500, the monthly fee is zero; otherwise, the fee is $10.

You can nest @IF statements to test a series of values:

```
@IF(C9>=75000;500;@IF(C9>=50000;350;@IF(C9>=25000;200;50)))
```

computes a series of bonus amounts.

# Getting Information about
# 1-2-3 @Functions

The best source of information about all the 1-2-3 @functions is 1-2-3's Help facility. There are two ways to find out about a particular @function:

- Choose the Help menu on the menu bar. Then go through a series of Help windows until you get to the one for the desired function. Use this procedure if you are not sure of the best @function for the formula.

- Select a cell containing a formula that includes the @function about which you wish to learn. Then press F1. This displays the Help Contents window. Then click on the @Functions button, select a category, and select the function. Figure 5.12 shows the @SUM help window.

When you choose Help ➤ Contents and click on the @Functions button, 1-2-3 displays the @Functions window (Figure 5.13) from which you can select any of four topics:

**What Are @Functions?**   to display an overview of @functions. From this window, you can return to the @Functions window or display the @Function Selector window.

**Descriptions of Individual @Functions**   to display an introductory window for the @Function Help facility. From this window, you can return to the @Functions window or display the 1-2-3 Release 4 Help Contents window.

1-2-3

**FIGURE 5.12**

The @SUM Help window, provides arguments, examples, related SmartIcons, similar @functions, other Help topics, and information about help in the *User's Guide*.

The Help menu bar

Help buttons

Click on to view a new Help topic.

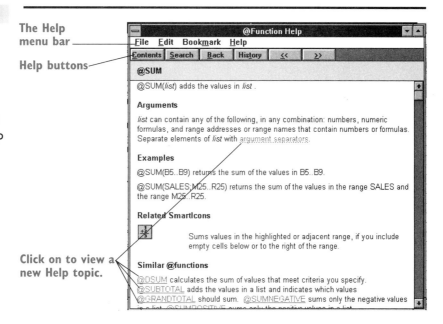

@**Function Categories**    to list the @function categories: Calendar, Database, Engineering, Financial, Information, Logical, Lookup, Mathematical, Statistical, and Text. From this window, you can display particular functions by category. You can also return to the @Functions window or display the @Function Selector window.

@**Function Selector**    to display help information about the @Function Selector in the edit line. From this window, you can return to the @Functions window.

**Alphabetical Listing of All @Functions**    to see instructions for viewing a list of all @ Functions.

To use the <u>H</u>elp menu to display help windows for @functions, follow these steps:

**1.** Choose <u>H</u>elp ➤ <u>C</u>ontents. 1-2-3 displays the @Functions window (Figure 5.13).

**2.** Choose one of four topics: What Are @Functions?, Descriptions of Individual @Functions, @Function Categories, or @Function Selector.

The @Functions Contents window, from which you can choose from four @function Help topics

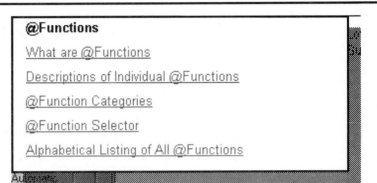

**3.** Continue to select @function Help windows until you accumulate the desired information.

 **NOTE**   **You can print a help topic by choosing <u>F</u>ile ➤ <u>P</u>rint Topic from the Help window menu bar.**

**4.** To return to the current spreadsheet, choose <u>F</u>ile ➤ E<u>x</u>it from the Help window menu bar or press Alt+F4.

For more information about using Windows help, see your Windows manuals.

**WORKING TOGETHER** ▲

# Constructing Calculation Applications

You can build your own calculators using the BUILD.SMM macro and following these steps:

1. Choose Tools ➤ Macros ➤ Playback or click on the appropriate SmartIcon in the Bonus Pack SmartIcons set. Ami Pro displays the Play Macro dialog box.

2. Choose BUILD.SMM and click on OK. Ami Pro displays the Calculation Application Builder dialog box. The first option button is selected.

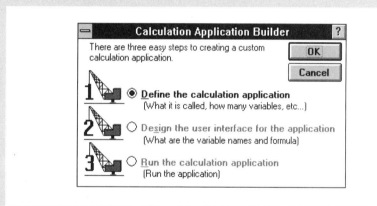

3. Click on OK. The macro displays the Define Application dialog box.

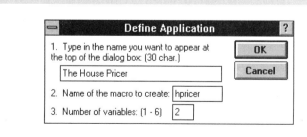

WORKING
TOGETHER
▲

**4.** Fill in the dialog box and click on OK. The macro returns to the Calculation Application Builder dialog box. The second option button is selected.

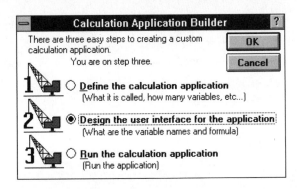

**5.** Click on OK. The macro displays the Design Dialog Box dialog box.

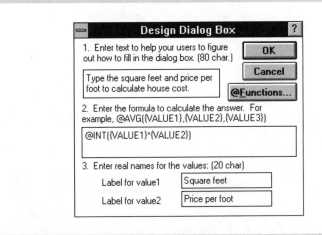

**6.** Fill in the dialog box. (To insert an @function in the text box in the middle of the dialog box, click on @Functions, make a selection, and click on OK.)

**WORKING TOGETHER**

▲

**7.** Click on OK. The macro returns to the Calculation Application Builder dialog box. The third option button is selected.

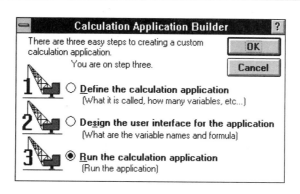

**8.** Click on OK.

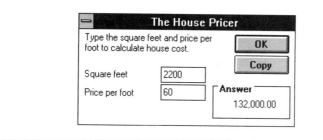

**9.** Run the macro by filling in the text boxes and evaluating the answer in the Answer box.

**10.** Click on OK to close the dialog box, or click on Copy to copy the contents of the Answer box to the Clipboard.

**11.** To copy the contents of the Clipboard into the current document, move the insertion point to the location in which you wish to insert the copied values.

**12.** Either choose Edit ➤ Paste, click on the Paste SmartIcon, or press Ctrl+V. The contents of the Clipboard are inserted at the insertion point.

# 6

# Editing and Formatting a Spreadsheet

In Chapters 4 and 5, you learned how to fill in a spreadsheet. Now that your spreadsheet is complete, you should think about how to handle future changes and how to present the spreadsheet to other people—in your company and outside.

In this chapter, you'll learn how to edit and format a spreadsheet—cell by cell to spreadsheet-wide. You'll find out how to add new cells, rows, and columns. You'll discover how to search for values and formats and how to replace values and formats. You'll find out how to automatically and manually recalculate, how to add objects (such as logos) to spreadsheets, how to view a spreadsheet before printing it, and how to take advantage of 1-2-3's printing options.

## Editing and Formatting Cells

There are two ways to edit a cell: in the cell itself and in the edit line. If you type a new value in a cell whose name or contents are part of a formula, 1-2-3 automatically recalculates the formulas and changes appropriate values in other cells.

  **If you edit a cell in which 1-2-3 calculated the value, the new value replaces the old, without any warning prompt. To undo the change (if it's the last action performed), choose Edit ➤ Undo or press Ctrl + Z.**

You can use the Edit menu to copy and paste and to cut and paste information from one location to another in a spreadsheet. You can also use the Windows drag and drop feature to move data. To learn more about these features, see Chapter 3.

In Chapter 3, you also learned how to apply formats to selected parts of a SmartSuite file. Use the same principles to format and/or enhance a 1-2-3 spreadsheet. Simply select one or more cells and click on a SmartIcon, choose a format command from the Style menu, or press a shortcut key or key combination.

In the following sections, you'll learn about editing and formatting techniques that are unique to 1-2-3.

## Clearing a Cell's Contents

 To delete the contents of a cell, select the cell and click on the Delete Smart-Icon, or choose either Edit ➤ Cut (or press Ctrl+X or Shift+Del) or Edit ➤ Clear (or press Del). Depending on the command that you choose or the key that you press, there are important differences:

- Choosing Edit ➤ Cut (or pressing Ctrl+X or Shift+Del) places the contents of the cell in the Clipboard so that you can paste the value into another cell. Remember that the Clipboard only keeps one item at a time; you can only retrieve the last cut you made. However, a range of cells can be cut to the Clipboard and retrieved later or even saved as a .CLP file for use much later.

- Pressing Del or clicking on the Delete SmartIcon permanently deletes the contents of the cell.

- Pressing Ctrl+Del clears both the contents of the cell and its formats.

- Choosing Edit ➤ Clear opens the Clear dialog box (Figure 6.1) from which you can clear the value in the cell (the default), the formatting style for the cell, or both. You learned about some formatting styles in Chapter 3, and you'll find out about the Style Gallery and Named styles in a following section of this chapter.

  **You cannot clear the contents of a cell in a protected spreadsheet, unless you have "unprotected" a specific range of cells.**

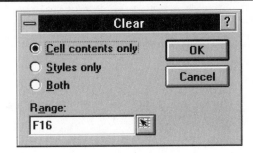

Remember that choosing Edit ➤ Undo or pressing Ctrl+Z reverses only the last action taken.

## Clearing a Cell's Formats

 In the previous section, you learned how to clear the contents of a cell. If you just clear the contents, any styles or formats remain although the cell looks empty. To clear a selected cell's styles, either click on the Delete Styles Smart-Icon, which automatically deletes the styles, or choose Edit ➤ Clear, which opens the Clear dialog box. Click on Styles Only and either click on OK or press ↵.

## Pasting One Cell's Formats to Another

 If you have spent a great deal of time formatting a cell or a range of cells, you can copy the styles to another cell. You can use a SmartIcon or commands from the Edit menu or Style menu.

To use the Copy Styles SmartIcon, click on the cell or select the range whose styles you wish to copy. Click on the Copy Styles SmartIcon. When the mouse pointer looks like a paint brush, click on the cell or drag across the range to which the styles are to be applied. The menu command equivalent is Style ➤ Fast Format.

To use the Edit menu to copy styles, follow these steps:

**1.** Select the cell or range whose styles you wish to copy.

**2.** Choose Edit ➤ Copy. You can also press Ctrl+C or Ctrl+Ins.

**3.** Select the cell or range to which you wish to apply the copied styles.

**4.** Choose Edit ➤ Paste Special.

**5.** In the Paste Special dialog box (Figure 6.2), click on Styles Only.

**6.** Either click on OK or press ↵.

**FIGURE 6.2**

The Paste Special
dialog box, in which
you can paste data,
styles, or formulas as
values from the
Clipboard to the
spreadsheet

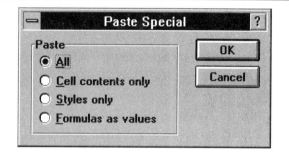

# Inserting, Deleting, and Moving Rows and Columns

When you create a spreadsheet, although you can plan and plan, quite often you'll find that you have missed an important element, have included an unnecessary element, or need to move a row or column to a new location. In this section, you'll find out how to handle these situations.

## Inserting New Rows

There are three ways to insert a new row: using a SmartIcon, a shortcut key combination, or a menu command. In any case, start by clicking anywhere in the row that will be pushed down by the new row (for example, if you wish to insert a new row 7, click on the current row 7).

**WORKING TOGETHER**
▲

# Copying Ami Pro
# Styles to 1-2-3 for Windows

To coordinate the look of reports and proposals, you can create 1-2-3 named styles from Ami Pro style sheets (either predefined or those that you define). Then you can apply those named styles to the spreadsheet. To create 1-2-3 named styles based on Ami Pro styles, follow these steps:

1. Open both Ami Pro and 1-2-3. (You must have 1-2-3 Release 4 or later.)

2. Open the spreadsheet to be "styled."

3. Open the document or style sheet containing the desired styles.

4. Choose Tools ➤ Macros ➤ Playback or click on the appropriate SmartIcon in the Bonus Pack SmartIcons set. Ami Pro displays the Play Macro dialog box.

**WORKING TOGETHER**

**5.** Choose 123STYLE.SMM and click on OK. Ami Pro displays the Convert Styles dialog box.

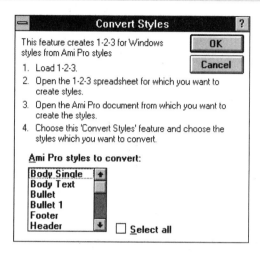

**6.** Click on the styles that you wish to convert or check the Select All check box to convert all styles.

**7.** Click on OK. The macro selects styles in the document and creates counterpart named styles in the spreadsheet. As the process goes on, you'll see menus and dialog boxes open and close.

**8.** Apply a named style to the spreadsheet by selecting cells to be styled, clicking on the named style button on the status bar, and selecting a named style from the list. For example, select a title and apply the Title style, and select row and column labels and apply the Subhead style

**9.** Repeat step 8 until you have styled the 1-2-3 spreadsheet.

If you run this macro more than once for a particular spreadsheet, you'll see duplicate styles on the Named Styles list. To remove a duplicate style, choose Style ➤ Named Style, and in the Named Style dialog box, select from the Existing Styles list and click on Clear.

**1-2-3**

After indicating the location of the new row, the quickest way to add it is to click on the Insert Row SmartIcon. To insert a row using a menu command or shortcut key combination, follow these steps:

**1.** Click on the location of the new row.

**2.** Choose Edit ➤ Insert or press Ctrl++ (on the numeric keypad).

**3.** In the Insert dialog box (Figure 6.3), click on Row.

**4.** Either click on OK or press ↵. Everything beyond the new row, which is blank, moves down one row. All the formulas in the old rows remain the same; they also move down one row.

 You might have to edit formulas to include any new data that you put into a new row. It depends on whether you used ranges or specific cell addresses in your formulas.

---

**FIGURE 6.3**

The Insert dialog box with which you can insert columns, rows, a selection, or an entire spreadsheet

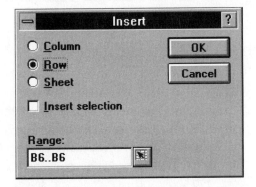

---

 To add more than one row at a time, in the Insert dialog box, type or select a range. For example, to insert three rows, select a range of three rows, such as A7..A9. You can also click on the Insert Rows SmartIcon three times quickly.

## Inserting New Columns

Inserting a new column works exactly the same way as inserting a new row; either use a SmartIcon, a shortcut key combination, or a menu command. However, this time click anywhere in the column that will be pushed to the right by the new column.

 After indicating the location of the new column, the quickest way to add a column is to click on the Insert Column SmartIcon.

To insert a column using a menu command or shortcut key combination, follow these steps:

**1.** Click on the location of the new column.

**2.** Choose Edit ➤ Insert or press Ctrl++ (on the numeric keypad).

**3.** In the Insert dialog box, click on Column.

**4.** Either click on OK or press ↵. Everything beyond the new column, which is blank, moves over one column to the right. All the formulas in the old columns remain the same; they also move over to the right.

  **To add more than one column at a time, in the Insert dialog box, type or select a range. You can also click on the Insert Rows SmartIcon the same number of times as the number of columns you wish to add.**

## Deleting Rows and Columns

To delete rows and columns, you use the same techniques but slightly different SmartIcons, menu commands, and shortcut key combinations as you did when inserting rows and columns. First, select the rows or columns to be deleted.

  **When deleting rows or columns, be careful not to delete cells that contain important formulas or that are referred to by other formulas.**

The quickest way to delete a row or column is to click on the Delete Row or Delete Column SmartIcon.

To delete a row or column using a menu command or shortcut key combination, follow these steps:

1. Click on the row or column to be deleted.

2. Choose Edit ➤ Delete or press Ctrl+− (on the numeric keypad).

3. In the Delete dialog box (Figure 6.4), click on Column or Row.

4. To delete more than one column or row at a time, type or select a range in the Range box.

5. Either click on OK or press ⏎. The remaining rows or columns fill in the space formerly taken by the deleted rows or columns.

## Moving Rows, Columns, and Ranges

In Chapter 3, you learned how to move selections by choosing Edit ➤ Cut and Edit ➤ Paste and by using drag and drop. You can use these techniques to edit your spreadsheet. However, when you move rows, columns, or ranges, you may have to reenter data or formulas. Please note the following:

■ you should not break up ranges of cells that are linked together by a formula.

■ if you move cells to an area that already contains data, 1-2-3 will overwrite those cells with the moved data. You may have to edit formulas having absolute cell references.

**FIGURE 6.4**

The Delete dialog box, with which you can delete columns, rows, a selection, or an entire spreadsheet

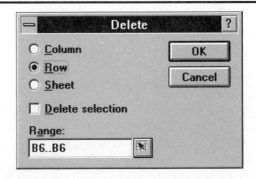

# formatting Cells, Ranges, and Spreadsheets

When you find an appealing combination of formats and enhancements, you can save them as a named style that you can use again and again. 1-2-3 allows you to save any combination of number formats, types, type sizes, underlining, text enhancements, colors, and alignment. Table 6.1 lists all the 1-2-3 Style menu formatting commands, shows you related SmartIcons, and describes the types of resulting formats.

**TABLE 6.1:** 1-2-3 Formatting SmartIcons and Menu Commands

| RELATED SMARTICON | COMMAND | DESCRIPTION |
|---|---|---|
| N/A | Style ➤ Number Format | Allows you to apply a number or text format to data in a cell |
| [icon] | Style ➤ Font & Attributes | Allows you to change the Face (font), Size, apply Attributes (Normal, Bold, Italics, or three types of Underline), and specify Color to a range of cells. |
| [icon] [icon] | Style ➤ Lines & Color | Allows you to specify a color or pattern to the foreground or background of a selection; define a border, line style, or line color for a selection; or select a designer frame and its color for a range of cells. |
| [icon] [icon] [icon] [icon] [icon] | Style ➤ Alignment | Allows you to align data horizontally and/or vertically, wrap data, or change the orientation of data for a range of cells. |
| [icon] | Style ➤ Gallery | Opens the Gallery dialog box so that you can format a range of cells using one of 14 predefined templates. |
| N/A | Style ➤ Named Style | Opens the Named Style dialog box so that you can name the style of a range of cells. Then you can apply the named style to other ranges of cells. |

## Defining and Naming Styles

It's simple to define and name a style: format a cell or range of cells and then follow these steps:

1. Select a cell or range that has the combination of formats to be saved.

2. Choose <u>S</u>tyle ➤ Named <u>S</u>tyle. 1-2-3 opens the Named Style dialog box (Figure 6.5).

3. In the Style <u>N</u>ame text box, type a style name, up to 35 characters.

4. To name the style but keep the Named Style dialog box open, click on the <u>D</u>efine button.

5. To name the style and close the Named Style dialog box, either click on OK or press ↵.

## Applying a Style to a Range

1-2-3 provides two ways to apply a named style to a selected cell or range: by choosing a menu command or by selecting from the status bar.

**FIGURE 6.5**

The Named Style dialog box allows you to define up to 16 styles

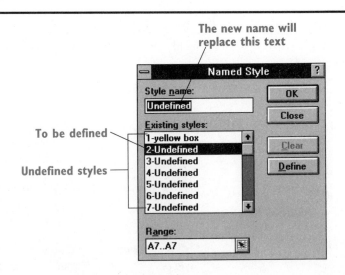

The new name will replace this text

To be defined

Undefined styles

To apply a style using <u>S</u>tyle ➤ Named <u>S</u>tyle, follow these steps:

1. Select the cell or range of cells to which you want to apply the style.

2. Choose <u>S</u>tyle ➤ Named <u>S</u>tyle.

3. Double-click on the desired style from the <u>E</u>xisting Styles list box. 1-2-3 applies the style to the selected cell or range.

To apply a style using the status bar, follow these steps:

1. Select the cell or range of cells to which you want to apply the style.

2. Click on the named style button on the status bar. 1-2-3 applies the styles to the selected cell or range.

 The fastest way to remove the formatting that you have applied by using a named style is to select a cell or range with the default formatting, click on the Copy Styles SmartIcon, and select the cell or range that you wish to format. To turn off the SmartIcon, click on it again.

## Removing a Named Style

When you no longer need a named style, delete it by following these steps:

1. Choose <u>S</u>tyle ➤ Named <u>S</u>tyle.

2. Select the style name listed in the <u>E</u>xisting Styles list box.

3. Click on <u>C</u>lear.

4. Either click on OK, press ↵, or click on Close.

 **NOTE** Any cells or ranges that you have already formatted with the named style keep the formats, even though the named style has been deleted.

## Formatting with the Style Gallery

1-2-3 provides predefined styles with which you can format a cell, range of cells, or even an entire spreadsheet. To use the Style Gallery, follow these steps:

1. Select a cell, range of cells, or the current spreadsheet.

 To select the entire spreadsheet, click on the button to the left of column A and above row 1. However, if you apply a style to an entire spreadsheet, the result may be a very large file that is slow to open, print, and so on.

2. Choose Style ➤ Gallery or click on the Style Gallery SmartIcon. 1-2-3 opens the Gallery dialog box (Figure 6.6).

3. From the Template scroll box, select a template. Notice that the Sample box shows you how your selection will look.

4. When you have found the appropriate style, either click on OK or press ↵. Figure 6.7 illustrates our sample spreadsheet formatted using the Picture1 style.

**FIGURE 6.6**

The Gallery dialog box, from which you can select a predefined style from a selected cell, range, or even the entire spreadsheet

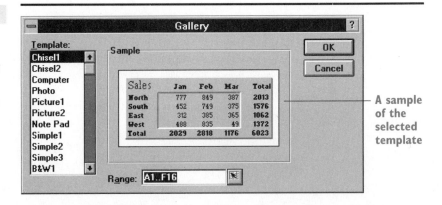

A sample of the selected template

**FIGURE 6.7**

The sample
spreadsheet in the
Picture1 style from
the Style Gallery

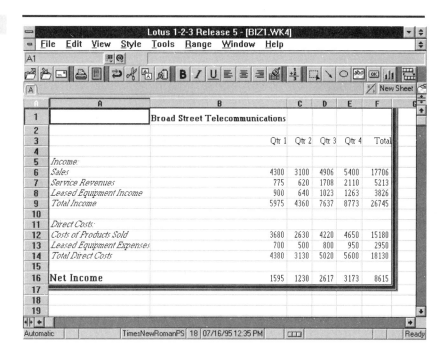

| | | Qtr 1 | Qtr 2 | Qtr 3 | Qtr 4 | Total |
|---|---|---|---|---|---|---|
| | Broad Street Telecommunications | | | | | |
| *Income:* | | | | | | |
| *Sales* | | 4300 | 3100 | 4906 | 5400 | 17706 |
| *Service Revenues* | | 775 | 620 | 1708 | 2110 | 5213 |
| *Leased Equipment Income* | | 900 | 640 | 1023 | 1263 | 3826 |
| *Total Income* | | 5975 | 4360 | 7637 | 8773 | 26745 |
| *Direct Costs:* | | | | | | |
| *Costs of Products Sold* | | 3680 | 2630 | 4220 | 4650 | 15180 |
| *Leased Equipment Expenses* | | 700 | 500 | 800 | 950 | 2950 |
| *Total Direct Costs* | | 4380 | 3130 | 5020 | 5600 | 18130 |
| **Net Income** | | 1595 | 1230 | 2617 | 3173 | 8615 |

# finding and Replacing in 1-2-3

At the end of Chapter 3, you read an overview of find and replace. Every
SmartSuite application (except for Freelance Graphics) has its own find and
replace facility. 1-2-3 allows you to find and replace characters in labels and
formulas for a selected range—but not the data in the range. 1-2-3 enables
you to search for characters in cells that you have hidden by choosing Style ➤
Number Format; however, you cannot search for characters in columns or
spreadsheets that you have hidden by choosing Style ➤ Hide.

## Finding Characters in a Spreadsheet

To find characters in a spreadsheet, follow these steps:

1. Select a cell, a range of cells, or the entire spreadsheet.

2. Choose Edit ➤ Find & Replace. 1-2-3 opens the Find & Replace dialog
   box (Figure 6.8).

**FIGURE 6.8**

In the Find & Replace dialog box, you can search for a search string and optionally replace it with the replace string.

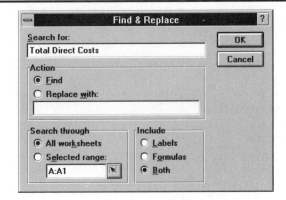

3. Type the *search string* (up to 512 characters) in the Search for text box.

4. In the Action group, click on Find.

5. In the Include group, click on Labels, Formulas, or Both.

6. In the Search through group, click on All Worksheets or Selected Range.

7. Either click on OK or press ↵. If 1-2-3 finds the search string, it highlights the search string and displays the Find dialog box (Figure 6.9).

**FIGURE 6.9**

The Find dialog box, with which you can continue or end a search

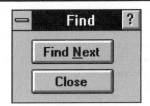

If 1-2-3 does not find the search string, it displays a message box:

8. If 1-2-3 finds the search string, either click on Find <u>N</u>ext to find the next occurrence of the search string or click on Close to end the search.

## Replacing Characters in a Spreadsheet

To replace characters in a spreadsheet, follow these steps:

1. Select a cell, a range of cells, or the entire spreadsheet.

2. Choose <u>E</u>dit ➤ <u>F</u>ind & Replace. 1-2-3 opens the Find & Replace dialog box.

3. Type the search string (up to 512 characters) in the <u>S</u>earch for text box.

4. Type the *replace string* (up to 512 characters) in the Replace <u>w</u>ith text box.

5. In the Include group, click on <u>L</u>abels, F<u>o</u>rmulas, or <u>B</u>oth.

6. In the Search Through group, click on All Wor<u>k</u>sheets or S<u>e</u>lected Range.

7. Either click on OK or press ↵. If 1-2-3 finds the search string, it high-lights the search string and displays the Replace dialog box (Figure 6.10).

   If 1-2-3 does not find the search string, it displays a message box:

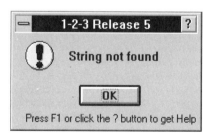

8. If 1-2-3 finds the search string:
   - click on <u>R</u>eplace to replace this occurrence of the search string.
   - click on Replace <u>A</u>ll to replace all occurrences of the search string.
   - click on Find <u>N</u>ext to search for the next occurrence of the search string without replacing this occurrence.
   - click on Close to end the search.

**FIGURE 6.10**

The Replace dialog box offers four buttons from which to choose.

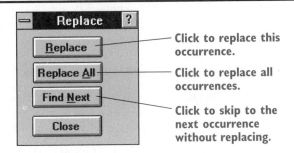

Click to replace this occurrence.

Click to replace all occurrences.

Click to skip to the next occurrence without replacing.

# Automatic vs. Manual Recalculation

By default, whenever you change a value in a cell or edit a formula, 1-2-3 automatically recalculates all the formulas and changes the results in the spreadsheet. However, if you plan to make many changes to formulas in the spreadsheet, you may want to stop calculation for a while. One reason is that while you're changing formulas, automatic recalculation produces meaningless error messages because you haven't completed your changes. Another reason is that constant recalculation while you're changing formulas wastes processing time.

To change to manual recalculation, follow these steps:

1. Choose Tools ➤ User Setup. 1-2-3 displays the User Setup dialog box (Figure 6.11).

2. Click on the Recalculation button. 1-2-3 displays the Recalculation dialog box (Figure 6.12).

3. In the Recalculation group, click on Manual.

4. Either click on OK or press ⏎.

Calc   To manually recalculate a spreadsheet, press F9 or click the Calc button on the status bar.

To reset recalculation to automatic, repeat the preceding steps, but select Automatic instead of Manual in the Recalculation group.

FIGURE 6.11

The User Setup dialog box allows you to customize 1-2-3 to suit your needs.

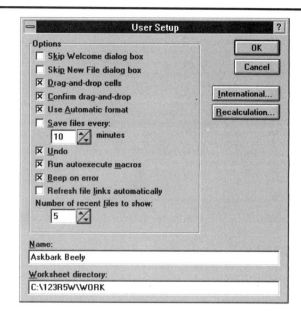

FIGURE 6.12

In the Recalculation dialog box, you can set recalculation options.

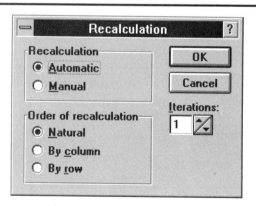

# Protecting Your Files

1-2-3 provides two ways to protect the data in a spreadsheet: you can hide the entire spreadsheet or parts of it, or you can protect the spreadsheet by setting a password.

## Hiding Parts of a Spreadsheet

To keep your data from being viewed by others, you can hide part of or an entire spreadsheet. There are two different ways to hide data: choose either Style ➤ Number Format or Style ➤ Hide.

### Assigning the Hidden Number Format

One way to hide any part of a spreadsheet—from a cell to the entire spreadsheet, is to select it and choose Style ➤ Number Format. When 1-2-3 opens the Number Format dialog box (Figure 6.13), select Hidden from the Format scroll box, and either click on OK or press ↵. A shortcut procedure is to click on the Number Format button on the status bar and select Hidden.

To reveal the hidden data, either change its number format to any format but Hidden, or choose Style ➤ Number Format and click on Reset in the Number Format dialog box.

**FIGURE 6.13**

The Number Format dialog box, which allows you to select a number format or reset selected data to their original formats

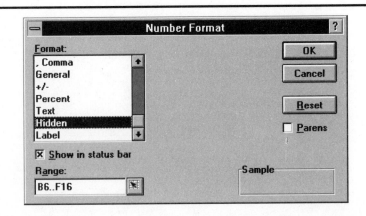

 When you select a cell in a hidden range, 1-2-3 reveals the contents of the cell in the Contents box of the edit line, unless you have sealed the spreadsheet.

## Hiding Data with a Menu Command

1-2-3 provides a more secure way to hide all or part (except for a row) of a spreadsheet. In fact, after hiding data in this way, you can't even move the cell pointer to the hidden parts of a spreadsheet; however, you can apply formats.

 **WARNING** Certain commands (e.g., some Edit and Range menu commands and others) allow you to overwrite hidden data. For a list of some of those commands, see the topic "Style Hide" in 1-2-3 Help.

To hide part or all of a spreadsheet, select it, and choose Style ➤ Hide. If the Hide dialog box appears (Figure 6.14), click on Column or Sheet. Either click on OK or press ↵.

To reveal part of a spreadsheet that you have hidden in this way, select the range; to reveal a hidden column (except for column A), select parts of the columns on either side. Then choose Style ➤ Hide, and click on the Show button. To reveal column A either by itself or as part of a hidden range, press Home before clicking on Show.

**FIGURE 6.14**

The Hide dialog box allows you to hide columns, ranges, or worksheets and to prevent printing.

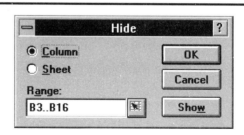

201

## Hiding Columns with the Mouse

You can hide a column using the mouse. Move the mouse pointer to the right border of the column that you wish to hide. When the mouse pointer changes to a double-headed arrow, drag the column border to the left. When the right border covers the left border of the column that you wish to hide, release the mouse button. Notice that the column label and the column itself are hidden. To reveal a column hidden this way, repeat the preceding instructions but drag the column border to the right. You cannot use the mouse to reveal a column hidden by choosing <u>S</u>tyle ➤ <u>H</u>ide.

  **If you try to hide a row using this mouse technique, you'll be unsuccessful; you'll just change the height of the row.**

## Sealing a File

Sealing a file protects the data from being changed; however, you and others can view the data. When you seal a file, the only way that you can edit data is to "unseal" it by using the same password that you used to seal the file.

The Protect dialog box also allows you to *reserve* a file (that is, you will be the only person who can edit this file and save the changes) if you are a member of a group that has access to the file. For more information, see *Reserving a File* in 1-2-3 Help.

 **Make sure that you remember the assigned password and its combination of upper- and lowercase letters. If you forget the password, you won't be able to edit the file.**

To seal a file, follow these steps:

1. Choose <u>F</u>ile ➤ <u>P</u>rotect. 1-2-3 opens the Protect dialog box (Figure 6.15).

2. Check the Seal file check box and either click on OK or press ↵. 1-2-3 displays the Set Password dialog box (Figure 6.16).

**FIGURE 6.15**

The Protect dialog box
allows you to seal or
"unseal" a file.

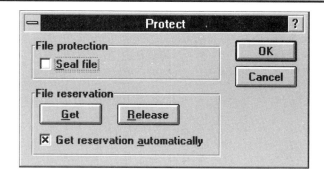

**FIGURE 6.16**

The Set Password
dialog box

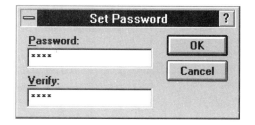

3. Type your password in the <u>P</u>assword text box. Then type the same password in the <u>V</u>erify text box. 1-2-3 replaces each character that you type with an asterisk (*).

4. Either click on OK or press ↵. 1-2-3 closes both dialog boxes and returns to the spreadsheet.

After sealing a file, whenever you or anyone else attempts to edit, 1-2-3 displays this message box:

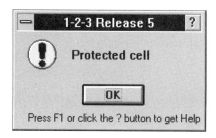

To remove the seal from a file, follow these steps:

1. Choose <u>F</u>ile ➤ P<u>r</u>otect. 1-2-3 opens the Protect dialog box.

2. Clear the Seal file check box and either click on OK or press ↵. 1-2-3 displays the Get Password dialog box (Figure 6.17).

3. Type your password in the <u>P</u>assword text box. 1-2-3 replaces each character that you type with an asterisk (*).

4. Either click on OK or press ↵. 1-2-3 "unseals" the file, closes both dialog boxes, and returns to the spreadsheet.

**NOTE** If you close a file from which you have removed a seal and do not save it, the next time you open the file, you'll find that it is sealed again.

**FIGURE 6.17**

The Get Password dialog box

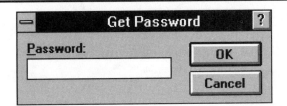

# Defining Multiple Spreadsheets in a File

One of the most powerful features of 1-2-3 is its ability to incorporate multiple spreadsheets in a single file. This means that you can save your actual figures for this year and budgeted figures for next year in the same file. In addition, you can keep all related charts and worksheets in one file, making it easy to find related information.

You can insert up to 256 spreadsheets (or pages) in a single file. Each page is represented on your desktop with a tab, which you can rename from the default name of A, B, C, and so on.

To add a new page to the current file, simply click on the New Sheet button on the right side of your desktop:

1-2-3 inserts a new blank spreadsheet and adds a new tab:

**NOTE** When a 1-2-3 file contains more than one spreadsheet, a cell or range of cells in the Contents box of the edit line changes. Instead of a cell address looking like A5, it is now preceded by its spreadsheet identifier (for example, for cell A5 in spreadsheet B, B:A5).

You can insert several new spreadsheets at a time by following these steps:

1. Choose Edit ➤ Insert or press Ctrl++ (on the numeric keypad). 1-2-3 displays the Insert dialog box.
2. Click on Sheet. 1-2-3 adds the Quantity text/scroll box to the dialog box.
3. Select or type a number of sheets (from 1 to 255).
4. Either click on OK or press ↵. 1-2-3 displays the new spreadsheets on the desktop.

To delete a spreadsheet, click on its tab to select it, and follow these steps:

1. Choose Edit ➤ Delete or press Ctrl+− (on the numeric keypad). 1-2-3 displays the Delete dialog box.
2. Click on Sheet.
3. Either click on OK or press ↵. 1-2-3 deletes the spreadsheet, and renames only the default tabs (e.g., if you remove spreadsheet E, 1-2-3 changes the name *F* to *E*, *G* to *F*, and so on).

## Moving among Spreadsheets in a File

To move from one spreadsheet to another, just click on the tab representing the desired spreadsheet. When the number of tabs in a file exceeds the width of the desktop, click on this button:

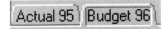

to display more tabs to the left or right of the current tab. Then click on a tab to display the desired spreadsheet page.

## Naming a Page

To change the name of a tab from the default letter, simply double-click on the tab, type the new name, and either press ↵ or click on another part of the spreadsheet. For a list of spreadsheet-naming guidelines, see Chapter 5 in the *Lotus 1-2-3 User's Guide*.

## Viewing Multiple Spreadsheets Simultaneously

You can view two or three spreadsheets at the same time. To view two spreadsheets horizontally (to compare rows) or vertically (to compare columns), drag the horizontal or vertical splitter until both spreadsheets are displayed as you wish. Figure 6.18 shows two spreadsheets, Actual 95 and Budget 96, displayed horizontally.

**TIP** When you see identical values in both panes, you are viewing the same spreadsheet. Click on a tab to view the second spreadsheet in one of the panes.

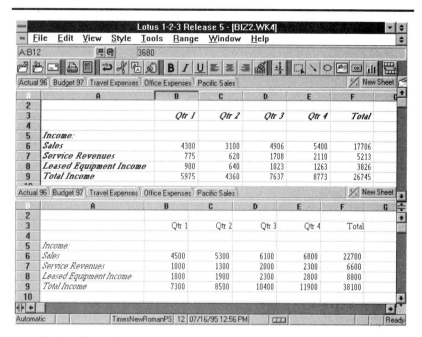

**FIGURE 6.18**

Two spreadsheets
displayed horizontally
on the desktop

To return to the display of a single spreadsheet, either drag the horizontal splitter up or down the desktop or drag the vertical splitter to the left or right. You can also choose View ➤ Clear Split.

The only way to show three spreadsheets at the same time is to display them in Perspective view. Just choose View ➤ Split, click on Perspective, and either click on OK or press ↵. Figure 6.19 shows three spreadsheets in Perspective view.

**NOTE** If you attempt to display a file containing fewer than three spreadsheets, 1-2-3 fills in the space with "dummy" spreadsheets.

# Viewing a Spreadsheet as It Will Print

Print Preview allows you to check a file before you print it. When you look at your file in the Print Preview window, you can check page layout, alignment,

**FIGURE 6.19**

Three spreadsheets
displayed in
Perspective view

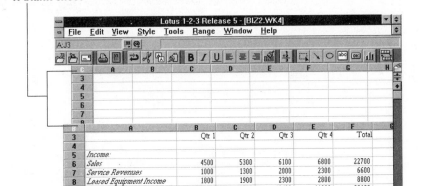

A blank sheet

formatting, and enhancements. Then you can correct any problems before
you print.

 To view your 1-2-3 file as it will print, choose File ➤ Print Preview, click on
the Print Preview SmartIcon, or click on the Preview button in the Print dialog box. In the Print Preview dialog box (Figure 6.20), select options, and
then either click on OK or press ↵.

The Print Preview window (Figure 6.21) provides a new set of SmartIcons,
described in Table 6.2.

 While you are viewing your file in the Preview window, you
can view details of the page by clicking on the + magnifying
glass SmartIcon to zoom the page. Then move around the
page by pressing ←, →, ↓, and ↑.

**FIGURE 6.20**

In the 1-2-3 Print Preview dialog box, you can select display options for a spreadsheet and change the page setup.

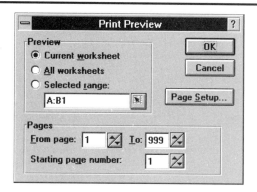

**FIGURE 6.21**

1-2-3's Print Preview window displays the spreadsheet and contains a new set of SmartIcons.

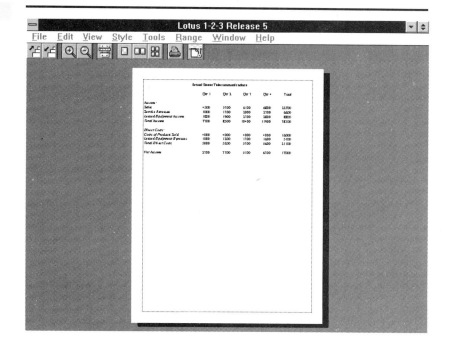

**TABLE 6.2:**   SmartSuite Print Preview SmartIcons

| SMARTICON | SHORTCUT KEY COMBINATION | DESCRIPTION |
|---|---|---|
| | ↵ or PgDn | Displays the next page |
| | PgUp | Displays the prior page |
| | – (numeric keypad) | Magnifies the display every time you click with a maximum of five levels of magnification. (Press * to unzoom.) |
| | + (numeric keypad) | Reduces the display every time you click with a maximum of five levels of reduction. (Press * to unzoom.) |
| | N/A | Displays the Page Setup dialog box so that you can modify options such as orientation, margins, and headers and footers |
| | N/A | Displays a full page, the default |
| | N/A | Displays two side-by-side pages, if the worksheet contains two or more pages |
| | N/A | Displays up to four pages, depending on the number of pages the worksheet contains |
| | N/A | Displays the Print dialog box so that you can modify print options and then print your selection |
| | | Enables you to close this window and display your file in the application window. |

# Selecting Page Setup Options

Whether you're viewing your spreadsheet on the Print Preview window or in the work area, or you're ready to print, you can specify the way the page is set up. 1-2-3 provides several choices for opening the Page Setup dialog box (Figure 6.22):

- Click on the Page Setup SmartIcon from the Print Preview window or from the work area.

- Choose File ➤ Page Setup.

- Click on the Page Setup button in the Print dialog box or Print Preview dialog box.

**FIGURE 6.22**

1-2-3's Page Setup dialog box, which offers a multitude of page setup options

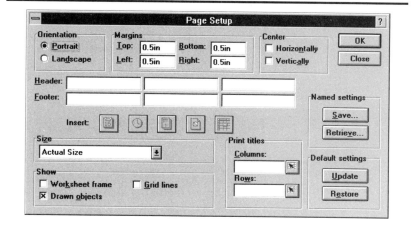

In the Page Setup dialog box, you can change page setup options, such as the orientation of the page, the margins around the border of the page, or the amount of data printed on the page. You can create headers and footers, insert information, show or hide spreadsheet elements, and so on. When you have completed filling out the dialog box and selecting options, you can save your settings so that you can reuse them at a later time. The following sections contain brief descriptions of each Page Setup dialog box option.

## Orientation

Click on Portrait to print the file with the same orientation as a letter or memo; click on Landscape to print the file oriented as a standard spreadsheet. Portrait orientation is longer than it is wide, and landscape orientation is wider than it is long. The default orientation is Portrait.

## Margins

Set the Top, Bottom, Left, and/or Right margins from 0.5 to 32 inches. The default for each margin is 0.5 inches. When setting margins, be sure to leave enough room for the printed data; For example, wide left and right margins can meet in the center of the page, leaving no space for the data.

## Center

Check Horizontally to center the contents of a page between the left and right margins, and/or Check Vertically to center the contents of a page between the top and bottom margins. The default is two cleared check boxes.

## Headers and Footers

In the three boxes next to Header and Footer, you can type and insert text. The leftmost box contains text aligned with the left margin, the center box contains text that is centered, and the rightmost box contains text aligned with the right margin. The default is no header or footer. Table 6.3 describes the buttons with which you include specific text in a header or footer.

**NOTE** Don't use | (vertical bar) in a header or footer, because it is reserved for 1-2-3 processing. If you need to insert a character (@, +, #, ^, or \) that 1-2-3 uses as a header of footer code, type an apostrophe (') and then type the character.

**TABLE 6.3:** 1-2-3 Insert Buttons

| BUTTON | INSERTED PLACEHOLDER SYMBOL | CLICK TO INSERT: | EXAMPLE |
|---|---|---|---|
|  | @ | the current computer system date, formatted *dd/mm/yy* (where *dd* is the day, *mm* is the month, and *yy* is the year) | 12/23/96 |
| | + | the current computer system time, formatted *hour:minutes:seconds* | 03:58 PM |
| | # | the current page number on every page | 1 |
| | ^ | the name of the current file | BIZ3.WK4 |
| | \ | the cell contents of a cell or range of cells that you type after the inserted backslash symbol (\) (for example, \a:b6) | 4300 |

**TIP** You can combine typed and inserted text. For example, to better identify the page number, type "Page", press the spacebar to insert a space, and then click on the Page Number button. The result is Page <u>n</u>, where <u>n</u> represents the current page

## Size

Click on this drop-down list box to reveal the choices described in Table 6.4. The default is Actual Size.

**TABLE 6.4:** 1-2-3 Page Setup Size Choices

| SIZE | DESCRIPTION |
|---|---|
| Actual Size | Prints the selection, starting at the upper-left corner of the page, in its full size |
| Fit All to Page | Fits the entire selection on a single page |
| Fit Columns to Page | Fits the selection so that all its columns fit a single page |
| Fit Rows to Page | Fits the selection so that all its rows fit a single page |
| Manually Scale | Sizes the selection to a percent (from 15 to 1000) that you enter |

## Show

Check or clear these check boxes to show or hide the Worksheet Frame (the column and row labels), Drawn Objects (objects that you have inserted into the spreadsheet), and Grid Lines (the boundaries of the cells).

## Print Titles

Select titles for rows and columns. In Columns, specify a cell containing a value displayed to the left of the column labels. In Rows, specify a cell containing a value displayed at the top of the row labels.

## Named Settings

Click on the Save button to open the Save Named Settings dialog box (Figure 6.23) in which you can save all the settings in the Page Setup dialog box. Save this file as you would any other file.

To retrieve a saved named setting, click on the Retrieve button. In the Retrieve Named Settings dialog box, select the name of the file to be retrieved.

**NOTE** The extension for a 1-2-3 Named Settings file is .AL3.

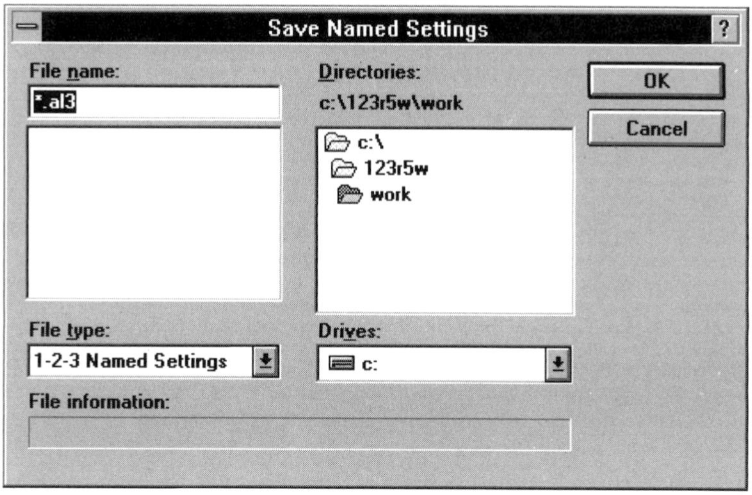

**FIGURE 6.23**

The Save Named
Settings dialog box
looks like most other
dialog boxes in which
you save files.

## Default Settings

Click on the Update button to make all the current page settings the default
for this file. Click on the Restore button to return to the current default page
settings for this file. For example, if you change the bottom margin to 0.75
inch but you have previously saved 1 inch margins using Update, clicking on
Restore returns to the 1 inch margins—not the original 0.5 inch setting.

# Setting Page Breaks

When you print a 1-2-3 spreadsheet, file, or range, both the way in which you
fill out the Page Setup dialog box and 1-2-3 defaults determine where one
printed page ends and another begins. The break between pages is a *page
break*. A 1-2-3-determined page break is a *soft page break*. To manually break
pages, you insert a *hard page break*—either horizontally (between rows) or vertically (between columns). If you remove or add rows or columns, 1-2-3 adjusts the location of a soft page break. However, a hard page break remains
until you delete it. There are two ways to insert a page break: by clicking on a
SmartIcon or by choosing a menu command and following a few steps.

To insert a hard page break using a SmartIcon, click on a cell before which the break should occur. Then click on the Vertical Break SmartIcon or the Horizontal Break SmartIcon.

To use a menu command to insert a hard page break, follow these steps:

1. Click on a cell before which the break should occur.

2. Choose Style ➤ Page Break. 1-2-3 displays the Page Break dialog box (Figure 6.24).

3. Click on Row or Column, for a horizontal or vertical break, respectively.

4. Either click on OK or press ↵. 1-2-3 displays a dotted line at the site of a hard page break.

To remove a hard page break, follow these steps:

1. Click on the cell either below the row or to the right of the column adjacent to the page break.

2. Either choose Style ➤ Page Break or click on the appropriate SmartIcon.

3. In the Page Break dialog box, clear the checked check box.

4. Either click on OK or press ↵.

## Selecting Print Options

Whether you decide to print from the Print Preview window, choose File ➤ Print, press Ctrl+P, or click on the Print SmartIcon, you have a choice of options for printing a 1-2-3 spreadsheet.

**FIGURE 6.24**

In the Page Break dialog box, you can choose the location of a hard page break—a row or column.

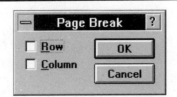

## Printing from the Print Dialog Box

This section provides a brief description of each 1-2-3 print option shown in the Print dialog box (Figure 6.25). After selecting options in the dialog box, either click on OK or press ↵.

**NOTE** The Print dialog box provides "gateways" to the Page Setup dialog box (click on Page Setup) and to the Print Preview window (click on Preview).

**FIGURE 6.25**

The Print dialog box allows you to select options to customize printing of a range, spreadsheet, or file.

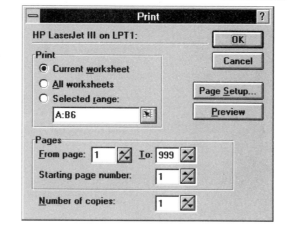

### Print

Click on Current Worksheet (the default) to print the current spreadsheet in the file, All Worksheets to print the entire file, or Selected Range to print a range of cells from either the current spreadsheet or several spreadsheets.

### Pages

Select or type a starting page number in the From Page text/scroll box; the default is 1. Select or type an ending page number in the To text/scroll box; the default is 999. Select or type the number of the first page to be printed in the Starting Page Number text/scroll box; the default is 1.

### Number of Copies

Select or type the number of copies (from 1 to 999) that you wish to print in the Number of Copies text/scroll box.

## Printing Formulas

You can print a list of the formulas in the current spreadsheet. This gives you a chance to review formulas for accuracy and effectiveness. To print a list of formulas, you actually create an audit report and then print it:

1. Choose Tools ➤ Audit.

2. In the Audit dialog box (Figure 6.26):

   ■ Click on All Formulas.

   ■ In the Produce a group, click on Report at Range and select a one-column range in which 1-2-3 will display the report. Be sure that the range is large enough to hold the complete list of formulas and that it's not occupied by values, labels, or titles.

   ■ Click on Current File.

**FIGURE 6.26**

In the Audit dialog box, you can produce several reports, including a list of all formulas.

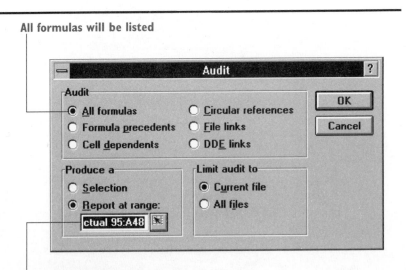

All formulas will be listed

The range in which the report will be inserted

3. Either click on OK or press ↵. 1-2-3 produces a report of all the formulas in the spreadsheet (Figure 6.27).

4. Select the cells containing the report.

5. Either click on the Print SmartIcon, choose File ➤ Print, or press Ctrl+P. 1-2-3 displays the Print dialog box.

6. If the Selected Range option button is not selected, click on it.

7. Either click on OK or press ↵. 1-2-3 prints the selected cells.

**FIGURE 6.27**

A partial report of the formulas in the sample spreadsheet.

```
Formulas
Current file
Actual 95:F6: @SUM(SALES)
Actual 95:F7: @SUM(SERVICE_REVENUE)
Actual 95:F8: @SUM(B8..E8)
Actual 95:B9: +B6+B7+B8
Actual 95:C9: +C6+C7+C8
Actual 95:D9: +D6+D7+D8
Actual 95:E9: +E6+E7+E8
Actual 95:F9: @SUM(B9..E9)
Actual 95:F12: @SUM(B12..E12)
Actual 95:F13: @SUM(LEASED_EXPS)
Actual 95:B14: +B12+B13
Actual 95:B16: +B9-B14
Actual 95:C14: +C12+C13
Actual 95:C16: +C9-C14
Actual 95:D14: +D12+D13
Actual 95:D16: +D9-D14
Actual 95:E14: +E12+E13
Actual 95:F14: @SUM(B14..E14)
```

Cell address        Formula

# Inserting an Object into a Spreadsheet

In Chapter 10, you will learn how to create a drawing and insert it into a SmartSuite application. In the meantime, this section explains how to insert an object into a spreadsheet. For example, if you create a logo using Windows Paintbrush, you can follow these steps:

1. Select the cell or location where the object is to be inserted.

2. Choose Edit ➤ Insert Object. 1-2-3 displays the Insert Object dialog box (Figure 6.28).

3. In the Object Type scroll box, double-click on the appropriate object type; in this case, Paintbrush Picture. A window (Figure 6.29) opens within 1-2-3.

4. In the object's application window, choose File ➤ Open or the command by which you can retrieve the object. The object's application may display a message (Figure 6.30).

5. Click on No. (You don't want to update a nonexistent object.) The object's application opens the Open dialog box or a dialog box with which you can retrieve the object.

6. In the File Name text/scroll box, either type or select the name of the object.

7. Either click on OK or press ↵. The object appears in its application window (Figure 6.31).

8. Select the object. In Paintbrush, "cut out" the object.

9. Choose Edit ➤ Copy (or press Ctrl+C or Ctrl+Ins) in the object's application.

10. Choose File ➤ Exit or press Alt+F4 to exit the object's application.

**FIGURE 6.28**

The Insert Object dialog box with Paintbrush Picture selected

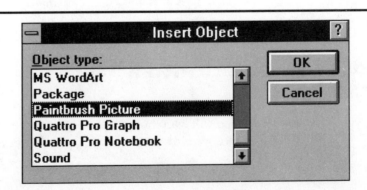

**FIGURE 6.29**

A Paintbrush window
opened within the
1-2-3 application
window

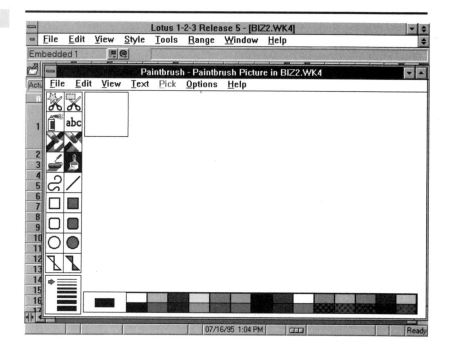

**FIGURE 6.30**

A message window
offering three choices.
Because the current
embedded object
doesn't exist,
select No.

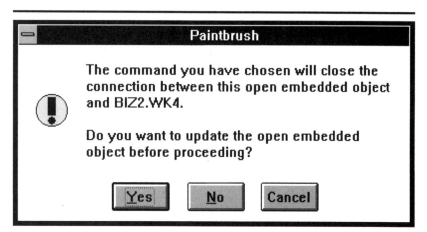

FIGURE 6.31

A retrieved object in its application window

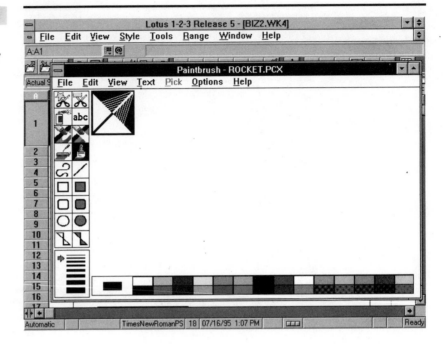

**11.** In 1-2-3, choose Edit ➤ Paste (or press Ctrl+V or Shift+Ins) to paste the object into the desired cell or location.

**12.** If the object (Figure 6.32) is not active (that is, it does not have handles), click on it. Notice that when a drawn object is active, 1-2-3 provides a set of drawing SmartIcons. Also notice the name <METAFILE> in the Contents box of the edit line.

**13.** To move the object, drag it to its new location. To size the object, drag on a handle. Figure 6.33 shows the sample spreadsheet with its new logo; a new font for its title; and bold, italicized column labels.

**FIGURE 6.32**

An object in the 1-2-3 spreadsheet

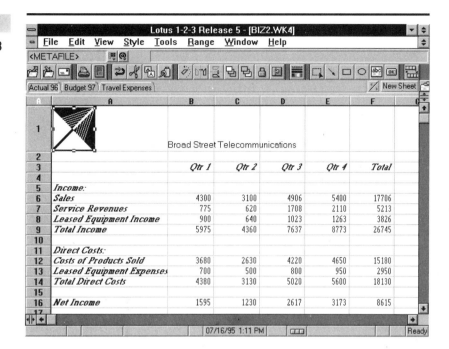

**FIGURE 6.33**

The sample spreadsheet with a logo, and a larger title

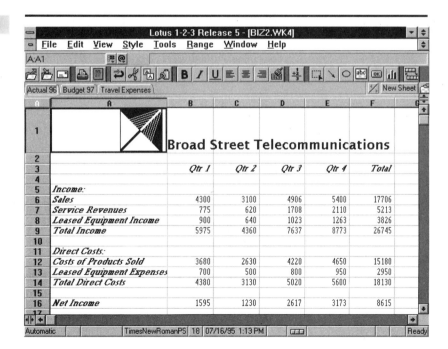

## CHAPTER SEVEN

# Analyzing and Graphing Your Data

This chapter concludes the 1-2-3 section of the book by providing information about two of the most important 1-2-3 features: Version Manager and charting.

First, you'll find out about Version Manager, which allows you to create several versions of data and build scenarios with which you can analyze and predict your financial future. In the second part of the chapter, you'll learn how to create *charts*, pictorial representations of your spreadsheet data.

## Analyzing Data with Version Manager

Version Manager makes it easy to perform what-if analysis. Using Version Manager, you can create several named sets of data to "plug in" to your spreadsheet. You can create sets of data that show you the highest possible income combined with the lowest expenses, the reverse income and expenses to show the worst results, and several points in between. Version Manager allows each member of your business team to create sets of data to aid in making informed decisions.

Each named set of data is a *version*, which is created using a named range. A version contains both data and styles for its range. Then, to take things one step further, you can create *scenarios*, named groups of versions. Version Manager has two elements: the Version Manager and the Version Manager Index. Use the Manager to work with or view just one version at a time (for creating, modifying, and deleting). Use the Index to work with or view one or more versions or scenarios at once (for creating, modifying, and deleting both versions and scenarios).

To open Version Manager, either choose <u>R</u>ange ➤ <u>V</u>ersion or click on the Version Manager SmartIcon. 1-2-3 displays either the Version Manager window (Figure 7.1) or the Version Manager Index window (Figure 7.2). When you start 1-2-3 the first time after installation, opening Version Manager reveals the Version Manager window. After that, opening Version Manager displays the last Version Manager window you used. To switch from the Version Manager window to the Version Manager Index window, click on the <u>T</u>o Index button (or press Alt+T). To switch from the Version Manager Index window to the Version Manager window, click on the <u>T</u>o Manager button (or press Alt+T). To switch between a Version Manager window and the spreadsheet, press Alt+F6.

To close a Version Manager window, double-click on the Control menu button or press Alt+F4.

**FIGURE 7.1**

The Version Manager window lets you create and edit a single version at a time.

**FIGURE 7.2**

The Version Manager Index window lets you create and edit one or more versions or scenarios.

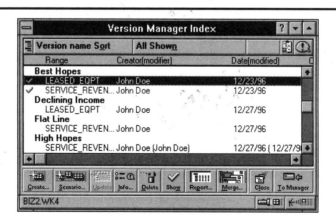

**TIP**  If you minimize a Version Manager window and attempt to restore or maximize it, it doesn't work. Choose <u>R</u>ange ➤ <u>V</u>ersion instead to redisplay the window.

The desktop can become very crowded with the 1-2-3 window, the Version Manager window, and a dialog box that you display from Version Manager, so you may have to drag both the dialog box and the Version Manager Index window to different locations, and size the window to accommodate the dialog box. For example, if you wish to view names of prior versions when you create new versions, you'll have to display the selected range in the spreadsheet, the scroll box in the middle of the Version Manager Index window, and the dialog box that you are filling in. This may require dragging both the dialog box and the Version Manager Index window to different locations, and reducing the size of the window to accommodate the dialog box.

The Version Manager window contains these elements:

- The Named <u>R</u>ange drop-down list box, which contains a list of named ranges that contain versions.
- The With <u>V</u>ersion(s) drop-down list box, which contains a list of versions for the selected named range.
- The scroll box, which contains comments about the listed versions.

Table 7.1 describes the buttons at the bottom of the Version Manager window.

**TABLE 7.1:** Version Manager Window Buttons

| BUTTON | NAME | SHORTCUT KEY | DESCRIPTION |
|--------|------|--------------|-------------|
| Create... | <u>C</u>reate | Alt+C | Displays the Create Version dialog box so that you can create a version of a named range |
| Update | <u>U</u>pdate | Alt+U | Updates one or more selected versions with both the styles and data in the spreadsheet |

**TABLE 7.1:** Version Manager Window Buttons (continued)

| BUTTON | NAME | SHORTCUT KEY | DESCRIPTION |
|---|---|---|---|
| Info... | Info | Alt+I | Displays the Version Info window so that you can change attributes for the selected version |
| Delete | Delete | Alt+D | Deletes one or more selected versions and/or scenarios |
| Close | Close | Alt+L | Closes Version Manager |
| To Index | To Index | Alt+T | Switches to the Version Manager Index window |
| | Highlight | Alt+H | Turns on or off version highlighting in the spreadsheet. Version highlighting shows named ranges containing one or more versions. |
| | Synchronize | Alt+K | Turns on or off tracking mode so that when you move the cell pointer to a named range in the spreadsheet, the same range is selected in the Named Range drop-down list box in the Version Manager window, allowing you to edit versions for that range. |

**NOTE** To see 1-2-3's description of a particular button, move the mouse pointer to the button and click the right mouse button. Then look in the title bar.

The Version Manager Index window displays a list of ranges, range addresses, and their related versions. It contains some Version Manager buttons, as well as additional buttons, which allow you to group versions into scenarios. Table 7.2 describes the buttons on the Version Manager Index window.

**TABLE 7.2:** Version Manager Index Window Buttons

| BUTTON | NAME | SHORTCUT KEY | DESCRIPTION |
|--------|------|--------------|-------------|
| | N/A | N/A | Shows either a complete list of range names and their versions, or a collapsed list of only range names |
| Version name Sort | Sort | N/A | Sorts the list by particular name and/or date information |
| All Shown | Shown | N/A | Displays or restricts the display to particular versions |
| | N/A | N/A | Copies the contents of the window to the Clipboard |
| | N/A | N/A | Reveals or hides the comment for the selected version |
| Create... | Create | Alt+C | Enables you to create a version of a named range |
| Scenario... | Scenario | Alt+S | Enables you to group versions into a scenario |
| Update | Update | Alt+U | Updates selected versions with both spreadsheet styles and data |

**TABLE 7.2:**   Version Manager Index Window Buttons (continued)

| BUTTON | NAME | SHORTCUT KEY | DESCRIPTION |
|---|---|---|---|
| | Info | Alt+I | Allows you to change attributes for the selected version |
| | Delete | Alt+D | Deletes one or more selected versions and/or scenarios |
| | Show | Alt+W | Selects a version so that its values are shown in the spreadsheet |
| | Report | Alt+P | Allows you to create a report showing the selected versions and optional information |
| | Merge | Alt+M | Merges selected versions and scenarios from other copies of the file into your master copy of the file |
| | Close | Alt+L | Closes Version Manager |
| | To Manager | Alt+T | Switches to the Version Manager window |
| | Highlight | Alt+H | Turns on or off version highlighting in the spreadsheet |
| | Synchronize | Alt+K | Turns on or off tracking mode |

1-2-3

In the Version Manager Index window,

■ Each range name is shown in boldface, with its range address enclosed in parentheses. 1-2-3 allows you to use ranges previously created by choosing Range ➤ Name, or you can create ranges using Version Manager.

■ Under each range name appears a list of its versions, the names of creators (and names of modifiers enclosed in parentheses), creation dates, (and modification dates enclosed in parentheses), and comments. When you sort, the headers for the display adjust for the sort.

■ A currently displayed version name appears in blue text and is preceded by a check mark.

■ If you have edited a version, the check mark that precedes the version name is drawn through and the text is italicized. To save your edits, click on the Update button, which displays a check mark as a reminder.

**When the Version Manager Index window first appears, all currently displayed versions are selected.**

## Creating a Version

You can create versions from either the Version Manager window or the Version Manager Index window by following these steps:

**1.** In the spreadsheet, type values for the new version.

**Before typing new values in this spreadsheet, if you have already filled in the spreadsheet, it's a good idea to save the current values as a version.**

**2.** Click on the Create button (or press Alt+C). 1-2-3 opens the Create Version dialog box (Figure 7.3) and highlights the contents of the Range Name text box. If you have previously named the range, its name will appear; otherwise, RANGE*n* (where *n* represents the suggested range number) is displayed.

**FIGURE 7.3**

The Create Version dialog box allows you to name a version and assign a range name, if one is needed.

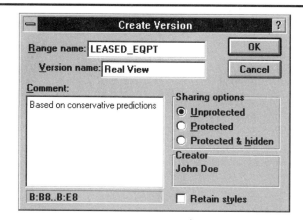

3. Either type a name (up to 15 characters with no embedded blanks) or accept the name in the Range Name text box.

4. Move the cursor to the Version Name box by double-clicking or by pressing Tab. Overtype Versionn (where n represents the suggested version number) with a name that better describes the version.

5. Type a comment in the Comment text box.

6. Either click on OK or press ↵. The new version appears in the Version Manager window and is highlighted in the spreadsheet.

 To edit a version, click on the Info button, fill in the Version Info dialog box (Figure 7.4), and either click on OK or press ↵.

## Viewing a Version

 Switching from one version to another makes it easy to view and edit values in the spreadsheet. If you click on the Highlighting and Synchronize buttons to turn highlighting and tracking on, you can synchronize cursor movement in the spreadsheet and in the Version Manager or Version Manager Index window.

If you are working in the Version Manager window, you can display a version by opening the Named Range drop-down list box and selecting the desired range. Then click on the With Version(s) drop-down box and select the desired version.

**FIGURE 7.4**

In the Version Info
dialog box, you can
edit a version.

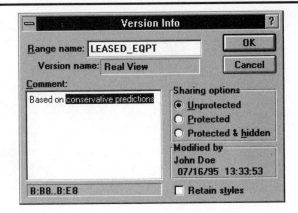

In the Version Manager window, you'll see the names of the range and version
and a checkmark in front of the selected version. In the spreadsheet, the range
of cells is highlighted, the version's values are displayed, and 1-2-3 recalculates the spreadsheet (if automatic recalculation is turned on).

If you are working in the Version Manager Index window, you can display a
version by double-clicking on the version name in the scroll box. In the Version Manager Index window, the selected version name is in blue text and is
preceded with a check. In the spreadsheet, the range of cells is highlighted,
the version's values are displayed, and 1-2-3 recalculates the spreadsheet (if
automatic recalculation is turned on).

## Sorting in the Version Manager Index Window

Once you have a list of versions, you can sort them by any of five criteria:
range, version, scenario, date, and contributor.

| CRITERIA | DESCRIPTION | DISPLAYS |
|---|---|---|
| Range Name | Sorts by range name and sorts the versions within each range | Version, Creator(modifier), Date(modified), Comment |

| CRITERIA | DESCRIPTION | DISPLAYS |
|---|---|---|
| Version Name | Sorts by version name and sorts the named ranges within each version | Range, Creator(modifier), Date(modified), Comment |
| Scenario Name | Sorts by scenario name and sorts the named ranges within each scenario | Range and Version, Creator(modifier), Date(modified), Comment |
| Date | Sorts by the creation date and sorts by creation time, from the newest to the oldest, within each date | Time, Range and Version, Creator(modifier), Comment |
| Contributor Name | Sorts by the contributor name and sorts by the version name within each contributor | Range and Version, Creator(modifier), Date(modified), Comment |

To sort, click on the Sort button (which shows you the current sort selection (for example, Range name Sort, Version name Sort, and so on); then select the sort criteria from the list:

```
Version name Sort
Range name
Version name
Scenario name
Date
Contributor name
```

## Creating Scenarios with Version Manager Index

Although you can create versions using either Version Manager, you can only group versions to form scenarios with the Version Manager Index.

**235**

**TIP**  A scenario can contain only one version of any named range. To ensure that you are selecting only one version from any range, it's best to sort the list of versions by range name.

To create a scenario, follow these steps:

1. Click on the <u>S</u>cenario button. 1-2-3 displays the Create Scenario dialog box (Figure 7.5).

2. Type a name (up to 32 characters and spaces) in the <u>S</u>cenario Name text box.

3. Fill up to eight lines of comments in the <u>C</u>omment text box.

4. Double-click on versions listed in the Available Versions scroll box. 1-2-3 copies the versions that you choose into the Selected <u>V</u>ersions box.

5. Either click on OK or press ↵. 1-2-3 closes the dialog box and returns to the Version Manager Index window.

Double-click on a scenario name to show its results in the spreadsheet (Figure 7.6).

---

**FIGURE 7.5**

The Create Scenario dialog box lets you name a new scenario, write a comment, and select versions.

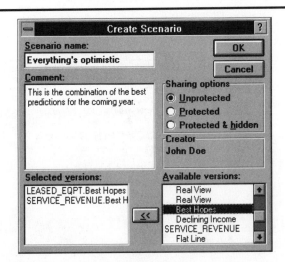

## FIGURE 7.6

The spreadsheet and Version Manager Index window with the current scenario shown

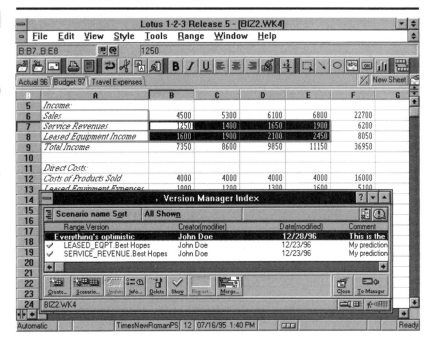

# Charting Data

A spreadsheet application would be incomplete without allowing you to create and edit charts. For example, our sample spreadsheet is quite small; you can see the entire spreadsheet on your screen. But, if you are working with a very wide spreadsheet, a chart might present the data in a format that's easier to understand. In fact, you might even detect a trend or a relationship between numbers by viewing a chart.

1-2-3 allows you to chart data from a spreadsheet using 12 chart types, including both two- and three-dimensional types. All chart types offer both horizontal and vertical versions. The list below covers the 1-2-3 chart types, shows the SmartIcons that you can use to create them, and describes how best to use each type.

**Line** Shows one or more series of data points over a period of time. Effective for charting many data points and for showing trends and

changes and for comparing series of data points. Individual values are de-emphasized.

**Area**    Shows one or more series of data points over a period of time. The filled part of the chart emphasizes the total of the series. Individual values are de-emphasized.

**Bar**    Shows individual values or magnitudes at a specific time and enables you to easily compare values. A vertical bar chart is the default chart type. A horizontal bar chart places a great emphasis on the flow of time. A stacked bar chart shows the relationship of each value to the whole.

**Pie**    Shows the parts of one data range as they compare to the whole. Note that a pie chart can only show positive values.

**XY**    Also known as a scatter chart, shows points of data drawn from two axes. If there is a correlation between two sets of values, data points cluster close to an imaginary line; otherwise, values appear all over the chart.

**HLCO**    Known as a High-Low-Close-Open chart or stock market chart, shows ranges of data and data points over time. You must arrange data series in this order:

**1.** One data series of high values shown as the top of a vertical line

**2.** One data series of low values shown as the bottom of a vertical line

**3.** One data series of closing values (optional) shown as a tick mark protruding to the right off the vertical line

**4.** One data series of opening values (optional) shown as a tick mark protruding left off the vertical line

**5.** One data series to plot in a bar chart (optional) below the HLCO portion

**6.** Additional data series to plot as lines (optional) below the HLCO portion

**Mixed** (no button)    Shows data series in any combination of bar, line, and/or area in order to emphasize particular traits of each series and relationships between them. Choose Chart ➤ Ranges and select the chart type for each data series.

**Radar**    Related to line (unfilled) and area (filled) charts, shows values drawn around a central point on the chart. Emphasizes the symmetry of data.

**3D Line**    A three-dimensional version of a line chart

**3D Area**    A three-dimensional version of an area chart

**3D Bar**     A three-dimensional version of a bar chart

**3D Pie**     A three-dimensional version of a pie chart

**NOTE** Some of the preceding SmartIcons are not on any of the SmartIcon sets added during 1-2-3 installation. However, 1-2-3 makes them available for an existing or new set. For information on creating a new set, see Appendix C.

Figure 7.7 shows a three-dimensional bar chart, which illustrates two data series over four quarters.

**FIGURE 7.7**

A typical 3-D bar chart showing income and direct costs for one year.

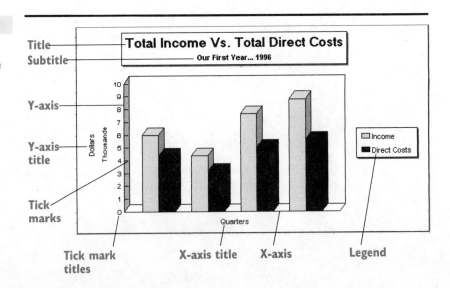

Most charts contain all or most of the elements shown in Table 7.3.

With 1-2-3, creating a chart is easy; all you do is choose one or more rows or columns, optionally choose the type of chart, and edit the chart elements. An extra bonus is that if the charted data changes, the chart automatically changes as well; you don't have to re-create the chart with its new values.

**TABLE 7.3:** Elements of a Chart

| ELEMENT | DESCRIPTION |
| --- | --- |
| Title | A chart heading |
| Subtitle | A chart subheading |
| X-Axis | The horizontal axis, used for time or areas |
| X-axis title | The title that you give to the x-axis |
| Y-axis | The vertical axis, used for units of measure, such as years, weights, or currency. You can add a second y-axis to a 1-2-3 chart by choosing Chart ➤ Axis ➤ 2nd Y-Axis. |
| Y-axis title | The title that you give to the y-axis |
| Plot | The core of the chart; the bars, lines, areas, or slices of pie. Each bar, line, area, point, or entire pie chart is based on a single spreadsheet row or column. |
| Legend | The key, which shows each data series and its color and/or pattern |
| Tick mark | A short line that identifies a value on a chart axis |
| Tick mark title | A title that identifies a specific tick mark |
| Gridline | A line that parallels an axis and either extends a tick mark across or down the chart |

## Planning a Chart

There are three important factors in planning a chart: the data, the purpose, and the chart type. Be sure to select appropriate data and leave out unimportant or inappropriate data. For example, don't combine column or row totals with cells whose contents are totaled. Ask yourself what you want to prove with the chart and what you want to show those who will view the chart. Finally, make sure that the chart type matches the selected data and purpose.

## Selecting Data for a Chart

You can select contiguous (adjacent) or noncontiguous rows or columns. To choose contiguous rows or columns, move the cell pointer to the first cell in a selection, press the left mouse button down, and drag to the last cell in a selection. To choose noncontiguous data, (e.g., all totals), drag to select the first applicable cells, press and hold down the Ctrl key, and select the next group of cells. Then repeat this process to include additional rows.

**NOTE**    **Be sure to select the row and column labels that you want the chart to use as its own labels. If you don't select labels, 1-2-3 supplies its own generic labels (for example Data A) and you'll have to edit them.**

## Creating a Chart

To create a chart, follow these steps:

1. Select one or more rows or columns.

 2. Choose Tools ➤ Chart or click the Chart SmartIcon.

 3. Move the mouse pointer to the starting point of the chart, press and hold down the left mouse button, and drag the mouse pointer diagonally to the ending point of the chart. (If necessary, you can always adjust the chart dimensions at a later time.)

**TIP**    **To use 1-2-3 default chart dimensions, simply click on the starting point of the chart.**

4. Release the mouse button. 1-2-3 draws the chart within the boundaries that you have set. Figure 7.8 shows the resulting chart, with all its defaults.

**FIGURE 7.8**

A default chart that contains three data series: Sales, Service Revenues, and Leased Equipment Income

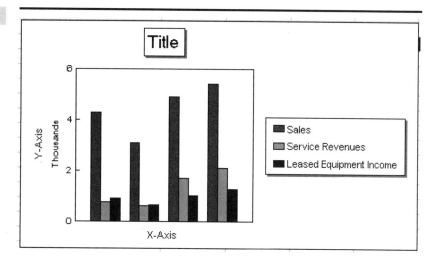

## Editing a Chart

As you can see, an unedited 1-2-3 chart is almost good enough to include in a report without further changes. However, to make a chart's contents more understandable, it's a good idea to edit and enhance it. This section will review the steps necessary for adding titles, changing the chart type, and editing other elements.

Table 7.4 lists the names of one or more chart elements on which you click and the names of the dialog box in which you select options and enter information.

**TABLE 7.4:** Shortcuts for Editing 1-2-3 Charts

| CHART ELEMENT | DIALOG BOX |
| --- | --- |
| Title | Headings dialog box |
| Y-axis, Y-axis title, or Y-axis subtitle | Y-Axis dialog box |
| X-axis, X-axis title, or X-axis subtitle | X-Axis dialog box |
| Plot | Lines & Color dialog box |
| Outside the plot but within the axes | Type dialog box |
| Line, bar, area, pie slice | Ranges dialog box |
| Data label | Data Labels dialog box |
| Legend | Legend dialog box |

**WORKING TOGETHER**
▲

# Using Lotus Map Viewer

You can graph data on a map of a selected region using the Lotus Map Viewer (a stand-alone application) and a set of country, state, and city maps. Lotus Map Viewer provides the following commands with which you can create and edit maps:

| | |
|---|---|
| Tools ➤ Map ➤ New Map | Inserts a new map based on a selected range and in the spreadsheet location that you have indicated |
| Tools ➤ Map ➤ Colors & Legend | Opens a dialog box in which you can change color settings, values, and legend labels for the selected map or start Lotus Map Viewer |
| Tools ➤ Map ➤ Patterns & Legend | Opens a dialog box in which you can change pattern settings, values, and legend labels for the selected map or start Lotus Map Viewer |
| Tools ➤ Map ➤ Ranges & Title | Opens a dialog box in which you can change range assignments (regions of a map, colors, patterns, and coordinates for pin characters) and the map title or start Lotus Map Viewer |
| Tools ➤ Map ➤ Set Redraw Preference | Opens a dialog box in which you can indicate whether 1-2-3 redraws maps automatically whenever you change data or redraws maps only when you choose Tools ➤ Map ➤ Redraw |
| Tools ➤ Map ➤ Redraw | Redraws all the maps in the current file |

**WORKING TOGETHER**
▲

Once you start Lotus Map Viewer, you can manage and modify the selected map using the following menu commands:

| | |
|---|---|
| File ➤ Update *application* | Updates the map in the spreadsheet, but Lotus Map Viewer remains open |
| File ➤ Exit & Return to *application* | Updates the map in the spreadsheet, closes Lotus Map Viewer, and returns to the spreadsheet |
| Edit ➤ Undo (Ctrl+Z) | Undoes the most recent change, if allowed |
| Edit ➤ Copy (Ctrl+C) | Copies the selected map to the Windows Clipboard, from which you can paste it into a Windows application |
| Edit ➤ Clear (Del) | Hides the selected title or legend. To reveal a hidden title or legend, in Lotus Map Viewer, choose View ➤ Set View Preferences and check the appropriate check box: Title, Color Legend, or Pattern Legend. |
| Edit ➤ Font & Attributes | Changes the font, font size, and/or attributes for the selected title or legend |
| View ➤ Zoom In (Ctrl+I) | Increases the size of the map in the window by 10% to a maximum of 400%. You can also zoom in to a specific part of the map by dragging the mouse to draw a sizing rectangle around the map. |
| View ➤ Zoom Out (Ctrl+O) | Decreases the size of the map in the window by 10% to a minimum of 25%. You can also zoom out by clicking the right mouse button and selecting Zoom Out from the menu. |

1-2-3

| | |
|---|---|
| View ➤ Reset (Ctrl+R) | Changes the size of the map in the window to the default display size |
| View ➤ Set View Preferences | Displays document information for a particular file |
| Map ➤ Add Overlay | Places a map overlay over the selected map. Map overlay files, which have the .TV extension, are stored in the \mapdata subdirectory if you accepted the suggested directories and subdirectories during installation. |
| Map ➤ Remove Overlay | Removes a map overlay from the selected map. |
| Help ➤ Contents | Lists the Lotus Map Viewer Contents from the Help facility |
| Help ➤ About Lotus Map Viewer | Displays Lotus Map Viewer version and copyright information |

Lotus Map Viewer also provides the following menu commands when you click the right mouse button:

| | |
|---|---|
| Recenter | Centers the selected map on the clicked-on location |
| Zoom Out | Reduces the size of the map and reveals more of it |
| Copy Region Code | Copies the code of the clicked-on region to the Windows Clipboard so that you can copy the code in 1-2-3 or in another Windows application |

**WORKING TOGETHER** ▲

| | |
|---|---|
| Copy Region Name | Copies the name of the clicked-on region to the Windows Clipboard so that you can copy the code in 1-2-3 or in another Windows application |
| Copy Coordinates | Copies the coordinates of the clicked-on region to the Windows Clipboard so that you can copy the code in 1-2-3 to define pin characters or in another Windows application |

To set up your data properly, follow these steps:

**1.** Define regions in the leftmost column: Either type names of regions or region codes.

**2.** Type values, codes, labels, pin characters, pin coordinates, or pin character colors in succeeding columns. Do not mix data types in a single column.

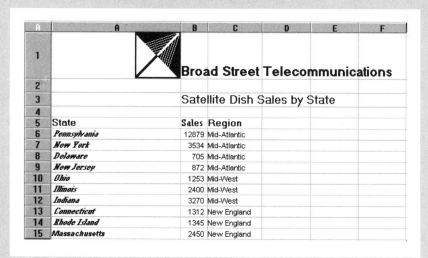

**WORKING
TOGETHER**
▲

To create a map, follow these steps:

1. Select a range of data to be mapped. Include the region names or region codes in the selection, but do not include new labels.

2. Choose <u>T</u>ools ➤ Map ➤ <u>N</u>ew Map.

3. Click in the cell that marks the upper-left corner of the map. Lotus Map Viewer then creates and displays the map. The map is color-coded to show ranges of data (in this case, the contents of column B) and is pattern-coded to show regions (in this case, the company divisions in column C).

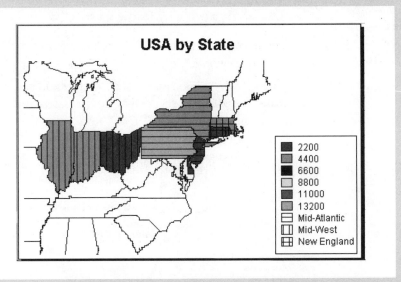

To edit a map, either double-click on it to start Lotus Map Viewer, or click on it, choose <u>T</u>ools ➤ Map, and then choose one of the commands on the submenu. To zoom in to the area being mapped to cut extraneous areas on the map, press the Ctrl key, click the left mouse button, and drag a rectangle around the area of the map that you wish to display. Be sure to select an area much larger than the region to be displayed. For detailed information about Lotus Map Viewer, see the *User's Guide* or look up "Lotus Map Viewer" in the Help facility.

## Editing Titles

In 1-2-3, you have the ability to add a chart title, a chart subtitle, an x-axis title, and y-axis titles. To add a title, either double-click on the element or choose Chart ➤ Headings. In the Headings dialog box (Figure 7.9), type a title in the Line 1 text box, and type a subtitle in the Line 2 text box. Then either click on OK or press ↵.

**FIGURE 7.9**

In the Headings dialog box, you can type and change the placement of a title and subtitle.

| Headings | ? |
|---|---|

**Title**
Line 1: Income for 1996          ☐ Cell
Line 2: _____          ☐ Cell
Placement: ○ Left  ● Center  ○ Right  ○ Manual

**Note**
Line 1: _____          ☐ Cell
Line 2: _____          ☐ Cell
Placement: ● Left  ○ Center  ○ Right  ○ Manual

OK
Cancel

To add titles for the y-axis, either click on its default title, Y-Axis, or choose Chart ➤ Axis ➤ Y-Axis. In the Y-Axis dialog box (Figure 7.10), type a new title in the Axis Title text box. Then either click on OK or press ↵.

To add an x-axis title, either click on the default x-axis title or choose Chart ➤ Axis ➤ X-Axis.

**NOTE**  You can also scale the chart manually and place tick marks at selected intervals.

**FIGURE 7.10**

In the Y-Axis dialog box, you can type a y-axis title, scale a chart manually, show major and minor tick marks, and place labels on the y-axis.

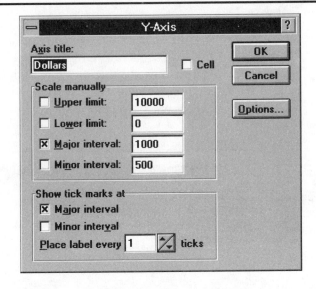

### Adding Grids

To add grids to a chart, choose <u>C</u>hart ➤ <u>G</u>rids. In the Grids dialog box (Figure 7.11), open the <u>X</u>-axis (to draw a vertical grid from the x-axis), <u>Y</u>-axis (to draw a horizontal grid from the y-axis), or <u>2</u>nd Y-axis drop-down list box (to draw a horizontal grid from the second y-axis). Select the interval at which you want 1-2-3 to draw a grid, and either click on OK or press ↵.

### Adding Extra Text to a Chart

You can emphasize a particular part of a chart by adding text and even illustrations. Chapter 10 covers how to draw in Ami Pro (and use the same skills to draw in other SmartSuite applications). To add text to a chart, click on

**FIGURE 7.11**

In the Grids dialog box, you can add horizontal and/or vertical grid lines to a chart.

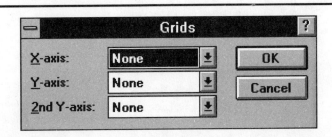

the Text Box SmartIcon. Move the mouse pointer to the chart and draw a text box. Then type your text:

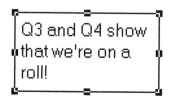

You can enhance or change the font or size of text in a text box. Make sure that the text box is active (there should be handles around the border), and either select options from the status bar or menu bar or press shortcut keys as you would for any text selection.

 To draw a line and arrow from a text box to another element in the chart, click on the Arrow SmartIcon, drag a line between the text box and chart, and release the left mouse button. You can move or size the text box or arrow until the chart looks just the way you want it (Figure 7.12).

**FIGURE 7.12**

The default chart shown in Figure 7.8 now shows much improvement.

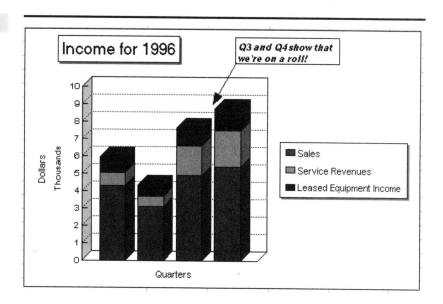

**TIP** When you have trouble selecting a text box, select another part of a chart (for example, the legend), and then return to the text box and click on it. The selection should be successful.

When dragging a chart to a new location, text boxes, lines, arrows, and other illustrations remain behind. Before moving a chart, group as many of these elements as you can. Click on the Select SmartIcon and draw a box around all the elements. When you have grouped items successfully, you'll see handles around the entire group.

## Changing to Another Type of Chart

When you want to change the chart type, make sure that you select a type that's appropriate to your data. To change the chart type, follow these steps:

**1.** Either click on the Type SmartIcon, double-click on the area within the axes but outside the *plot* (the lines, bars, or slices of pie), or choose Chart ➤ Type. 1-2-3 displays the Type dialog box (Figure 7.13) with the current chart type selected and illustrated.

**2.** To change to another type of chart, click on an option button in the Types group. 1-2-3 changes the illustrations in the middle of the dialog box.

**3.** Optionally, click on one of the illustrations to select the best look for your chart.

**4.** Either click on OK or press ↵. 1-2-3 closes the Type dialog box and changes the chart to its new type.

## Naming a Chart

The main reason for naming a chart is to be able to use the name as a memory tool to find the chart in a very large file. When you create a file, 1-2-3 automatically names it CHART *n*, where *n* represents a number. 1-2-3 names the first chart in the file CHART 1, the second CHART 2, and so on. When you delete a chart in the middle of a group of charts, 1-2-3 does not reuse the number when naming the next chart. Instead, it adds one to the highest numbered chart in the file.

To specify a chart name, select a chart and choose Chart ➤ Name. In the Name dialog box (Figure 7.14), type the desired name (up to 15 characters and spaces) in the Chart Name text box, which contains the name of the selected chart. Click on the Rename button, and 1-2-3 renames the chart.

**1-2-3**

**FIGURE 7.13**

In the Type dialog box, you can select a new chart type or another version of the current type.

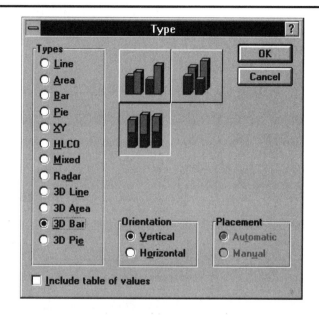

**FIGURE 7.14**

The Name dialog box, which contains all the names of the charts in the current file

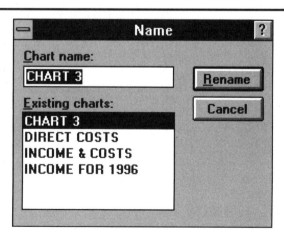

## Finding a Chart

When you create a series of charts, there may be one or two that you'd like to edit, rename, or even delete. In the frenzy of creation, you may have placed a chart in a remote area of a spreadsheet and now you can't find it. To find a particular chart, choose Edit ➤ Go To or press F5. In the Go To dialog box (Figure 7.15), open the Type of Item drop-down list box if needed, and select Chart. Then either double-click on the name of the desired chart, or select the chart name and either click on OK or press ↵.

## Deleting a Chart

To delete a chart, select it (notice the handles around the borders of the chart) and press Del.

FIGURE 7.15

The Go To dialog box, with which you can find a particular chart

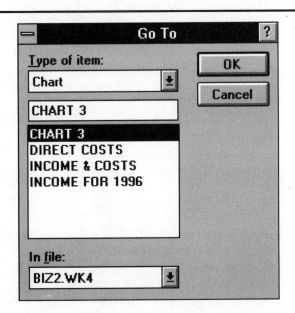

# Processing Words
with Ami Pro

Part Three introduces you to Ami Pro, a full-featured yet easy-to-use word processor. In this part, you'll learn about creating and editing documents, and formatting—of words, paragraphs, and the entire document. You'll find out how to check your words with the thesaurus and grammar checker. As a grand finale, you'll learn how to use Ami Pro's drawing tools to create pictures that you can use in your Ami Pro documents as well as in your other SmartSuite and Windows files.

Table III.1 illustrates and describes many Ami Pro SmartIcons.

# Ami Pro SmartIcons

| SMARTICON | DESCRIPTION |
|---|---|
| **Common Ami Pro SmartIcons** | |
| | Opens an existing file. [File ➤ Open] *Shortcut:* Ctrl+O |
| | Saves the current file. [File ➤ Save] *Shortcut:* Ctrl+S |
| | Prints the current file using the options in the Print dialog box. [File ➤ Print] *Shortcut:* Ctrl+P |
| | Prints an envelope. [File ➤ Print Envelope] |
| | Toggles between viewing the current file in full page and layout views. [View ➤ Full Page/View ➤ Layout Mode] *Shortcut:* Ctrl+D |
| | Undoes the last action, if allowed. [Edit ➤ Undo] *Shortcut:* Ctrl+Z |
| | Cuts the selection and places it in the Clipboard. [Edit ➤ Cut] *Shortcut:* Ctrl+X or Shift+Del |
| | Copies the selection to the Clipboard. [Edit ➤ Copy] *Shortcut:* Ctrl+C or Ctrl+Ins |
| | Pastes the contents of the Clipboard into the file at the current cursor location. [Edit ➤ Paste] *Shortcut:* Ctrl+V or Shift+Ins |
| **B** | Applies or removes boldface from the selection. [Text ➤ Bold] *Shortcut:* Ctrl+B |
| *I* | Applies or removes italics from the selection. [Text ➤ Italic] *Shortcut:* Ctrl+I |
| U | Underlines or removes the underline from the selection. [Text ➤ Underline] *Shortcut:* Ctrl+U |

Toggles between applying the character or paragraph format of the selection to text in the current document or returning to edit mode. [Text ➤ Fast Format] *Shortcut:* Ctrl+T

 Aligns the selection to the left margin of the cell. [Text ➤ Alignment ➤ Left] *Shortcut:* Ctrl+L

 Aligns the selection between the left and right margins of the cell. [Text ➤ Alignment ➤ Center] *Shortcut:* Ctrl+E

 Toggles between showing and hiding the ruler. [View ➤ Show Ruler/View ➤ Hide Ruler]

 Inserts a frame at the insertion point. [Frame ➤ Create Frame]

 Inserts a table at the insertion point. [Tools ➤ Tables]

 Runs the spell checker on the current selection or file. [Tools ➤ Spell Check]

 Runs the grammar checker on the current selection or file. [Tools ➤ Grammar Check]

 Runs the thesaurus for the current selection. [Tools ➤ Thesaurus]

 Displays the drawing SmartIcons so that you can create a picture. [Tools ➤ Drawing]

Opens the Chart dialog box so that you can create a chart with selected data or data that you enter. [Tools ➤ Charting]

AmiPro

# Ami Pro SmartIcons

| SMARTICON | DESCRIPTION |
|---|---|
| **Common Ami Pro SmartIcons (continued)** | |
| | Displays the next set of SmartIcons. [Tools ➤ SmartIcons] |
| | Toggles between outline and layout mode (the default). [View ➤ Layout Mode/View ➤ Outline Mode] |
| | Toggles between a desktop with and without a title bar, menu bar, SmartIcons, and status bar. [View ➤ Show Clean Screen] |
| | Displays the Font dialog box from which you can change the attributes of the selected text. [Text ➤ Font] |
| | Justifies the selection between the left and right margins of the cell. [Text ➤ Alignment ➤ Justify] *Shortcut:* Ctrl+J |
| | Displays the Modify Style dialog box so that you can modify the selected paragraph style. [Style ➤ Modify Style] *Shortcut:* Ctrl+A |
| | Displays the Modify Page Layout dialog box. [Page ➤ Modify Page Layout] |
| | Goes to a particular page or item. [Edit ➤ Go To] *Shortcut:* Ctrl+G |
| | Searches for and optionally replaces a search string. [Edit ➤ Find & Replace] *Shortcut:* Ctrl+F |
| | Inserts a note at the insertion point. [Edit ➤ Insert ➤ Note] |

**Common Ami Pro SmartIcons (continued)**

 Opens the Modify Frame Layout dialog box so that you can change the attributes for the selected frame. [Frame ➤ Modify Frame Layout]

 Creates a frame using the same attributes as the previous frame that you created. [Frame ➤ Create Frame]

 Moves the selected frame to the front of the layers of frames. [Frame ➤ Bring to Front]

 Moves the selected frame to the back of the layers of frames. [Frame ➤ Send to Back]

 Groups or ungroups selected frames. [Frame ➤ Group]

 Imports a picture to be inserted at the insertion point. [File ➤ Import Picture]

 Opens the Graphics Scaling dialog box so that you can scale the selected picture. [Frame ➤ Graphics Scaling]

 Toggles between showing and hiding all the pictures in this document. [View ➤ View Preferences; then check or clear Pictures]

 Toggles between viewing the current file in draft and layout views. [View ➤ Layout Mode/View ➤ Draft Mode] *Shortcut:* Ctrl+M

Inserts a floating header or footer into the current document. [Page ➤ Header/Footer; then click on Floating Header/Footer]

# Ami Pro SmartIcons

| SMARTICON | DESCRIPTION |
|---|---|
| **Common Ami Pro SmartIcons (continued)** | |
| | Inserts a page break at the current insertion point. [Page ➤ Breaks; then click on Insert Page Break] |
| | Inserts page numbers in the current document. [Page ➤ Page Numbering] |
| | Opens a pane so that you can insert a footnote in the current document. [Tools ➤ Footnotes] |
| | Opens the Mark Index Entry dialog box so that you can insert an index entry. [Edit ➤ Mark Text ➤ Index Entry] |
| | Opens the Insert Glossary Record dialog box so that you can insert a glossary item. [Edit ➤ Insert ➤ Glossary Record] *Shortcut:* Ctrl+K |
| | Toggles between revision marking and insert typing modes. [Tools ➤ Revision Marking] *Shortcut:* Ins button on status bar |
| | Opens the TOC, Index dialog box so that you can generate a table of contents or an index [Tools ➤ TOC, Index] |
| | Starts 1-2-3. |
| | Starts Freelance Graphics. |
| | Starts Lotus SmarText (if installed). |
| | Starts Lotus Notes (if installed). |
| | Starts Lotus cc:Mail (if installed). |

Starts Organizer.

Opens an MS-DOS window. (Type **Exit** to return.)

Opens Windows File Manager.

Inserts a copyright symbol at the insertion point.

Inserts a registered trademark symbol at the insertion point.

Inserts a trademark symbol at the insertion point.

Replaces quotation marks, dashes, and apostrophes with comparable typeset symbols.

Reduces the point size of the selected text by two points. [Text ➤ Font; then select a new point size]

Increases the point size of the selected text by two points. [Text ➤ Font; then select a new point size]

Displays the entire page from left margin to right margin using the FIT2SCRN.SMM macro application. [View ➤ Fit to Screen]

Opens the Select Pages to Print dialog box so that you can print selected pages.

Prints the current document with all the current print defaults. [File ➤ Print] *Shortcut:* Ctrl+P

Opens the View Preferences dialog box so that you can determine how you view files on the desktop. [View ➤ View Preferences]

AmiPro

# Ami Pro SmartIcons

Compares two documents and marks differences with revision marks. [Tools ➤ Doc Compare]

Shows or hides nonprinting symbols—tab and paragraph marks (carriage returns). [View ➤ View Preferences; then check or clear Tabs & Returns]

Shows or hides symbols representing column breaks, page breaks, inserted ruler, inserted page layout, floating header and footer, and DDE text links. [View ➤ View Preferences; then check or clear Marks]

Overrides the default hyphenation. [Edit ➤ Mark Text ➤ No Hyphenation]

Displays the Lines & Color dialog box so that you can change table lines (position and style) and color. [Table ➤ Lines & Color]

Displays the Column/Row Size dialog box so that you can change the size of table columns, rows, and gutters between table cells. [Table ➤ Column/Row Size]

Connects the selected table cells. [Table ➤ Connect Cells]

Inserts a row in a table. [Table ➤ Insert Column/Row; then select Rows]

Inserts a column in a table. [Table ➤ Insert Column/Row; then select Columns]

Deletes a row from a table. [Table ➤ Delete Column/Row; then select Delete Row]

**Common Ami Pro SmartIcons (continued)**

   Deletes a column from a table. [Table ➤ Delete Column/Row; then select Delete Column]

  Deletes the selected table. [Table ➤ Delete Entire Table]

  Sends mail, if you have the capability.

  Allows you to create a Lotus Mail message in Ami Pro.

  Allows you to create a calendar using information from Organizer.

  Allows you to copy styles from Ami Pro to 1-2-3.

AmiPro

# 8

# Planning and Creating Your First Document

In this chapter, you'll create a report. As you work, you'll find out about the elements of the Ami Pro application window and certain important word processing features: the ruler, WYSIWYG, insert and overtype modes, the spell checker, thesaurus, and grammar checker. Remember that you can learn the basics of opening and saving files by reviewing Chapter 2, and Chapter 3 covers editing concepts.

## Introducing Ami Pro

Ami Pro is an easy-to-use and extensive word processor that enables you to create a wide range of documents—from a simple one-page memo to a heavily illustrated manual with a table of contents, footnotes, and an index. Regardless of the type of document that you create, before you send it to the outside world, you can use the built-in spell checker, grammar checker, and thesaurus to proof and refine your work.

Using Ami Pro, you can do the following:

- Create a business plan or report that incorporates 1-2-3 charts and spreadsheet data, drawings and clip art, Approach database information, and even Calendars from Organizer.

- Print a handout that accompanies a Freelance Graphics presentation.

- Work with other SmartSuite applications using the Working Together macros. For example, you can coordinate the exchange of data between Approach and 1-2-3, you can link or import a spreadsheet or chart, compute mortgage payments, or even build a custom calculator—all from within Ami Pro.

## Reading and Writing Common File Formats

Ami Pro reads the following file formats: 1-2-3 (including releases 3, 4, and 5), AdvanceWrite, Ami Pro Macro, ASCII (text), dBASE, DCA/FFT, DCA/RFT, DIF, DisplayWrite, E-Mail, Enable, Excel (including 3.0, 4.0, and 5.0), Exec MemoMaker, Manuscript, Microsoft Word, MultiMate, Navy DIF, Office Writer, Organizer, Paradox, PeachText, Professional Write, Rich Text Format, Samna Word, SmartWare, SuperCalc, Symphony Document, Wang (IWP), Windows Write, Word for Windows (both 1.x and 2.0), WordPerfect (both 4.2 and 5.x), WordStar, and WS 2000 (both versions 1.0 and 3.0).

Ami Pro writes to these file formats: AdvanceWrite, Ami Pro, Ami Pro Macro, ASCII (text), DCA/FFT, DCA/RFT, DisplayWrite, E-Mail, Enable, Exec MemoMaker, Manuscript, Microsoft Word, MultiMate, Navy DIF, Office Writer, PeachText, Professional Write, Rich Text Format Samna Word, SmartWare, Symphony Document, Wang (IWP), Windows Write, Word for Windows (both 1.x and 2.0), WordPerfect (both 4.2 and 5.x), WordStar, and WS 2000 (both versions 1.0 and 3.0).

 **NOTE** Even if you are not currently working on an Ami Pro document, you can use Ami Pro as a file converter. In Ami Pro, open a file in one format and save it to another format.

# Viewing the Ami Pro Window

The Ami Pro application window (Figure 8.1) contains many elements that you found out about in Chapter 2. Since it is a word processing application, its window includes unique elements to make your job easier, as well as common elements about which you have already learned.

 **NOTE** When you start Ami Pro, the Ami Pro SwitchKit window may appear on your desktop. To close it, click on the rightmost icon at the bottom of the SwitchKit window.

## FIGURE 8.1

The Ami Pro application window provides many helpful elements to help you create and edit documents.

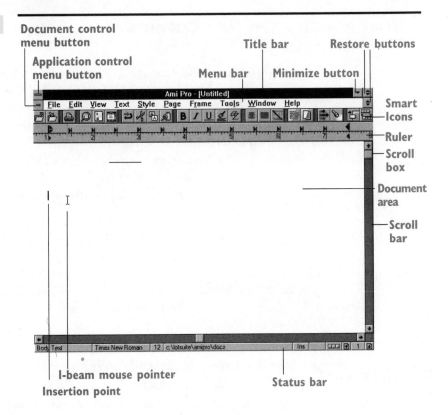

## Ami Pro SmartIcons

The pages starting Part Three (the beginning of the Ami Pro section) show all the SmartIcons for Ami Pro. To learn how SmartIcons work, see Chapter 2. When you start Ami Pro for the first time, the Default SmartIcons appear. From then on, the SmartIcons set with which you end an Ami Pro session are the same ones that appear when you start a new session.

## Using the Ruler

The ruler (Figure 8.2) displays the current margin and tab settings. Use the ruler to change these settings, to determine paragraph indentation (if any), and to widen or narrow columns of text. You'll learn about using the ruler in Chapter 9.

FIGURE 8.2

**FIGURE 8.2**

The Ami Pro ruler displays and defines margins and tab positions.

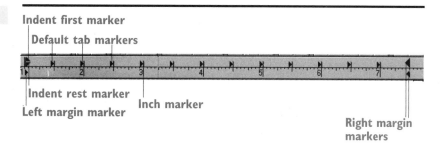

Ami Pro replaces the Show Ruler command with Hide Ruler. To hide the ruler, choose View ➤ Hide Ruler.

## The Document Window

The document area (Figure 8.3) displays your document as you work. The vertical blinking line is the *insertion point*, which shows the location of the next character that you type. Don't confuse the insertion point with the I-beam mouse pointer; use the I-beam to point to the area in a page of text to which you want to move the insertion point. Notice that the document area includes both a vertical and a horizontal scroll bar.

**FIGURE 8.3**

In the Ami Pro worksheet window, you can type and edit each document.

## The Ami Pro Status Bar

The Ami Pro status bar (Figure 8.4) allows you to change to a different para-graph style, font, or point size; check the current date and time, the current path, or current location of the insertion point; check for mail (if cc:Mail or Notes is installed); switch typing modes; display a set of SmartIcons; and dis-play the current page number (if you are in Layout mode) or go to a specific page or screen.

The Ami Pro status bar provides these buttons:

**Style status button**   Click on this button to reveal a list of paragraph styles (Figure 8.5).

**Face button**   Click on this button to reveal a list of the installed fonts (Figure 8.6) on your computer system.

**FIGURE 8.4**

The Ami Pro status bar consists of various buttons with which you can change styles, fonts, and point sizes, and check your current status.

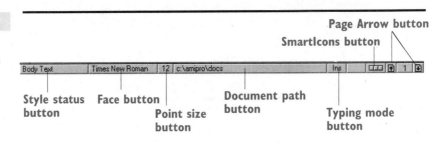

**FIGURE 8.5**

The list of Ami Pro paragraph styles from which you can select

**FIGURE 8.6**

A list of some of the fonts installed on one computer system.

**Point Size button**   Click on this button to display a list of point sizes for the selection.

AmiPro

**Document Path/date-time/insertion point indicator**    Click on this button to either display the document path, the computer system date and time, or the current line number, column number, and position (using the current unit of measure) of the insertion point

c:\amipro\docs

12/31/96 11:46 AM

Line 1        Col 1        Pos: (1.00,1.00)

**Mail Notification button**    If you have cc:Mail or Notes and you see an envelope on this button, click to read your mail.

Ins   **Typing mode button**    Click on this button to switch among Insert (Ins), Overtype (Type), and Revision Marking (Rev) modes. Table 8.1 describes each mode.

Caps   **Caps Lock**    This indicator shows whether Caps Lock is active. If the indicator is blank, uppercase letters are not locked.

**SmartIcons selector**    Click on this button to display a list of Smart-Icons (Figure 8.7). (The highlighted list item is the current SmartIcons set.) Click on Hide SmartIcons to remove all SmartIcons from the desktop. Select Bonus Pack to work with other SmartSuite applications from within Ami Pro.

**PgUp Arrow button**    Click on this button to move to the previous page (in Layout mode) or screen (Draft mode), unless you are on the first page or screen.

1   **Page Status**    Click on this button, which shows the current page number in Layout mode (but is blank in Outline and Draft modes), to display the Go To dialog box (Figure 8.8).

**TABLE 8.1:**   Ami Pro Typing Mode Buttons

| INDICATOR | MODE | DESCRIPTION |
|---|---|---|
| Ins | Insert | As you type a character or space, all characters and spaces to the right of the insertion point are pushed ahead; no text is deleted as you type. Insert mode is the default typing mode. To switch between Insert mode and Overtype mode, press the Ins key. To cycle through all typing modes, click on the Typing mode button. |
| Type | Overtype | As you type a character or space, the character or space to the right of the insertion point is erased. |
| Rev | Revision Marking | As you type a character or space, Ami Pro marks it with attributes or colors that you specify. This means that you can more easily identify the text that you edit during a particular Ami Pro session. |

**FIGURE 8.7**

The nine 1-2-3 SmartIcons sets from which you can choose and the option that hides SmartIcons

 **PgDn Arrow button**   Click on this button to move to the next page (in Layout mode) or screen (Draft mode), unless you are on the last page or screen.

**FIGURE 8.8**

The Go To dialog box, which allows you to move to a particular page or item in the current document

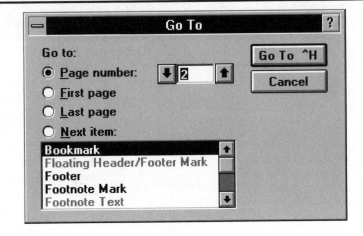

# What Is WYSIWYG?

Ami Pro allows you to view a document as it will look when printed. This technology is known as WYSIWYG (What You See Is What You Get).

# Creating a Document

Once you start Ami Pro, you can just start typing in the document window using a default template or style. You can modify or select a new style sheet if desired. See the sidebar called "Creating a Document with an Ami Pro Style Sheet" later in this chapter.

As you type, the text seems to push the insertion point along the line toward the right margin. When the text reaches the end of the line, you don't have to press ↵ to start a new line. Ami Pro has *word wrap*, which means that if a word that you are typing won't fit on the line, Ami Pro moves the word to the beginning of the next line.

# Ami Pro Style Sheets

When you start a new Ami Pro document, you have a choice of style sheets. Normally, you'll choose Default, which has the most frequently used paragraph styles. However, if you want to create a certain type of document, Ami Pro might provide a "pre-built" style for that document. The following table lists the style sheet files and describes each one.

**Article (_article.sty)**   A template for an article, including your name and address, the number of words in the article, and an article layout.

**Basic (_basic.sty)**   A set of basic paragraph styles for body text.

**Calendar (_calday.sty)**   Today's calendar with half-hourly appointments from 7:00 AM to 7:30 PM; spaces for notes, contacts, expenses, and tasks; and your name, address, and telephone number.

**Calendar (_calmon.sty)**   A blank calendar for a month and year that you specify, printed in landscape orientation.

**Calendar (_calorg.sty)**   A monthly calendar for a month and year that you specify, using Organizer appointments, printed in portrait orientation.

**Calendar (_calwk.sty)**   A weekly calendar with hourly appointments from 8:00 AM to 6:00 PM; your name, address, and telephone number; and room for a list of tasks.

**Default (_default.sty)**   A set of the most frequently used paragraph styles. This is the default style.

**Dissertation (_dissert.sty)**   A set of paragraph styles for theses and dissertations.

**Envelope (_envelop.sty)**   An envelope with your name and return address, if you choose. When you print, be sure to choose File ➤ Print Envelope.

**WORKING TOGETHER** ▲

**Expense Report (_expense.sty)** An expense report with self-totaling columns and rows.

**Fax (_fax1.sty)** A plain fax cover sheet with your name, business name, address, telephone number, and today's date.

**Fax (_fax2.sty)** A fax cover sheet with black borders at top and bottom. Also included are your name, business name, address, telephone number, and the current date and time.

**Fax (_fax3.sty)** A fax cover sheet with a gray-to-black border at the top. Also included are your name, business name, address, telephone number, and the current date and time.

**Handout (_handout.sty)** A handout based on a Freelance Graphics presentation.

**Index (_index.sty)** An index for long documents.

**Invoice (_invoice.sty)** An invoice form with self-totaling columns. Also included are your name, business name, address, telephone number, and today's date.

**Label (_label.sty)** A label based on an Avery label that you specify.

**Letter (_letter1.sty)** A business letter with a globe graphic. Also included are your name, business name, address, telephone number, and today's date.

**Letter (_letter2.sty)** A business letter with a border around the page. Also included are your name and title, business name, address, telephone number, and today's date.

**Letter (_letter3.sty)** A business letter, using a sans serif font, with your name and title, business name, address, telephone number, and today's date.

**Letter (_letter4.sty)** A business letter, using a serif font, with your name and title, business name, address, telephone number, and today's date.

**Loan Payment Table (_loanpay.sty)**    A loan payment table based on minimum and maximum amounts and time.

**Macro sheet (_macro.sty)**    A sheet used for writing macros.

**Memo (_memo1.sty)**    A memorandum with a line down the left margin. The From and Date areas are filled in for you.

**Memo (_memo2.sty)**    A memorandum with the word *MEMO* in large font in a gray frame. The From and Date areas are filled in for you.

**Memo (_memo3.sty)**    A memorandum with a line above and below the word *Memorandum*. The From and Date areas are filled in for you.

**Memo (_memo4.sty)**    A memorandum with a sawtooth line at the top margin. The From and Date areas are filled in for you.

**Memo (_memo5.sty)**    A memorandum with the word *Memo* in white text on a black background at the left margin and a gray bar to the right margin. The From and Date areas are filled in for you.

**Memo (_memo6.sty)**    A memorandum with a diamond line at the top margin and the centered word *MEMORANDUM*. The From and Date areas are filled in for you.

**Merge data file (_mergdat.sty)**    A data file with merge field names and delimiters.

**Merge letter (_merglet.sty)**    _LETTER.STY with merge fields included.

**Mortgage (_mortgag.sty)**    A real estate mortgage calculation form.

**Newsletter (_newslt1.sty)**    A two-column newsletter, with a centered title between two lines and two frames for graphics.

**Newsletter (_newslt2.sty)**     A one-column newsletter, with the left-aligned title in a gray frame.

**Newsletter (_newslt3.sty)**     A three-column newsletter with a centered title between two lines, with two small frames for graphics.

**Newsletter (_newslt4.sty)**     A three-column newsletter with a white title in a black frame, with a frame spanning columns 2 and 3.

**Newsletter (_newslt5.sty)**     A two-column newsletter with a centered title and with a graphic of a fountain pen.

**Outline (_outlin1.sty)**     Paragraph styles for an outline.

**Outline (_outln2.sty)**     Paragraph styles for an outline; style specifies a large left margin, left-aligned heading, and a line across the top of the page.

**Outline (_outln3.sty)**     Paragraph styles for an outline; style specifies a large left margin.

**Outline (_outline.sty)**     Paragraph styles used in Outline mode.

**Overhead (_overhd1.sty)**     An overhead in portrait orientation, with room for a large headline on a number graphic and a large centered title.

**Overhead (_overhd2.sty)**     An overhead in landscape orientation, with a title and page heading and a large gray arrow.

**Overhead (_overhd3.sty)**     An overhead in landscape orientation with a starburst graphic.

**Overhead (overhd4.sty)**     A simple overhead, 8.5" × 8.5".

**Overhead (_overhd5.sty)**     An overhead with a top line, 8.5" × 8.5".

**Phone list (_phonlst.sty)**     A two-column phone list with last name, first name, and phone number in a small font.

**WORKING TOGETHER** ▲

**Press Release (_press1.sty)**    A press release with gray lines above and below the left-aligned heading.

**Press Release (_press2.sty)**    A press release with a right-aligned text graphic containing the words *NEWS RELEASE.*

**Proposal (_propos1.sty)**    A proposal with a medium-width black line above the title and a fine black line between the title and first heading.

**Proposal (_propos2.sty)**    A two-column proposal with section headings and dotted section underlines.

**Report (_report1.sty)**    A plain report with the only line between the title and first heading.

**Report (_report2.sty)**    A two-column report with white section headings in black frames.

**Report (_report3.sty)**    A two-column report with a centered title in a shadow frame.

**Report (_report4.sty)**    A report with white section headings in black boxes stretching from left to right margin.

**Term Paper (_termppr.sty)**    Paragraph styles for a term paper.

**Title Page (_title1.sty)**    A title page within a gray frame with a black shadow. Included is your name, title, company name, address, and today's date. A blank page follows.

**Title Page (_title2.sty)**    A title page with a triple line and single line border. Included is your name, company name, and address. A blank page follows.

**Title Page (_title3.sty)**    A title page with a gray frame with a black shadow. Included is your name, title, company name, address, and today's date. A blank page follows.

AmiPro

**WORKING TOGETHER** ▲

**Table of Contents (_toc.sty)**    A table of contents for long documents.

**Envelope (~amienv.sty)**    A style sheet used to automatically print envelopes.

**Mercury Sports (murclet.sty)**    A demonstration letter with a graphic.

# Checking Your Document

Part of the editing process is running Ami Pro's spell checker, thesaurus, and grammar checker.

As you have learned in Chapter 2, four of the five SmartSuite applications have access to the central spell checker. To learn how to use the spell checker, see Chapter 2. These are the proofing tools that are unique to Ami Pro:

- a thesaurus, which helps you find the best synonym (and sometimes antonym) for a selected word
- a grammar checker, which you can set to different levels of formality and which can display readability statistics

**WORKING TOGETHER** ▲

## Creating a Document with an Ami Pro Style Sheet

A *style sheet* is a template with built-in paragraph styles and a page layout. When you create or edit a document in Ami Pro, a style sheet is always available. Unless you specifically select or create another style sheet, you will use the _default.sty paragraph styles and page layout.

**WORKING TOGETHER**

When you start a new document, select options in the New dialog box and then work in the document using the styles that you have selected. To create an Ami Pro document using a particular style sheet (in this example, _fax3.sty), follow these steps:

**1.** Choose File ➤ New. Ami Pro displays the New dialog box.

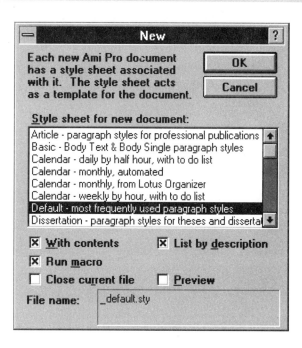

**2.** Check the With Contents check box if you wish the style sheet to open with defined contents.

**3.** Check the Run Macro check box to run any macros associated with the style sheet. If you check this check box, Ami Pro may display a series of dialog boxes to be filled in or accepted by clicking on OK.

AmiPro

**4.** Check the Close Current File check box to close the current document.

**5.** Check the List by Description check box to list the style sheets in this dialog box by description rather than by file name.

**6.** Select a style sheet by clicking on it.

**7.** Check the Preview check box to see a preview of the selected style sheet.

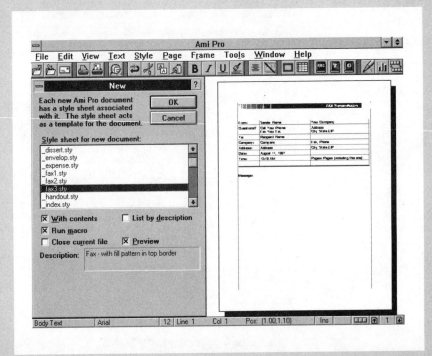

**8.** Click on OK. For some style sheets, Ami Pro displays the Default Information dialog box, in which you either verify or type name, address, and telephone information.

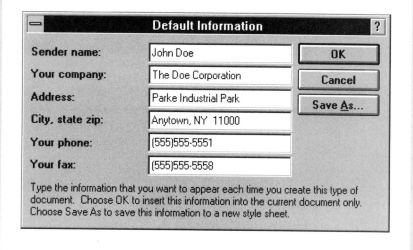

9. Click on OK. For some style sheets, Ami Pro displays the Optional Information dialog box, in which you enter recipient information.

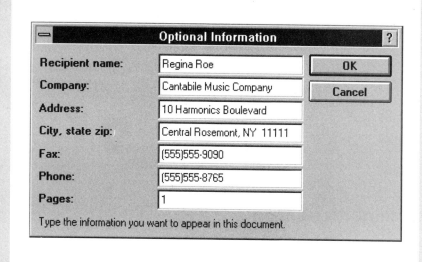

**WORKING TOGETHER** ▲

**10.** Fill in the dialog box and click on OK. Ami Pro fills in the information and the document is ready to print.

A quick way of formatting a document is to apply styles. Simply select a paragraph, click on the Style Status button on the status bar, and select a style.

For more information about using style sheets, see Chapter 9 in the *User's Guide.*

## Using the Thesaurus

Use the thesaurus to substitute synonyms for overused words in a document. You can also use the thesaurus to find a better word— one that conveys your meaning with greater clarity.

Place the insertion point immediately before or after the first or last character in the word, or click on any character within the word, and choose Tools ➤ Thesaurus or click on the Thesaurus SmartIcon. Ami Pro displays the Thesaurus dialog box (Figure 8.9).

**FIGURE 8.9**

The Thesaurus window displays words from which you can choose.

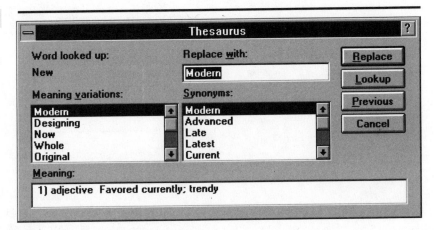

## Running Collect & Copy for 1-2-3

You can link to 1-2-3 in order to insert ranges of contiguous and non-contiguous data from one or more 1-2-3 spreadsheets into an Ami Pro document. To use Collect & Copy for 1-2-3 for Windows, follow these steps:

**1.** Choose Tools ➤ Macros ➤ Playback. Ami Pro displays the Play Macro dialog box. You can also click on the appropriate Smart-Icon in the Bonus Pack SmartIcons set to bypass this dialog box and immediately start the macro.

**2.** Choose 123COPY.SMM and click on OK. Ami Pro starts 1-2-3 for Windows and displays the Collect & Copy dialog box.

**3.** Open a file and select ranges of data while the dialog box remains on display.

**4.** Click on Copy to Ami Pro in the dialog box. In the background, the macro copies the data to Ami Pro.

**5.** Repeat steps 3 and 4 until you have copied all the data that you wish to Ami Pro.

**WORKING TOGETHER** ▲

**6.** Click on Done. A new Collect & Copy dialog box appears.

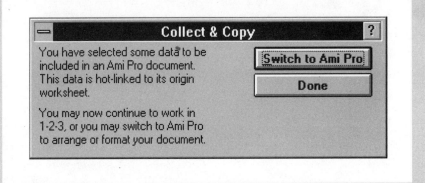

**7.** Click on <u>S</u>witch to Ami Pro to return to Ami Pro. (Otherwise, click on Done to continue working in 1-2-3.) Ami Pro opens a new document and inserts the ranges.

The range or ranges are linked to 1-2-3. To edit the linked data, double-click on it in the Ami Pro document, and 1-2-3 opens for editing.

Use the IMPRCOPY.SMM macro to collect and copy data from Lotus Improv, if it's installed on your computer system.

The Thesaurus window provides these options:

**Word Looked Up:** An area in which the word or phrase that you selected is displayed. If there is no synonym for a selected word, Ami Pro displays an information box (shown on the following page).

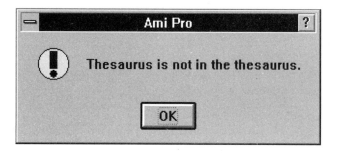

**Replace With**    A text box that displays the suggested replacement word.

**Meaning Variations**    A text box that displays a list of replacement words. When you click on a new word in this list, the Replace With text box also displays the new word.

**Synonyms**    A scroll box that displays a list of synonyms starting with the word in the Replace With and Meaning Variations boxes. When you click on a different word in the Meaning Variations box, the list of synonyms changes.

**Meaning**    A box that displays the part of speech and definition of the highlighted word in the Meaning Variations box.

**Replace**    A button on which you click to replace the selected word in the document with the word in the Replace With text box. Click on Cancel to close the dialog box and return to the document with the re-placement word in place.

**Lookup**    A button on which you click to change the looked-up word and all the other words, lists, and meanings in the dialog box, to the word in the Replace With text box.

**Previous**    A button on which you click to return to the previous looked-up word (and to the other prior words, lists, and meaning). Click repeatedly until the thesaurus displays the first looked-up word.

**AmiPro**

**WORKING TOGETHER**

# Running Collect & Copy for Freelance Graphics

Use the FLWCOPY.SMM macro to switch to Freelance Graphics to insert pages from a Freelance Graphics presentation into an Ami Pro document. To use Collect & Copy for Freelance Graphics for Windows, follow these steps:

1. Start Freelance Graphics and open the desired presentation.

2. Return to Ami Pro and choose Tools ➤ Macros ➤ Playback or click on the appropriate SmartIcon in the Bonus Pack. Ami Pro displays the Play Macro dialog box. You can also click on the appropriate SmartIcon in the Bonus Pack SmartIcons set to bypass this dialog box and immediately start the macro.

3. Choose FLWCOPY.SMM and click on OK. The macro displays Freelance Graphics and displays the Collect & Copy dialog box.

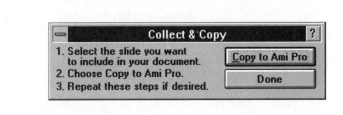

4. Select a page presentation while the dialog box remains on display.

5. Click on Copy to Ami Pro in the dialog box. In the background, the macro copies the data to Ami Pro.

6. Repeat steps 4 and 5 until you have copied all the pages that you wish to have in Ami Pro.

**WORKING TOGETHER** ▲

**7.** Click on Done. A new Collect & Copy dialog box appears.

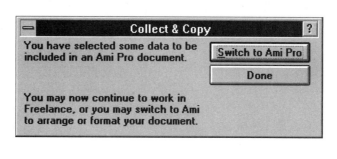

**8.** Click on Switch to Ami Pro to return to Ami Pro. (Otherwise, click on Done to continue working in Freelance Graphics.) Ami Pro opens a new document and inserts the pages.

Once you collect and copy a page, it becomes an Ami Pro graphic and is not linked to Freelance Graphics. If you wish to edit, you can either remain in Ami Pro and edit it as an Ami Pro graphic, or you can return to Freelance Graphics. To edit the page in Freelance Graphics, run FLWCOPY.SMM and re-insert the modified page.

## Checking Your Grammar

An important step in editing your document is to check its grammar—following a set of stringent or casual rules or somewhere in-between. You can also specify that the grammar checker produce a list of readability statistics after it evaluates the document.

 Choose Tools ➤ Grammar Check or click on the Grammar Check SmartIcon to display the Grammar Check dialog box (Figure 8.10).

**AmiPro**

FIGURE 8.10

In the Grammar Check
dialog box, you can
select and customize a
set of rules and set
preferences.

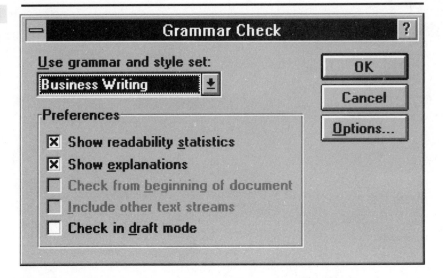

The Grammar Check dialog box contains these options:

**Use Grammar and Style Set**     A drop-down list box that shows eight
sets of grammar (usage and punctuation), sentence style, and word order
(split infinitives, consecutive nouns, and prepositional phrases) rules. Select the set that most closely follows the rules that you want to apply to
the current document. Click on the Options button to view or customize the selected set of rules.

**Show Readability Statistics**     Check this check box to indicate
whether you want to show readability statistics: Gunning's Fog Index,
Flesch-Kincaid Score, Flesch Reading Ease Score, and Flesch Reading
Ease Grade Level. To learn more about these statistics, select the Help
topic *Understanding Readability Statistics*.

**Show Explanations**     Check this box to have the grammar checker dis-
lay explanations of errors and examples of correct usage.

**Check from Beginning of Document**     Check this check box to have
the grammar checker evaluate the complete document from top to bottom.

**Include Other Text Streams**     Check this check box to have the grammar checker evaluate the sentences in the *text stream* (block of text within a frame, header, footer, footnote, or entire document) in which the insertion pointer is located, and to check lower priority text streams as well.

**Check in Draft Mode**     Check this check box to have Ami Pro switch to draft mode before the grammar checker starts its evaluation. If this check box is clear and if the document contains multiple columns or multiple pages, the grammar checker may not evaluate a complete text stream.

Either click on OK or press ↵ to start the grammar checker.

## Running the Grammar Checker

After you start the grammar checker, it will run behind the scenes until it finds a sentence to be brought to your attention. At this point, the grammar checker highlights the sentence in question and displays the Grammar Checker dialog box (Figure 8.11).

These are the options in the Grammar Checker dialog box:

**Suggestions**     A scroll box containing a list of suggestions and explanations.

**Sentence**     A text box in which the sentence appears. The grammar checker highlights the questionable word or phrase.

**FIGURE 8.11**

When the grammar checker finds potential problems with your document, Ami Pro opens the Grammar Checker dialog box.

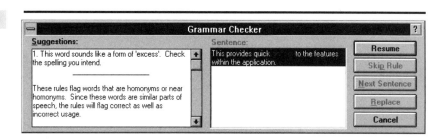

**WORKING TOGETHER** ▲

# Creating an Organization Chart in Ami Pro

You can create an organization chart in an existing Ami Pro document using Freelance Graphics. To use the FLWORG.SMM macro, follow these steps:

1. Move the insertion point to the desired location in your Ami Pro document.

2. Choose Tools ➤ Macros ➤ Playback or click on the appropriate SmartIcon in the Bonus Pack. Ami Pro displays the Play Macro dialog box. You can also click on the appropriate SmartIcon in the Bonus Pack SmartIcons set to bypass this dialog box and immediately start the macro.

**Replacement Options**    A list of suggested replacement sentences from which you can choose.

**Resume**    A button on which you click to ignore the selected sentence and find the next sentence with a possible problem.

**Skip**    A button on which you click to ignore the selected sentence and find the next sentence with a possible problem (including a sentence having the same sort of problem just identified).

**Skip Rule**    A button on which you click to ignore the selected sentence and find the next sentence with a possible problem. (The checker will ignore all further sentences with that sort of problem).

**Next Sentence**    A button on which you click to check the next sentence. This takes some control from the grammar checker, which may have ignored this sentence in its evaluation.

**Replace**    A button on which you click to replace the selected sentence with a replacement sentence in the Replacement Options box.

**3.** Choose FLWORG.SMM and click on OK. The macro opens Freelance Graphics and displays the Organization Chart Gallery dialog box.

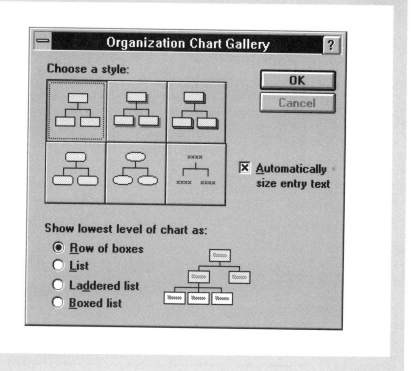

AmiPro

Once the Grammar Checker dialog box appears, the grammar checker evaluates the entire selection or document. At the end of its evaluation, the grammar checker displays the Readability Statistics dialog box (Figure 8.12)

**4.** Choose an organization chart style, lowest level format, and click on OK. Freelance Graphics opens the Organization Chart Entry List.

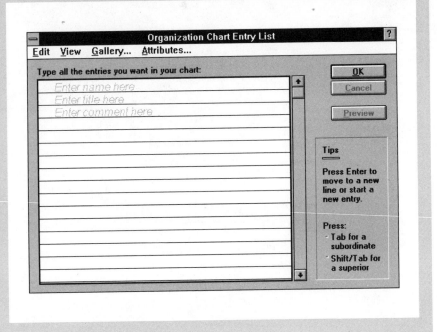

---

**FIGURE 8.12**

The Readability Statistics dialog box shows the word, sentence, paragraph, syllable, and three-syllable word count.

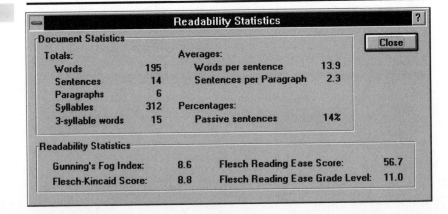

**WORKING TOGETHER** ▲

**5.** Type the name at the top of the organization chart on the Enter Name Here line, press ↵, type the title on the Enter Title Here line, press ↵, and, optionally, type a comment on the Enter Comment Here line, and press ↵. The macro displays the next three lines in the organization chart.

**6.** Type the next name, title, and comment information, pressing ↵ after each line.

**7.** Press Tab to enter information for a subordinate, one level below the current entry. Press Shift+Tab to enter information for a superior, one level above the current entry. You cannot insert more than one top level entry.

**8.** Repeat steps 6 and 7 until you have typed all the organization chart information.

**9.** Click on OK. The macro inserts the organization chart in a frame into your document at the insertion point.

When you create an organization chart, the original remains in Freelance Graphics. You can save it or close Freelance Graphics without saving it.

**TIP**

To keep track of the current page number in a long document, look at the Page Status button on the right side of the status bar.

## Customizing Grammar Checker Rules

You can adjust the grammar checker rules to fit your grammatical strengths and weaknesses. When you have finished checking or clearing the check boxes for a particular set of rules, you can select another set and repeat the process. If you have a question about any of the options, click on it and read the text in the Explanation box. When you have finished, click on Save to save the set under its original name or Save as to save the set under a new name.

**AmiPro**

# Using Ami Pro's Equation Editor

You can enter equations in an Ami Pro document by using the Equation editor. Choose Tools ➤ Equations, and Ami Pro adds a new set of icons to the application window. To use the Equation editor to build an equation, click on one icon at a time, and then fill in the input blocks within the templates. To edit an existing equation, double-click on it, and Ami Pro displays the Equation editor icons to the application window.

The Equation editor offers six categories of icons:

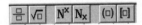

The template icons are the building blocks of the equation. Click on an icon and fill in the input boxes with your values. As you add to your equation, the Equation editor adjusts the size of the templates. From left to right, template icons are Fraction, Radical, Superscript, Subscript, Parentheses, and Brackets.

The operator icons create summation and integral operators at the insertion point:

The toggle icons allow you to switch between inserting mathematical symbols (red italicized characters) and text (black normal characters).

Clicking on the asterisk icon enables you to show and hide input boxes and matrix lines.

The dialog box icons open dialog boxes from which you can select special symbols, matrices, functions, space, labels, and so on:

The symbol icons allow you to insert one of 18 common symbols into a formula:

The pulldown box icons open boxes from which you can select lowercase Greek, uppercase Greek, binary operators, binary symbols, single and bi-directional arrows, miscellaneous characters, and left and right delimiters to be inserted into a formula:

For more information about using the Equation editor, see Chapter 30 of the *User's Guide* or look up *Equations Contents* in the Help facility, if you are using the Equation Editor, or *Creating an Equation* if you are not.

**AmiPro**

**WARNING** Clicking on the <u>S</u>ave button changes a set of rules permanently. It's far safer to click on the Save <u>a</u>s button and save
the set under a new name. This action preserves the original
settings.

These are the grammar checker sets:

**All Rules**     20 of 20 grammar rules checked, 20 of 20 style rules
checked, flags all split infinitives, flags 3 or more consecutive nouns,
flags 3 or more prepositional phrases in a row

**Technical Writing**     20 of 20 grammar rules checked, 18 of 20 style
rules checked, flags split infinitives with 3 or more intervening tokens,
flags 5 or more consecutive nouns, flags 5 or more prepositional phrases
in a row

**Business Writing**     20 of 20 grammar rules checked, 14 of 20 style
rules checked, flags all split infinitives, flags 4 or more consecutive
nouns, flags 4 or more prepositional phrases in a row. Figures 8.13, 8.14,
and 8.15 show grammar rules, style rules, and word order rules for business writing.

**FIGURE 8.13**

The Grammar and
Style Options dialog
box showing the
grammar rules for
business writing

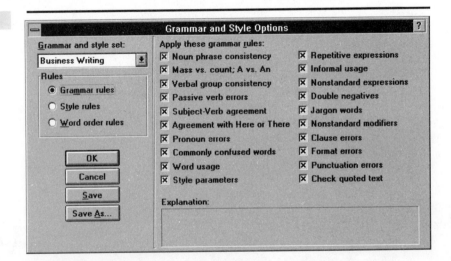

**FIGURE 8.14**

The Grammar and
Style Options dialog
box showing the style
rules for business
writing

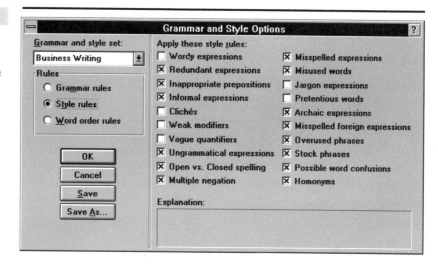

**FIGURE 8.15**

The Grammar and
Style Options dialog
box showing the
word order rules for
business writing

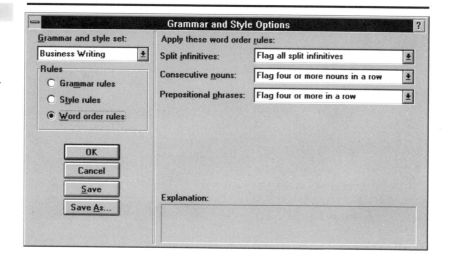

**AmiPro.**

**Formal Writing**    20 of 20 grammar rules checked, 18 of 20 style rules
checked, flags all split infinitives, does not flag consecutive nouns, does
not flag prepositional phrases

**Academic Writing** 19 of 20 grammar rules checked, 18 of 20 style rules checked, flags all split infinitives, flags 3 or more consecutive nouns, flags 3 or more prepositional phrases in a row

**Legal Writing** 19 of 20 grammar rules checked, 16 of 20 style rules checked, flags all split infinitives, flags 4 or more consecutive nouns, flags 3 or more prepositional phrases in a row

**Casual Writing** 15 of 20 grammar rules checked, 8 of 20 style rules checked, flags split infinitives with 2 more intervening tokens, flags 5 or more consecutive nouns, flags 5 or more prepositional phrases in a row

**Fiction Writing** 15 of 20 grammar rules checked, 11 of 20 style rules checked, does not flag split infinitives, does not flag consecutive nouns, does not flag prepositional phrases

To customize rules for the grammar checker, follow these steps:

1. Choose Tools ➤ Grammar Check. Ami Pro displays the Grammar Check dialog box.

2. Click on the Options button. Ami Pro opens the Grammar and Style Options dialog box.

3. If the selection in the Grammar and Style Set drop-down list box is not your choice, choose another level of grammar and style rules.

4. Select settings in the Apply These Grammar Rules check boxes to ease or tighten the rules. When you check or clear a check box, Ami Pro explains the option.

5. If you want to reset the rules to the default settings, select from the Grammar and Style Set drop-down list box.

6. When you have completed customizing the rules, Select OK or press ↵. Ami Pro returns to the Grammar/Options dialog box.

7. Select OK or press ↵. Ami Pro returns to the Grammar dialog box.

8. Click on Close.

## Checking Document Information

Ami Pro automatically tracks your document by keeping information such as the date and time of creation, the date and time of your last revision, the total number of revisions, and the time that you have spent in working on the document. You can also see the number of pages, words, and characters, and the size of the document (in kilobytes).

To open the Doc Info dialog box (Figure 8.16), choose File ➤ Doc Info. Then type a description and keywords in the Description and Keywords text boxes so that you can find the file at a later time. Whenever you open the dialog box, click on the Update button to update the information in the Statistics group.

**FIGURE 8.16**

The Doc Info dialog box displays and allows you to add information about the current document.

| Doc Info | |
|---|---|
| File name: | MEMO0810.SAM |
| Directory: | C:\AMIPRO\DOCS |
| Style sheet: | None |

Description:

Memo to Asbark Beeley

Keywords:

☐ Lock for annotations
☐ Lock revision marking on
☒ Run frame macros

Import files:

**Statistics**

| | | | | |
|---|---|---|---|---|
| No. of pages: | 1 | Size (K): | 5 | |
| No. of words: | 95 | | | |
| No. of chars: | 511 | Update | | |

| | |
|---|---|
| Date created: | 8/10/97 |
| Time created: | 1:43 PM |
| Date last revised: | 8/10/97 |
| Time last revised: | 1:47 PM |
| Total revisions: | 1 |
| Total editing time: | 3 |

OK
Cancel
Other Fields...

**AmiPro**

# 9

# Formatting and Editing a Document

Once you have typed a document, your work is far from done. You'll want to change the typeface (font) and size of some text, such as headings and special terms; center or justify the alignment of selected paragraphs; or even add page numbers and headers and footers.

In this chapter, you'll find out about many of Ami Pro's formatting and editing functions (and some special shortcuts). Remember that if you have any questions about editing features common to most SmartSuite applications, you can turn to Chapter 3.

 **In most cases, you must be in Layout Mode to format text and paragraphs. To check your current mode, open the View menu and look for a checkmark preceding the Layout Mode command. If the checkmark precedes another command, choose View ➤ Layout Mode to change the mode.**

## formatting Text

Ami Pro has three basic levels of formatting: document-wide (page), paragraph, and character. *Document-wide formatting* encompasses the entire document page by page; *paragraph formatting* changes the appearance of one or more selected paragraphs; and *character formatting* determines the appearance of selected characters, words, lines, or sentences. You'll find all Ami Pro character and paragraph formatting commands on the Text menu, and the document-wide or page formatting commands on the Page menu.

Document-wide formatting controls margins, paper dimensions and orientation, the insertion of headers and footers, page and line numbering, and other attributes that apply to every page of a document.

**TIP** Choose Tools ➤ User Setup and click on the Options button to change default document-wide attributes. For example, you can specify hyphenation options, control widows and orphan lines, and set kerning (the space between characters in a line). For information about customizing the environment for each of the SmartSuite applications, see Appendix C.

Paragraph formatting controls selected text, as short as a one-word heading or as long as the entire document, ending with a paragraph mark. Using paragraph formatting, you can align text against the left or right margin, both margins, or from the center point between the margins; you can control indentation—of the first line of a paragraph, all but the first line, or all lines; and the spacing between lines in the selection.

Character formatting changes the way that selected text looks. Ami Pro allows you to enhance characters (with boldface, italics, single underlines, or color), apply special effects (such as superscript, subscript, double underlines, and strikethroughs), and modify the design and size of the characters (by changing the font or point size).

## Enhancing Text

Several Text menu commands allow you to enhance text in a document. To change the look of text in an Ami Pro document, select it, and either click on a SmartIcon, choose a menu command, or press a shortcut key. Table 9.1 describes Ami Pro's text enhancement commands.

**NOTE** Some of the SmartIcons in Table 9.1 are available only if you choose Tools ➤ SmartIcons and insert these custom SmartIcons in a set. For instructions on customizing your SmartIcons, see Appendix C.

Figure 9.1 shows a memorandum with some character enhancements that emphasize the message.

**AmiPro**

**TABLE 9.1:** Ami Pro's Text Enhancement Options

| SMARTICON | ENHANCEMENT | COMMAND | SHORTCUT KEY |
|---|---|---|---|
| | Changes the font, point size, or color | Text ➤ Font | N/A |
| | Increases the point size | Text ➤ Font, then select Size or Points; or, Text ➤ Font Up (displayed once you click on the SmartIcon) | N/A |
| | Decreases the point size | Text ➤ Font, then select Size or Points; or Text ➤ Font Down (displayed once you click on the SmartIcon) | N/A |
| | Removes boldface, italics, and underlines | Text ➤ Normal | Ctrl+N |
| | Applies or removes boldface | Text ➤ Bold | Ctrl+B |
| | Applies or removes italics | Text ➤ Italic | Ctrl+I |
| | Applies or removes single underlines | Text ➤ Underline | Ctrl+U |
| | Applies or removes an underline from selected words | Text ➤ Word Underline | Ctrl+W |
| | Displays selected characters in uppercase | Text ➤ Caps ➤ Upper Case | N/A |
| N/A | Displays selected characters in lowercase | Text ➤ Caps ➤ Lower Case | N/A |

**TABLE 9.1:** Ami Pro's Text Enhancement Options (continued)

| SMARTICON | ENHANCEMENT | COMMAND | SHORTCUT KEY |
|---|---|---|---|
| Abc | Displays selected words with initial uppercase and remaining lowercase | Text ➤ Caps ➤ Initial Caps | N/A |
| N/A | Displays selected characters in small uppercase | Text ➤ Caps ➤ Small Caps | N/A |
| Sˢ | Displays selected characters either above or on the baseline | Text ➤ Special Effects; check or clear Superscript | N/A |
| Sₛ | Displays selected characters either below or on the baseline | Text ➤ Special Effects; check or clear Subscript | N/A |
| U | Applies or removes a double underline | Text ➤ Special Effects; check or clear Double Underline | N/A |
| N/A | Applies or removes a line through the selection | Text ➤ Special Effects; check or clear Strikethrough | N/A |
| N/A | Applies or removes a defined character overstriking the selection | Text ➤ Special Effects; check or clear Overstrike character and enter a character in the text box | N/A |
| | Applies the format of the prior selection to the next selection | Text ➤ Fast Format | Ctrl+T |

**FIGURE 9.1**

A sample
memorandum with
several kinds of
character
enhancements

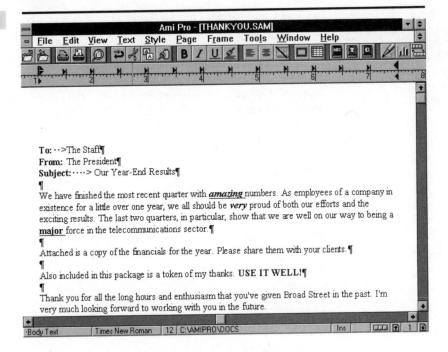

## Using the Fast Format Feature

Using either a SmartIcon or a menu command, you can copy all the formats from a selection to another selection in any open Ami Pro document. Note that

- If your selection contains separate formats (for example, the first word selected is boldfaced, and the second word is italicized), Fast Format uses the formats of the first word selected.

- If you select either a paragraph or less than one word, Ami Pro displays a dialog box (Figure 9.2).

To use the Fast Format feature, simply follow these steps:

**1.** Select a word that has the formats to be copied.

 **2.** Either click on the Fast Format SmartIcon, choose <u>T</u>ext ➤ Fas<u>t</u> Format, or press Ctrl+T.

**FIGURE 9.2**

The Fast Format dialog box prompts you to make the proper selection for fast formatting.

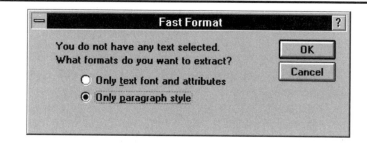

**3.** Drag the paint brush mouse pointer across any text that you wish to reformat.

**4.** When you are finished, click on the Fast Format icon or press Esc to turn off fast formatting.

## Adding Special Characters

In many documents, you'll need to add a character that you won't find on your keyboard. For example, three very common special characters are the copyright symbol, the trademark, and the registered trademark. If you are writing a technical manual or self-publishing a book, you'll need to embed at least one of these symbols—the copyright. Another reason for inserting special characters in a document is for emphasis. For example, you may wish to point to an important paragraph by placing a symbol, such as a Windows Wingdings arrow, to its left.

Ami Pro provides three methods to add special characters: by clicking on a SmartIcon, using the Windows Character Map, and inserting an ANSI (American National Standards Institute) symbol via the numeric keypad.

### Inserting Special Characters with SmartIcons

Ami Pro provides SmartIcons on which you can click to add a copyright, registered copyright, or trademark, respectively, to your document at the insertion point. You can click on the Typeset SmartIcon to convert the quotation marks, dashes, and apostrophes in the current document to their typeset equivalents, as shown in Table 9.2.

**AmiPro**

**TABLE 9.2:** Typographic Symbols

| NAME | TYPOGRAPHIC SYMBOL | CONVERTED FROM |
|------|--------------------|----------------|
| Apostrophe | ' | ' |
| Quotation Marks | " " | " " |
| Dash | – | - |
| Em Dash | —— | -- |

## Inserting Special Characters with the Windows Character Map

With Character Map, Windows provides as many groups of special characters as you have fonts installed on your computer system. To insert a special character, follow these steps:

1. Press either Alt+Esc or Ctrl+Esc to return to Program Manager. (For information about running Windows, see Appendix B.)

2. Open the Accessories Group window in which Character Map appears as a default.

3. Double-click on the Character Map icon. Windows opens the Character Map application window (Figure 9.3).

4. Select the desired font from the Font drop-down list box. Whenever you select a different font, some of the characters displayed in the application window disappear and new characters appear, because not every font can support every special character.

5. Double-click on the special character, or click on the character and then click on the Select button. (To see an enlarged view of a character, move the mouse pointer to the desired character and then click the left mouse button.) Windows moves the character into the Characters to Copy text box.

**FIGURE 9.3**

The Character Map
window

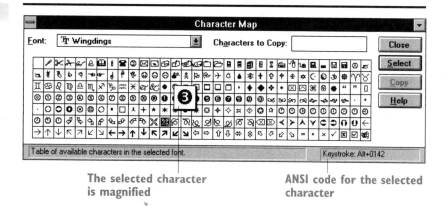

The selected character
is magnified

ANSI code for the selected
character

**TIP**   To see the keystroke equivalent and ANSI code of the character, see the bottom-right side of the screen. You can refer to this code when embedding characters with the numeric keypad.

**6.** Repeat steps 2 and 3 to accumulate as many characters as you want.

**WARNING**   If you change to a different font after selecting one or more characters, all the accumulated characters in the Characters to Copy text box disappear.

**7.** Select the Copy button to copy the characters to the Clipboard.

**8.** Press Alt+Esc or Ctrl+Esc to return to your document.

**9.** Move the insertion point to the location in which you want the characters placed.

**10.** Choose Edit ➤ Paste, click on the Paste button, or press Ctrl+V.

## Inserting Special Characters Using the Numeric Keypad

Most standard text fonts have their own unique set of ANSI symbols. When you find a chart with the symbol that you wish to embed, make sure that you

change the surrounding text to that font (otherwise, you may embed a different symbol), and then follow these steps:

1. Press the NumLock key (because the number keys on the numeric keypad must be active).

2. Press and hold down the Alt key.

3. On the numeric keypad, type the three- or four-digit ANSI code for the special character.

4. Release the Alt key. Ami Pro displays the symbol that you entered.

5. Make sure that you press the NumLock key again to turn off the numeric keypad letter keys.

# Viewing and Hiding Nonprinting Symbols

Ami Pro allows you to show nonprinting symbols such as paragraph marks, tab symbols, page breaks, and embedded headers, footers, and rulers. For example, Figure 9.1 shows a document as it will print; there are no nonprinting symbols in evidence. Figure 9.4 shows the same document with nonprinting symbols turned on. Revealing nonprinting symbols allows you to verify why a page has ended and another started, or the location of a DDE link. Table 9.3 illustrates each nonprinting symbol and how it is embedded in the document.

To reveal or hide paragraph nonprinting symbols, either choose View ➤ View Preferences or click on the View Preferences SmartIcon. In the View Preferences dialog box (Figure 9.5), check or clear Tabs & Returns and/or Marks.

If you want to reveal or display tabs and paragraph returns or marks (column breaks, page breaks, inserted page layouts, inserted rulers, floating headers and footers, and DDE text links), click on the Tabs & Returns or Marks SmartIcons, respectively.

**FIGURE 9.4**

The sample memorandum with non-printing symbols displayed

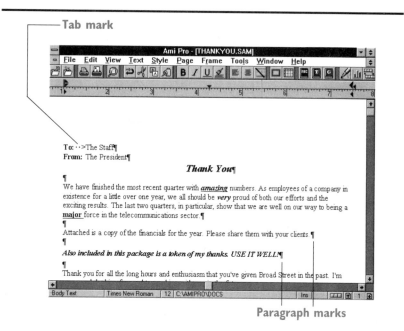

Tab mark

Paragraph marks

**TABLE 9.3:** Ami Pro Nonprinting Symbols

| SYMBOL | TYPE OF MARK | HOW IT'S INSERTED |
|---|---|---|
| ¶ | Paragraph mark | Press ↵. |
| · · · ·≻ | Tab mark | Press Tab. |
| ▥ | Inserted ruler | Select a paragraph and change a margin setting or tab stop on the ruler. |
| ↯ | Page break | Select a location for the break, choose Page ➤ Breaks, and click on Insert Page Break. |
| ⊞ | Column break | Select a location for the break, choose Page ➤ Breaks, and click on Insert Column Break. |

AmiPro

**TABLE 9.3:** Ami Pro Nonprinting Symbols (continued)

| SYMBOL | TYPE OF MARK | HOW IT'S INSERTED |
|---|---|---|
| ⬜ | Inserted page layout | Select a location for the layout, choose Page ➤ Insert Page Layout ➤ Insert. |
| ⬚ | Floating header | Select a location for the header, choose Page ➤ Header/Footer, click on Floating Header/Footer, select Insert and Floating Header. |
| ⬚ | Floating footer | Select a location for the footer, choose Page ➤ Header/Footer, click on Floating Header/Footer, select Insert and Floating Footers. |
| ◣ | DDE link | In another Windows application, select an object to be linked, choose Edit ➤ Copy, and minimize or keep the application running. In Ami Pro, select a location for the link, and choose Edit ➤ Paste Link. |

**FIGURE 9.5**

The View Preferences dialog box in which you can customize many viewing options

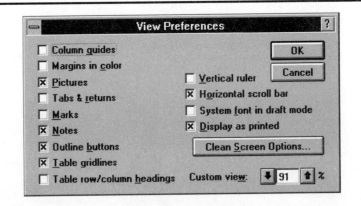

# formatting a Paragraph

Paragraph formatting determines the alignment of text between the left and right margins, the space between the lines of text in the paragraph, page breaks that occur within the paragraph, paragraph indentations, and paragraph enhancements (borders, lines, and shading).

To format one paragraph, place the insertion point anywhere in the paragraph. To format multiple paragraphs, make sure that you select all or part of them all using either the mouse or the keyboard. Ami Pro provides several methods for applying most paragraph formats: the ruler, SmartIcons, keyboard shortcuts, or the Text menu.

## Aligning Paragraphs

Unless you specifically change settings, Ami Pro aligns text along the left margin and does not align with the right margin. Figure 9.6 shows you a sample of each type of paragraph alignment. Table 9.4 summarizes Ami Pro's paragraph alignments.

 **NOTE** Some of the SmartIcons in Table 9.4 are available only if you choose Tools ➤ SmartIcons and insert these custom SmartIcons in a set. For instructions on customizing your SmartIcons, see Appendix C.

## Changing the Spacing between Lines

In this section, you'll find out how to adjust the *leading*, which is the spacing between the lines within a paragraph. Leading not only includes the text on a line but also the white space between the top of the characters in the line to the bottom of the characters in the previous line. As you increase the point size of selected characters, Ami Pro adds extra white space.

For most business documents, you'll use single spacing, but for manuscripts, double spacing is the rule. You can use line spacing to emphasize a particular

**AmiPro**

**315**

**FIGURE 9.6**

A sample document showing the four types of paragraph alignment

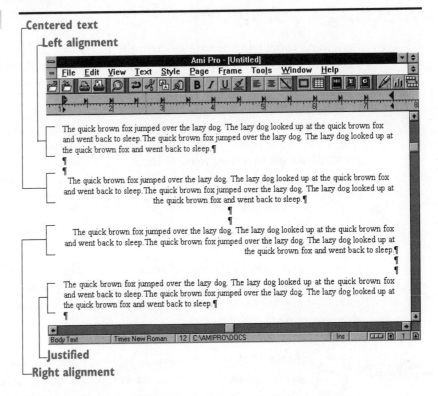

Centered text

Left alignment

Justified

Right alignment

**TABLE 9.4:** Ami Pro's Paragraph Alignment Options

| SMARTICON | FORMATTING | COMMAND | SHORTCUT KEY |
|---|---|---|---|
| | Align the text in the selected paragraphs with the left margin, leaving the text at the right margin ragged. | Text ➤ Alignment ➤ Left | Ctrl+L |
| | Align the text in the selected paragraphs along the center point of the page, leaving the text at both the left and right margins ragged. | Text ➤ Alignment ➤ Center | Ctrl+E |

**TABLE 9.4:** Ami Pro's Paragraph Alignment Options

| SMARTICON | FORMATTING | COMMAND | SHORTCUT KEY |
|---|---|---|---|
|  | Align the text in the selected paragraphs with the right margin, leaving the text at the left margin ragged. | Text ➤ Alignment ➤ Right | Ctrl+R |
|  | Align the text in the selected paragraphs with both the left and right margins. | Text ➤ Alignment ➤ Justify | Ctrl+J |

paragraph within a document. For example, if you are quoting a reviewer or introducing a new product, inserting extra space above and below the selected paragraph almost forces the reader to look at the important text. Ami Pro's default line-spacing setting is single spacing.

Choose Text ➤ Spacing to choose line spacing. In the Spacing dialog box (Figure 9.7), choose from one of these options:

| | |
|---|---|
| Single | single spacing, the default |
| 1½ | an extra half line between the selected lines of text |
| Double | an extra line between the selected lines of text |
| Custom | a measurement that you set (0.05–22 inches) |
| in | click to cycle through the measurement units listed in Table 9.5. |
| Revert to Style | returns to the spacing for the style of the paragraph |

**AmiPro**

**317**

FIGURE 9.7

The Spacing dialog box, which provides options buttons for setting line spacing for a selection

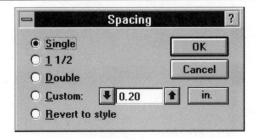

**TABLE 9.5:** Ami Pro's Units of Measure

| NAME | TYPE OF MEASURE | EQUIVALENT IN INCHES |
|------|-----------------|----------------------|
| in. | inches (the default) | N/A |
| cm. | centimeters | .3937 inch |
| picas | picas | $\frac{1}{6}$ inch |
| pt. | points | $\frac{1}{72}$ inch |

## Indenting Paragraphs

Paragraph indentation moves either the entire paragraph or the first line away from the left and/or right margin. You can indent selected paragraphs from 0 inches to 22 inches.

Ami Pro provides three ways to indent paragraphs: SmartIcons, the Text menu, and the ruler. Table 9.6 describes three paragraph indentation types: block indents, first line indents, and hanging indents.

### Indenting Paragraphs with SmartIcons

Use the SmartIcons documented in Table 9.6 to indent in 0.5 inch increments. Select a paragraph and repeatedly click on a SmartIcon to increase the indentation setting.

## Indenting Paragraphs with a Menu Command

Choose Text ➤ Indention to open the Indention dialog box (Figure 9.8), which allows you to indent using precise measurements.

**TABLE 9.6:** Ami Pro's Paragraph Indentation

| SMARTICON | NAME | DESCRIPTION | EXAMPLE OF USAGE |
|---|---|---|---|
| | Block Indent | Indents all lines in a paragraph from the left margin and/or right margin | Use block indents to emphasize the paragraph and make it stand out. |
| | First Line Indent | Indents just the first line in a paragraph | Use the first-line indent when there is little or no spacing between paragraphs and you want to differentiate between paragraphs. |
| | Hanging Indent | Indents the first line in a paragraph closer to the left margin than the rest of the lines | Hanging indents are ideal for bulleted and numbered lists. |

**FIGURE 9.8**

The Indention dialog box, which is set for a first line ident

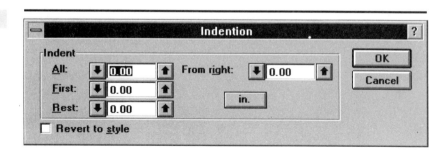

319

Using a SmartIcon to indent a selected paragraph fills in the All, First, and Rest text/list boxes in the Indentation dialog box. This means that you can open the Indentation dialog box, read the current values, and figure out how to change the settings for the desired type of indentation.

To create a block indent, select or type a value from 0 to 22 in the All text/list box. (You can also set a block indent by selecting or typing identical numbers in the First and Rest text/list boxes.) The higher the number you type, the farther the indent is from the left margin.

To create a hanging indent, make sure that the number you select or type in the Rest text/list box is greater than the value in the First text/list box.

To create a first line indent, make sure that the number you select or type in the First text/list box is greater than the value in the Rest text/list box.

To indent selected paragraphs from the right margin, type or select a value from 0 to 22 in the From Right text/list box. The higher the number you type, the farther the indent is from the right margin.

## Indenting Paragraphs with the Ruler

The quickest (and most visual way) to indent paragraphs is to use the ruler (Figure 9.9). Move the mouse pointer on the ruler and drag the small markers until you set the selected indents as desired.

**FIGURE 9.9**

The Ami Pro ruler showing margin, indent, and tab markers

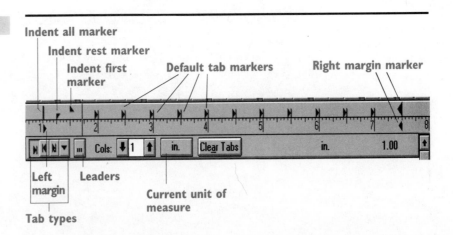

At the left margin of the ruler are two markers—the top marker is the first-line indent marker, and the bottom marker is the left margin marker. To indent paragraphs from the left or the right, simply drag the markers on the ruler to the desired indentation location.

To set a block indent from the left margin, point to the left side of the first-line marker or left margin marker and drag. Both markers move simultaneously.

To set a hanging indent, first set a block indent that marks the indentation of all the lines except the first in the paragraph. Then point to the right side of the first-line marker and drag to the left (toward the left margin).

To set a first line indent, first set a block indent that marks the indentation of all the lines except the first in the paragraph. Then point to the right side of the first-line marker and drag to the right (away from the left margin).

At the right margin is a single right margin marker. To indent paragraphs from the right, move the right margin marker.

 **You can also set a first-line indent for a paragraph by pressing the Tab key with the insertion point in front of the first character in the paragraph.**

## Setting and Using Tabs

Although you can indent paragraphs by pressing the Tab key, the most important use for tabs is to align text within paragraphs. For example, you can use tabs to align the To, From, and Subject lines. To insert a tab, move the insertion point to the desired location and press the Tab key.

Use the ruler to set and clear tab positions, to determine the type of *leader* (the dotted lines between a title and a page number in some tables), and to change tab alignment: left, right, numeric (decimal), or center. Table 9.7 describes each tab type and its button on the ruler.

  **If the ruler is not displayed between the SmartIcons and document area, choose Yiew ➤ Show Ruler. (To hide the ruler, choose Yiew ➤ Hide Ruler.)**

**TABLE 9.7:** Ami Pro's Tab Types

| BUTTON | TAB TYPE | DESCRIPTION |
|---|---|---|
| ⊩ | Left tab | The first character in the character string following the tab symbol aligns with the tab position; the remaining characters flow toward the right margin. |
| ⊩ | Right tab | The last character in the character string preceding the tab symbol aligns with the tab position; the remaining characters flow toward the left margin. |
| ⊮ | Numeric (decimal) tab | Any decimal point is aligned with the tab position. The remaining digits flow both left and right from the decimal point. If there is no decimal point, the character string is aligned as if the numeric tab were a right tab. |
| ▼ | Center tab | The character string is centered on the tab stop. |

To set tab positions, follow these steps:

**1.** Click on the ruler to display additional buttons.

**2.** Click on a tab type button, if needed.

**3.** Move the mouse pointer to the top part of the ruler and click on the desired position of the new tab. You can also drag existing tabs along the ruler to new locations.

**4.** Repeat the preceding steps to insert additional tabs.

To clear an individual tab symbol, just drag it off the ruler. To clear all tab symbols, click on the ruler, and click on the Clear Tabs button.

## Using Paragraph Styles

Ami Pro provides predetermined paragraph styles and allows you to create and modify styles. (These styles are described in Table 9.8) For detailed information on Ami Pro styles, see Chapter 9 in the *User's Guide* and the Help topic "Modifying a Paragraph Style."

**TABLE 9.8:** Ami Pro Predefined Paragraph Styles

| STYLE | SHORTCUT KEY | ATTRIBUTES |
|---|---|---|
| Body Text | F2 | Times New Roman, 12 point type, left aligned |
| Body Single | F3 | Times New Roman, 12 point type, left aligned |
| Bullet | F4 | bulleted list having small bullets |
| Bullet I | F5 | bulleted list having diamond-shaped bullets |
| Number List | F6 | numbered list |
| Subhead | F7 | bold italicized Times New Roman, 12 point |
| Title | F8 | bold centered Arial, 18 point |
| Header | F9 | floating Times New Roman, 12 point |
| Footer | F11 | floating Times New Roman, 12 point |

**AmiPro**

## Applying Paragraph Styles

To apply a paragraph style, follow these steps:

1. Select the paragraph to be styled and click on the Style Status button. Ami Pro opens the Style Status button list.

2. Click on a style name. Ami Pro changes the style for the selected paragraph, closes the Style Status button list, and displays the name of the style on the Style Status button.

**WORKING TOGETHER** ▲

# Using Elements from Ami Pro Style Sheets in Your Other Documents

Ami Pro style sheets include built-in elements that you can add to other documents. For example, using the _calday.sty style sheet, you can start with a table filled with gray rather than choosing Table ➤ Lines & Color to define the fill pattern.

Ami Pro style sheets offer these elements and attributes:

**_calday.sty** or **_calwk.sty**     A three-column table with the first column filled with gray and the second and third with printed horizontal lines. (You could use this style sheet to create a shopping list.)

**_calmon.sty**     A month calendar with landscape orientation. Elements include black bar with reverse video and a grid into which you can insert numbers.

**_fax2.sty**     A fax cover sheet, which you can convert to letterhead stationery.

**_fax3.sty**     A fax cover sheet with a series of graphics ranging from light gray to black. Insert the graphics at the top of letterhead stationery.

**_invoice.sty**     An invoice style sheet with self-totaling columns. Use this to accumulate the totals from any list.

**_memo2.sty**     A memorandum style sheet, which contains a shadow box with the word *MEMO*. Copy the shadow box into another document and change the word *MEMO* to other text.

**_memo3.sty**     A memorandum style sheet with a double-line border. Copy the border into a letterhead document.

**_memo4.sty**     A memorandum style sheet with a sawtooth border. Copy the border into a letterhead document.

**WORKING TOGETHER**

**_memo5.sty**     A memorandum style sheet with a black box and filled border. Copy both elements into a document in which you want to have a unique letterhead.

**_memo6.sty**     A memorandum style sheet, with a diamond border. Copy the border into a letterhead document.

**_newslt2.sty**     A newsletter style sheet with a filled rectangle with rounded corners. Copy the rectangle into a memo or document in which you want to highlight text.

**_newslt5.sty**     A newsletter style sheet with a pen graphic. Insert the graphic into a document as you would a piece of clip art.

**_overhd1.sty**     An overhead style sheet with a numbered graphic. Insert the graphic into a document and type in text.

**_report2.sty**     A report style sheet, with reverse video headings in boxes. Use the boxes to hold headings in another document.

**_report3.sty**     A report style sheet, with the main heading in a shadow box. Use the shadow box as the heading for a formal invitation.

**_report4.sty**     A report style sheet, with reverse video headings in wide boxes. Use the boxes to hold headings in another document.

**AmiPro**

## Creating a Style

There are two ways to create a new paragraph style:

- Base the style on the format that you or someone else have applied to a selected paragraph.
- Base the style on an existing style, and then modify the new style.

### Creating a Style Based on Selected Text

To create a style based on formatted text, follow these steps:

**1.** Format the text on which you'd like to define the new style.

**2.** Select the newly formatted text.

**3.** Choose <u>S</u>tyle ➤ <u>C</u>reate Style. Ami Pro displays the Create Style dialog box (Figure 9.10).

**4.** Type the new style name in the <u>N</u>ew Style text box.

**5.** Click on Selected <u>T</u>ext.

**6.** Click on <u>C</u>reate. Ami Pro assigns a function key to the new style, adds the new style name (and its assigned function key) to the Style Status button list, and closes the dialog box.

### Creating and Modifying a Style Based on an Existing Style

To create a style based on an existing style, follow these steps:

**1.** Choose <u>S</u>tyle ➤ <u>C</u>reate Style. Ami Pro displays the Create Style dialog box.

**2.** Type the new style name in the <u>N</u>ew Style text box.

**3.** Click on <u>S</u>tyle and select the style on which you wish to base the new style.

**4.** Click on Modify. Lotus opens the Modify Style dialog box (Figure 9.11).

To open the Modify Style dialog box, move the mouse pointer to any part of the current document and click the right mouse button, press Ctrl+A, or click on the Modify SmartIcon.

**5.** Click on a button in the Modify group:

◼ Font enables you to modify the font (Face), the point size (Size and Points), colors, and enhancement attributes.

◼ Alignment enables you to change, add, or clear tab stops, change or clear paragraph indentation, and modify paragraph alignment.

◼ Spacing enables you to modify line spacing, paragraph spacing, and kerning.

◼ Breaks enables you to set page and column breaks before, after, or within paragraphs, and to keep this paragraph with the previous paragraph and/or the next paragraph.

◼ Bullets & Numbers enables you to change attributes for bulleted and numbered lists.

**FIGURE 9.11**

The Modify Style dialog box allows you to change font, alignment, spacing, breaks, bullets and numbers, lines, and tables.

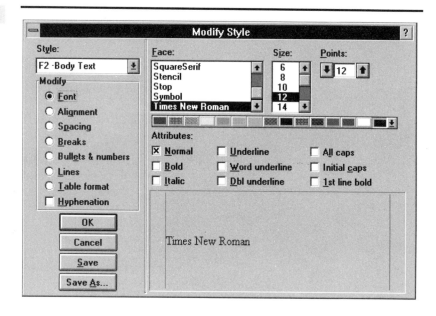

■ Lines enables you to add lines above and/or below a paragraph and to change line attributes.

■ Table Format enables you to define cell attributes for tables.

■ Hyphenation enables you to set or clear hyphenation.

Ami Pro opens the Modify Style dialog box for the selected Modify option. Figure 9.12 shows the Modify Style dialog box for bullets and numbers.

6. When you have completed your style changes, click on OK to save the style and close the dialog box, Save to save the style and keep the dialog box open, or Save as to save the style under a new name and keep the dialog box open. Ami Pro assigns a function key to the new style, and adds the new style name (and its assigned function key) to the Style Status button list.

Figure 9.13 shows the sample memorandum with both text and paragraph formats.

**FIGURE 9.12**

The Modify Style dialog box, in which you can define attributes for bulleted and numbered lists

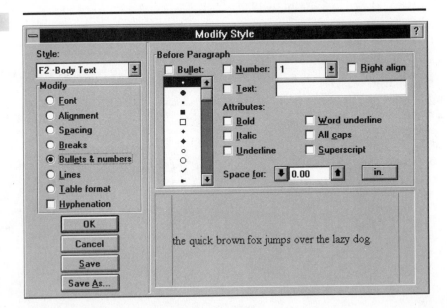

**FIGURE 9.13**

The sample memorandum with both text and paragraph formats applied

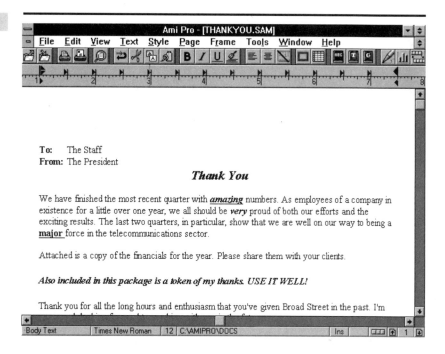

## formatting a Document

Document-wide (page) formatting controls the look of all the pages in a document. You can specify document-wide formats by using SmartIcons, the Page menu, and in many cases the ruler.

### Specifying Margins

Margins determine the space between the edge of the page and the text on the page. Ami Pro's initial margin settings for all four margins—top, bottom, left, and right—are 1 inch. The total of the left and right margin settings cannot be greater than the width of the paper, and the total of the top and bottom margin settings cannot be greater than the length of the paper.

Ami Pro allows you to set all four margins by clicking on the Modify Page Layout SmartIcon or choosing Page ➤ Modify Page Layout. You can use the ruler to set the left and right margins.

**WORKING TOGETHER**

# Creating a Newsletter with an Ami Pro Style Sheet

Ami Pro offers you a choice of five newsletter style sheets, ranging from one to three columns and incorporating frames for graphics. Creating a newsletter is just like creating another Ami Pro document using a style sheet; select the style, supply the information in dialog boxes, and fill in the document itself. To create a newsletter using the _newslt4.sty style sheet, follow these steps:

**1.** Choose File ➤ New. Ami Pro displays the New dialog box.

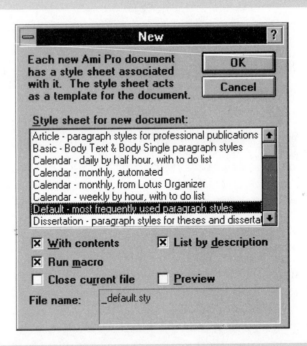

**WORKING TOGETHER** ▲

2. Select a style sheet (i.e., newslt4.sty)by double-clicking on it. The style sheet macro displays the Default Information dialog box.

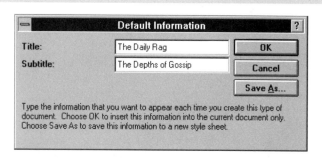

3. Fill in the Title and Subtitle text boxes and click on OK. The macro displays the Optional Information dialog box.

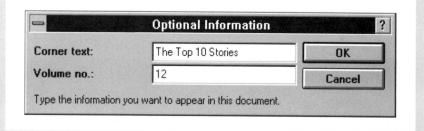

AmiPro

## Setting Margins with the Modify Page Layout Command

You can change margins whether or not there is a document in the document area. To change margins using the Modify Page Layout command, follow these steps:

1. Choose Page ➤ Modify Page Layout or click on the Page Layout Smart-Icon. Ami Pro opens the Modify Page Layout dialog box (Figure 9.14). The Modify Page Layout dialog box for Margins and Columns is the default.

WORKING TOGETHER

▲

**4.** Click on OK. Ami Pro displays the partially filled-in document.

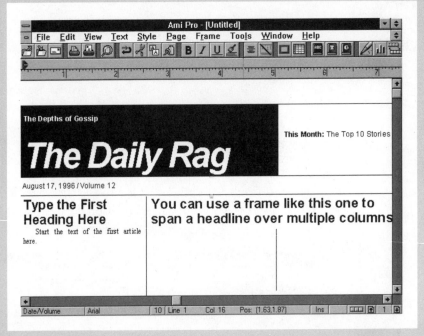

**5.** Add your articles and graphics, and print.

**TIP**

To quickly open the Modify Page Layout dialog box, move the mouse pointer within a margin and click with the right mouse button.

**2.** In the Modify group, click on the <u>M</u>argins & Columns option button.

**3.** In the Margins group, type or select a measurement in the <u>L</u>eft, <u>R</u>ight, <u>T</u>op, and/or <u>B</u>ottom text/list boxes. As you change any margin setting, the sample page in the lower right corner of the dialog box changes its

**FIGURE 9.14**

The Modify Page
Layout dialog box for
Margins and Columns,
in which you can
specify margin and
column settings

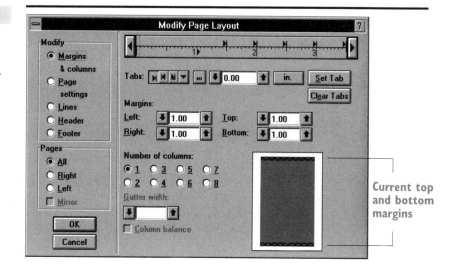

**Current top
and bottom
margins**

appearance. As you change the left or right margin, the markers on the
ruler at the top of the dialog box move.

**4.** Either click on OK or press ⏎.

## Setting Margins with the Ruler

If you have a document in the document area, you can change the left and
right margins and see how the document looks as a result. On the ruler, you'll
find the black left and right margin markers below the blue tab and indent
markers.

To adjust the left margin, drag the left margin marker along the ruler. To
change the right margin, drag the right margin marker on the ruler. As you
drag, Ami Pro shows a line representing the current margin location, opens
the bottom part of the ruler, shows the current margin measurement on the
ruler, and moves the tab markers. After you release the mouse button, your
document changes to reflect the new margins.

 **NOTE**    **If you can't see the ruler in the application window, choose
View ➤ Show Ruler.**

**AmiPro**

## Setting Page Dimensions

You can adjust page size to match the dimensions of the paper on which you are printing and, of course, the capacity of your printer. Simply follow these steps:

1. Choose Page ➤ Modify Page Layout, click on the Page Layout Smart-Icon, or click in any margin. Ami Pro displays the Modify Page Layout dialog box.

2. In the Modify group, click on the Page Settings option button.

3. In the Modify Page Layout dialog box for Page Settings (Figure 9.15), click on an option button in the Page Size group. As you select a page size, the dimensions in the text/list boxes change. Ami Pro allows custom page dimensions from 2.05 by 2.05 inches to 22 by 22 inches.

4. When you have completed filling in the dialog box, either click on OK or press ↵.

**FIGURE 9.15**

In the Modify Page Layout dialog box for Page Settings, you can specify page size, orientation, and the pages for which the settings apply.

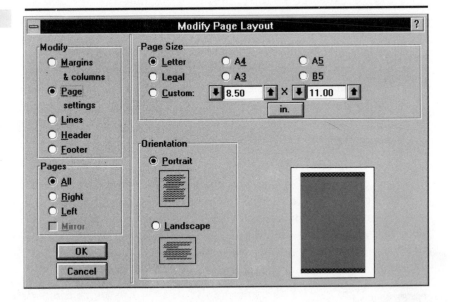

## Setting Page Orientation

Page orientation enables you to print on a page that is longer than it is wide (Portrait) or wider than it is long (Landscape). Examples of portrait orientation are reports, letters, and memoranda. A spreadsheet is the most common landscape document.

To change the page orientation for the current document, follow these steps:

1. Choose Page ➤ Modify Page Layout, click on the Page Layout Smart-Icon, or click in any margin. Ami Pro displays the Modify Page Layout dialog box.

2. In the Modify group, click on the Page Settings option button.

3. In the Modify Page Layout dialog box for Page Settings, click on Portrait (the default) or Landscape. Ami Pro changes the look of the sample page in the lower-right corner of the dialog box.

4. When you have completed filling in the dialog box, either click on OK or press ↵.

## Laying Out All, Right, or Left Pages

Ami Pro allows you to lay out all pages in a document identically, or specify separate page layouts for right (even-numbered) pages and left (odd-numbered) pages. This enables you to change margins on a left page and keep the original settings on a right page, or insert borders of different colors on each type of page. In fact, you can differentiate between left and right pages in every way except page size and orientation. Probably the most important reason for page differentiation is to allow you to have unique headers and footers for left and right pages.

  **Ami Pro numbers the pages of a document internally whether or not you insert printed page numbers. Therefore, when you identify left or right pages for floating headers and/or footers, you need not insert page numbers.**

To differentiate between left and right pages, follow these steps:

1. Choose Page ➤ Modify Page Layout, click on the Page Layout Smart-Icon, or move the mouse pointer to a margin and click the right mouse button. Ami Pro displays the Modify Page Layout dialog box.

2. Click on Margins & Columns, Lines, Header, or Footer option buttons. Remember that the only settings that you can't change are page size and orientation.

3. Select options and fill out text boxes in the Modify Page Layout dialog box. Make sure that you click on an option button in the Pages group.

4. When you have completed the dialog box, either click on OK or press ↵.

## Using Headers and Footers

Headers and footers are lines of text within the top and bottom margins, respectively. For a longer document, headers and footers aid the reader in identifying the page or chapter, and even the date and/or time of printing. Ami Pro offers two types of headers and footers: fixed and floating.

*Fixed headers* and *fixed footers* can appear on every page, only left (odd-numbered) pages, only right (even-numbered) pages, left and right pages (with different text on each), or on all except the first page of a document. Selecting All, Right, or Left in the Pages group of the Modify Page Layout dialog box determines the pages on which a header or footer appear.

*Floating headers* and *floating footers* allow you to insert header or footer information on any page of your document. For example, for a long document with several chapters, you can produce different floating headers and floating footers for the beginning of every chapter. The new header/footer signals the end of the previous one. Floating headers and floating footers can appear on every page, only left (odd-numbered) pages, only right (even-numbered) pages, left and right pages (with different text on each), or on all but the first page of the section in which you insert it.

 To insert a fixed or floating header or footer, choose Page ➤ Header/Footer or click on the Header/Footer SmartIcon.

To make sure that you are actually working within the top or bottom margins, it's a good idea to display the margins in color. To do so, choose <u>V</u>iew ➤ View Preferences or click on the View Preferences SmartIcon. In the View Preferences dialog box, place a check mark in the Margins in <u>C</u>olor check box.

## Inserting Fixed Headers and Footers

Inserting fixed headers and fixed footers in the current document is an easy operation. To insert a fixed header or fixed footer on every page of a document, move the insertion point within the top or bottom margin and type one or two lines of header or footer text.

If you plan to have different headers or footers on left or right pages, on all pages but the first, or on every page of the document, follow these steps to insert fixed headers or fixed footers:

1. Choose <u>P</u>age ➤ <u>H</u>eader/Footer. Ami Pro opens the Headers & Footers dialog box (Figure 9.16).

2. To specify that you are inserting a header or footer, click on Header or Footer.

3. Either click on OK or press ↵. Once you have inserted a header or footer, Ami Pro dims the Header or Footer option buttons.

 **TIP** **If you open the Headers & Footers dialog box and find that one or more of the buttons is dimmed, there is either a header or footer in your document or the insertion point is located in the top or bottom margin. To remove a header or footer, delete its text by pressing Backspace or Del. Then either click within the document or press Esc.**

Once you have inserted a header or footer, type and edit text using the same methods you use for any other part of a document. In a later section, you'll discover how to insert page numbers and the date and time in a header or footer.

**AmiPro**

**FIGURE 9.16**

The Headers &
Footers dialog box,
from which you can
specify a fixed header,
fixed footer, floating
header, or floating
footer

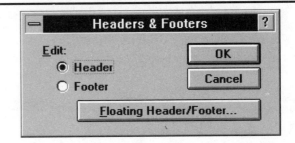

## Inserting Floating Headers and Footers

The steps involved in embedding floating headers and footers in a document
is almost identical to those used in adding fixed headers and footers. To insert
a floating header or footer, follow these steps:

1. Choose Page ➤ Header/Footer. Ami Pro opens the Headers & Footers
   dialog box.

2. Click on Floating Header/Footer. Ami Pro displays the Floating
   Header/Footer dialog box (Figure 9.17).

3. Click on Insert and choose either Floating Header or Floating Footer.

4. Apply the headers or footers to specific pages in the document by clicking on All Pages, Right Pages, or Left Pages.

5. Either click on OK or press ↵.

6. Repeat steps 1–6 to insert a footer or header.

**FIGURE 9.17**

In the Floating
Header/Footer dialog
box, you can define or
remove a floating
header or footer.

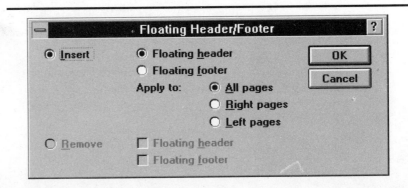

Just as you did for the fixed headers and footers, type one or two lines of text. In the following section, you'll learn how to insert page numbers and the date and time in a header or footer.

## Numbering Pages

When you add a page number to a header or footer (or another part of your document), Ami Pro automatically inserts the correct number on each page. You can indicate the page on which the first page number is printed and specify the beginning number. You can also include a text prefix with the page number.

To insert page numbers in a document, follow these steps:

**1.** Move the insertion point to the desired page number location.

**2.** Choose Page ➤ Page Numbering. Ami Pro opens the Page Numbering dialog box (Figure 9.18).

**3.** Open the Style drop-down list box, and select a style (1, I, i, A, or a).

**4.** To start numbering on a specific page, check the Start on Page check box, and type or select a number in the text/list box.

**5.** To start with a specific page number, check the Start with Number check box, and type or select a number in the text/list box.

**FIGURE 9.18**

The Page Numbering
dialog box

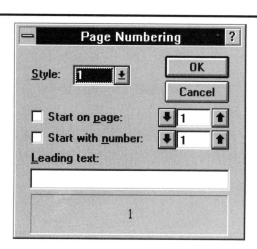

AmiPro

**6.** Type the text preceding the number in the Leading Text text box. To have a space between the leading text and the number, be sure to press the spacebar after typing the last character.

**7.** Either click on OK or press ↵.

Figure 9.19 shows one page from the sample memorandum with a header, which includes a page number.

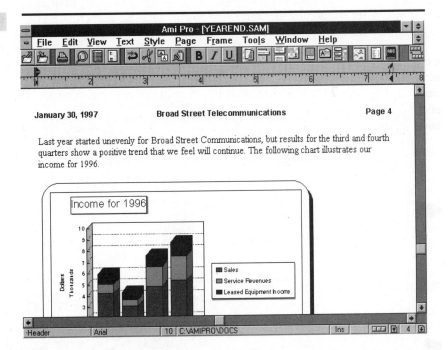

## Inserting Hard Page Breaks

As you add text to a document, Ami Pro inserts page breaks (known as *soft page breaks*) by computing the length of a page and the space taken by the top and bottom margins. When you want to end a page at a particular place in the text (for example, at the end of a section or chapter, or before the next paragraph begins), you can insert a page break (a *hard page break*).

To embed a hard page break, follow these steps:

1. Move the insertion point to the exact point at which you would like the break to occur.

2. Choose Page ➤ Breaks or click on the Breaks SmartIcon. Ami Pro displays the Breaks dialog box (Figure 9.20).

3. Click on Insert Page Break and either click on OK or press ↵. Ami Pro inserts the page break and closes the dialog box.

**FIGURE 9.20**

The breaks dialog box, in which you can insert or remove either page breaks or column breaks

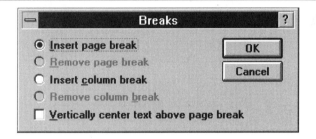

**To replace a soft page break with a hard page break, move the insertion point toward the top of the document and insert the break. The only way to fit more text on a particular page is to decrease one or more margins, lessen line spacing, change to a more condensed font, or decrease the point size.**

**For information about columns and column breaks, see the User's Guide or Inserting a Manual Page and Column Break in Help.**

## Removing Hard Page Breaks

There are three ways to remove a page break:

■ Place the insertion point after the last character on the prior page and either choose Page ➤ Breaks or click on the Breaks SmartIcon. Click on

AmiPro

the Remove Page Break option button and either click on OK or press ↵. (If the Remove Page Break option button is dimmed, move the insertion point so that it's immediately after the last character on the page.)

■ Place the insertion point after the last character on the prior page and press Del. Ami Pro then displays a message box; click on <u>Y</u>es.

■ Move the insertion point before the first character on the new page and press the Backspace key. Ami Pro then displays a message box, in which you should click on <u>Y</u>es.

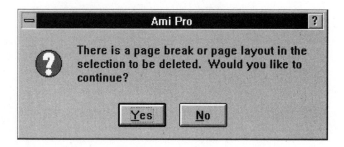

## Controlling Page Breaks within Paragraphs

A page break sometimes splits a paragraph between two pages. When the break occurs in the middle of a paragraph, usually there's no problem. However, when a single line is left at the bottom of a page (an *orphan*) or at the top of a page (a *widow*), it's best to adjust the break.

To prevent widows and orphans, follow these steps:

1. Choose Too<u>l</u>s ➤ <u>U</u>ser Setup. Ami Pro opens the User Setup dialog box (Figure 9.21).

2. Click on the <u>O</u>ptions button. Ami Pro displays the User Setup Options dialog box (Figure 9.22).

3. Check the Widow/Orphan Control check box.

4. Either click on OK or press ↵.

5. Either click on OK or press ↵ again.

**FIGURE 9.21**

The User Setup dialog box allows you to customize your Ami Pro environment.

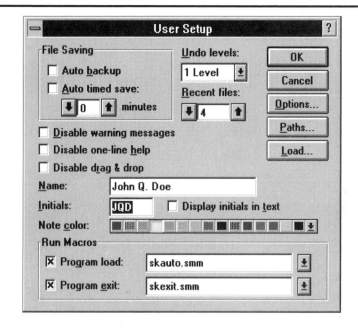

**FIGURE 9.22**

The User Setup Options dialog box allows you to set typographic and speed options for Ami Pro.

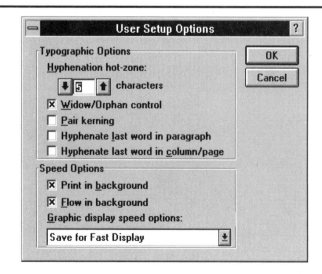

## Going to Pages and Items

 On the Edit menu, Ami Pro offers a navigation command, common to many Windows applications (including 1-2-3). If you choose Edit ➤ Go To, click on the Go To SmartIcon, or press Ctrl+G, Ami Pro opens the Go To dialog box (Figure 9.23).

These are the options in this dialog box:

**Page Number**   Click on this option button (the default) and either type or select a page number from 1 to 9999 in the text/list box.

**First Page**   Click on this option button to go to the top of the first page of the document.

**Last Page**   Click on this option button to go to the top of the last page of the document.

**Next Item**   Click on this option button and select an item from the scroll box to go to the next occurrence of the item.

Either click on the Go to ^H button or press ↵ to go to the next page or item that you specified. To use the same "go to" options to go to the next occurrence of the page or item, press Ctrl+H. Whenever you want to specify a new page or item, open the dialog box and select different options.

**FIGURE 9.23**

Ami Pro's Go To dialog box allows you to either specify an option for going to a page or any one of 13 items in a document.

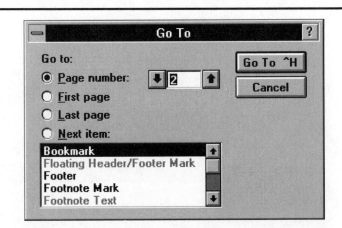

**TIP** To go to the top of the first page of the current document, press Ctrl+Home; to go to the end of the last page of the current document, press Ctrl+End.

# finding and Replacing

Find and replace features enable you to make wholesale changes to text and formats in a document. For example, if you move to another state, you can go through all your documents, searching for your old address and replacing it with the new address automatically. Ami Pro also lets you find and replace characters not on your keyboard and paragraph styles. In this section, you'll learn all about finding and replacing.

Whether you are performing a search or a search and replace, you'll use the same opening steps.

To begin, place the insertion point in the area of the document in which you wish to search. For example, you can move the insertion point to a header to search for header text only, or you can place the insertion point in the document to search in the entire document, including frames, headers, and so on.

Choose Edit ➤ Find & Replace, click on the Find & Replace SmartIcon, or press Ctrl+F to display the Find & Replace dialog box (Figure 9.24). Type the *search string*, the characters for which you are looking, in the Find text box. If you wish to replace the search string, type a *replace string* in the Replace with text box.

**FIGURE 9.24**

The Find & Replace dialog box is the starting dialog box for finding and optionally replacing text, non-printing characters, or styles.

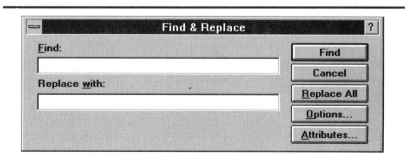

AmiPro

You can replace not only text, but also enhancements. Click on <u>A</u>ttributes to open the Find & Replace Attributes dialog box (Figure 9.25), in which you can specify enhancements for the search. For example, you can search for a boldfaced or italicized search string. You can check or clear any combination of attributes in the Find Attributes and/or the Replace Attributes groups.

To further refine your search, click on <u>O</u>ptions to open the Find & Replace Options dialog box (Figure 9.26).

These are the options in this dialog box:

| OPTION | ACTION, IF CHECKED | SEARCH STRING | RESULT |
|---|---|---|---|
| <u>W</u>hole Word Only | searches for a whole word only | the | finds "the" but not "theater" |
| <u>E</u>xact Case (for both find and replace) | searches for an exact match of upper- and lower-case characters | HELP | finds "HELP" but not "help" or "Help" |
| Exact <u>A</u>ttributes (for both find and replace) | searches for an exact match of attributes speci-fied in the Find & Replace Attri-butes dialog box | ***HELP*** | finds "**HELP**," but not "HELP," "*help*," or "Help" |

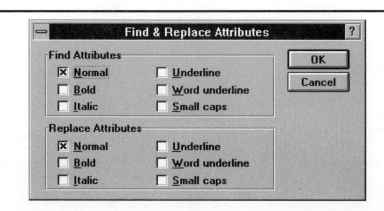

**FIGURE 9.26**

In the Find & Replace Options dialog box, you can specify options to refine your search.

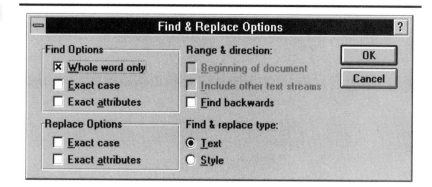

## Finding Text

To find text, follow these steps:

**1.** Move the insertion point to the location in which you want to search.

**2.** Choose Edit ➤ Find & Replace, click on the Find & Replace Smart-Icon, or press Ctrl+F. Ami Pro displays the Find & Replace dialog box.

**3.** Type the search string in the Find text box.

**4.** Either click on Find or press ↵. If Ami Pro finds the search string, it displays another Find & Replace dialog box (Figure 9.27). Otherwise, it displays a message in the status bar.

**5.** Click on Find Next to find the next occurrence. When the search is complete, Ami Pro displays a message in the status bar:

Find/Replace Results: 8 found 0 replaced

## Finding and Replacing Text

To find and replace text, follow these steps:

**1.** Move the insertion point to the location in which you want to search.

**2.** Choose Edit ➤ Find & Replace, click on the Find & Replace Smart-Icon, or press Ctrl+F. Ami Pro displays the Find & Replace dialog box.

**AmiPro**

FIGURE 9.27

Another Find &
Replace dialog box
with which you can
control a search

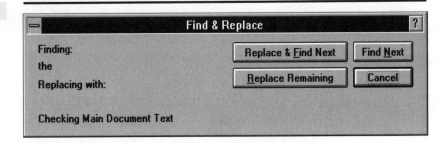

3. Type the search string in the Find text box.

4. Type the replace string in the Replace with text box.

5. To replace every occurrence of the search string with the replace string, click on Replace All. Ami Pro displays the results in the status bar.

6. To search and replace one occurrence at a time, click on Find. Ami Pro displays another Find & Replace dialog box.

7. To replace this occurrence with the replace string and continue the search, click on Replace & Find Next.

8. To replace this occurrence and the remaining occurrences with the replace string, click on Replace Remaining. Ami Pro displays the results in the status bar.

## Finding and Replacing Nonprinting Characters and Paragraph Styles

You can search for and replace nonprinting characters in your document. Table 9.9 provides examples of Ami Pro nonprinting character codes that you can insert in the Find and/or Replace with text boxes in the Find & Replace dialog box. Other than the special codes, the find and replace processes are exactly the same as those for text.

## Selecting Print Options

 Whether you decide to print by choosing File ➤ Print, pressing Ctrl+P, or clicking on the Print SmartIcon, you have a choice of options that are tailored

**TABLE 9.9**    Examples of Ami Pro Nonprinting Character Find and Replace Codes

| CODE | NONPRINTING CHARACTER |
|------|----------------------|
| <ANSI symbol> | an ANSI symbol |
| function key | a paragraph style |
| Ctrl+↵ | a carriage return symbol |
| Ctrl+Tab | a tab mark |
| abc* | abc followed any characters |
| *abc | abc preceded by any characters |
| *abc* | abc preceded and followed by any characters |
| ???ab | three characters followed by ab |
| ab?? | ab followed by two characters |
| *wn?? | any characters, followed by wn, ending with two characters |
| <*> | an asterisk |
| <?> | a question mark |

**AmiPro**

for printing an Ami Pro document. This section provides a brief description of each Ami Pro print option shown in the Print dialog box (Figure 9.28). After selecting options in the dialog box, either click on OK or press ↵.

**NOTE**    The Print dialog box provides "gateways" to the Setup dialog box (click on Setup) for the active printer and to the Print Options dialog box (click on Options).

## Number of Copies

Select or type the number of copies (from 1 to 9999) that you wish to print in the Number of Copies text/scroll box.

**FIGURE 9.28**

The Print dialog box allows you to select options to customize the printing of a document.

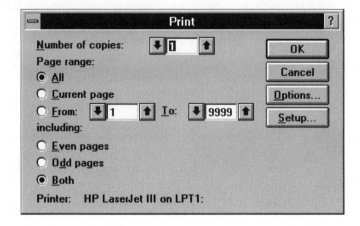

## Page Range

To specify the range of pages to print, click on one of the following options:

| | |
|---|---|
| Ａll | to print the entire document. This is the default. |
| Current Page | to print only the page in which the insertion point is located |
| From | to print a range starting with the page number in the first text/list box and ending with the page number in the To text/list box |
| Even Pages | to print only the even pages in the preceding range of pages |
| Odd Pages | to print only the odd pages in the preceding range of pages |
| Both | to print all the pages in the preceding range of pages. This is the default. |

**WORKING TOGETHER**

# Printing Envelopes in Ami Pro

There are two ways of printing envelopes in Ami Pro: by choosing the _envelope.sty style sheet if there is no open document, or by choosing File ➤ Print Envelope when you have an open document.

If you use _envelope.sty, Ami Pro will guide you through envelope creation. First, you'll get the chance to fill in or edit the contents of the Default Information dialog box.

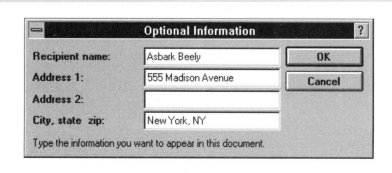

After completing the dialog box, click on OK. The style sheet macro then displays the Optional Information dialog box, in which you can give recipient information.

**AmiPro**

**WORKING TOGETHER** ▲

After completing the dialog box, click on OK. The style sheet macro adds the recipient information to the document in the document window. Choose File ➤ Print Envelope. The Print Envelope dialog box appears.

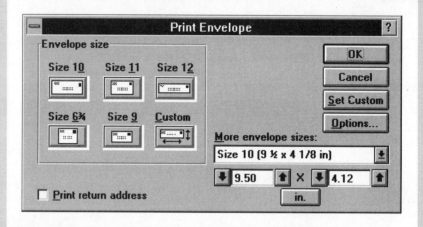

Select a size from the Envelope Size group. (If you click on Print Return Address, a return address section is added to the dialog box.) Click on OK.

At this point, you must know how your printer handles envelopes. For example, if you are manually feeding an envelope into a laser printer, know the direction the envelope should be facing, and open the back door, if necessary, to feed the envelope through a straight path. For more information, see your printer manual.

If you choose File ➤ Print Envelope, Ami Pro looks for a three- to five-line address with no spaces between the lines. If it finds one, Ami Pro highlights the address and opens the Print Envelope dialog box. Click on OK, and feed the envelope in. Refer to your printer manual if you have problems.

## Options

Click on the Options button to reveal the Print Options dialog box (Figure 9.29).

With the Print Options dialog box, you can select additional print options.

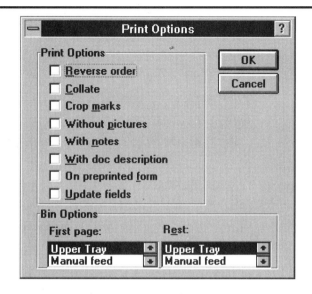

The Print Options dialog box contains these print options:

**Reverse Order**    Check this check box to print the last page in the document, followed by the next to last page, and so on, until the first page is printed.

**Collate**    Check this check box to print all the pages of a document, starting with the first page and ending with the last page (unless you have also checked Reverse Order) before starting to print the next copy.

**Crop Marks**    Check this check box to print lines that indicate the finished dimensions of the page when cropped for binding.

**Without Pictures**    Check this check box to print frames but not the pictures within the frames.

**With Notes**    Check this check box to print the document and the notes (both initialed and numbered) inserted in the document.

**WORKING TOGETHER**

# Using Ami Pro's File Manager

You can manage your Ami Pro files by choosing File ➤ File Management. Ami Pro starts the Ami Pro File Manager, a stand-alone application, which displays the files in the current directory.

Ami Pro File Manager provides the following commands with which you can manage your files:

**File ➤ Copy**   Copies a file, keeping all its formats and related files.

**File ➤ Move**   Moves a file, keeping all its formats and related files.

**File ➤ Delete**   Deletes any file except read-only files.

**File ➤ Attributes**   Changes a file from Read-Write to Read Only or from Read Only to Read-Write.

**File ➤ Change Directory**   Changes to a different directory so that you can change to a different list of file names.

**File ➤ Exit**   Exits from Ami Pro File Manager.

**View ➤ *.S?M Files**   Displays all the files with a *.S?M extension, including *.SAM and *.SMM.

**View ➤ All**   Displays all files in this directory. This is equivalent to displaying *.* files.

**View ➤ Partial**   Opens the Partial dialog box, with which you can search for files in any directory using the asterisk (*) wildcard character.

**View ➤ Doc Info**   Displays document information for a particular file.

**Help ➤ Contents**   Lists the File Management Contents from the help facility.

**WORKING TOGETHER** ▲

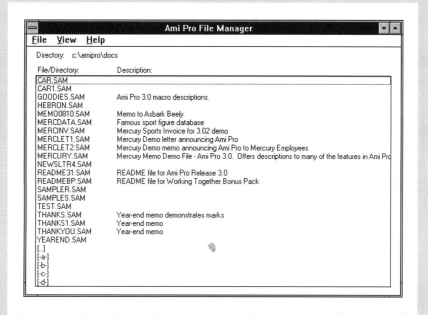

For more information about File Management, see Chapter 29 of the *User's Guide* or look up *Managing Files in the Help facility.*

**With Doc Description**     Check this check box to print the information about this document: file name and directory; style sheet; your description; keywords that you have typed; import files; page, word, and character counts; the size of the file; the date and time created and last revised, the number of revisions, and the time you have spent working on this file (in minutes). (To display the Doc Info dialog box, choose File ➤ Doc Info.)

**On Preprinted Form**     Check this check box to print all the text in the document stripped of lines and patterns.

**Update Fields**     Check this check box to update power fields and print the results.

10

# Creating Pictures

■

In the last two chapters, you learned how to create, edit, and format documents using Ami Pro. In this chapter, you'll find out how to create drawings and import pictures from other Windows applications in order to improve your documents. This chapter provides an overview of drawing in Ami Pro. For more detailed information, either see the *User's Guide* or search for graphics and drawing topics in Ami Pro's Help facility. To get drawing help quickly, double-click inside the frame and press F1.

**NOTE** **To create Ami Pro drawings, you must have a mouse installed and working. Although you can modify drawings using menu commands, drawing tools are only available through clicking on buttons.**

Whether you create or import them, drawings in Ami Pro are *objects*—individual parts of an application, file, or even a drawing. Other examples of objects are fields in Approach, charts and pieces of charts in 1-2-3, dialog boxes, SmartIcons, boxes, and buttons.

Both 1-2-3 and Freelance Graphics have drawing features and share many of the same drawing tools; you can apply the information in this chapter to other SmartSuite applications. And because you are running under Windows, you can create a drawing in one application (whether or not it's a SmartSuite application) and use it in another. Table 10.1 illustrates and describes common SmartSuite drawing tools, and shows examples of using each.

**TABLE 10.1:** SmartSuite Drawing Tools

| SMARTICON | DESCRIPTION | APPLICATIONS | EXAMPLE |
|---|---|---|---|
| | Selects an object in a drawing (Press Shift and click to add the next object to the selection.) | Ami Pro, Approach, Freelance Graphics | |
| | Selects all the drawn objects | 1-2-3 | |
| | Draws a straight line | Ami Pro, 1-2-3, Approach, Freelance Graphics | |
| | Draws a line made up of segments | Ami Pro, 1-2-3, Freelance Graphics | |
| | Draws a polygon | Ami Pro, 1-2-3, Freelance Graphics | |
| | Draws a rectangle or square | Ami Pro, 1-2-3, Approach, Freelance Graphics | |
| | Draws a rectangle or square with rounded corners | Ami Pro, 1-2-3, Approach | |
| | Draws an ellipse or circle | Ami Pro, 1-2-3, Approach, Freelance Graphics | |
| | Draws an arc | Ami Pro, 1-2-3, Freelance Graphics | |
| abc | Inserts text in a drawing | Ami Pro, 1-2-3, Approach, Freelance Graphics | text |

**TABLE 10.1:** SmartSuite Drawing Tools (continued)

| SMARTICON | DESCRIPTION | APPLICATIONS | EXAMPLE |
|---|---|---|---|
| | Draws an arrow pointing forward | 1-2-3, Freelance Graphics | |
| | Draws a double-headed arrow | 1-2-3 | |
| | Draws freehand | 1-2-3, Freelance Graphics | |
| | Draws a macro button in a drawing | 1-2-3 | Button |
| | Draws an open curve | Freelance Graphics | |

Drawing in Ami Pro (and Freelance Graphics) involves using SmartIcons; Ami Pro's Draw menu provides editing commands only. However, 1-2-3 has not only drawing SmartIcons but also its own set of drawing commands. Table 10.2 presents the list of 1-2-3 drawing commands.

**TABLE 10.2:** 1-2-3 Drawing Menu Commands

| SMARTICON | MENU COMMAND | DESCRIPTION |
|---|---|---|
| | <u>T</u>ools ➤ <u>D</u>raw ➤ <u>L</u>ine | Draws a straight line |
| | <u>T</u>ools ➤ <u>D</u>raw ➤ <u>P</u>olyline | Draws a line made up of segments |
| | <u>T</u>ools ➤ <u>D</u>raw ➤ <u>A</u>rrow | Draws an arrow pointing forward |
| | <u>T</u>ools ➤ <u>D</u>raw ➤ <u>R</u>ectangle | Draws a rectangle or square |

**TABLE 10.2:** 1-2-3 Drawing Menu Commands (continued)

| SMARTICON | MENU COMMAND | DESCRIPTION |
|---|---|---|
| ▢ | <u>T</u>ools ➤ <u>D</u>raw ➤ Roun<u>d</u>ed Rectangle | Draws a rectangle or square with rounded corners |
| ◝ | <u>T</u>ools ➤ <u>D</u>raw ➤ Ar<u>c</u> | Draws an arc |
| ○ | <u>T</u>ools ➤ <u>D</u>raw ➤ <u>E</u>llipse | Draws an ellipse or circle |
| ◿ | <u>T</u>ools ➤ <u>D</u>raw ➤ <u>P</u>olygon | Draws a polygon |
| ∿ | <u>T</u>ools ➤ <u>D</u>raw ➤ <u>F</u>reehand | Draws freehand |
| abc | <u>T</u>ools ➤ <u>D</u>raw ➤ <u>T</u>ext | Inserts a text box in a drawing |
| OK | <u>T</u>ools ➤ <u>D</u>raw ➤ <u>B</u>utton | Draws a macro button in a drawing |

## Creating Pictures in Ami Pro

Start the Drawing feature by clicking on the Drawing SmartIcon or by choosing <u>T</u>ools ➤ <u>D</u>rawing. Ami Pro adds a drawing toolbar:

and inserts a frame at the insertion point:

The frame has handles at each corner and along each side so that you can change its dimensions. Changing the size of the frame has no effect on the size of the objects enclosed. However, when you move the sides of a frame over an object, the object remains in its original location; that section just seems to disappear. To avoid this, move the sides of the frame off the object.

 **To keep the dimensions of the frame in their original proportions, drag a corner handle rather than one of the handles on the sides, top, or bottom.**

To move from the frame to your document, click outside the frame. The handles and drawing toolbar disappear and the insertion point is outside the frame. To select the frame, click within its borders; black handles appear. To edit a frame, double-click within its borders; the handles turn gray and the drawing toolbar appears.

When you start the drawing function, Ami Pro also adds the Draw menu to the menu bar. The Draw menu provides editing commands for drawings, listed in Table 10.3.

**TABLE 10.3:** Ami Pro Draw Menu Commands

| SMARTICON | MENU COMMAND | DESCRIPTION |
| --- | --- | --- |
| | Draw ➤ Line Style | Opens the Line Styles dialog box so that you can select a line style and line endings |
| | Draw ➤ Fill Pattern | Opens the Fill Pattern dialog box so that you can select a fill pattern and/or a color for the fill pattern |
| | Draw ➤ Extract Line & Fill | Copies the line styles, line endings, and fill patterns from the selected object |
| | Draw ➤ Apply Line & Fill | Applies the copied line styles, line endings, and fill patterns to the selected object |
| | Draw ➤ Rotate | Rotates the selected object 10 degrees clockwise |
| | Draw ➤ Flip ➤ Horizontal | Flips the selected object on the horizontal axis |
| | Draw ➤ Flip ➤ Vertical | Flips the selected object on the vertical axis |
| | Draw ➤ Snap To | Snaps or does not snap future drawing objects to the grid (whether or not it appears within the frame) |
| | Draw ➤ Show Grid; Draw ➤ Hide Grid | Displays or hides the grid within the frame |

**AmiPro**

**363**

**TABLE 10.3:** Ami Pro Draw Menu Commands (continued)

| SMARTICON | MENU COMMAND | DESCRIPTION |
|---|---|---|
| N/A | Draw ➤ Grid Settings | Opens the Grid Settings dialog box so that you can set grid spacing, define the grid line as dots or a dotted line, or make the grid setting the default. |
| | Draw ➤ Select All | Selects all the objects within the frame |
| | Draw ➤ Group | Groups the selected objects, or ungroups the selected group |
| | Draw ➤ Bring to Front | Moves the selected object to the front of the layers of objects |
| | Draw ➤ Send to Back | Moves the selected object to the back of the layers of objects |

## Using the Drawing Tools

To use a drawing tool, click on it. This selects the tool and deselects any other tool. Then place the mouse pointer inside the frame and start working. Ami Pro provides several mouse pointers, depending on the selected tool. Table 10.4 shows each mouse pointer and lists the associated tools for it.

## Selecting Objects

There are two Ami Pro selection tools. To select an object in the drawing, click on the Selection Arrow or choose Draw ➤ Select All; then click on the object. Ami Pro displays handles around the outside of the object. Once you have selected an object, you can delete it (press Del) or move it (drag it within its borders). To add another object to the selection, press and hold down the Shift key and click on the object. You can continue this until every

TABLE 10.4: Ami Pro Drawing Tool Mouse Pointers

| MOUSE POINTER | ASSOCIATED TOOLS |
|---|---|
|  | Select tool |
| | Hand tool |
| | Line tool, segmented line tool, polygon tool, rectangle tool, rounded rectangle tool, ellipse tool, arc tool |
| | Text block tool |

object is selected (that is, every selected object has handles). To "deselect" a selection, click outside the object.

 To select every object within the frame, click on the Select All drawing tool.

**NOTE**  **To select the frame and its contents, move the mouse pointer to the left of the frame and press Shift + →. You can also move the mouse pointer to the right of the frame and press Shift + ←.**

## Cropping Drawings

Use the Hand tool to select and move the entire picture within the frame. Moving the picture shows only part of the picture (that is, the picture is *cropped*). You can start with a picture that looks like this:

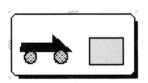

then looks like this as it is dragged:

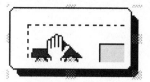

and ends up looking like this:

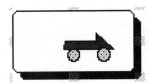

You can recover the cropped part of the picture—even if you have saved your document and exited Ami Pro—by clicking on the Hand tool again and moving the picture back to its original position.

## Drawing Lines and Arcs

Ami Pro provides two line drawing tools—Line and Polyline—and one arc drawing tool.

 To draw a straight line, click on the Line tool. Move the cross-hatch mouse pointer to one end of the line, press down the left mouse button, drag to the other end of the line, and release the mouse button. To draw a line horizontally, vertically, or at a 45 degree angle, press the Shift key while you are drawing.

 To draw a segmented line, click on the Polyline tool and draw the first segment as you did the straight line. To draw a new segment, move the mouse pointer to the ending point and click. Ami Pro joins the end of the previous segment with the end of this segment. As long as the Polyline tool is active ("pressed down"), you will continue to add segments. To inactivate the tool, click on another button. Your best choice is the Selection Arrow, since it does not add more objects to your drawing, nor does it change the drawing.

Drawing an arc is very similar to drawing a straight line; in fact, you can draw a straight line using the Arc tool. To draw an arc, click on the Arc tool. Move the cross-hatch mouse pointer to where you want the arc to begin, press down the left mouse button, drag to where you want the arc to end, and release the mouse button. If you drag directly horizontally or vertically from the starting point, you'll draw a straight line. However, if you drag diagonally from the starting point, you form the arc. To adjust the arc's curve, click on a section of the curve and drag it one way if you want more curve and the other if you want less.

## Drawing Polygons

To draw a polygon, which is a closed object with three or more straight lines, click on the Polygon tool and move the cross-hatch mouse pointer to the starting point in the drawing. Draw the polygon using the same techniques as you did for the segmented line. The only difference is that after you have drawn at least two sides of the polygon, Ami Pro will close the object with a final line for you. All you have to do is signal that you are finished with the other sides: click either on another drawing tool or outside the borders of the frame.

## Drawing Rectangles, Rounded Rectangles, and Ellipses

Drawing rectangles, rounded rectangles, and ellipses involves almost identical procedures. Click on the drawing tool, move the mouse pointer to a starting point, and drag diagonally until the object is the desired size. To draw a square or a circle, press the Shift key while dragging. To draw a square, press down on the Shift key, click on the Rectangle tool, and Ami Pro always keeps the sides of the object the same length. To draw a circle, press down on the Shift key, click on the Ellipse tool, and as you draw, Ami Pro always keeps the object a circle.

## Inserting Text in a Drawing

To insert text, click on the Text drawing tool, move the mouse pointer to the drawing, click, and start typing. To change text attributes, choose Text ➤ Font. In the Font dialog box (Figure 10.1), change the font, point size, or text color of text that you are about to type or that you have highlighted. Once you have typed text, you can select it (it must be surrounded by handles) and click on the Bold, Italics, and Underline SmartIcons; click on the status bar buttons; or press shortcut keys such as Ctrl+B, Ctrl+I, or Ctrl+U.

To start a new line of text, press ↵.

In the Font dialog box, you can change the attributes of text in a drawing.

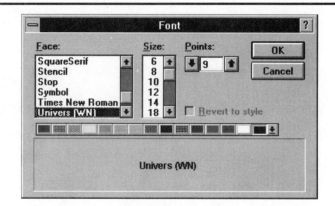

## Copying, Cutting, and Pasting Objects

You can use SmartIcons to copy, cut, and paste a selected object. You can also use the Copy, Cut, and Paste commands on the Edit menu (or press Ctrl+C, Ctrl+X, or Ctrl+V, respectively) to copy, cut, and paste. Simply select the object and either copy or cut it to the Clipboard. Then paste it back into the drawing. Ami Pro will paste the copy on top of the original object. To move the copy to another location in the drawing, drag it.

 Deleting a character or block of text (by pressing the Del key) is different from cutting the same character or text. A cut selection of text can be pasted back into the document, as long as no other Cut or Copy operation has been performed. You can undo a deletion as long as you haven't performed another action, but after that, a deleted selection is gone forever.

# Modifying Pictures

Once you have inserted objects in a drawing, you'll probably want to change them in some way. Before you can edit an object, you must select it by clicking directly on it. Ami Pro places handles around the selected object:

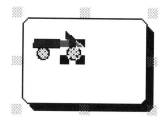

In this section, you'll learn how to use the editing buttons on the Drawing toolbar.

## Grouping and Ungrouping Objects

Grouping objects allows you to define several objects as a single object. This command is very useful when you must move several objects that form one part of a drawing (Figure 10.2).

**FIGURE 10.2**

The polygon and circles look like a single unit, but are actually three objects.

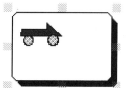

 Before grouping objects in a drawing, click on the Select All tool or choose <u>D</u>raw ➤ S<u>e</u>lect All. Ami Pro selects all the objects (and places handles on each selected object):

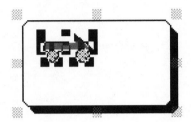

 Then click on the Group tool or choose <u>D</u>raw ➤ <u>G</u>roup. After you group an object, the Group tool changes to show that the next click will ungroup the grouped object (which now has just eight handles):

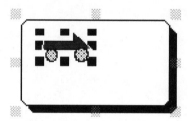

When you want to work with one part of a grouped object (for example, to change its color or to delete it), click on the Group tool or choose <u>D</u>raw ➤ <u>G</u>roup again. This ungroups the group into the individual objects with which you started.

## Using the Bring to Front and Send to Back Tools

As you add objects to the same general location in a drawing, you'll find that the new objects partially or completely overlap older objects (shown on following page).

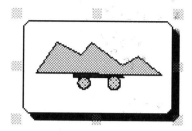

 Select the object that you want to bring to the front of the drawing, and click on the Bring to Front tool or choose <u>D</u>raw ➤ Bring to <u>F</u>ront.

**NOTE**  **You can press Ctrl+Z or choose <u>E</u>dit ➤ <u>U</u>ndo to undo your last action. If things really look desperate and the drawing is a total mess, you can choose <u>F</u>ile ➤ <u>C</u>lose and answer No to the save prompt. (This works only if you've previously saved a successful version of your work. If you haven't saved your work, you won't have anything left to work with.)**

 To send an object to the bottom layer of the drawing, click on the Send to Back tool or choose <u>D</u>raw ➤ Send to <u>B</u>ack.

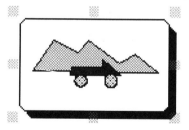

## Rotating an Object

To rotate an object, click on the Rotate tool or choose <u>D</u>raw ➤ <u>R</u>otate. Each click on the Rotate tool rotates the object 10 degrees. So, to rotate an object completely around to its starting position, click 36 times. If you choose <u>D</u>raw ➤ <u>R</u>otate, Ami Pro opens the Rotate dialog box (Figure 10.3). In the dialog

AmiPro

box, you can set rotation (from 0 to 359 degrees), specify the direction (Clockwise or Counterclockwise), and see the effects as you choose.

The Rotate dialog box with a clockwise rotation of 40 degrees selected

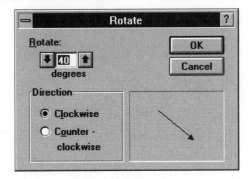

**TIP** You can also rotate an object by double-clicking on it. Ami Pro displays the center point around which you can rotate the object. You can also move this center point to change the path of rotation. To rotate an object, point to the small double-pointed arrow and drag. As you rotate the object, a box shows you the current degree of rotation.

An object rotated 40 degrees looks like this:

## Flipping an Object

To flip an object horizontally from this position:

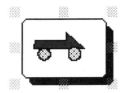

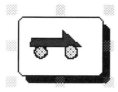 select it and click on the Flip Horizontally tool or choose <u>D</u>raw ➤ <u>F</u>lip ➤ Horizontal. The end result looks like this:

To flip an object vertically from this position:

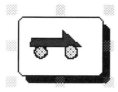 select it and click on the Flip Vertically tool or choose <u>D</u>raw ➤ <u>F</u>lip ➤ Vertical. The end result looks like this:

**AmiPro**

## Using the Grid

As you draw an object, you may not be able to control the final size of the object; the lines may seem to *snap* (jump) to another point in the frame. This seeming lack of control is caused by *snapping to the grid*. In this section, you'll find out how to control snapping to the grid, how to view or hide the grid, and how to change grid attributes.

### Snapping to the Grid

If you need to line up several objects in a flow chart, the Snap to Grid option is a great help. However, if you are making a drawing in which you create an object, size it, and then place it, Snap to Grid could be a disadvantage.

 To turn on or off the Snap to Grid feature, either click on the Snap to tool or choose <u>D</u>raw ➤ <u>S</u>nap to. Click on the top left SmartIcon to turn on Snap to Grid; click on the bottom left SmartIcon to turn it off.

### Viewing the Grid

 After you have turned on Snap to Grid, it's a good idea to actually see the grid within the frame. To show (or hide) the grid, click on the Show/Hide Grid tool. When the grid appears (with its default settings), the frame looks like this:

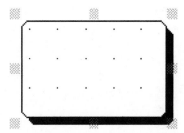

### Changing Grid Attributes

You can set grid spacing, change the look of the grid line, and make the new settings the default. To do this, select <u>D</u>raw ➤ Gri<u>d</u> Settings. The Grid

Settings dialog box (Figure 10.4) offers these options:

**Fine**    Click on this option button to set grid spacing to 0.1 inches apart.

**Medium**    Click on this option button to set grid spacing to 0.2 inches apart. This is the default.

**Coarse**    Click on this option button to set grid spacing to 0.5 inches apart.

  **You can refine the measurement by typing or selecting a value in the text/list box at the bottom of the group.**

**Dots at Intersect**    Click on this option button to show the grid as a series of dots at the intersection of the invisible vertical and horizontal lines that comprise the grid. This is the default.

**Dotted Line**    Click on this option button to show the grid as dotted vertical and horizontal lines.

**Make Default**    Check this check box to make the new settings the default grid display.

**FIGURE 10.4**

The Grid Settings dialog box enables you to specify new grid settings and save them as the default.

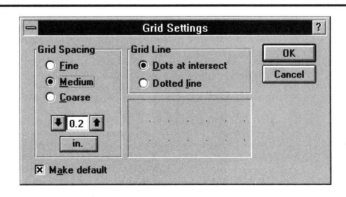

Figure 10.5 shows two figures—one not snapped to the grid and the other snapped to the grid.

**FIGURE 10.5**

Figures that illustrate the difference between snapping and not snapping to the grid.

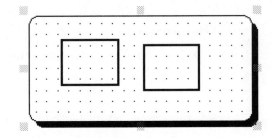

## Specifying Line Style, Fill Pattern, and Color

The last four tools on the Drawing toolbar allow you to define these aspects:

- line or border style (dashed or solid)
- line endings (arrow heads, and so on)
- line or border color (including white, which means no line or border at all)
- fill (interior of an object) color
- fill pattern

## Copying Line and Fill Attributes from One Object to Another

Copying the line and fill attributes from one object to another is a two step process.

 Select the object whose attributes you wish to copy, and click on the Extract Line & Fill tool or choose Draw ➤ Extract Line & Fill.

 Select the object whose attributes you wish to change (in this case, this is a grouped object), and click on the Apply Line & Fill tool or choose $\underline{D}$raw ➤ $\underline{A}$pply Line & Fill. The end result looks like this:

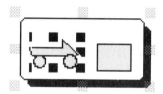

## Modifying Line and Border Attributes

 You can change line and border attributes for future drawn objects. Either click on the Line Style tool or choose $\underline{D}$raw ➤ $\underline{L}$ine Style. Ami Pro displays the Line Styles dialog box (Figure 10.6).

**FIGURE 10.6**

In the Line Styles dialog box, you can define the line or border style, line endings, and line and border colors.

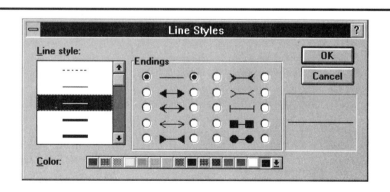

AmiPro

The Line Styles dialog box offers these options:

**Line Style**    Scroll through the line styles in the scroll box and click on your choice.

**Endings**    Click on one option button on the left side of the illustrations and one option button on the right side. You can select one type of ending for the left side of a line and another type for the right side.

**Color**    Click on a box in the color palette. Note that the box in the upper-right corner is the current selection; it looks as though it is pressed down.

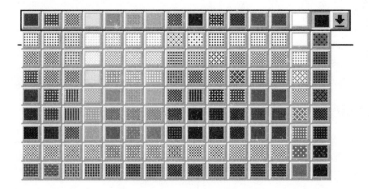

    You can "load" the top row of color buttons with your own 15 color choices. Then you don't have to open the color palette to make a selection; this becomes the default top row. To add a color to the top row, click on a button in the top row. If you haven't opened the palette, do so, and then click on your choice. The selected color replaces the color in the clicked-on button in the top row.

## Modifying Fill Attributes

You can change fill attributes for future drawn objects. Either click on the Fill Pattern tool or choose Draw ➤ Fill Pattern. Ami Pro displays the Fill Pattern dialog box (Figure 10.7).

**FIGURE 10.7**

In the Fill Pattern dialog box, you can define the color and pattern for the interior of future objects.

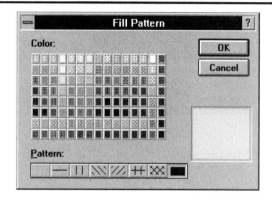

The Fill Pattern dialog box offers these options:

**Color**   Click on a box in the color palette.

**Pattern**   Click on a pattern. Use the leftmost button to apply white, regardless of the chosen color. Use the rightmost button to apply the chosen color and pattern from the Color palette. Clicking on the remaining buttons combines the pattern and chosen color.

# Scaling an Object

Ami Pro provides two ways to *scale* (increase or decrease the size of) an object: dragging on its handles, or clicking on a SmartIcon and then filling in a dialog box.

## Scaling with Handles

To scale a selected object using its handles, it's a good idea to move the object to a part of the frame that will accommodate the final size.

**AmiPro**

In many applications, when you click on a handle, the mouse pointer changes to a double-headed arrow. In Ami Pro, the mouse pointer does not change, but a sizing border replaces the handles:

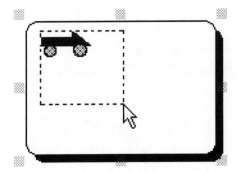

When you release the mouse button, the object changes size to fill the area defined by the final size of the sizing border:

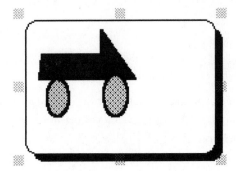

## Scaling with the Scaling SmartIcon

 To scale an object by the numbers (that is, using its measurements as a guide), click on the Scaling SmartIcon. You don't have to select the object if it's the only object in the drawing. In the Graphics Scaling dialog box (Figure 10.8), select from these options:

> **Original Size**    Click on this option button to return to the starting size of the selected object.

**Fit in Frame**   Click on this option button to fit the object within the frame. If you change the dimensions of the frame, the object changes as well.

**Percentage**   Click on this option button and then scroll through the choices (from 1 to 790) in the text/list box.

**Custom**   Click on this option button to specify a custom width and height for the object. Valid values for both width and height are from 0.05 to 22 inches.

**Maintain Aspect Ratio**   Check this check box to ensure that the original proportions of the object are maintained. For example, if the current object is 0.84 by 0.72 inches, at 50%, it should be very close to 0.42 by 0.36 inches.

**Rotate**   Type or select a value in this text/list box. Valid values are 0–359.

 **The only way to open the Graphics Scaling dialog box is to click on the Scaling SmartIcon.**

The Graphics Scaling dialog box allows you to scale the selected object or the contents of the frame.

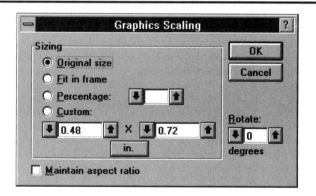

**AmiPro**

# Creating and Editing Frames

When you start the Drawing feature, Ami Pro inserts a frame in which you can draw objects. This type of frame prevents text from wrapping close to its left and right margins. Now you'll find out about a different type of frame that does not provide drawing tools but allows text to wrap close to all four sides. You can insert objects, such as completed drawings and text, into this frame, or you can keep it empty as a placeholder for later use. You can add a frame to an empty or text-filled document.

## Adding a Frame to a Document

 To insert a frame in a document using the mouse, click on the Frame Smart-Icon. Then move the mouse pointer, which changes to a miniature frame, into the document. Click at the starting corner, and drag diagonally toward the opposite corner.

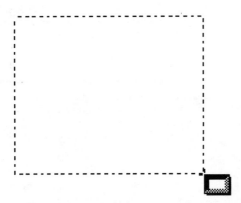

When the bounding box reaches the desired dimensions, release the mouse button. Notice that the frame looks exactly the same as the drawing frame.

To insert a frame using specific measurements, choose Frame ➤ Create Frame and fill in the Create Frame dialog box (Figure 10.9).

**FIGURE 10.9**

The Create Frame
dialog box

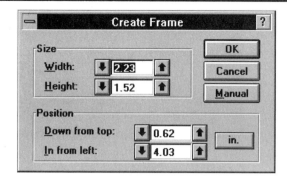

These are the options in the Create Frame dialog box:

Width             Type or select a value in the current unit of
                  measure for the width of the frame.

Height            Type or select a value in the current unit of
                  measure for the height of the frame.

Down from Top     Type or select a value in the current unit of
                  measure for the distance from the top of the page
                  to the top of the frame.

In from Left      Type or select a value in the current unit of
                  measure for the distance from the left border of the
                  page to the left border of the frame.

Manual            Click on this button to close the dialog box and
                  draw the frame with the mouse.

To insert a frame that is the exact duplicate of the last frame you inserted
(before you changed its dimensions), click on the Add a Frame SmartIcon.

**AmiPro**

## Modifying a Frame

In this section, you'll learn about the four versions of the Modify Frame Layout dialog box and their options.

To modify a frame, either click on the Modify Frame Layout SmartIcon, choose F<u>r</u>ame ➤ <u>M</u>odify Frame Layout, or select the frame and click the right mouse button. The left side of each Modify Frame Layout dialog box (Figure 10.10) contains the Frame group, which you use to display a particular version of the dialog box, and three command buttons. Once you make changes to any version of the dialog box, click on <u>M</u>ake Default to save the settings as your new frame default.

| CLICK ON: | TO SELECT: |
|-----------|-----------|
| <u>T</u>ype | a text wrap option, a display option, and frame placement |
| <u>S</u>ize & Position | the frame size, position on the page, and the size of the margins |
| <u>L</u>ines & Shadows | the location and look of lines, and the location and look of the shadow |
| <u>C</u>olumns & Tabs | the number of columns in a frame, column attributes, and column margins |

The Modify Frame Layout dialog box for frame type

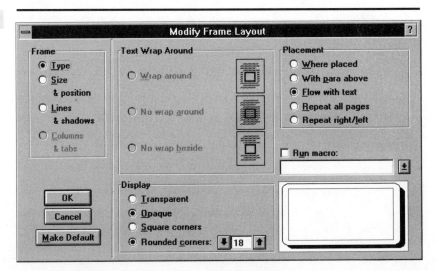

## Modifying Frame Type

These are the options in the Modify Frame Layout dialog box for frame type:

**Wrap around**     Click on this option button to have text wrap around all sides of the frame. This is the default text wrap option.

**No Wrap around**     Click on this option button to have text continue over the frame. This option ignores the existence of the frame.

**No Wrap beside**     Click on this option button to allow text wrap at the top and bottom of the frame but not on the left or right.

**Transparent**     Click on this option button to make the frame transparent; you can see all text and other objects under the frame.

**Opaque**     Click on this option button to make the frame opaque; you can't see text or objects underneath. This is the default display option.

**Square Corners**     Click on this option button to square the corners of the frame.

**Rounded Corners**     Click on this option button to round the corners of the frame. In the text/list box, type or select a value from 0 (rectangular) to 100 (oval) to specify the amount of rounding for any lines that you define around the frame. This is the default frame corner type.

**Where Placed**     Click on this option button to anchor the frame in this position on the page, despite the editing around the frame and throughout the document. This is the default placement option.

**With Para above**     Click on this option button to anchor the frame to the preceding paragraph. The frame can move horizontally but cannot move vertically.

**Flow with Text**     Click on this option button to anchor the frame to the last character in the preceding paragraph. The frame can move vertically but not horizontally.

**Repeat All Pages**     Click on this option button to display the frame and the objects within it on every page of the document in the same position.

AmiPro

**Repeat Right/Left**    Click on this option button to display the frame and the objects within it on every other page (either all odd-numbered or all even-numbered) of the document.

**Run Macro**    Check this check box and select a macro from the drop-down list box. When someone clicks inside the frame, Ami Pro runs the specified macro.

## Modifying Frame Size and Position

These are the options in the Modify Frame Layout dialog box for frame size and position (Figure 10.11):

**Width**    Type or select a value for the width of the frame. A frame can be almost as wide as the paper on which it is printed. Valid values depend on the defined paper size. The default width is 1.81 inches.

**Height**    Type or select a value for the length of the frame. A frame can be almost as long as the paper on which it is printed. Valid values depend on the defined paper size. The default height is 1.26 inches.

**FIGURE 10.11**

The Modify Frame Layout dialog box for frame size and position allows you to specify frame size, position on the page, and margin sizes.

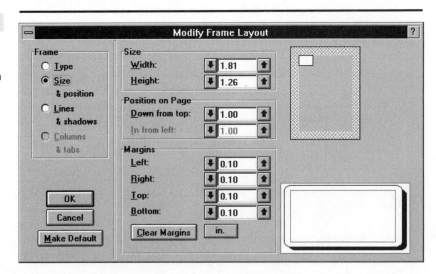

**Down from Top**     Type or select a value for the measurement from the top of the page. The default value is 1.00 inches. Valid values range from the top edge to the bottom edge of the page.

**In from Left**     Type or select a value for the measurement from the left margin. The default value is 1.00 inches. Valid values range from the left edge to the right edge of the paper.

 **NOTE**     **Certain laser printers do not allow you to print within one-half inch of any edge of the paper.**

**Left**     Type or select a value for the left margin within the frame. The default value is 0.10 inches. Valid values are 0 to 1.70 inches, depending on the value of the right margin. The higher the value of the right margin, the lower the maximum value of the left margin.

**Right**     Type or select a value for the right margin within the frame. The default value is 0.10 inches. Valid values are 0 to 1.70 inches, depending on the value of the left margin. The higher the value of the left margin, the lower the maximum value of the right margin.

**Top**     Type or select a value for the top margin within the frame. The default value is 0.10 inches. Valid values are 0 to 1.25 inches, depending on the value of the bottom margin. The higher the value of the bottom margin, the lower the maximum value of the top margin.

**Bottom**     Type or select a value for the bottom margin within the frame. The default value is 0.10 inches. Valid values are 0 to 1.25 inches, depending on the value of the top margin. The higher the value of the top margin, the lower the maximum value of the bottom margin.

**Clear Margins**     Click on this button to set the left, right, top, and bottom margins to 0.

**In**     Click on this button to cycle through the units of measure: inches, centimeters, picas, and points.

AmiPro

## Modifying Frame Lines and Shadows

These are the options in the Modify Frame Layout dialog box (Figure10.12) for frame lines and shadows:

**All**    Check this check box to draw lines around all sides of the frame. This is the line default.

**Left**    Check this check box to draw a line on the left side of the frame.

**Right**    Check this check box to draw a line on the right side of the frame.

**Top**    Check this check box to draw a line on the top side of the frame.

**Bottom**    Check this check box to draw a line on the bottom side of the frame.

**Line**    Open on this drop-down list box, to select a color for the lines around the frame. The default color is black.

**Shadow**    Open on this drop-down list box to select a color for the shadow specified in the Shadow group of this dialog box. The default color is black.

**FIGURE 10.12**

The Modify Frame Layout dialog box for frame lines and shadows

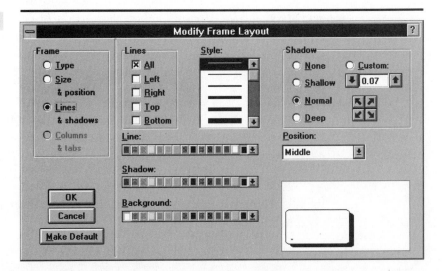

**Background**    Open on this drop-down list box, to select a color for the background of the frame. The default color is white.

**Style**    Select a line style for the lines around the frame from the scroll box.

**None**    Click on this option button to have no shadow.

**Shallow**    Click on this option button to have a shadow measuring 0.04 inches.

**Normal**    Click on this option button to have a shadow measuring 0.07 inches. This is the default shadow size.

**Deep**    Click on this option button to have a shadow measuring 0.12 inches.

**Custom**    Click on this option button to define a custom shadow measuring from 0 to 0.22 inches.

**Position**    Select from this drop-down list box to specify the position of lines as they relate to the margins within the frame. Choices allow you to change the display of lines on the margins (Inside) to outside the frame (Outside). Middle, which displays the lines between the margins and outside the frame, is the default.

## Modifying Frame Columns and Tabs

These are the options in the Modify Frame Layout dialog box for columns and tabs (Figure 10.13):

**Tabs**    Select the type of tab and define up to 22 tab stops for the text in the frame.

**Set Tab**    Click on this button to set the newly defined tab.

**Clear Tabs**    Click on this button to clear all tabs.

**Column Balance**    Check this check box to balance the length of the columns as equally as possible.

**Gutter Width**    Select the width of the space between columns. Valid values are 0 to 0.25 inches. The default is 0.17 inches.

AmiPro

**FIGURE 10.13**

The Modify Frame Layout dialog box for frame columns and tabs

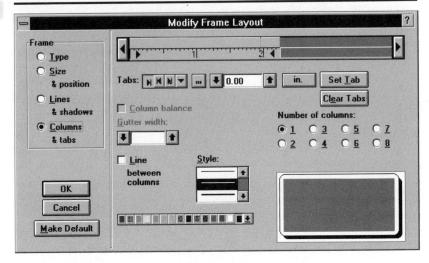

**Line between Columns**    Check this check box to place a vertical line between columns.

**Style**    Select a line style for the line between the columns. Select a color from the palette below the Style scroll box.

**Number of Columns**    Click on an option button to select the number of columns (from 1 to 8).

# Importing a Picture into Ami Pro

Ami Pro allows you to import a variety of pictures into your documents. You can import pictures having any of the following file types:

| | |
|---|---|
| AmiDraw (.SDW) | HPGL |
| AmiEquation | Lotus PIC |
| AutoCAD | PCX |

CGM                     TIFF

DrawPerfect             Windows Bitmap (.BMP)

EPS                     Windows Metafile (.WMF)

Freelance

You can also use the Edit menu in most Windows applications to copy and paste pictures into Ami Pro or from Ami Pro into another Windows application. Whether you paste or import a picture, pictures must be inserted into frames. You can either create a frame or have Ami Pro create the frame while the picture is being pasted or imported.

To import a picture into an Ami Pro document, follow these steps:

**1.** Choose File ➤ Import Picture. Ami Pro opens the Import Picture dialog box (Figure 10.14).

**2.** Select a file type from the File Type scroll box. For example, if you choose AmiDraw, you'll see a list of more than 100 pieces of clip art located in the \drawsym subdirectory.

**3.** If no list appears in the Files scroll box, you may need to change directories.

**4.** Select a file from the Files scroll list.

---

**FIGURE 10.14**

In the Import Picture dialog box, you can select a picture to be imported.

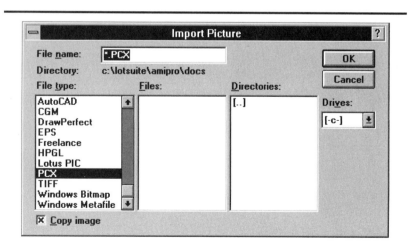

---

**5.** Either click on OK or press ↵. If you have not created a drawing frame, Ami Pro creates one and imports the picture into it.

Figure 10.15 shows the top of a document with three frames: one with a logo drawn in Windows Paintbrush, one holding the company name, and the third with a piece of AmiDraw clip art.

**FIGURE 10.15**

A sample document with three frames, one for the letterhead, and one for the graphic

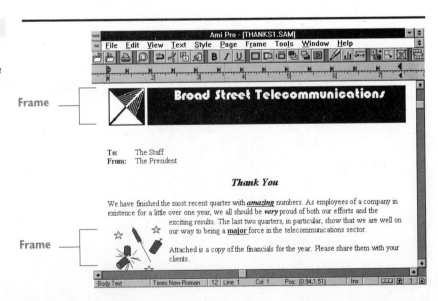

# PART FOUR

# Organizing Information with Approach

In Part Four, you'll find out how to organize and report on your data with Approach, Lotus's relational database application. First, you'll create a database and assign data types, and you'll learn about manipulating data by sorting and searching. In the process, you'll master database and Approach basics. You'll learn how to take advantage of Approach's strengths as a relational database by using the types of files that work together most efficiently. You'll discover how easy it is to create and edit standard, columnar, and summary reports. Finally, you'll learn how to quickly create merge documents and labels to fully automate your mailings.

Table IV.1 illustrates and describes the Approach SmartIcons.

# Approach SmartIcons

| SMARTICON | DESCRIPTION |
|---|---|
| **Approach SmartIcons** | |

Opens an existing file. [File ➤ Open] *Shortcut:* Ctrl+O

Saves the current Approach file. [File ➤ Save Approach File] *Shortcut:* Ctrl+S

Sends mail, if a mail application is installed. [File ➤ Send Mail]

Prints the current view. [File ➤ Print] *Shortcut:* Ctrl+P

Goes to Preview. [File ➤ Preview] *Shortcut:* Ctrl+Shift+B

Goes to the first record. *Shortcut:* Ctrl+Home

Goes to the previous record. *Shortcut:* PgUp or the left arrow on the status bar

Goes to the next record. *Shortcut:* PgDn or the right arrow on the status bar

Goes to the last record. *Shortcut:* Ctrl+Home

Goes to Design. [View ➤ Design] *Shortcut:* Ctrl+D

Goes to Browse. [View ➤ Browse] *Shortcut:* Ctrl+B

Finds a set of records. [Browse ➤ Find] *Shortcut:* Ctrl+F

Finds all the records in the file. [Browse ➤ Show All] *Shortcut:* Ctrl+A

Sorts records in ascending order. [Browse ➤ Sort ➤ Ascending]

**Approach SmartIcons (continued)**

| | |
|---|---|
| | Sorts records in descending order. [Browse ➤ Sort ➤ Descending] |
| | Creates a new record. [Browse ➤ New Record] *Shortcut:* Ctrl+N |
| | Deletes the selected record. [Browse ➤ Delete Record] *Shortcut:* Ctrl+Del |
| | Duplicates the current record. [Browse ➤ Duplicate Record] |
| | Inserts today's computer system date. [Browse ➤ Insert ➤ Today's Date] *Shortcut:* Ctrl+Shift+D |
| | Inserts today's computer system time. [Browse ➤ Insert ➤ Current Time] *Shortcut:* Ctrl+Shift+T |
| | Duplicates a value from the last changed record. [Browse ➤ Insert ➤ Previous Value] *Shortcut:* Ctrl+Shift+P |
| | Runs the spell check. [Tools ➤ Spell Check] *Shortcut:* Ctrl+K |
| | Enters the new record in the database or performs the find. *Shortcut:* ⏎ |
| | Undoes the last action, if allowed. [Edit ➤ Undo] *Shortcut:* Ctrl+Z |
| | Cuts the selection and places it in the Clipboard. [Edit ➤ Cut] *Shortcut:* Ctrl+X or Shift+Del |

Approach

# Approach SmartIcons

| SMARTICON | DESCRIPTION |
|---|---|
| | Approach SmartIcons (continued) |

Copies the view or all views to the Clipboard. [Edit ➤ Copy View] *Shortcut:* Ctrl+C or Ctrl+Ins

Pastes the contents of the Clipboard into the file. [Edit ➤ Paste] *Shortcut:* Ctrl+V or Shift+Ins

In Design, applies the format of the selection to new selections. [Object ➤ Fast Format] *Shortcut:* Ctrl+M

In Design, opens the InfoBox. [Object ➤ Style & Properties] *Shortcut:* Ctrl+E

In Design, brings the selected object one layer toward the front. [Object ➤ Arrange ➤ Bring Forward]

In Design, sends the selected object one layer toward the back. [Object ➤ Arrange ➤ Send Backward]

In Design, groups the selected objects. [Object ➤ Group] *Shortcut:* Ctrl+G

In Design, ungroups the selected object. [Object ➤ UnGroup] *Shortcut:* Ctrl+U

In Design, displays the grid. [View ➤ Show Grid]

Displays the ruler. [View ➤ Show Ruler] *Shortcut:* Ctrl+J

Displays the drawing tools. [View ➤ Show Drawing Tools] *Shortcut:* Ctrl+L

Zooms in. [View ➤ Zoom In]

Zooms out. [View ➤ Zoom Out]

| SMARTICON | DESCRIPTION |
| --- | --- |

**Approach SmartIcons (continued)**

Displays the next set of SmartIcons. [Tools ➤ SmartIcons]

Aligns the selection to the left margin of the field. [Object ➤ Align; then click on Left.] *Shortcut:* Ctrl+l

Centers the selection between the left and right margins of the field. [Object ➤ Align; then click on Center.] *Shortcut:* Ctrl+l

Aligns the selection to the right margin of the field. [Object ➤ Align; then click on Right.] *Shortcut:* Ctrl+l

Specifies single spacing for the selected lines. [Text ➤ Style & Properties; then click on the Text tab and select from line spacing.]

Specifies double spacing for the selected lines. [Text ➤ Style & Properties; then click on the Text tab and select from line spacing.]

 In Design, inserts a field. [Form ➤ Add Field; Report ➤ Add Field; Letter ➤ Add Field; Mailing Label ➤ Add Field; or Object ➤ Add Field]

# Planning and Creating Your First Database

In this chapter, you'll get acquainted with Approach. First, you'll find out some basic facts about databases. Then you'll learn how to plan, create, edit, and delete a database. Remember that you can learn the basics of opening and saving files by reviewing Chapter 2, and you can review editing concepts in Chapter 3.

## Introducing Approach

Approach is an easy-to-use and powerful relational database. *Relational databases* allow you to work simultaneously with multiple database files to get to and report on the information you need. For example, you can retrieve name and address information from one file, inventory items from another file, and vendor data from a third file.

Using Approach, you can do the following:

- print reports of customer or employee names, addresses, and telephone numbers.
- track all goods sold or not sold, including length of time on the market, asking price, and so on.
- match a vendors database with your inventory database to find out from whom to order.
- retrieve a list of employees who meet certain criteria. For example, you could retrieve a list of salespeople located in one region and experienced in selling a particular item.
- create a mail merge to all customers who meet income, education, or residence criteria.
- print inventory reports based on the entire inventory or categories of items. You can age the inventory or find out how popular certain items are.

## Reading and Writing Common File Formats

Approach reads Approach, dBASE III+ and IV, FoxPro, Query, Oracle, Paradox, 1-2-3 Ranges, SQL Server, DB2-MDI, Lotus Q+E dBASE, Access, ODBC Data Sources, ODBC: Lotus Q+E dBASE, ODBC Access, Text - Delimited, Text - Fixed-Length, Excel, and Lotus 1-2-3 files.

  **There are some restrictions on field definitions and limits on files, records, and fields.**

Approach writes to Approach files.

**WORKING TOGETHER**

# SmartSuite Initialization Files

Initialization (*.INI) files contain software and hardware information and current defaults. The following is a list of selected SmartSuite INI files, their directory locations, and descriptions.

| FILE | DIRECTORY | DESCRIPTION |
| --- | --- | --- |
| ACODES.INI | \amipro\macros | A list of area codes and associated data for the Ami Pro ACODES.SMM macro |
| ALASKA.INI | \123r5w\mapdata | Information about the Alaska map. There are other map .INI files in this subdirectory. |
| AMICALC.INI | \windows | A list of Ami Pro calculation functions |

**Approach**

| FILE | DIRECTORY | DESCRIPTION |
| --- | --- | --- |
| AMIDRAW.INI | \windows | A list of the current Ami Pro Drawing settings |
| AMIDW.INI | \windows | Information about the Ami Pro DisplayWrite 4 filter |
| AMIEQN.INI | \windows | The settings for the Ami Pro Equation editor |
| AMIFONT.INI | \windows | The default Ami Pro Roman, Swiss, Modern, Script, Decorative, and symbol fonts |
| AMIIWP.INI | \windows | Information used by Ami Pro's Wang (IWP) import filter |
| AMILABEL.INI | \windows | Information used for printing labels in Ami Pro |
| AMIOW.INI | \windows | Information used to map printer fonts from Office Writer to Ami Pro |

**WORKING
TOGETHER**
▲

| FILE | DIRECTORY | DESCRIPTION |
|---|---|---|
| AMIPRO.INI | \windows | A list of many Ami Pro elements and defaults, such as Ami Pro components, paths and directories, user information, grammar checker, filters, and SmartIcons |
| AMIPRO2.INI | \windows | A list of more Ami Pro elements and defaults, including current template information |
| AMIWP.INI | \windows | A list of fonts associated with exporting to WordPerfect |
| APPRCH2.INI | \approach \tutorial | Information about the Approach tutorial attributes: fonts, font sizes, positions of window elements, colors, and so on |
| APPROACH.INI | \windows | A list of many Approach elements and defaults, such as most recently used files, colors, fonts, point size, and SmartIcons |

Approach

| FILE | DIRECTORY | DESCRIPTION |
| --- | --- | --- |
| EBTIF9.INI | \lotusapp\filters | Information about the TIFF export filter |
| FILLS.INI | \123r5w\programs | Information about Fill-by-Example custom fills |
| FLW2.INI | \windows | A list of many Freelance Graphics elements and defaults, such as paths and directories, most recently opened files, fonts, import and export extensions, and SmartIcons |
| INSTALL.INI | \123r5w | Information about 1-2-3 installation file sets—their directories and purpose |
| INSTALL.INI | \123r5w | A brief history of the 1-2-3 installation program and country information |
| IRTIF9.INI | \lotusapp\filters | Information about the TIFF import filter |

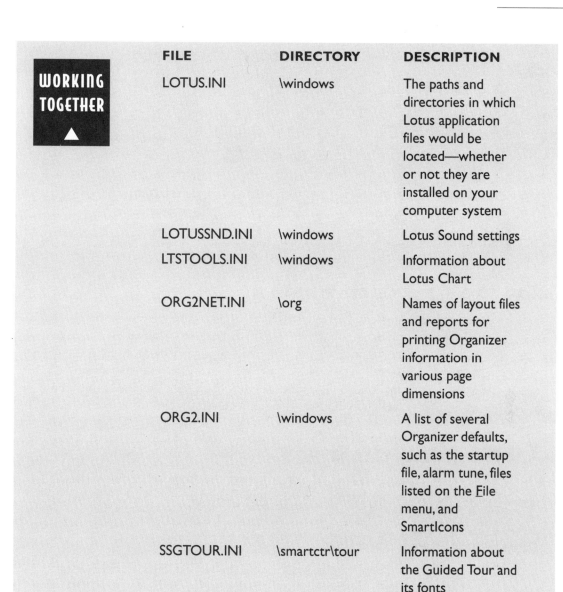

| | FILE | DIRECTORY | DESCRIPTION |
|---|---|---|---|
| **WORKING TOGETHER** ▲ | LOTUS.INI | \windows | The paths and directories in which Lotus application files would be located—whether or not they are installed on your computer system |
| | LOTUSSND.INI | \windows | Lotus Sound settings |
| | LTSTOOLS.INI | \windows | Information about Lotus Chart |
| | ORG2NET.INI | \org | Names of layout files and reports for printing Organizer information in various page dimensions |
| | ORG2.INI | \windows | A list of several Organizer defaults, such as the startup file, alarm tune, files listed on the File menu, and SmartIcons |
| | SSGTOUR.INI | \smartctr\tour | Information about the Guided Tour and its fonts |

Approach

| | FILE | DIRECTORY | DESCRIPTION |
|---|---|---|---|
| **WORKING TOGETHER** ▲ | WIN.INI | \windows | Windows environment settings, including information about Windows applications— directories, paths, and extensions |

# Viewing the Approach Window

The Approach application window (Figure 11.1) contains many of the elements that you found out about in Chapter 2. Because you are now working in a database application, its window includes unique elements to help make your job easier, as well as common elements about which you have already learned. In this section, you'll get an overview of all the elements of the application window and find out about the Approach status bar.

## Approach SmartIcons

The pages starting Part Four (the beginning of the Approach section) show all the Approach SmartIcons. To learn how SmartIcons work, see Chapter 2.

## The Work Area

The work area displays records and forms as you work. Notice that the document area includes both a vertical and a horizontal scroll bar.

FIGURE 11.1

The Approach
application window
provides many helpful
elements to assist you
in creating and editing
databases.

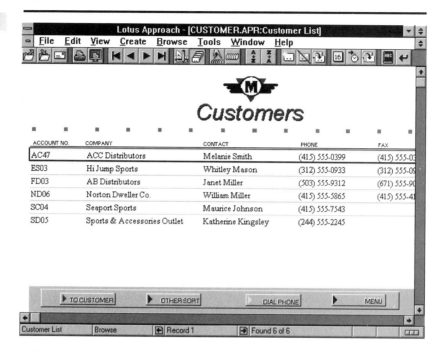

## The Approach Status Bar

The Approach status bar (Figure 11.2) allows you to change to a different
view or environment, or to display a set of SmartIcons. Depending on the
current environment, you might be able to magnify or reduce the form on the
screen, see the page or record number, or go to a specific record.

FIGURE 11.2

The Approach status
bar consists of buttons
with which you can
change the view, the
environment, or the
record.

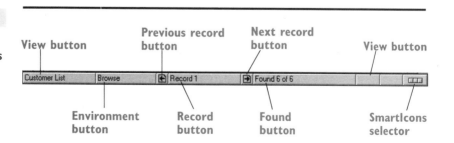

Approach

The Approach status bar provides these buttons:

**View**    Click on this button to reveal a list of views for the current database (Figure 11.3).

**Environment**    Click on this button to reveal a list of the environments (Figure 11.4) to which you can go.

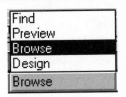

**Previous Record**    Click on this button to move to the previous record, unless you are on the first record.

**Record Status**    Click on this button, which shows the current record number, to display the Go To Record dialog box (Figure 11.5).

 **Next Record**    Click on this button to move to the next record, unless you are on the last page or screen.

**FIGURE 11.5**

The Go To Record
dialog box allows you
to move to a record in
the current database.

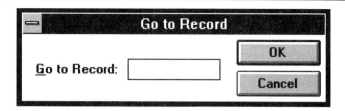

**Found**    Displays the number of records you have found. If you have
not explicitly found any records, Approach states that all the records are
found.

**View**    In Design and Preview, displays the size at which you are currently
viewing this record, form, report, or page. For example, if you see 50% on this
button, you are viewing at half the size of the printed page. Click on this button to choose from a list of percentages (Figure 11.6).

**FIGURE 11.6**

The list of viewing
percentages

**Dimensions**    In Design, you can always be aware of the current cursor
location and size of the page or a box that you are drawing. The number
after *W* shows the location of the mouse pointer between the left and
right margins. The number after the *H* shows the location of the mouse
pointer between the top and bottom margins.

**NOTE**    **In Design, you can change the font or font size and/or apply
or remove boldface, italics, or underlines.**

**Approach**

409

**SmartIcons selector**      Click on this button to display a list of Smart-Icons (Figure 11.7). Click on Hide SmartIcons to remove all SmartIcons from the desktop.

**NOTE**   Another way to display the SmartIcon set related to a specific environment (for example, Browse, Design, Preview, or Find) is to click on the appropriate SmartIcon.

The SmartIcon sets you can choose in Design and the line that hides SmartIcons

# Learning about the Elements of a Database

A *database* contains groups of organized information, which can be sorted, retrieved, reported on, and/or copied into letters and mailing labels. To make an analogy, a database is like a file cabinet drawer loaded with letters and documents. If each folder in the drawer is arranged in some sort of order, you'll be able to find the information you are looking for almost instantaneously. On the other hand, if you have high stacks of correspondence and reports piled on your desk and waiting to be filed, you won't be able to find a crucial document when your manager urgently needs it. So one of the most important elements of a database is organization—ensuring that each drawer and folder is just so.

## Field

A *field*, which is the smallest piece of a database, is the area into which you type a single piece of information. A field is one piece of information on a form or letter in the file drawer. For example, one field on an employment application includes the name of the college that an applicant attended and another field holds the applicant's first name.

To describe the contents of a field and tell Approach how it can use the information, assign a *field type*. For example, you can define Date as a date field (especially if you calculate the difference between that date and the date of hire to track the weeks, months, or years that it takes for a prospective employee to become an actual employee). Last Name, First Name, Street, City, and state are all text fields. Approach can use the information in a date field for computation but cannot compute the contents of a text field.

A *field label* is the name that you give to a field; it helps the person entering data to identify what kind of information the field contains. Returning to our analogy, examples of field labels are *College or University* and *First Name*. It's very clear that the applicant is expected to write the name of his or her alma mater in the first field and his or her first name in the second field.

## Record

A *record* contains a group of related fields. In other words, one application for employment is a record, and as you remember, every piece of information on the application is a field. It's a record of the meaningful information about an individual. Examples of other records are a time card, a trip report, and a passport application.

## Form

A *form* is a record layout that allows for easy and efficient data entry. For example, you'll place name and address information so that you can type information in the order with which you are most comfortable. In most cases, you'll type the first and last name, then the street address, followed by the city, state, and zip code.

**Approach**

# Approach

## Planning and Designing a Database

In this section, you'll plan, design, and create a sample database, STAFF, which contains employee information. In many cases, you'll be able to use one of the Approach database templates rather than designing and creating your own. You'll find the templates in the \samples subdirectory.

If you plan to create a database based on your design, devote some time to planning. Although Approach makes it easy to fine-tune and redesign an existing database on the fly, it is a good idea to develop the habit of using pencil and paper to plan. All you have to do is write down the name of each field and its length. After you learn about field types in "Specifying Field Types" later in this chapter, you'll add the appropriate type next to each field label. You'll learn how to design a form later in this chapter, so all you need at this point is a list of fields—nothing more.

As you plan any database, review the following questions:

- What are the main reasons for creating this database? Will you create mailing labels, are you gathering information for reports, or both?
- What fields does this database need? When developing your list of fields, are you thinking about your company or department's growth and plans for the future? For example, do you have room for several telephone numbers: for voice, fax, and modem?
- Do you need to reserve space for new fields, or is it more practical to create a new database?
- Are the fields arranged so that data entry is easy? Are related fields grouped together?
- What information types should you assign to each field? What fields are used for calculations? for sorting? for indexes?
- How many ways do you need to sort the information in the database? How many subsets of records do you wish to retrieve?
- Should the database include room for addresses outside your home country?

Other factors to consider:

- Give a database an easy-to-remember name. For example, the names TRAVEL or even EMP_TRAV are better reminders that a database contains travel information than EMP_09AB.

- Keep it simple and small! You can add complex computations and multiple pages of fields after you spend time learning Approach. In fact, because Approach is a relational database, there is never a need for a gigantic database; it's much easier to work with a set of joined databases instead.

- For better sorting and retrieving, each field should be the smallest possible component of the database. For example, instead of a Name field containing Mr. Thomas Jones, Jr., define Title (Mr.), First Name (Thomas), and Last Name (Jones). In fact, if your database will include many names (e.g., a list of registered voters or licensed drivers), consider adding a suffix field for Jrs, IIIs, and so on.

- It is a good idea to include a field with a unique identifier for each record. If you are building a company database, you can use the employee's identification number. But if you are compiling a list of clients, consider combining the last name with the year and date (e.g., SMIL950712). An ID field makes it more difficult to duplicate records accidentally. When you create the STAFF database, you'll see two built-in identifiers: the employee number and the key name.

# Specifying Field Types

When you design an Approach database, the two important pieces of information you'll provide for a field are its name and its type. Selecting the correct field type ensures that you see the contents of a field in a familiar format (e.g., a typical date field looks like *Apr 17, 1998*, or a zip code field keeps its leading zeroes), you'll be able to calculate numbers when needed (e.g., to determine an employee's years of service or to compute a commission in dollars for a paycheck), and you can define a field so that it contains a graphic (e.g., to display your company logo on a report or mailing label).

The list below summarizes each of the Approach field types.

**Text**    Alphanumeric information, such as names, addresses, cities, and company names

**Memo**    Alphanumeric information, such as notes, descriptions, and supplemental information

**Numeric**    Numeric information, such as percentages, currency, quantities, units, discount rates, multipliers, bonus factors, measures, zip codes, telephone numbers, and social security numbers

**Date**    Date information, for date formatting

**Time**    Time information, for time formatting

**Calculated**    Formulas; the results appear in the field

**Boolean**    Answers to Yes/No, True/False, or 0/1

**PicturePlus**    Objects, such as graphics, charts, spreadsheet ranges, and sound files from Windows applications supporting OLE

**Variable**    Information stored temporarily for any field type that you define

## Text Field Type

The most common field type is text, which is the default. Text fields accept any combination of characters—alphabetic, numeric, punctuation, or special symbols—and can have up to 255 characters. (For longer fields, use the Memo field type instead.) Use this field type for any data that you either won't use for calculations or don't want Approach to format as money, a date, or a time. Other examples of text fields are identification numbers, last name, address, city, and state. In the STAFF database, every field that does not fall into another field type category is a text type. To see how to specify a format for a text field, see "Selecting a Format for a Field," later in this chapter.

## Memo Field Type

A close, but much larger, relative of the text field is the memo field type. Like a text field, a memo field accepts any combination of characters. A memo field can be up to 5 (dBASE III) or 64 (dBASE IV) kilobytes in length. When you enter information in a memo field, Approach stores it in a separate file.

# Numeric Field Type

The numeric field type is the all-purpose field type for numbers that will be calculated or numerically sorted but cannot be categorized as date or time. Approach does not accept non-numeric characters typed in a numeric field, except for negative signs and decimal points, which indicate negative numbers and numbers that are not integers (e.g., −101.34), respectively. Don't type commas or currency symbols; you'll select a format to do that. Typing commas into a number field is not necessary because Approach removes or adds them depending on the format defined for that number field.

Normally, Approach does not accept leading zeroes (e.g., 0566.80) in a number field; after you type a leading zero, Approach removes it (e.g., 566.80). However, if you format a numeric field as a zip code, for example, Approach allows leading zeroes. Examples of number fields are percentages, quantities, units, discount rates, multipliers, bonus factors, measures, zip codes, currency, telephone numbers, and social security numbers. The Commission field in the STAFF database, which is a percentage, is a numeric field, as are the SS Number, Zip, and Salary fields. To see how to specify a format for a numeric field, see "Selecting a Format for a Field," later in this chapter.

# Date Field Type

Selecting the date field type ensures that appropriate numbers and characters typed in a field are converted to a date format. The default date format is the current Windows date format. (To change the default Windows date format, select the International icon in the Control Panel. For more Windows information, see Appendix B.) You can have Approach automatically enter the date in date fields. Your choices are the date on which the record was created or the date on which it was modified.

Approach can calculate date fields. For example, you can have Approach compute the number of years that an employee has worked for your company by subtracting the date of hire from today's date, or you can calculate someone's age by subtracting a birthday field from the current date. To see how to specify a format for a date field, see "Selecting a Format for a Field," later in this chapter.

Approach

## Time Field Type

The time field type ensures that Approach formats numbers entered in the field as a time. The only non-numeric characters that you can type in a time field are AM and PM. You can have Approach automatically enter the time in time fields. Your choices are the time at which the record was created or the time at which it was modified.

Approach can calculate time fields. For example, an employee can track his or her hours by having Approach subtract a login time from a logout time. The STAFF database does not have a time field. To see how to specify a format for a time field, see "Selecting a Format for a Field," later in this chapter.

## Calculated Field Type

Use a Calculated field type to hold the results of a formula written in the field at the same time you define the field. Approach formulas can hold constants or references to another field (for example, Price * .07).

## Boolean Field Type

You can use the Boolean field type to answer questions to which the answer is Yes or No, True or False, or 0 or 1. For example, in the STAFF database, a Yes/No field shows whether an employee travels or not. *Yes, y, True, T,* or *1* indicates that the employee travels; otherwise, the answer is *No, n, False, F,* or *0.* If you use a check box or option box for a Boolean field, the person entering data can just click on a choice.

## PicturePlus Field Type

Approach uses the PicturePlus field type to define a field in which you will embed or paste a graphic or object from an application that supports Object Linking and Embedding (OLE). In addition to pictures, PicturePlus fields can hold charts, spreadsheet ranges, and sound files. Supported picture formats are .BMP, .DIB, .EPS, .GIF, .PCX, .TGA, .TIF, and .WMF. Approach supports any sound files for which you have an OLE server.

## Variable Field Type

Approach uses the Variable field type to temporarily store information. The contents of a Variable field are very similar to the contents of the Windows Clipboard; it's a storage place used to hold information temporarily. When you turn off your computer, the contents of the Variable field, like those of the Clipboard, disappear permanently. When you define a Variable field, identify the field type of the information that it will hold.

# (reating a Database

In this section, you can create a database. If you wish, you can use the sample database STAFF.DBF:

| FIELD LABEL | DESCRIPTION | FIELD TYPE |
| --- | --- | --- |
| SS Number | Employee social security number | Numeric |
| Hire Date | Date employee started work | Date |
| First Name | Employee's first name | Text |
| Last Name | Employee's last name | Text |
| Address 1 | First line of employee's street address | Text |
| Address 2 | Second line of employee's street address (e.g., apartment number or post office box number) | Text |
| City | City or town in which the employee resides | Text |
| State | State in which the employee resides | Text |
| ZIP | Zip code | Numeric |
| Department | The department to which the employee is assigned | Text |

| FIELD LABEL | DESCRIPTION | FIELD TYPE |
|---|---|---|
| Title | The employee's job title or position | Text |
| Extension | The employee's telephone extension | Text |
| Salary | The employee's current gross salary | Numeric |
| Commission | A computed percentage of sales for which the employee is totally or somewhat responsible. | Numeric |
| Calc_Commission | The calculated dollar commission | Calculated |
| Travel | A yes or no answer to whether the employee travels for the company | Boolean |

Once you have decided on the fields and their field types, the next step is to create the database. To create a new database, start Approach and follow these steps:

1. In the Welcome dialog box, double-click on Blank Database. (If you have turned off the Welcome dialog box, choose File ➤ New.) Approach then opens the New dialog box (See Figure 11.8)

**FIGURE 11.8**

The New dialog box with the name of a new database already typed in

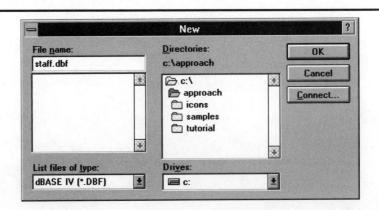

2. To store the new file in a different location, select from the choices in the Directories box and the Drives drop-down box.

3. In the File Name text box, type a filename (e.g., STAFF).

4. Click on OK or press ⏎. You don't have to type an extension after the filename; Approach assigns the .DBF (dBASE IV) extension. Approach then opens the Creating New Database dialog box (Figure 11.9), in which you define the field.

**FIGURE 11.9**

The Creating New Database dialog box is used for defining fields for a new database.

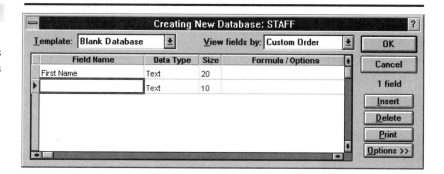

5. Type a Field Name in the Field Name column.

6. Assign a field type by clicking in the Data Type text box, clicking on the downward-pointing arrow to the right of the Type drop-down list box, and clicking on your choice. For instructions on entering a formula in a calculated field, see the following section.

 **TIP** **You can select a field type quickly by highlighting the Type drop-down list box and entering the first character of the type name.**

7. Fill in a field length in the Size column. Try to be accurate in determining length, but don't underestimate.

**Approach**

**NOTE** If you are filling in a numeric field, the number to the left of the decimal point in the Length text box represents the number of digits to the left of the decimal point, not the total length of the number.

**8.** After clicking in the next empty Field Name cell, repeat steps 5-7 to add the next fields.

**9.** When you have defined the last field, click on OK. Approach displays the record in the default format and changes to Browse. Figure 11.10 shows the almost-completed database in the Creating New Database dialog box. Figure 11.11 shows the database form in the Browse environment.

**NOTE** You can use the preceding steps to add a field to a database at any time.

**FIGURE 11.10**

The Field Definition dialog box with several fields in STAFF displayed in the Database Fields box

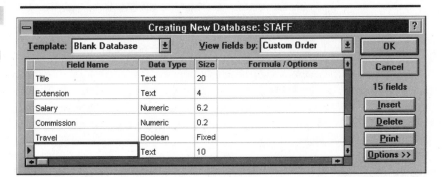

## Defining a Calculated Field

Defining a calculated field in the Creating New Database dialog box is very similar to defining any other field, until you select the field type. (If you have already saved the database, choose Create ➤ Field Definition to reopen the Field Definition dialog box.) When you select Calculated, Approach adds to the Creating New Database dialog box (Figure 11.12). Assemble the formula by clicking on fields, operators, and functions. For example, to create the

## FIGURE 11.11

The new STAFF database as it is displayed in Browse. If you wish, you can start typing data.

**Lotus Approach - [STAFF.APR:Form 1]**

File  Edit  View  Create  Browse  Tools  Window  Help

| Form 1 | Worksheet 1 |

**Form 1**

| SS Number | Hire Date | First Name | | Last Name |

| Address 1 | | Address 2 |

| City | | State | ZIP | Department |

| Title | | Extension | Salary | Commission | Travel |

Form 1     Browse     Record 1     Found 0 of 0

Calc_Commission formula, click on Salary, click on the multiplication operator, and click on Commission. Then click on OK. In the Add Field dialog
box, drag the new field onto the form. Notice that Approach differentiates between calculated fields and all others by displaying the field in italics. Close
the Add Field dialog box by selecting Close from the Control menus or pressing Alt+F4.

## Selecting a Format for a Field

You can ensure that the value entered in a field looks like a date, time, money,
or one of three text formats. Just click on Design in the Status bar, click on a
field, choose <u>O</u>bject ➤ <u>S</u>tyle & Properties, or press Ctrl+E. Fill in the InfoBox
(Figure 11.13), and click on OK.

**You can also open the InfoBox by double-clicking on a field
that you wish to format.**

Approach

**FIGURE 11.12**

The Field Definition dialog box with the Calc_Commission formula defined

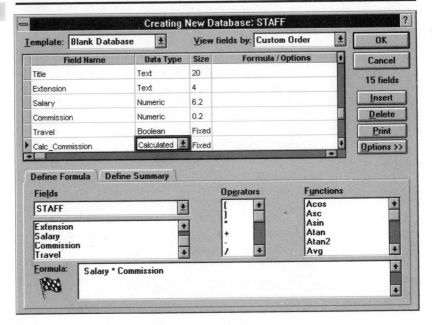

**FIGURE 11.13**

The InfoBox, in which you can change a design format for a selected field or other object

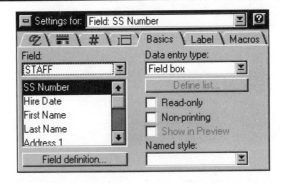

These are the categories in the InfoBox:

**Text**    Click on this tab to change the font, style, font size, alignment, text color, and text relief.

**Lines and Colors**    Click on this tab to change the border width, border color, fill color, shadow color, type of frame, and border lines.

**Format**     Click on this tab to change the format for the current field.

**Dimensions**     Click on this tab to change the width, height, and position of the object in the work area or when printing.

**Basics**     Click on this tab to select a field, open the Field Definition dialog box, select or define a data entry type, check field attributes, and name a style.

**Label**     Click on this tab to specify label attributes: the font, style, font size, alignment, text, position, color, and text relief.

**Macros**     Click on this tab to specify what triggers the running of a macro attached to the selected field or to define a macro.

When you open the InfoBox and click on the Format tab, Approach displays *Display as Entered* or the format type for the selected field. Display as Entered formats the value in the selected field just as you entered it. This is the default for any field.

Approach date formats are as follows:

**Date Format**     Click on this option button to select a custom date format or create a custom date format after you click on the Other option button. The list below shows an example of each date format.

| FORMAT | EXAMPLES |
|---|---|
| Day-Month-Year | Monday, 23 January, 1995 *or* Mon, 23 01, 1995 *or* Mon, 23 Jan 95 |
| Month-Day-Year | Monday, January 23, 1995 *or* Mon, 01 23, 1995 *or* Mon, Jan 23, 95 |
| Year-Month-Day | Monday, 1995 January, 23 *or* Mon, 1995 01, 23 *or* Mon, 95 Jan, 23 |
| Other | 11 other formats or your own custom format |

The list below describes the syntax for each component of a date:

| PART OF DATE | OPTIONS |
| --- | --- |
| Day of Week | 3-character (e.g., Mon) or full name (e.g., Monday) |
| Day | Day without leading zero inserted, if needed (e.g., 2 or 25), or day with leading zero inserted, if needed (e.g., 02 or 25) |
| Month | Month without leading zero inserted, if needed (e.g., 1 or 12), or month with leading zero inserted, if needed (e.g., 01 or 12), or 3-character month (Jan or Dec), or full name (January or December) |
| Year | 2-digit year (95), or 4-digit year (1995) |

**Time Format**    Click on this option button to select a time format. The list below shows an example of each time format:

| FORMAT | EXAMPLE (12-HOUR TIME) | EXAMPLE (24-HOUR TIME) |
| --- | --- | --- |
| Hour:Minute: Second:Hundredth AM I PM | 4:20:07:00 PM | 16:20:07:00 |
| Hour:Minute:Second AM I PM | 4:20:07 PM | 16:20:07 |
| Hour:Minute AM I PM | 4:20 PM | 16:20 |
| Hour AM I PM | 4 PM | 16 |

**Numeric Format**    Approach numeric format types are Integer, General, Currency, Currency with decimals, Percent, Percent with decimals, Telephone, Social Security, Scientific, and Zip code. Click on this option button to select a numeric format, or create a custom numeric format by overtyping the value in the <u>N</u>umeric Format text/drop-down list box.

The list below describes each numeric format:

**#,##0;(#,##0)**     For the Integer format, Approach inserts commas to indicate thousands. Digits following decimal points are not included in the display. Negative numbers are enclosed in parentheses.

**#,##0.00;(#,##0.00)**     For the General format, Approach inserts commas to indicate thousands. Digits following decimal points are included in the display. Negative numbers are enclosed in parentheses.

**$#,##0;($#,##0)**     For the Currency format, Approach inserts a dollar sign preceding the numbers and commas to indicate thousands. Digits following decimal points are not included in the display. Negative numbers are enclosed in parentheses.

**$#,##0.00;($#,##0.00)**     For the Currency with decimals format, Approach inserts a dollar sign preceding the number and commas to indicate thousands. Digits following decimal points are included in the display. Negative numbers are enclosed in parentheses.

**0%**     For the Percent format, Approach inserts a percent sign following the number. Digits following decimal points are not included in the display. Negative numbers are preceded by minus signs.

**0.00%**     For the Percent with decimals format, Approach inserts a percent sign following the number. Digits following decimal points are included in the display. Negative numbers are preceded by minus signs.

**7 (###)""000-0000 or 7 000-0000**     For the Telephone format, Approach formats the number as a U.S. telephone number (for example, (555) 555-5555).

**000-00-000**     For the Social Security format, Approach formats the number as a social security number (for example, 555-55-5555).

**0.00e+00**     For the Scientific format, Approach formats the number as an exponential number.

**5 00000-0000 or 00000**     For the Zip Code format, Approach formats the number as a 9- or 5-digit zip code.

The list below presents the syntax used for Approach numeric formats:

**#**     A placeholder for an optional number. If the number isn't large enough to include a digit other than 0, Approach omits the digit.

**0**     A placeholder for a required number. If the number isn't large enough to include a digit other than 0, Approach inserts a 0.

**.**     A decimal point.

**,**     A comma, which separates thousands. If a number isn't large enough to include a thousands separator, Approach omits it.

**;**     A semicolon, which separates two related syntaxes. For example, a semicolon separates positive and negative syntaxes in some numeric formats.

**$**     A dollar sign, which is inserted in the place it appears in the syntax.

**%**     A percent sign, which is inserted in the place it appears in the syntax.

**+**     A plus sign, which is inserted in the place it appears in the syntax, if the number is positive.

**−**     A minus sign, which is inserted in the place it appears in the syntax, if the number is negative.

**()**     Parentheses, which are inserted in the places they appear in the syntax, if the number is negative.

**:**     A colon, which is inserted in the place it appears in the syntax; normally used to separate digits in a date or time.

**Text Format**     Click on this option button to select a text format: ALL CAPITALIZED, all lowercase, or First Capitalized.

You'll learn more about using the InfoBox later in this chapter. In the meantime, go through the sample database and format the fields (for example, format ZIP as a Zip Code Field and SS Number as a Social Security field).

# Using Forms

Once you have created a database, you can start typing information into the form. However, Approach provides a better way: you can design and create a customized form, which should make data input a much more pleasant experience.

## Planning and Designing a Form

Although you can accept the default form, arranging the fields in the order in which you would add information is important. For example, most people are so accustomed to filling out forms in a "name, address, city, state, zip code" order that it makes sense to arrange fields in the same order.

In sketching out your own database design on paper, plan for easy data entry by spreading fields out (from the left margin to the right margin, and from the top of the screen to the bottom). Make sure there is room for adding lines and boxes. Use white space (areas that don't contain text or graphics), boxes, and lines to group similar or related fields and to separate dissimilar fields. Be sure to leave enough room to add a new field to groups of related fields.

When you design a form, you can use all the fields in the database or just a few. If you plan to use several types of information from a database (e.g., to create special mailing labels or a unique report), create a form for each purpose.

## Creating a Form

When you create a form, you'll start working with the Form Assistant. First, you'll select a form and then you'll identify the fields that you wish to have in the form, clicking on the Add button after selecting the fields. (If you wish to remove any of your selections, click on it and then click on the Remove button.) After you have selected the last field for the form, click on the Done button.

To create a new form for your new database, open the STAFF database (or the database with which you are working) and follow these steps:

1. Choose Create ➤ Form. Approach displays the Form Assistant dialog box (Figure 11.14).

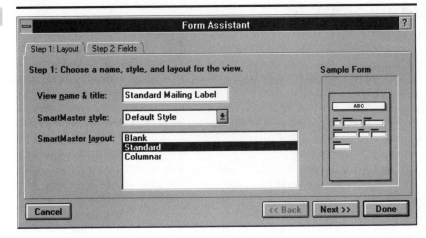

**FIGURE 11.14**

The Form Assistant dialog box with Step 1 filled in

2. Type the name of the form in the View Name & Title text box. Select Standard from the SmartMaster Layout list box. Click on the Next button. Approach changes to Step 2 in the Form Assistant dialog box (Figure 11.15).

3. Select a field to be added to the form.

4. Click on the Add button to add the selected field to the form.

5. To remove a field from the form, select it and click on the Remove button.

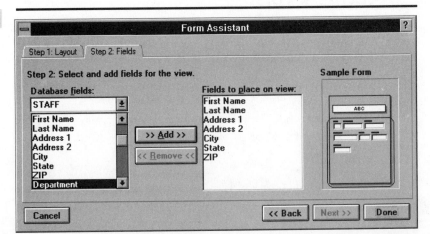

**FIGURE 11.15**

The Form Assistant dialog box with Step 2 completed

6. Repeat steps 3 and 4 to add more fields to the new form.

7. When you have added all the desired fields to the new form, click on Done. Approach closes the dialog box, displays the selected fields arranged in the work area as you specified, and displays the form name on the view button.

If you wish, you can edit the form by using the InfoBox or by changing the location and/or size of fields.

## Editing a Form

Approach provides a great deal of flexibility in form design. After you add the desired fields to a form, you can change their sizes, move them around the form, and enhance them.

Sizing a field box is quite easy. First, click on the field to be changed. When Approach adds handles to the field, point to a handle and drag it until it reaches the desired size.

It's easy to rearrange the form so that objects, such as fields, are logically placed and data entry is as easy as possible. To move an object, press and hold down the mouse button anywhere within its boundaries. When the mouse pointer looks like a hand, drag the object to its new location, and release the mouse button. When you drag a field, you also drag its field label.

Before moving the first object, particularly for a very crowded form, review these notes:

- If an object is one of the last to be moved, temporarily drag it to an empty space, preferably at the bottom of the form. This gets it out of the way, leaving you with more workspace.

- Before starting to move objects around the form, turn the grid on by choosing <u>V</u>iew ➤ Show Grid. To have objects align with, or *snap to*, the grid, choose <u>V</u>iew ➤ Snap to Grid, or press Ctrl+Y.

- You can refine the grid so that fine adjustments in movement are possible. Choose <u>T</u>ools ➤ Preferences, and click on the Display tab, if needed. Open the Grid <u>W</u>idth drop-down list box, select values from $\frac{1}{16}$ to $\frac{1}{2}$ inch, and either click on OK or press ↵.

■ If you know that you will be increasing the length of a field in its final location, be sure to leave extra room on the form. In fact, if the field will be quite long, don't drag another object to the same horizontal grid line.

■ If you know that you will shorten the length of a field, you can squeeze more objects in the same area and adjust the length later.

■ Although it's very useful to group related objects (by selecting the objects and then choosing Object ➤ Group or pressing Ctrl+G), there is a disadvantage. Before you can add or remove room from an object in a group, you must ungroup. There is enough fine-tuning to each field and field label on a form that grouping can be counterproductive. Therefore, it is good to do your grouping as one of your later steps.

To enhance fields, use the InfoBox. Table 11.1 lists and describes the InfoBox elements used to enhance objects, including fields, and provides examples.

Figure 11.16 shows the completed Standard Mailing Label form for the STAFF database.

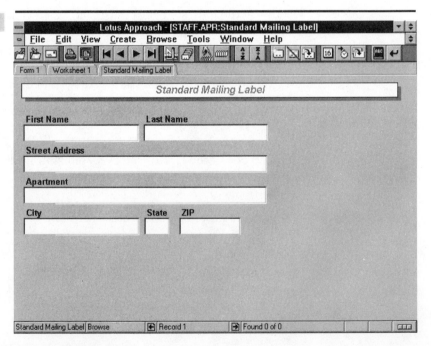

**FIGURE 11.16**

The Standard Mailing Label form with fields enhanced and in new positions

**TABLE 11.1:** Approach InfoBox Styles and Enhancements

| INFOBOX TAB | INFOBOX ELEMENT | DESCRIPTION |
| --- | --- | --- |
| Text | Font Name drop-down list box | Specifies the font for the selected text |
| Text | Style/Effect scroll box | Specifies the style (that is, Bold, Italic, Underline, or Strikethrough) of the selected text |
| Text | Size drop-down list box | Specifies the font size of the selected text |
| Text | Alignment buttons | Specifies the alignment (that is, left-aligned, center-aligned, or right-aligned) of the selected text |
| Text | Text Color drop-down list box | Applies a color to the selected text |
| Text | Text Relief drop-down list box | Specifies whether the selected text looks flat, embossed, or carved into the surface |
| Text | Line Spacing buttons | Specifies the spacing (that is single, one-and-one-half, and double) between text lines |
| Lines and Colors | Fill Color drop-down list box | Specifies the color within the borders of an object (for example, the box that contains the contents of a field) |
| Lines and Colors | Border Width drop-down list box | Specifies the thickness of the defined border |
| Lines and Colors | Frame drop-down list box | Changes the look of the frame surrounding the field contents |

**Approach**

**TABLE 11.1:** Approach InfoBox Styles and Enhancements (continued)

| INFOBOX TAB | INFOBOX ELEMENT | DESCRIPTION |
|---|---|---|
| Lines and Colors | Borders check boxes | Specifies whether left, right, top, bottom, and baseline borders are present or absent |
| Label | Label Font drop-down list box | Specifies the font for the selected label |
| Label | Style/Effect scroll box | Specifies the style (that is, Bold, Italic, Underline, or Strikethrough) of the selected label |
| Label | Size drop-down list box | Specifies the font size of the selected label |
| Label | Alignment buttons | Specifies the alignment (that is, left-aligned, center-aligned, or right-aligned) of the selected label |
| Label | Label Text | Changes the text for the selected label |
| Label | Label Position | Specifies the presence or position (that is, No Label, Above, Below, Left, Right) of the selected label with its field |
| Label | Label Color drop-down list box | Applies a color to the selected label |
| Label | Text Relief drop-down list box | Specifies whether the selected label looks flat, embossed, or carved into the surface |

## Specifying Cursor Movement in a Form

Normally, as you press the Tab key in an input form, the cursor moves from field to field in a left-to-right, top-to-bottom pattern. However, sometimes this does not happen or you want to change the order of movement. For example, as you drag fields around a form, their old tab order remains with them. To change tab order, in Design, choose View ➤ Show Data Entry Order and type new numbers on the tab symbols.

**NOTE** You can specify different tab orders for different input forms.

When you show the tab order for a specific input form, tab symbols are superimposed over the fields on the input form (Figure 11.17). As you press Shift

**FIGURE 11.17**

A form showing the default tab order

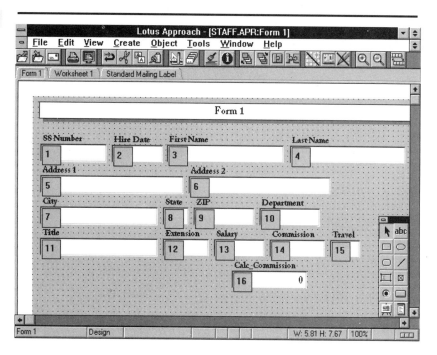

during data entry, the cursor travels from 1 to 2 to 3, and so on. You can view and/or change tab order for the current input form by following these steps:

1. Go to Design by clicking on the Design SmartIcon, selecting Design from the View list on the status bar, choosing <u>V</u>iew ➤ Design, or pressing Ctrl+D.

2. Choose <u>V</u>iew ➤ Data <u>E</u>ntry Order. Approach overlays tab symbols on the input form.

3. Select the number on the tab symbol you wish to change, and type a new number.

**NOTE** Sometimes Approach fills in the new number as you highlight the old; if you have eliminated a number and have created a gap between numbers, as you highlight the next number, Approach fills in the missing number.

4. Repeat step 3 until you have made all the desired changes.

5. Choose <u>V</u>iew ➤ Data <u>E</u>ntry Order or change to Browse. Approach removes the tab symbols from the form and implicitly saves the new tab order.

## Renaming a Form

Sometimes it's necessary to rename a view to better explain its purpose. For example, you might have accepted the default name of Form 3, or now you have two versions of a mailing label, one named Label and the other Form 6. To rename a view, follow these steps:

1. Select the view that you wish to rename by clicking on the View button on the status bar and selecting from the list or by clicking on the appropriate View tab.

2. Click on the form title at the top of the form.

3. Open the InfoBox by clicking on its SmartIcon, by choosing <u>O</u>bject ➤ Style & Properties, pressing Ctrl+E, or double-clicking on the form title.

4. Click on the Basics tab, if needed.

**5.** Open the Settings for drop-down list box, and select Form: *form name*.

**6.** In the Form Name text box, type the new name. Figure 11.18 shows the InfoBox as a view is renamed.

**7.** Close the InfoBox by clicking on its Control menu and selecting Close, or pressing Alt+F4.

**8.** Save the Approach file.

**FIGURE 11.18**

The InfoBox showing a
View being renamed

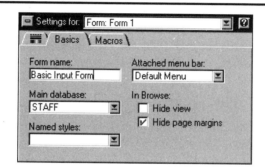

**NOTE** To change the title text at the top of the form, repeatedly click on the title until it's surrounded by a blue border. (However, don't click too rapidly. If Approach interprets your clicking as a double-click, it opens the InfoBox.) Then edit the title as you would any text.

## Deleting a Form

When you decide to move to a better form design or you change a database in such a way that a form is obsolete, it's better to remove it than to keep it. To remove a form, follow these steps:

**1.** Make active the soon-to-be-deleted form in the Design Input Forms area by selecting it from the drop-down list box on the tool bar.

**Approach**

2. Choose Edit ➤ Delete Form. (If you're deleting a report, form letter, or mailing label, this command changes to Delete Report, Delete Form Letter, or Delete Mailing Label.) Approach displays a message box that prompts you to confirm the deletion.

3. To delete the form, click on Yes. If you change your mind, click on No.

4. Save the Approach file.

12

# Entering
# Data

Although you can retrieve records, create reports, design input forms, and change a database's structure in Approach, most of your time is spent entering data—either by adding new records or by editing existing records. In this chapter, you'll find out all about entering data—preparing to enter data, entering data in different types of fields, and using special methods to save time.

# Displaying Records

You can view a record in two different ways: as a form or as a worksheet. As you learned in the last chapter, in a form you see all or part of one record at a time. A form displays the fields in various locations in the work area. A worksheet shows you several records at once, in a format that is very similar to a spreadsheet. In a worksheet, there is one record per row and one field per column. Regardless of the way that you view your database, you enter data in the same way. The only difference is the layout of fields and records.

A newly created Approach database starts with two basic views: Form 1, which is your first form, and Worksheet, the first worksheet. To choose one of these views, either click on the View button in the status bar and select or click on one of the tabs right below the SmartIcons.

## Displaying a Database as a Form

When you display a form, you can move fields to any location on the form. As you learned in the previous chapter, you can move the fields with the mouse and alter their fonts and field box sizes using the InfoBox. You can design and create several forms for a database—each for its own purpose. Figure 12.1 displays an employee information form from Approach's EMPLOYEE template. Notice that there is only one record on display.

FIGURE 12.1

The EMPLOYEE
Employee Info form

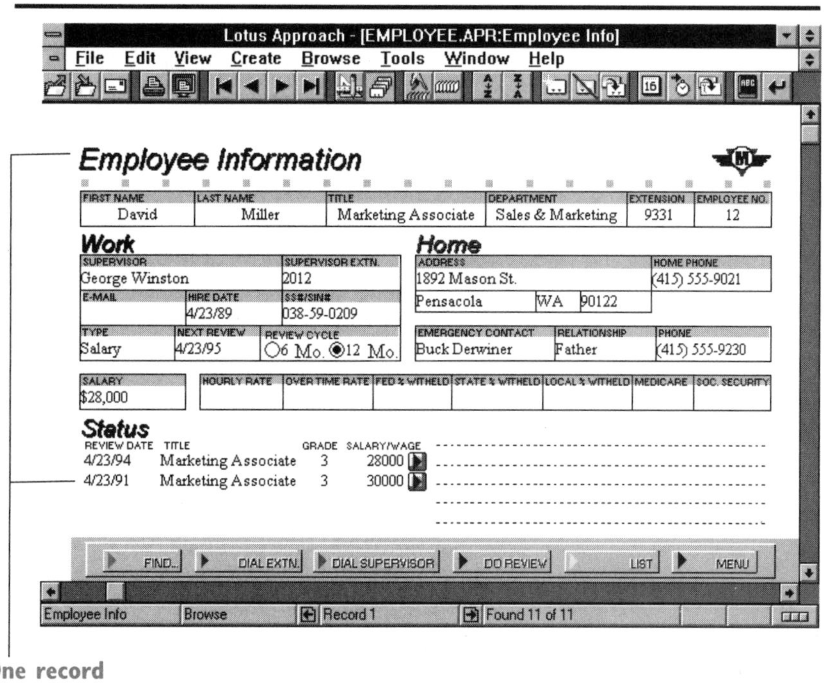

One record

## Displaying a Database as a Worksheet

Worksheet view displays fields as columns in a spreadsheet or table, and each record of the database is displayed as a row. Since you can see more than one record at a time, Worksheet view offers a more complete look at your database. Figure 12.2 shows a list from the EMPLOYEE template.

# Adding Records to a Database

A carefully designed form is the best way to add records to a database. Working with a form allows you to see the overall record before you start to fill in the next one. However, you can also add records in Worksheet view. For example, if you are entering many records at once and the contents of many fields will be the same (for example, the same city, state, and zip code), simply select a worksheet

Approach

**FIGURE 12.2**

The Employee List
from the EMPLOYEE
template

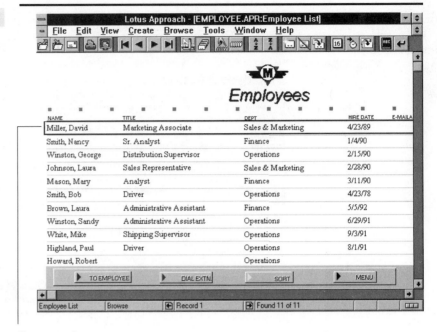

One record

or form and start typing information. You can add records to a database in either Form view or Worksheet view by following these steps:

1. If you are not in the Browse environment, either click on the Browse SmartIcon, click on the Environment button in the status bar and select Browse from the list, choose View ➤ Browse, or press Ctrl+B.

2. Click on the New Record SmartIcon, choose Browse ➤ New Record, or press Ctrl+N. This displays a blank form in Form view or a blank row in Worksheet view, and places your cursor in the first field of the new record.

3. Add the appropriate data in the new record, either clicking on each new field or pressing Tab or Shift-Tab to move through the record.

4. Repeat steps 2 and 3 until you have completed the last record. As you enter information in a record, Approach automatically saves it. Whenever you change to a different mode or start to add another record, Approach automatically saves your changes or additions up to that point.

**WORKING TOGETHER** ▲

# Securing Your SmartSuite Data

Each of the SmartSuite applications provides a way in which you can protect your data—either by using a password, hiding the data, or defining a file as read-only. The following is a list of security features for each SmartSuite application.

**1-2-3: Save a file with a password**    Choose File ➤ Save As, type a file name, and check the With Password check box. In the Set Password dialog box, type a password in the Password text box, type it again in the Verify text box, and click on OK. When someone attempts to open the protected file, the Get Password dialog box appears.

**1-2-3: Seal a file**    Choose File ➤ Protect, and in the Protect dialog box, check the Seal File check box and click on OK. In the Set Password dialog box, type a password in the Password text box, type it again in the Verify text box, and click on OK. The next time you open the sealed file, 1-2-3 does not allow you to edit. To unseal the file, clear the Seal File check box in the Protect dialog box and click on OK.

**1-2-3: Protect a style**    Choose Style ➤ Protection to protect a style, but not the data, before you seal a file.

**1-2-3: Hide data**    Select the data and choose the Hidden format from the Number format button in the status bar.

**1-2-3: Hide a column or sheet**    Choose Style ➤ Hide and either select the range and the column or select the sheet. Then click on OK. To reveal the hidden data, choose Style ➤ Hide and click on Show.

**1-2-3: Hide a column**    Drag the right border over to the left border. To reveal the column, drag the left border of the preceding column toward the right, or choose Style ➤ Column Width, type a value greater than zero, and click on OK.

Approach

**WORKING TOGETHER**

**Ami Pro: Save a file with a password**     Choose File ➤ Save As, type a file name, and check the Password Protect check box. In the Password Protect dialog box, type a password, and click on OK. In the next Password Protect dialog box, retype the password, and click on OK. When someone attempts to open the protected file, the Password Protect dialog box appears.

**Ami Pro: Define a file as read only**     Choose File ➤ File Management, select the file, choose File ➤ Attributes, click on the Read Only option button, and click on OK. Choose File ➤ Exit to exit from Ami Pro File Manager and return to Ami Pro.

**Approach: Save a database file with a password**     Open a database file and choose Tools ➤ Preferences. In the Preferences dialog box, click on the Password tab and type the password in the Password for This Approach File text box. Approach places a check mark in the check box. In the Confirm Password dialog box, type the password again and click on OK. Click on OK to close the Preferences dialog box. When someone attempts to open the protected file, the Enter dBASE Password dialog box appears.

**Approach: Give a read/write password to a database**
Open a database file and choose Tools ➤ Preferences. In the Preferences dialog box, click on the Password tab and type the password in the Read/Write text box. Approach places a check mark in the check box. In the Confirm Password dialog box, type the password again, and click on OK. Click on OK to close the Preferences dialog box.

**Approach: Give a read-only password to a database**
Open the database file and choose Tools ➤ Preferences. In the Preferences dialog box, click on the Password tab and type the password in the Read-Only Password text box. Approach places a check mark in the check box. In the Confirm Password dialog box, type

**WORKING TOGETHER** ▲

the password again, and click on OK. Click on OK to close the Preferences dialog box. When someone attempts to open the protected file, the Enter dBASE Password dialog box appears.

**Approach: Hide records**      Select the records to be hidden. Choose Browse ➤ Hide Record or press Ctrl+H. To reveal hidden records, choose Browse ➤ Show All or press Ctrl+A.

**Freelance Graphics: Make a file read only**      Choose File ➤ Network Options. In the Network Options dialog box, click on the Release and the Manual option buttons, and click on OK. Then when someone edits the file, she or he cannot close the file and save the editing changes. This works only until you close the file; when you open the file again, the file is no longer read only.

**Organizer: Define a password for a file**      Choose File ➤ Organizer Preferences ➤ User Access, or press Ctrl+U. In the User Access dialog box, click on Password. In the Password dialog box, type a password, and click on OK. Verify the password by retyping it in the Verify Password dialog box. Then click on OK three times.

## Duplicating a Record

When the current record contains much of the information in the previous record, an easy method for data entry is to duplicate the last active record and then change the appropriate fields. Start by adding a new record; then select Browse ➤ Duplicate Record. Approach copies the data from the most recently added or edited record to the current one.

To create a duplicate record, follow these steps:

1. Add a record by clicking on the New Record SmartIcon, choosing Browse ➤ New Record, or pressing Ctrl+N.

**Approach**

**2.** Choose <u>B</u>rowse ➤ <u>D</u>uplicate Record to duplicate all information from the previous added or edited record in the new record.

## Setting Initial Values for a Field

Approach allows you to have data already in a field when you add a record. For example, if you add a record for every new contact, Approach can enter today's date for you. This ensures that the date is accurate (if your computer system date is accurate) and also saves time. You can also have Approach insert a value that automatically increases for each new record. This is a good way of inserting a unique identifier, such as a contact ID, for each record in a database.

To insert initial values, choose <u>C</u>reate ➤ Field <u>D</u>efinition to open the Field Definition dialog box (Figure 12.3).

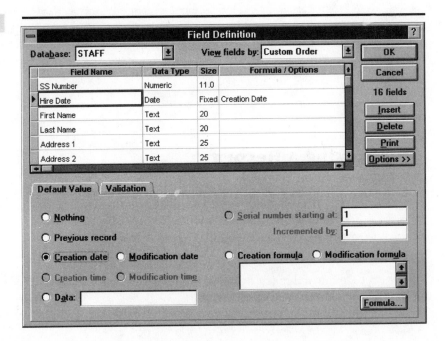

Select a field, click the <u>O</u>ptions button, and Approach adds a new section to the dialog box. You can specify a value or formula for the field by clicking on one of these option buttons:

<u>N</u>othing    Click on this button to leave the field blank.

<u>P</u>revious Record    Click on this button to insert the contents of the previous active record in the selected field.

<u>C</u>reation Date    Click on this button to insert the system date in the selected field when you add the record. Use this initial value only with date fields (although other field types accept this value).

<u>M</u>odification Date    Click on this button to insert the system date in the selected field when you modify the record. Use this initial value only with date fields (although other field types accept this value).

Creation <u>T</u>ime    Click on this button to insert the system time in the selected field when you add the record. Use this initial value only with time fields (although other field types accept this value).

Modification Tim<u>e</u>    Click on this button to insert the system time in the selected field when you modify the record. Use this initial value only with time fields (although other field types accept this value).

<u>D</u>ata    Click on this button to insert the data that you type in the text box in the selected field.

**TIP**

**You can use this option to automate data entry. For example, if you know that you will add 50 records with identical values in the City and State fields, set the values using the <u>D</u>ata option. When you have finished adding these records, remove these initial values.**

<u>S</u>erial Number Starting at    Click on this button to insert a number *incremented* (increased) or *decremented* (decreased) by the positive or negative number in the Incremented <u>b</u>y text box. This initial value is a *counter* (a number that is changed by a certain value each time it is

used). If you start numbering at 1 and increment by 1, the first record that you add has 1 in the selected field, the second record has 2, and so on. You can increment a number by a value up to 2147483647 or decrement a number by a value up to −2147483647.

 You cannot increment a number by 0, so if you want to insert the same number in a field in every new record, enter the value in the **D**ata option button and text box.

To create initial values for a field, use the following steps:

1. Go to Design view, if needed, by clicking on the Design SmartIcon, choosing **V**iew ➤ **D**esign, or pressing Ctrl+D.

2. Choose **C**reate ➤ Field **D**efinition. Approach displays the Field Definition dialog box.

3. In the Field Name column, click on the field that will contain the initial value.

4. Click on the **O**ptions button. Approach adds the section to the dialog box.

5. Click on an option button in the Default Value section. If you click on **D**ata or **S**erial Number Starting at, enter values in the appropriate text boxes.

6. Click on OK to close the dialog box and save your changes.

## Validating Values in a Field

The Field Definition dialog box also allows you to check information as you enter it. You can check to see if a value is unique in the database, is one of a list of values, fits within a range of values, or exists at all.

To check entered data, open the Field Definition dialog box (Figure 12.4), click on the Options button, click on the Validation tab, and check or select an option:

**Unique**   Check this check box to ensure that the value in the selected field is unique in the database.

**FIGURE 12.4**

In the extended Field Definition dialog box, you can validate values for fields.

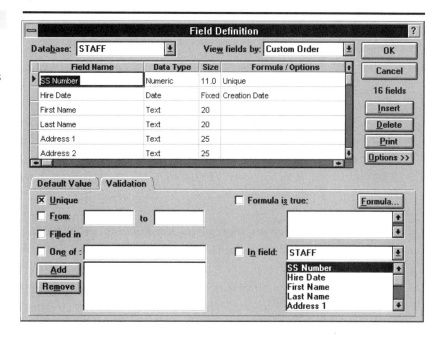

**From/To**   Check this check box to ensure that the value in the selected field is within the values entered in the From text box and the To text box.

**Filled in**   Check this check box to ensure that there is a value in the selected field.

**One of**   Check this check box to ensure that the value in the selected field is one of the values listed in the drop-down list box.

**Formula Is True**   Check this check box to ensure that the value in the selected field is true when the formula in the text box is calculated.

**In Field**   Check this check box to ensure that the value in the selected field matches the value in the selected field in the database that you selected from the drop-down list box.

**Approach**

To validate values in a field, use the following steps:

1. Go to Design view, if needed, by clicking on the Design SmartIcon, choosing <u>V</u>iew ➤ <u>D</u>esign, or pressing Ctrl+D.

2. Choose <u>C</u>reate ➤ <u>F</u>ield Definition. Approach displays the Field Definition dialog box.

3. Click on the <u>O</u>ptions button.

4. Click on the Validation tab.

5. In the Field Name column, click on the field to be validated.

6. Click on the <u>O</u>ptions button. Approach adds a section to the dialog box.

7. Click on one or more check boxes in the Validation section. If you click on On<u>e</u> of or <u>F</u>rom, enter values in the appropriate text boxes.

8. If you check Formula I<u>s</u> True, click on the <u>F</u>ormula button to create a formula.

9. Click on OK to close the dialog box and save your changes.

## Creating a List of Values for a Field

You can limit the choices to be entered in a particular field by creating a list of values from which the person entering data must choose. For example, you can list only the current departments in your company or the states in which your company is located. This prevents entering invalid information and also speeds up data entry. It's much easier to select from a list than to type the information character by character.

To create a list of values, follow these steps:

1. From Design view, select the field for which you want the list.

2. Open the InfoBox by double-clicking on the object, clicking on its SmartIcon, by choosing <u>O</u>bject ➤ <u>S</u>tyle & Properties, or pressing Ctrl+E.

3. Click on the Basics tab, if needed.

4. From the Data Entry Type drop-down list box, select Drop-Down List. Approach displays the Drop-Down List dialog box (Figure 12.5).

FIGURE 12.5

In the Drop-Down List
dialog box, you can
enter a list of values
for a field.

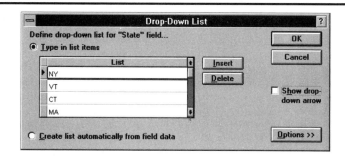

**TIP** A shortcut for opening the InfoBox is to double-click on a field while in Design.

5. Type a list in the List scroll box.

6. To insert a new item at a particular place on this list, click on the value before which you want the new item, click on the Insert button, and type the new value.

7. To delete an item, select it, and click on the Delete button.

8. To always display an arrow button in the field box, check the Show Drop-Down Arrow check box. To only display the arrow button when you have clicked in the field box, clear the Show Drop-Down Arrow check box.

9. Click on OK.

10. Save the Approach file. Figure 12.6 shows a value list in a form.

**NOTE** The next time you need to edit the list, open the InfoBox and click on the Define List button under the Data Entry Type drop-down list box.

## Entering Data into Different Types of Fields

As you enter data, the data is accepted differently for each field type. If you type a number with a leading zero in a number field, Approach removes the

**FIGURE 12.6**

The State field with an open value list

leading zero from the data. However, if you type a number with a leading zero in a text field or a numeric field formatted as a Zip Code, the leading zero remains. For example, in the STAFF database, if you type **02139** in the ZIP field (a numeric field with a Zip Code format), Approach will not remove the leading zero.

## Entering Data in Text and Memo Fields

You can type text, numbers, and dates into a text field and the data's appearance will not be changed from the way in which you entered it. However, these entries are no longer considered dates, times, and numbers and probably won't calculate properly. If you select ALL CAPITALIZED, all lowercase, or First Capitalized for a field, you can type data any way you wish, and Approach will format it as you have defined. For example, if you select ALL CAPITALIZED and type **indy** in the First Name field, Approach changes the entry to **INDY**.

## Entering Data in Numeric Fields

You can only type numeric values in a number field; Approach issues an error message if you type any other characters. Remember that Approach removes leading zeroes from numbers, unless you specifically choose a format that allows them. If you enter numbers with values to the right side of the decimal point, you must enter the decimal points. If you choose a numeric format that adds comma separators, Approach adds commas automatically; otherwise, comma separators are not inserted. If you enter numbers that you want to be formatted as currency, select an appropriate numeric format.

## Entering Data in Date Fields

You can type a value in a date field using *mm/dd/yy | yyyy*, where *mm* represents the number of the month from 01 or 1 to 12, *dd* represents the number of the day from 01 or 1 to 28, 29, 30, or 31 (depending on the month), *yy* or *yyyy* represents the year—either the last two digits or the full four digits. Separate each element of a date with a non-numeric character, such as a dash, slash, or comma. You can type as many as 10 characters in a date field. An invalid value in a date field triggers an error message.

## Entering Data in Time Fields

When you type a time (or have Approach automatically enter a time) in a time field, Approach automatically converts your data to the time format set in the Field Format dialog box. You can type using the *hh*, *hh:mm*, *hh:mm:ss*, or *hh:mm:ss.00* format. You can type a time value in either military (for example, 1700) or standard (for example, 5:00 PM) format. If you type a time in standard format and do not follow it with either AM or PM, Approach defaults to AM. You can type as many as 12 characters in a time field.

## Entering Data in Calculated Fields

Approach calculates formulas and places the results in calculated fields. Therefore, there is no data entry for these fields.

## Entering Data in Boolean Fields

Boolean fields allow you to only use a few affirmative and negative entries: Yes, No, Y, N, 1, and 0. Any entries besides these automatically put a Yes in the field.

## Entering Data in PicturePlus Fields

PicturePlus fields can only contain graphical images—.BMP, .EPS, .GIF, .PCX, .TGA, .TIF, and .WMF—sound files, and other OLE objects pasted from the Windows Clipboard or imported from other Windows applications. To place a picture in a PicturePlus field, copy and paste it just as you learned in Chapter 3. If you choose the Edit ➤ Paste Special command, you can embed the picture as an OLE object (when the source application supports OLE).

If the picture is an OLE object, you can edit the picture using the source application while you remain in Approach.

 **TIP** You can use drag and drop to copy a picture from the Windows File Manager to a PicturePlus field. Have both the File Manager window containing the icon which represents the picture file and the Approach PicturePlus field displayed on the desktop at the same time. Then drag the File Manager icon to the PicturePlus field.

## Entering Data in Variable Fields

Remember that variable fields are temporary fields of any type. To enter data in a variable field, follow the instructions in this section for that type of field.

## Entering Data into Restricted Fields

When you restrict input in a field using the extended Field Definitions dialog box, the condition of the check boxes in the Check Entered Data group determines whether you can type certain data in a field. For example, if you check the From check box and enter a range of A–M for Department, Approach will not allow you to enter values of N–Z.

# Deleting a Record

 Whether you have just added a record, the record has been in your database for years, or you are in the middle of adding the record, you can delete it by clicking on the Delete Record SmartIcon, by choosing Browse ➤ Delete Record, or by pressing Ctrl+Del. Answer Yes to the prompt, and Approach permanently deletes the record. Once you have responded to the prompt, you cannot undo the deletion.

# 13

# Retrieving and Sorting Data and Joining Databases

Like any good filing system, Approach can search for and update the records already entered into a database. With Approach, you can easily select the specific records you want to retrieve for viewing, printing, reporting, or editing.

The Approach find process allows you to specify particular records to be viewed, edited, or included in a report. For example, you can find all active employees who have worked for you for more than three years and who have a salary less than $30,000. With a paper filing system, this task probably requires going through each record—a lengthy process if you have many employees. With Approach, the retrieval is immediate.

# finding Records in a Database

When you want to get a set of records to view, print, or edit, you must find them by comparing them against a set of criteria by which you define the records to be fetched. When you find records, Approach gets the records you specified, called a *found set*. The status bar shows the number of records you have found out of the total number of records in the database. To retrieve a found set of records, follow these steps:

**1.** If you are not in the Browse environment, either click on the Environment button and select Browse from the list, choose View ➤ Browse, or press Ctrl+B.

**2.** Click on the Find SmartIcon, click on the Environment button on the status bar and choose Find, choose Browse ➤ Find, or press Ctrl+F. Approach displays a find request (Figure 13.1) and a new group of SmartIcons.

**3.** Type the find criteria you want into the appropriate fields.

4. Click on the OK button or click on the ↵ SmartIcon. The status bar reports on the number of records that have been found and the total number of records in the database. Record 1 of the found set appears in the work area.

To return to the full database, click on the Show All SmartIcon, choose Browse ➤ Show All, or press Ctrl+A.

**TIP** When retrieving records, normally you view the work area in Form view. However, you can also view retrieved records in Worksheet view. Since you can see more than one record at a time in Worksheet view, displaying the found set is often more efficient than using Form view.

## Creating a Find Request

When you run a search, Approach searches through every record in the database and selects all the records that meet the conditions in the find request.

**FIGURE 13.1**

The Approach find request form with two fields filled in

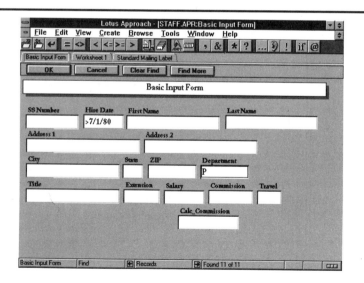

**Approach**

You can specify single or multiple conditions in one or more fields. Table 13.1 shows the SmartIcons and operators that you can use to create conditions.

## Setting Conditions for a Search

You request certain records in Approach the same way that you might request a set of paper records. For example, to get all the records in which *Tom* is the value in the First Name field, simply type the following:

```
=Tom
```

in the First Name field of the find request.

**TABLE 13.1:** Approach Find Request SmartIcons and Operators

| SMART-ICON | KEY(S)/DESCRIPTION | EXAMPLE |
| --- | --- | --- |
| ↵ | ↵ Enters the new record in the database or starts the find. | N/A |
| = | = Finds items that are equal to the find request, or when entered by itself finds blank fields. | The find request **=99** finds a record when the selected field contains 99. |
| <> | <> Finds items that are not equal to the find request, or when entered by itself finds non-blank fields. | The find request **<>99** finds a record when the selected field contains every value except 99. |
| < | < Finds items that are less than the find request. | The find request **<99** finds a record when the selected field contains 98, 97, 96, 95, and so on. |
| <= | <= Finds items that are less than or equal to the find request. | The find request **<=99** finds a record when the selected field contains 99, 98, 97, 96, 95, and so on. |

**TABLE 13.1:** Approach Find Request SmartIcons and Operators (continued)

| SMART-ICON | KEY(S)/DESCRIPTION | EXAMPLE |
|---|---|---|
| `>=` | `>=` Finds items that are greater than or equal to the find request. | The find request **>=99** finds a record when the selected field contains *99, 100, 101, 102, 103,* and so on. |
| `>` | `>` Finds items that are greater than the find request. | The find request **>99** finds a record when the selected field contains *100, 101, 102, 103,* and so on. |
| `,` | `,` Retrieves a record when the item matches condition 1 *or* condition 2. | The find request **VT, NY** finds a record when the selected field contains *VT* or *NY*. |
| `&` | `&` Retrieves records when the item matches condition 1 *and* condition 2. | The find request **\*computer\*&\*table\*** finds a record when the selected field contains the words *computer* and *table* in any order or location. |
| `*` | `*` Finds items with any character(s) at the location of the asterisk in the find request. You can use a combination of asterisks and question marks in the find request. If you enclose text with asterisks, Approach finds records that contain the word in any location in the search field. | The find request **th\*** finds a record when the selected field contains *the, them, those, thesaurus, thanksgiving,* and so on. |

Approach

**TABLE 13.1:** Approach Find Request SmartIcons and Operators (continued)

| SMART-ICON | KEY(S)/DESCRIPTION | EXAMPLE |
|---|---|---|
| **?** | **?** Finds an item with any character at the location of the question mark in the find request. You can search using a combination of asterisks and question marks. | The find request **the?** finds a record when the selected field contains *thee*, *them*, *then*, and *they*. |
| **...** | **...** Finds items within the range specified in the find request. | The find request **A...S** finds a record when the selected field contains *Alfred*, *Don*, *Monty*, *Stuart*, and so on. |
| 👂 | **~** Finds items that sound like the find request. | The find request **~Manetenince** finds a record when the selected field contains *Maintenance*. |
| **!** | **!** Finds items that match by case in the find request. | The find request **!Bart** finds a record when the selected field contains *Bart*, but not *BART*, *bart*, *bArT*, and so on. |
| **if** | **If** Retrieves a record when the expression in the find request is true. | The find request **If(Bonus>Salary)** finds a record when the contents of the Bonus field are greater than the contents of the Salary field. |
| **@** | **@** Retrieves a record when the value returned by the function in the find request is not equal to 0. | The find request **>@Pi()** finds a record when the selected field contains a value greater than 3.14159. |

## Finding Text and Memo Fields

Text fields are the most straightforward of the field types. The information that you type in a text field for a retrieval is the information that Approach retrieves.

### Using Wildcards to Find Text

Approach allows you to use the wildcard characters * and ? to find groups of similar records or to find records containing words whose spelling you don't remember completely. Use *wildcards* as a placeholder for one character or several characters at the beginning, middle, or end of a word in a find request.

To find any number of unknown characters, use the asterisk. Here are some examples:

| FIND REQUEST | FINDS | EXAMPLES |
|---|---|---|
| *s* | text that begins with any number of unknown characters or no characters, includes an *s*, and ends with any number of unknown characters or no characters | baseball, Oslo, satisfaction, *s* |
| s*o | text that begins with an *s*, includes any number of unknown characters or no characters, and ends with an *o* | *so, solo, scenario, stiletto* |
| s* | text that begins with an *s* and ends with any number of unknown characters or no characters | *s, so, solo, scenario, stiletto, satisfaction, serious* |

**Approach**

| FIND REQUEST | FINDS | EXAMPLES |
|---|---|---|
| *s | text that begins with any number of unknown characters or no characters and ends with an *s* | s, serious, harass, videos |

To find a set number of unknown characters, use the question mark. Here are some examples:

| FIND REQUEST | FINDS | EXAMPLES |
|---|---|---|
| s??? | text that begins with *s* and ends with three unknown characters | solo, sans, sole, sale |
| s?le | text that begins with *s*, includes one unknown character, and ends with *le* | *sole, sale* |
| ?ale? | text that begins with one unknown character, includes *ale*, and ends with one unknown character | s*ale*s, S*ale*m, m*ale*s |

## Finding Sounds-Like Text

You can use a special operator that finds values that sound similar to the find request. Just type a tilde (~) in front of what you think the value sounds like. For example, to find all records with Last Name fields that sound something like *Donovan*, type any of the following:

```
~donvan
~donvin
~donvn
~donovan
```

and you will find records with the Last Name value of *Donovan*.

## Finding Numeric Fields

Finding numeric fields is almost as easy as searching for text fields. Just type a number (without characters such as dollar signs, commas, dashes, slashes and so on) into the numeric field and Approach retrieves only the records that contain that value. For example, to retrieve the records with the value of *80,000.00*, type the following:

80000

You enter only the numbers for which you are searching because field formats, such as the dashes between numeric social security numbers (e.g., 123-45-6789) are not saved with the data (e.g., 123456789) in a field. Therefore, when Approach searches for data in this type of field, it searches only for the numbers, not for the combination of numbers and characters. So, if you fill in a find request and include the separator characters, Approach will not find your data. However, if you define a social security number as a text field and enter a combination of numbers and dashes, you must type the numbers and the dashes as entered to search successfully.

## Finding Date Fields

When finding dates, you can use any numeric date format typed using your current Windows short date default (e.g., *mm/dd/yy*). For example, you could find the following:

01/01/95
1-1-1995

You cannot use this search string:

January 1, 1995

Approach also carefully checks the numbers that you type. For example, typing a month greater than 12 or a day greater than 31 produces an error message. In fact, Approach even checks the month against the day, so you can't type **2/29** except in leap years.

## Finding Time Fields

You can enter time in a find request using either military or standard format:

```
18:00
6:00 PM
```

## Finding Exact Matches

An exact match finds records that strictly match the conditions entered in a find request. For example, if you enter either of these lines:

```
=123 Main Street
123 Main Street
```

Approach finds only records that contain exactly that text. Notice that the equal sign is not required in an exact match find request.

## Finding Ranges of Information

Range find requests allow you to find records that contain values that fall within a range specified in the retrieval spec. For example, you can find all the cities between Albuquerque and Boston in an alphabetical list by typing this:

```
Albuquerque...Boston
```

or you can find salaries greater than $16,000 but less than $70,000 by typing this:

```
16000...70000
```

 **You can also find ranges of dates and times.**

## Specifying More Than One Condition in a Search

There are several ways to search using more than one condition. You can combine search criteria in one find request by entering values in several fields at once. For example, you can find all the records that have a value of *VT* in the State field and a value less than *$25,000* in the Salary field. Simply type the two search criteria in the appropriate fields; type **VT** in the State field and **>25000** in the Salary field.

You can combine search criteria in a single field by separating the values with commas. For example, you can find all the records that have a value of *VT* or *NY* in the State field by typing **VT, NY** in the State field.

Another way to combine several search criteria is to create several find requests before pressing ↵ or clicking on the Enter SmartIcon. Begin by filling in the first find request as you learned earlier. Then either choose Records ➤ Find More or press Ctrl+F, and create the next find request. You can repeat this as often as you wish. (Note that you won't see the Find More command on the Browse menu until you start the second search; it replaces the Find command at that point.) When you have finished filling in the last find request, either press ↵ or click on the Enter SmartIcon.

You can create an If statement to create a find request. An If statement tests conditions and returns either Yes or No. A value of Yes adds a record to the found set. Following are some examples of If statements:

**If(Bonus>Salary)**    Tests whether the value in the Bonus field is greater than the value in the Salary field. If Bonus is greater than Salary, Approach returns Yes, thereby adding the record to the found set.

**If((State=VT) And (Last Name=A…L))**    Tests whether the value in the State field is *VT* and whether the value in the Last Name field starts with A–L. If both these conditions are true, Approach returns Yes, thereby adding the record to the found set.

**If((State=VT) Or (Last Name=A…L))**    Tests whether the value in the State field is *VT* or whether the value in the Last Name field starts with A–L. If either of these conditions is true, Approach returns Yes, thereby adding the record to the found set.

**Approach**

## Repeating a Search

During this work session, you can repeat a search using the same criteria and conditions that you used in the last search. Just choose <u>B</u>rowse ➤ Find Again. Approach displays the most recent find request, which you can edit. Then click on OK or the ↵ SmartIcon or press ↵.

## Finding Fields with Duplicate Values

Approach provides a feature that searches through all active records (that is, every record in the database or every found record) and finds records with duplicate values in selected fields. To search for duplicate values, follow these steps:

1. Find a group of records or show all the records in the current database.

2. Choose <u>B</u>rowse ➤ Find Spe<u>c</u>ial. Approach displays the Find Special dialog box (Figure 13.2).

3. Click on Find <u>D</u>uplicate Records in the Current Found Set option.

4. If you wish, check the <u>E</u>xclude First Record Found in Each Set of Duplicates check box. This skips marking the first record in a set of duplicates as a duplicate.

5. In the Database <u>F</u>ields scroll box, select a field and click on <u>A</u>dd to add it to the Fields to <u>S</u>earch list.

 **A quick way to add a field to the Fields to C<u>h</u>eck list is to double-click it in the <u>F</u>ields scroll box.**

6. Repeat step 3 until you have added all the desired fields to the list.

7. To clear the Fields to <u>S</u>earch box, click on <u>C</u>lear All.

8. To remove a field from the Fields to <u>S</u>earch box, select it and click on <u>R</u>emove.

9. Click on OK. Approach finds the duplicate records.

FIGURE 13.2

In the Find Special
dialog box, start the
search for duplicate
values in selected fields.

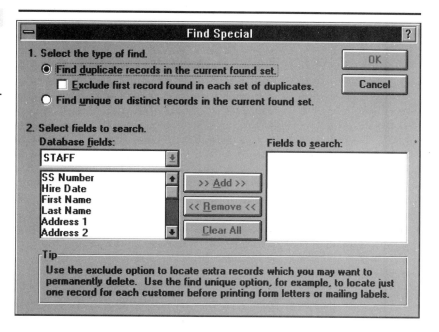

# Sorting Records

Now that you know about retrieving records, you are ready to learn about displaying records in a sorted order. When retrieving records, Approach can arrange the records in various orders depending on the field type. Text, memo, and Boolean fields are sorted in alphabetical order; numeric fields are sorted in numeric order; and dates and times are sorted in chronological order. You can sort records in *ascending* (A to Z or 0 to 9) order, or in *descending* (Z to A or 9 to 0) order. You cannot sort PicturePlus fields. All sorts are temporary; when you click on the Show All icon, choose Browse ➤ Show All, or click on Ctrl+A, the records return to the order in which you added them.

**NOTE**  To permanently keep records in their sorted order, export them to a new database. Choose File ➤ Export Data, specify a new file name, choose a database file type, select whether to export the found records or all the records, move the fields to be exported, and click on OK.

# SmartSuite Commands for Importing and Exporting

You can import and export information and objects to and from Smart-Suite applications using the following commands:

**Importing a file:** *1-2-3, Ami Pro, Approach, Freelance Graphics*    Choose File ➤ Open. Type or select the file name, select the file type, and click on OK.

**Exporting a file:** *1-2-3, Ami Pro, Approach, Freelance Graphics*    Choose File ➤ Save As. Type or select the file name, select the file type, and click on OK.

**Importing an object:** *1-2-3*    Choose Edit ➤ Insert Object. Select the object type and click on OK. The application from which you will import opens. Select the object or open the file and click on OK.

**Importing a picture:** *Ami Pro*    Choose File ➤ Import Picture. Type or select the file name, select the file type, and click on OK.

**Importing data:** *Approach*    In Browse, choose File ➤ Import Data. Select a file name and file type; then click on OK. Fill in the appropriate Options dialog box and click on OK. Fill in the Import Setup dialog box and click on OK.

**Importing an Approach file:** *Approach*    Go to Design and choose File ➤ Import Approach File. Select a file name and click on OK. In the Import Approach File Setup dialog box, map the fields and click on OK.

**Exporting data:** *Approach*    In Browse, choose File ➤ Export Data. Select the fields to export and select the file to which the information will be exported. Click on OK.

**Importing a graphic or ASCII file:** *Freelance Graphics*
In Current Page view, go to the page into which you wish to import. Choose File ➤ Import. Type or select a file name and type. Click on OK.

**Importing a chart:** *Freelance Graphics*     In Current Page View, go to the page into which you wish to import. Choose File ➤ Import Chart. Type or select a file name and type. Click on OK.

**Exporting a graphic or ASCII file:** *Freelance Graphics* Choose File ➤ Export. Type or select a file name and file type. Then click on OK.

**Importing an object:** *Freelance Graphics*     In Current Page View, go to the page into which you wish to import. Choose Edit ➤ Insert Object. Select the object type and click on OK. The application from which you will import opens. Select the object or open the file and click on OK.

**Importing a file:** *Organizer*     Choose File ➤ Import. Choose an Organizer section to which to import, type or select a file name, choose an import format (.CSV, .DBF, or .ORG), and click on OK. If prompted, map the fields and click on Import. Note that you can map more than one field to an Organizer time, date, or text field.

**Exporting a file:** *Organizer*     Choose File ➤ Export. Choose an Organizer section from which to import, type or select a file name, choose an export format (.CSV, dBASE, Cardfile, or Organizer), and click on OK. If prompted, map the fields and click on Export.

For more information about importing and exporting, see the appropriate *User's Guide* or search in the appropriate Help facility.

To run a simple ascending or descending sort, follow these steps:

**1.** Select the field by which you wish to run the sort.

**2.** Either click on the Ascending Sort or Descending Sort SmartIcons, or choose Browse ➤ Sort ➤ Ascending or Browse ➤ Sort ➤ Descending. Approach runs the sort and displays the first record in the new order.

**Approach**

To define a sort with multiple fields, follow these steps:

**1.** Choose <u>B</u>rowse ➤ Sort ➤ De<u>f</u>ine or press Ctrl+T. Approach opens the Sort dialog box (Figure 13.3).

**2.** In the Database <u>F</u>ields scroll box, select a field and click on <u>A</u>dd to add it to the Fields to <u>S</u>ort on list.

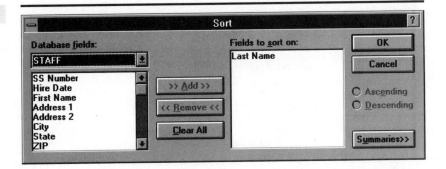

  **A quick way to add a field to the Fields to <u>S</u>ort on list is to double-click it in the Database <u>F</u>ields box.**

**3.** Click on As<u>c</u>ending or <u>D</u>escending to determine the order of the sort.

**4.** Repeat steps 2 and 3 until you have added all the desired fields to the sort.

**5.** To clear the Fields to <u>S</u>ort on box, click on <u>C</u>lear All.

**6.** To remove a field from the Fields to <u>S</u>ort on box, select it and click on <u>R</u>emove.

**7.** Click on OK. Approach changes the order of the records.

**8.** To return to the original order, either click on the Show All SmartIcon, choose <u>B</u>rowse ➤ Show <u>A</u>ll, or press Ctrl+A.

# Joining Two Databases

As you learned in Chapter 11, Approach is a relational database in which you can have several databases working together to produce reports, mailing labels, and form letters.

## Designing Databases for Joining

Before joining databases and designing the databases that will form a related set of databases, determine the *join field*, the field that connects the databases; it is essentially the same field in the joined databases. For example, in the STAFF database, the join field should be SS_NO, the social security number. Even though you may have employees with the same first and last names, or the same address, the social security number is unique.

Let's say that you will design a database that holds travel information for your employees. Other than adding SS_NO, the join field, you don't need to duplicate any other fields. For example, if you periodically send a travel report to your employees, you can incorporate the name and address from the *main database* STAFF with the information in the *detail database* TRAVEL.

There are three possible types of relationships between the main database and detail databases: one-to-one, one-to-many, and many-to-one.

- The *one-to-one* relationship associates one record from each database. This enables you to look up and possibly display the contents of the looked-up record in a database when you type an identifier in a field in the other database.
- The *one-to-many* relationship associates one record in one database and several records in the other database.
- The *many-to-one* relationship associates several records in one database with one record in the other.

Figure 13.4 shows a filled-in data entry form for the detail database TRAVEL. Notice that this database has one field, SS_NO, in common with the main database STAFF.

Approach

**WORKING TOGETHER**

## Importing 1-2-3 Data into an Approach Database

You can import data from 1-2-3 into an Approach database. Before you start, define a database file with fields that match the fields in the 1-2-3 spreadsheet. For example, if your database file contains Last Name, First Name, Address, City, State, and Zip fields, the 1-2-3 spreadsheet should contain these or comparable fields in the top row of the spreadsheet.

Then follow these steps:

1. In Approach, go to Browse and choose File ➤ Import Data. Approach displays the Import Data dialog box.

2. Type the name of the file, choose the path and directory, and select the type for the file to be imported. Then click on OK. Approach opens the Select Range dialog box, in which you select the spreadsheet or fields in the spreadsheet to be imported into the database. Approach opens the Import Setup dialog box; the blue arrows show how the contents of the 1-2-3 spreadsheet will be mapped to the database.

3. Click on blue arrows of any fields you don't want mapped to the database.

**WORKING TOGETHER**

4. Click on OK. Approach closes the dialog box and adds the records to the database.

5. Carefully review the new records and delete or edit as needed.

You can also create a new Approach database using a 1-2-3 file. Create and save a 1-2-3 spreadsheet, making sure to define the field labels in the top row. In Approach, choose File ➤ Open. In the Open dialog box, select the 1-2-3 file, file type (Lotus 1-2-3(*.WK*)), and the directory in which the file is located; then click on OK. In the Select Range dialog box, select the spreadsheet or range of fields, check First Row Contains Field Names, and click on OK. In the Convert To dialog box, type a database file name, select a file type (if needed), select a directory in which the file will be stored, and click on OK.

**FIGURE 13.4**

The detail database TRAVEL form

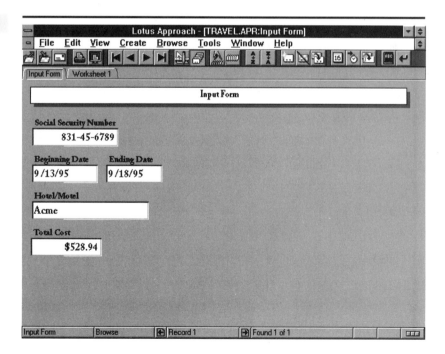

**Approach**

## Joining Databases

Approach allows you to join up to 10 databases to a view file. To join two database files, follow these steps:

1. Open the main database and go to Design.

2. Choose Create ➤ Join. Approach displays the Join dialog box (Figure 13.5), which shows the name of the main database and lists its fields.

**FIGURE 13.5**

The Join dialog box, in which you join two or more databases

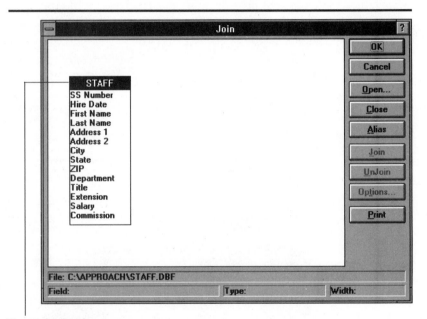

The main database

3. Either click on Open or press ↲. Approach displays the Open dialog box (Figure 13.6), which lists the available database files.

4. Double-click on a detail database name in the File Name text/scroll box. Approach adds the list of detail database fields to the Join dialog box.

5. Click on the join fields in both lists and click on the Join button. Approach draws a line between the join fields (Figure 13.7).

6. To join more databases, repeat steps 3, 4, and 5.

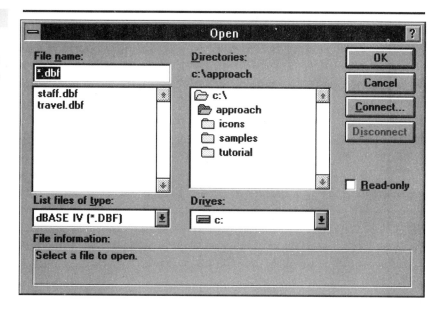

FIGURE 13.6

The Open dialog box, from which you select a detail database to be joined to the main database

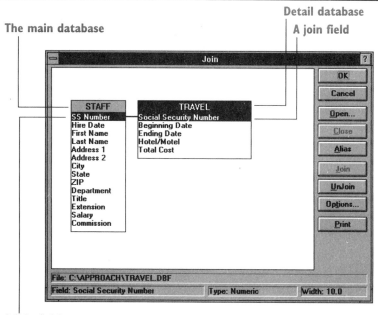

FIGURE 13.7

The Join dialog box, with the detail database added

7. When you have finished joining databases, click on OK. (If OK is dimmed, the joins are not valid. Refer to Chapter 3 in the *User's Guide*, or "How Databases Are Joined" and "Joining Database Files" in Help.)

## Adding a Repeating Panel to a Form

Once you have joined databases, you can display the data from the detail database in a repeating panel in the main database. A *repeating panel* displays records in a one-to-many relationship. Once you display a record on your desktop, the repeating panel displays one of possibly many records related to the current record. To add a repeating panel, follow these steps:

1. Open the main database and go to Design.

2. Choose Create ➤ Repeating Panel. Approach displays the Add Repeating Panel dialog box (Figure 13.8).

**FIGURE 13.8**

The Add Repeating Panel dialog box, with four fields defined for a repeating panel

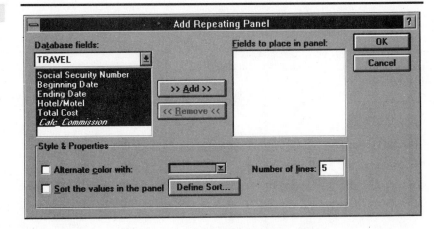

3. In the Number of Lines text box, type the number of records (as individual lines) to be displayed in the repeating panel at one time.

4. Choose the name of the detail database from the Database Fields drop-down list box. This step is necessary when there is more than one detail database joined to the main database.

5. Select a field to be included in the repeating panel and click on Add (or just double-click on the field name). Approach adds the field name to the Panel Fields box (Figure 13.9).

6. When you have completed your selection, click on OK. Approach adds the repeating panel to the main database form.

**FIGURE 13.9**

The Add Repeating Panel dialog box with fields selected for the repeating panel

The fields that will appear in the repeating panel

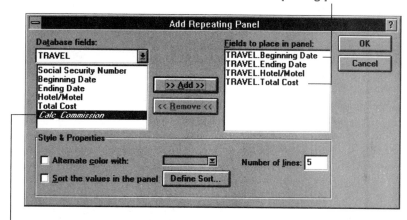

A field that will appear in the repeating panel

7. If needed, drag the repeating panel to a new location on the form. It's best to drag it by its bottom border.

8. If needed, resize the repeating panel by pressing and holding down the Ctrl key and clicking in the top part of the panel. When the top part of the panel is surrounded by a double-border and the mouse pointer changes to a double-headed arrow, drag a side of the panel until it's the desired size (Figure 13.10).

9. If needed, format the fields in the repeating panel using the InfoBox or by clicking the right mouse button to reveal a pop-up menu. Figure 13.11 shows an example of a repeating panel at the bottom of the STAFF Basic Input Form.

**Approach**

**FIGURE 13.10**

Drag the edge of a
repeating panel to
change its dimensions

**FIGURE 13.10**

Drag the edge of a
repeating panel to
change its dimensions

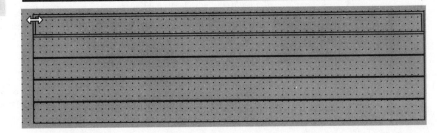

**FIGURE 13.11**

The STAFF repeating
panel in Browse

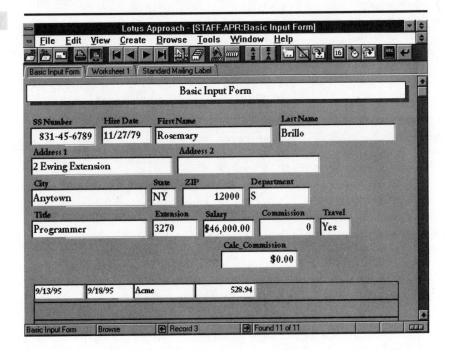

14

# Reporting on
# Your Database

W e've covered entering, finding, and sorting Approach data. In this chapter you'll find out how to display that information in reports. As you know, Approach displays a database in either Form view or Worksheet view. In this chapter, you'll create standard and columnar reports using SmartMasters and then edit and format a report. Finally, you'll learn about calculating in Approach reports and creating a summary report using calculations.

## Approach Reports

In Approach, there are seven types of reports available to you: blank (for custom reports), standard, columnar, four summary reports, and a repeating panel report. The most common reports are described below.

### The Standard Report

The standard report shows selected data from the current database with fields from each record in their own section. The contents of each record are separated by a heavy horizontal line.

The standard report looks like a form. Figure 14.1 shows you a page from a standard report.

### The Columnar Report

The columnar report arranges fields in columns; each column holds the contents of the same field from different records. Rows hold all the selected fields from individual records. Figure 14.2 displays a columnar report.

**FIGURE 14.1**

A standard report displays selected fields a few records at a time.

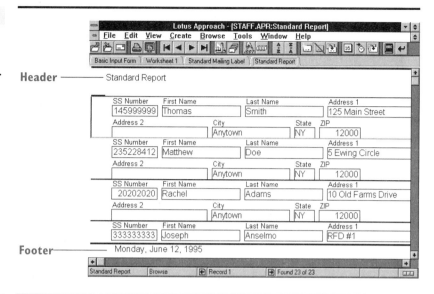

Header ──── Standard Report

Footer ──── Monday, June 12, 1995

**FIGURE 14.2**

A columnar report displays fields in columns and records in rows.

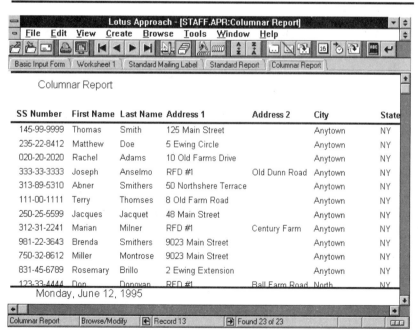

Approach

**479**

## The Summary Report

Summary reports display summary information for a group of records. Depending on the type of report you select, Approach shows or does not show other details from the database. Figure 14.3 displays a summary report and details from the database.

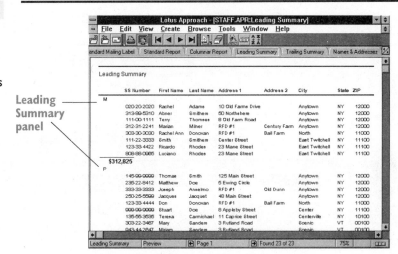

# Creating a Standard Report

To create a standard report, follow these steps:

1. Open the database for which you want to create a report and go to Design.

2. Choose Create ➤ Report. Approach displays the Report Assistant dialog box (Figure 14.4).

3. Type the report name in the View Name & Title text box.

4. Select a style from the SmartMaster Style drop-down list box.

5. Click on Standard in the SmartMaster Layout scroll box.

6. Click on the Next button. Approach displays the Step 2: Fields section (Figure 14.5) of the dialog box.

FIGURE 14.4

In the Report Assistant
dialog box, you can
create custom,
columnar, standard,
and several types of
summary reports.

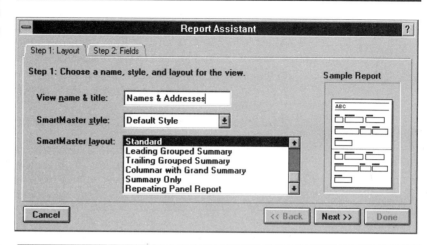

FIGURE 14.5

Define report fields in
the Step 2: Fields
section of the Report
Assistant dialog box.

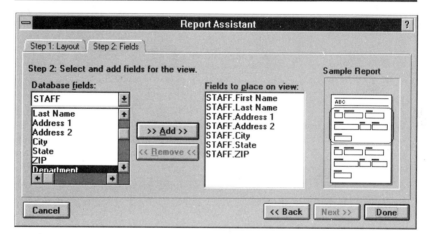

**7.** From the Database Fields scroll box, click on a field to be displayed and
click on <u>A</u>dd to insert a field in the Fields to <u>P</u>lace on View box. (You can
also insert a field in the Fields to <u>P</u>lace on View box by double-clicking
on it.)

**8.** Select the remaining fields for the report, in the order in which you
want them to appear, from left to right and from top to bottom.

**Approach**

9. Click on Done. Approach closes the dialog box, displays the report in Design, and inserts the report name on the View list on the status bar and on a tab right below the SmartIcons. Figure 14.6 shows a formatted Standard report in Preview.

10. Save the Approach file.

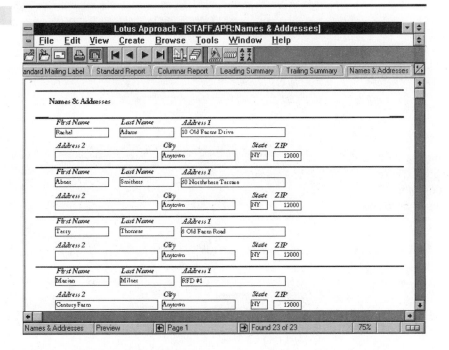

# Creating a Columnar Report

To create a columnar report, follow these steps:

1. Open the database for which you want to create a report and go to Design.

2. Choose Create ➤ Report. Approach displays the Report Assistant dialog box (Figure 14.7).

3. Type the report name in the View Name & Title text box.

4. Select a style from the SmartMaster Style drop-down list box.

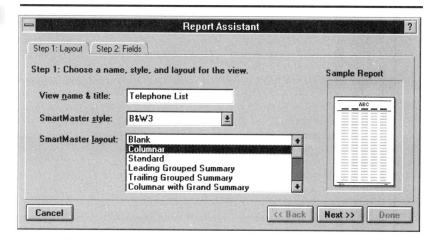

**FIGURE 14.7**

The Report Assistant dialog box with a report name, style, and layout selected.

5. Click on Columnar in the SmartMaster Layout scroll box.

6. Click on the Next button. Approach displays the Step 2: Fields section of the dialog box.

7. From the Database Fields scroll box, click on a field to be displayed and click on Add to insert the field in the Fields to Place on View box. (You can also insert a field in the Fields to Place on View box by double-clicking on it.)

8. Select the remaining fields for the report, in the order in which you want them to appear, from left to right.

9. Click on Done. Approach closes the dialog box, displays the report in Design, and inserts the report name on the View list on the status bar and on a tab right below the SmartIcons. Figure 14.8 shows a formatted columnar report in Preview.

10. Save the Approach file.

**TIP** The easiest way to sort a columnar report by a specific field is to go to Design. Click in the column of the field to be sorted, choose Object ➤ Sort ➤ Ascending for an ascending sort or Object ➤ Sort ➤ Descending for a descending sort.

Approach

**FIGURE 14.8**

An example of a
formatted columnar
report in Preview

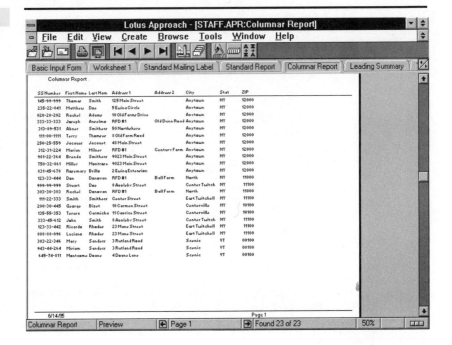

Before printing a sorted report, make sure that the fields are in the original
sorted order. If you have produced multiple reports and have sorted or grouped
by different fields, fields in this report may have been resorted or regrouped.

# Editing a Report

Approach enables you to add information to reports by using headers, footers,
and title pages. You can also add columns to a standard report, adjust the spacing between columns, and fill in or remove blank spaces. In this section, you'll
learn how to edit reports.

**To enhance a report (for example, to change the font, apply
boldface, reduce the point size, etc.), use the InfoBox. For a
synopsis of Approach InfoBox formats, see Table 11.1.**

## Inserting Headers and Footers

In standard and summary only reports, Approach automatically adds headers and footers. In columnar reports, Approach adds column headers. The *header*, which is an area at the top of each page, and *footer*, which is an area at the bottom of the page, contain information that appears on every page (for example, the date, your name, report name, page number, or your company name).

To customize, turn off, or turn on a header or footer, follow these steps:

1. Open the database for which you have created a report and go to Design.

2. Click on the tab for the report and choose Report ➤ Add Header or Report ➤ Add Footer to add or remove a header or footer, respectively. (A checkmark preceding the menu command indicates that Approach has added a header and/or footer.

 3. To insert an object in a header or footer, click on the Text Block button in the drawing tools. Draw a box in the header or footer pane by clicking one side of the box and dragging diagonally to the opposite corner.

4. To enter text, click within the text box and start typing.

5. To insert the page number in the header or footer, click within the text box, and choose Report ➤ Insert ➤ Page #.

 **TIP**  Because you can also type normal text in the text box, you can type the word "Page" and then insert the page number.

6. To insert your current computer system clock date, click within the text box and choose Report ➤ Insert ➤ Date.

7. To embed an object such as a Paintbrush picture, copy and paste using the Clipboard and the Copy, Cut, and/or Paste commands from the Edit menu. (Remember that you can double-click on an embedded object to edit it in the application in which it was created while remaining in the current application.)

**Approach**

## Adding a Title Page

You can create a unique first page for a report. The page looks like every other page in the report, but can contain its own header and/or footer and report information. To add a title page to a report, follow these steps:

1. Open the database for which you want to create a report and go to Design.

2. Choose Report ➤ Add Title Page to insert new header and footer panes on the first page of the report. Approach places a checkmark in front of the Add Title Page command.

3. Follow steps 3–7 in the preceding section to embed text, the page number, today's date, or a graphic in the header and/or footer pane.

Choose Report ➤ Add Title Page to remove a title page. Approach removes the checkmark that precedes the Add Title Page command.

## Moving and Resizing Fields or Parts of a Report

Blank spaces occur in an Approach report when the font size is decreased, the body panel is too large, or the data in a field is much shorter than the maximum size of a field.

To move or resize a field, go to Design, click on the field and drag it to its new location.

You can only change the size of a section by moving its bottom border up or down. To change the size of a section in a report, click within the section, and move the mouse pointer to the bottom border. Move the mouse pointer until it changes to a double-headed arrow. Then drag the bottom border until the size of the section is appropriate.

To adjust the size of a field box so that its contents fit properly, click on the field and move the mouse pointer to a handle. When the mouse pointer changes to a double-headed arrow, drag the handle to change the field box.

To adjust the size of a column in a columnar report, click anywhere within the column. Move the mouse pointer to the right side of the selected column. When the mouse pointer changes to a double-headed arrow, drag to reduce or increase the width of the column. Approach adjusts the position of the columns to the right of the column that you changed.

To move a column in a columnar report, click anywhere within the column. Move the mouse pointer within the column. When the mouse pointer looks like a hand, drag the column to the left or right. Approach adjusts the position of the columns to the right of the column that you changed.

## Changing the Number of Columns in a Standard or Columnar Report

You can change the number of columns on a page for a standard or columnar report. For example, if the report extends only from the left margin to the center of the page, you might be able to print two columns and save paper. To change the number of columns in a standard report, follow these steps:

1. Open the database, click on the tab for the report, and go to Design.

2. Double-click on a report element to open the InfoBox (Figure 14.9).

**FIGURE 14.9**

In the InfoBox, you can change the appearance or the number of columns in a report.

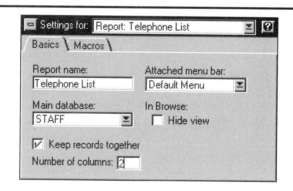

3. Select Report: *reporttitle* from the Settings For drop-down list box.

4. Select the number in the Number of Columns text box and overtype a new number.

5. Close the InfoBox. Approach converts the report to a two-column format. Figure 14.10 shows a two-column standard report in Preview.

FIGURE 14.10

A formatted
two-column standard
report

Title page
header

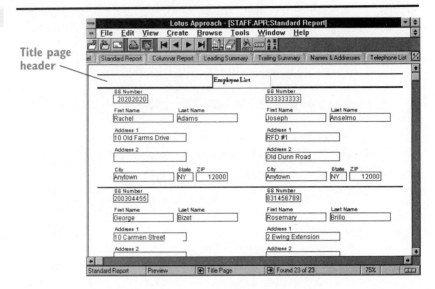

# Summarizing Your Data

Approach provides four types of summary reports. Summary reports can also contain leading or following calculations for numeric fields. These are the Approach summary reports:

**Leading Grouped Summary**    Contains one or more groups of like fields led by a summary panel with one or more field labels for each group.

**Trailing Grouped Summary**    Contains one or more groups of like fields followed by a summary panel with one or more field labels for each group.

**Columnar with Grand Summary**    Is a columnar report with a single grand calculation in a following position.

**Summary Only**    Contains one or more summary panels without detail lines.

You can either use the Report Assistant to create a basic summary report, or you can choose Create ➤ Summary to open the Summary dialog box (Figure 14.11) in which you can select options to produce custom summary reports.

In the Summarize group, there are three option buttons:

**Every n Records**    Click on this option button to summarize the values before or after every nth record in the database or to create a group of n records, where n represents a number from 1 (the default) to 999.

**All Records**    Click on this option button to summarize the values before or after the active group of records—either the entire database or those in the found set. This is the default.

**Records Grouped by**    Click on this option button to either group values without a summary or summarize the values before or after each group of records sorted by a selected field. You can select a field from a selected main or detail database.

At the bottom of the dialog box, there are two sets of option buttons and a check box:

**Left, Center, Right**    Click on one of these option buttons to indicate the location to display the panel on the report page. Center is the default.

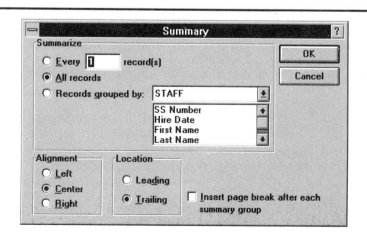

**Leading, Trailing**  Click on one of these option buttons to indicate whether to diplay the panel before or after the group being summarized. Trailing is the default.

**Insert Page Break**  Check this check box to insert a page break between summary items. This ensures that only one summary occurs on a page. The default is a cleared check box, or no page break between summary items.

## Creating a Summary Report with the Report Assistant

Creating a summary report with the Report Assistant is just like producing any other Approach report. However, instead of the two steps used to make a standard or columnar report, Approach adds a third step with which you select a grouping and/or select a field to be calculated and the type of calculation. To create a summary report with the Report Assistant, follow these steps:

1. Open the database for which you want to create a report and go to Design.

2. Choose Create ➤ Report. Approach displays the Report Assistant dialog box.

3. Type the report name in the View Name & Title text box.

4. Select a style from the SmartMaster Style drop-down list box.

5. Click on Leading Grouped Summary, Trailing Grouped Summary, Columnar with Grand Summary, or Summary Only in the SmartMaster Layout scroll box.

6. Click on the Next button. Approach displays the Step 2: Fields section of the dialog box for all but the Summary Only report. For the Summary Only report, skip to step 10.

7. From the Database Fields scroll box, click on a field to be displayed and click on Add to insert a field in the Fields to Place on View box. (You can also insert a field in the Fields to Place on View box by double-clicking on it.)

8. Select the remaining display fields for the report, in the order in which you want them to appear, from left to right.

**9.** Click on the Next button. Approach displays the Step 3 (for Summary Only reports, Step 2) section.

**10.** Click on a field by which records are grouped. Approach places a check mark in the check box.

**11.** In the Calculate drop-down list box, select a calculation, and in the Field scroll box, click on a field to be calculated.

**12.** Click on Done. Approach closes the dialog box, displays the report in Design, and inserts the report name on the View list on the status bar and on a tab right below the SmartIcons. Figure 14.12 illustrates a summary only report.

**13.** Save the Approach file.

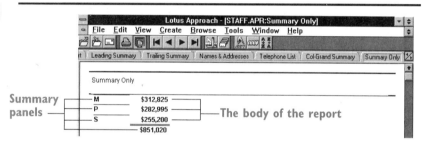

Summary panels — The body of the report

**NOTE** You can view a summary only report in Preview, Find, or Design. Browse is not available.

**TIP** To sort a summary report by one or two fields within each group, press Ctrl+T, choose Browse ➤ Sort ➤ Define in Browse or Preview, or choose Report ➤ Sort ➤ Define in Design. In the Sort dialog box, you'll find the field by which the report is grouped in the Fields to Sort on box. Just add other fields by clicking on the field in the Database Fields scroll box and clicking on the Add button. When you have completed specifying the fields on which to sort, select a sort order, and click on OK.

Approach

## Adding a Summary to a Report

You can add a summary to an Approach report in three ways:

- Choose Create ➤ Summary and fill in the Summary dialog box.
- Click in a column to be calculated, choose Object ➤ PowerClick, and either select a calculation type or the placement of the summary.
- Click in a column to be calculated, and click on the appropriate PowerClick SmartIcons.

Table 14.1 illustrates and describes the PowerClick SmartIcons and commands.

**TABLE 14.1:** Approach PowerClick SmartIcons and Commands

| SMARTICON | COMMAND | DESCRIPTION |
|---|---|---|
| 1 +2 3 | Object ➤ PowerClick ➤ Sum | Sums the values in a group of numeric fields |
|  | Object ➤ PowerClick ➤ Average | Calculates the average of the values in a group of numeric fields |
|  | Object ➤ PowerClick ➤ Count | Counts the fields in a group |
| N/A | Object ➤ PowerClick ➤ Minimum | Finds the minimum value in a group of numeric fields |
| N/A | Object ➤ PowerClick ➤ Maximum | Finds the maximum value in a group of numeric fields |
| N/A | Object ➤ PowerClick ➤ Standard Deviation | Calculates the standard deviation of the values in a group of numeric fields |

**TABLE 14.1:** Approach PowerClick SmartIcons and Commands (continued)

| SMARTICON | COMMAND | DESCRIPTION |
|---|---|---|
| N/A | Object ➤ PowerClick ➤ Variance | Calculates the variance of the values in a group of numeric fields |
| | Object ➤ PowerClick ➤ Leading Summary | Places a summary panel before a group of records |
| | Object ➤ PowerClick ➤ Trailing Summary | Places a summary panel after a group of records |

## Adding a Report Summary using the Summary Dialog Box

To add a report summary using the Summary dialog box, follow these steps:

1. Open the database containing the report and go to Design.

2. Open a report for which you want to add a summary.

3. Choose Create ➤ Summary. Approach displays the Summary dialog box (Figure 14.11).

4. In the Summarize group, choose whether you wish to summarize for every record, all records, or by a group of fields.

5. In the Alignment group, select the alignment for the summary panel.

6. In the Location group, choose whether the summary leads or follows the group(s) of records.

7. Check or clear the Insert Page Break after Each Summary Group check box to specify whether a page break is inserted after each summary group.

8. When you have filled in the dialog box, click on OK or press ↵. Approach adds summary panels to the report (Figure 14.13), and marks the parts of the report.

**Approach**

**FIGURE 14.13**

A zoomed portion of a columnar report with trailing summary panels

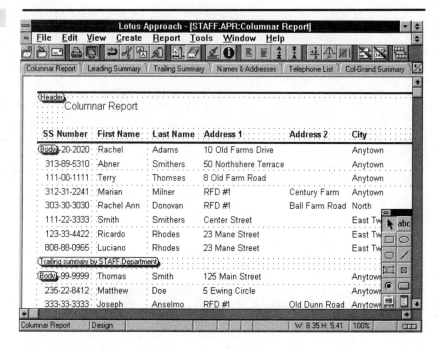

## Adding a Report Summary using the PowerClick Feature

To add a report summary using the PowerClick feature, follow these steps:

1. Open the database containing the report and go to Design.

2. Create a columnar report. (For more information, see "Creating a Columnar Report," earlier in this chapter.)

3. Click in the column that holds the field by which you wish to group the report records. Click on the Trailing Summary SmartIcon. Approach asks if you wish to sort the field that you will group.

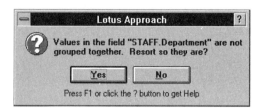

4. Click on <u>Y</u>es. Approach sorts and groups the records by the selected field, leaving a space between groups.

5. Optionally, click in the column holding a field by which you wish to sort within the group. Then click on either the Ascending Sort or Descending Sort SmartIcon.

6. Click in the field for which you want a summary.

7. Click on the Total SmartIcon. Approach calculates a total for each group in the report. Figure 14.14 shows part of a formatted report in Preview.

8. Save the Approach file.

# Creating and Editing Mail Merge Documents

One of the most important reasons for maintaining a database is that you can use it to send out mass mailings. In Approach, you can prepare both form letters and mailing labels. In addition to names and addresses, mail merge documents can contain almost any other information that you can direct to a specific individual. By using Approach's mail merge feature, you can automate yet personalize a large mailing.

The basic components of mail merge are database fields, which are merged into the finished form letter, and a form letter. For the most part, the starting form letter is like any other letter. It contains text for your entire audience, but omits unique information, such as the name, address, city, state, and zip code of the recipient. You can create a letter document from scratch either in

**FIGURE 14.14**

Part of a formatted
report grouped by
Department and with
salaries totaled by
Department

Salaries by Department

| SS Number | First Name | Last Name | Dept | Title | Salary |
|---|---|---|---|---|---|
| 220-20-2020 | Rachel | Adams | M | Administrative | 27,000 |
| 303-30-3030 | Rachel Ann | Donovan | M | Administrative | 24,000 |
| 312-31-2241 | Marian | Milner | M | Vice President | 52,000 |
| 123-33-4422 | Ricardo | Rhodes | M | Personnel Mgr. | 46,250 |
| 308-88-0965 | Lucinne | Rhodes | M | Purchasing Mgr. | 42,500 |
| 313-89-5310 | Abner | Smithers | M | Vice President | 50,000 |
| 111-22-3333 | Smith | Smithers | M | Production Mgr. | 46,000 |
| 111-00-1111 | Terry | Thomas | M | Administrative | 25,075 |
| | | | | | $312,825 |
| 333-33-3333 | Joseph | Anselmo | P | Mechanic | 33,750 |
| 135-55-3535 | Terom | Carmichael | P | Inspector | 33,000 |
| 235-22-8412 | Matthew | Doe | P | Sales Associate | 35,000 |
| 999-99-9999 | Stuart | Doe | P | Assembler | 27,545 |
| 123-33-4444 | Don | Donovan | P | Assembler | 26,000 |
| 250-25-5555 | Jacques | Jacquet | P | Inspector | 34,500 |
| 303-22-3467 | Mary | Sanders | P | Inspector | 33,575 |
| 343-44-2647 | Miriam | Sanders | P | Inspector | 33,575 |
| 145-99-9999 | Thomas | Smith | P | Mechanic | 26,050 |
| | | | | | $282,995 |
| 200-30-1455 | George | Baret | S | Computer Operator | 28,000 |
| 331-45-6789 | Rosemary | Brillo | S | Programmer | 46,000 |
| 545-74-8111 | Montgomery | Doane | S | Programmer | 48,000 |
| 750-32-8612 | Miller | Montrose | S | Programmer | 44,075 |
| 333-45-6125 | John | Smith | S | Programmer | 45,050 |
| 781-22-3643 | Brenda | Smithers | S | Programmer | 44,075 |
| | | | | | $255,200 |

Approach or in a word processor, such as Ami Pro, or by editing an existing document.

The database fields, from Approach or even another database program, contain the unique information about the recipient of each letter. In addition to the name and address information previously mentioned, other typical fields merged into a form letter are amount owed, credit and sales history, and date of last contact.

# Ami Pro's Mail Merge Facility

Ami Pro provides a mail merge feature. To perform a mail merge from within Ami Pro, start Ami Pro, and then follow these steps:

1. Choose File ➤ Merge. Ami Pro displays the Welcome to Merge dialog box.

2. Click on the Select, Create, or Edit a Data File option button. A data file contains the unique information to be inserted into the merge document. Click on OK.

3. In the Select Merge Data File dialog box, select or name a file. Valid file types include 1-2-3, Ami Pro, Comma delimited, dBASE, DIF, Excel, Filed Length ASCII, Organizer, Paradox, and SuperCalc. Click on OK. Ami Pro displays the Welcome to Merge dialog box again.

4. Click on the Create or Edit a Merge Document option button, if needed. Click on OK. Ami Pro prompts you to accept the current document as the merge document.

5. Click on Yes to use the current document. (If you already have created a merge document, click on No to open the Merge Document dialog box from which you can choose the merge document.)

6. In the Insert Merge Field dialog box, select a field name to be merged into the merge document; click on Insert. It's easier to select fields in the order in which you want them to appear in the merge document. Since the Insert Merge Field dialog box remains in the document window, you can create and edit the merge document and add fields at the same time. For example, you can add spaces between fields, if needed.

7. Continue writing your merge document and adding fields.

8. When you have completed the merge document, click on Continue Merge. Ami Pro displays the Welcome to Merge dialog box again.

Approach

**WORKING TOGETHER** ▲

**9.** Click on the Merge and Print the Data and the Document option buttons and click on OK. Ami Pro opens the Merge dialog box.

**10.** Click on the Merge & Print (to merge and print), Merge, View & Print (to merge, preview the document, and then print), or Merge & Save As (to merge and save for later printing) option button; then click on OK.

For more information about the Ami Pro SmartMerge function, see Chapter 28 in the *User's Guide* and *Understanding Merge* or *SmartMerge* in the Help facility.

## Creating a Form Letter

The Form Letter Assistant guides you through writing a form letter and selecting the fields to be inserted in the letter. To create a form letter, follow these steps:

**1.** Open the database for which you want to create a form letter and go to Design.

**2.** Choose Create ➤ Form Letter. Approach displays the Step 1: Layout section of the Form Letter Assistant dialog box (Figure 14.15).

**3.** Type the form letter name in the View Name & Title text box.

**4.** Select a style from the SmartMaster Style drop-down list box.

**5.** Choose a layout from the SmartMaster Layout box, and click on the Next button. Approach displays the Step 2: Return Address section of the Form Letter Assistant dialog box (Figure 14.16).

**FIGURE 14.15**

In the Step 1: Layout section of the Form Letter Assistant dialog box, choose a name, style, and layout.

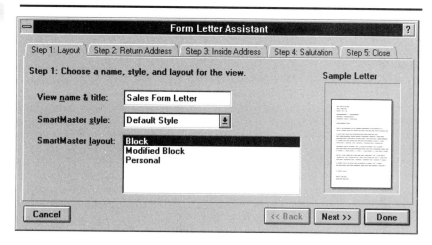

**FIGURE 14.16**

In the Step 2: Return Address section, either type your return address or leave it blank.

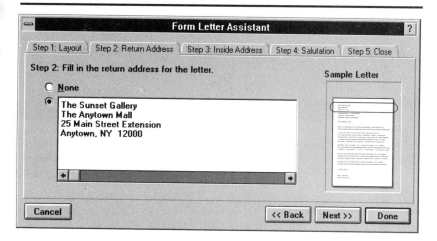

6. Type the return address. (If you use letterhead stationery, leave the box blank.) Click on Next. Approach displays the Step 3: Inside Address section of the Form Letter Assistant dialog box (Figure 14.17).

7. Select a layout from the Address Layout drop-down list box. Notice that Approach changes the look of the Fields for the Address box.

A filled-in Step 3: Inside
Address section of the
Form Letter Assistant
dialog box

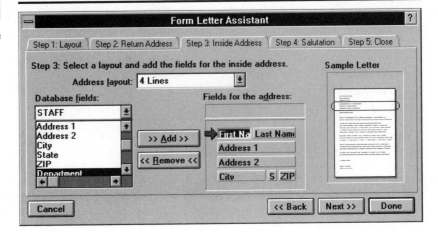

8. In the Database Fields scroll box, click on the first field of the inside address and click on <u>A</u>dd to insert a field in the Fields for the A<u>d</u>dress box. (You can also insert a field in the Fields for the A<u>d</u>dress box by double-clicking on it.)

9. Select the remaining fields for the inside, in the order in which you want them to appear. Click on Next. Approach displays the Step 4: Salutation section of the Form Letter Assistant dialog box (Figure 14.18).

A filled-in Step 4:
Salutation section of
the Form Letter
Assistant dialog box

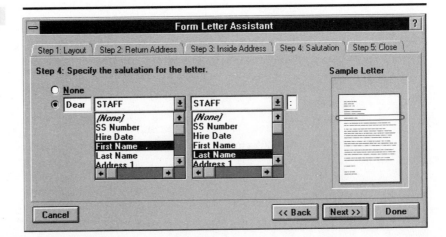

**10.** If desired, type another salutation in the Dear text box. Click on a field, such as First Name, in the first scroll box. Optionally, click on a field, such as Last Name, in the second scroll box. Optionally, change the punctuation in the small text box to the right of the second scroll box. Then click on Next. Approach displays the Step 5: Close section of the Form Letter Assistant dialog box (Figure 14.19).

**FIGURE 14.19**

The Step 5: Close section of the Form Letter Assistant dialog box with the defaults

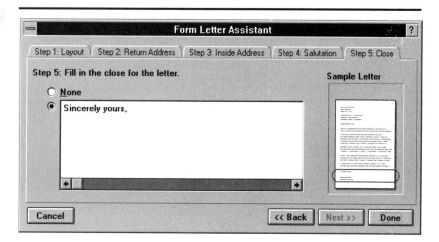

**11.** Fill in the close for your letter, and click on Done. Approach displays the form letter with the address, fields, saluation, and close (Figure 14.20).

## Editing a Form Letter

To write a form letter, follow these steps:

**1.** In Design, select the desired form letter from the View list on the status bar by clicking on its name or by clicking on its tab immediately below the SmartIcons.

**2.** Repeatedly click on the text box if it is not active. When a blue border appears, you can start typing. (Remember not to click too rapidly. If Approach senses a double-click, the InfoBox appears.)

Approach

FIGURE 14.20

A form letter ready to
be filled in with its
body text

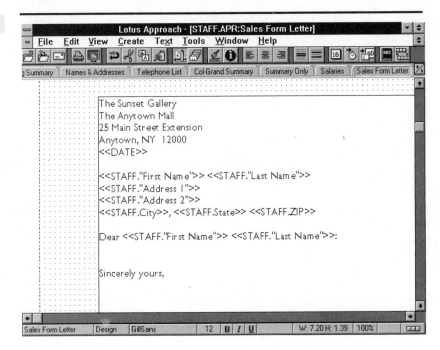

**3.** Type the letter just as you would any letter.

**4.** Either type around the fields, or insert fields into the letter.

When working on a form letter, note the following:

- You can use a field more than once in a letter.

- When inserting two fields side by side (for example, First Name and Last Name), insert a space between the fields. If you forget to insert the space, the second field will begin immediately after the last character in the first field.

- Periodically check the appearance of the form letter by looking at it in Browse view. Approach will have already filled in the letter with the results of the fields.

- To copy a field to another part of the letter, select the field, choose Edit ➤ Copy (or press Ctrl+C), move the insertion point to the desired location, and choose Edit ➤ Paste (or press Ctrl+V).

■ To move a field to another part of the letter, select the field, choose <u>E</u>dit ➤ Cu<u>t</u> (or press Ctrl+X), move the insertion point to the desired location, and choose <u>E</u>dit ➤ <u>P</u>aste (or press Ctrl+V).

■ To insert a field into the letter, point to the location in which you want to insert the field, choose Tex<u>t</u> ➤ <u>I</u>nsert ➤ <u>F</u>ield, select the field from the Insert Field dialog box, and click on OK.

■ To insert a page number into the letter, make sure that the Text Smart-Icon is pressed down, point to the location in which you want to insert the page number, and choose Tex<u>t</u> ➤ <u>I</u>nsert ➤ <u>P</u>age #.

■ To insert today's date (from your computer system clock) into the letter, make sure that the Text SmartIcon is pressed down, point to the location in which you want to insert the date, and choose Tex<u>t</u> ➤ <u>I</u>nsert ➤ <u>D</u>ate.

■ To insert an object into the upper-left corner of the letter, choose Edit ➤ Paste from <u>F</u>ile, and click on OK.

■ To format the entire letter at one time, choose <u>E</u>dit ➤ Select <u>A</u>ll.

Figure 14.21 shows a completed form letter.

**FIGURE 14.21**

The completed form letter in Preview

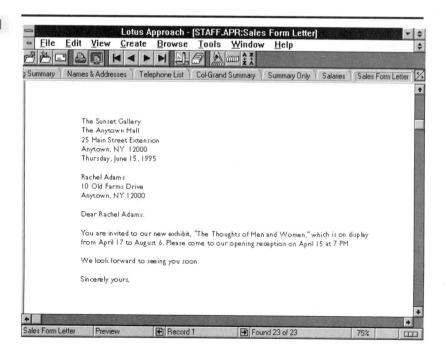

Approach

## Creating Mailing Labels

Using almost the same techniques that you used to produce a form letter, you can create mailing labels. Approach provides predefined label formats, or you can create your own. To create mailing labels, follow these steps:

1. Open the database for which you want to create a mailing label and go to Design.

2. Choose Create ➤ Mailing Label. Approach displays the Mailing Label dialog box (Figure 14.22).

3. Type the mailing label name in the Mailing Label Name text box.

4. Select a database from the Database drop-down list box. You can create a mailing label using fields from several joined databases.

5. In the Database Fields scroll box, double-click on fields for the label in the order in which you want them to appear. As you double-click, Approach adds the fields in the Fields to Place on Label box.

**FIGURE 14.22**

In the Mailing Label Assistant dialog box, you can name a mailing label and select the fields to be merged into it.

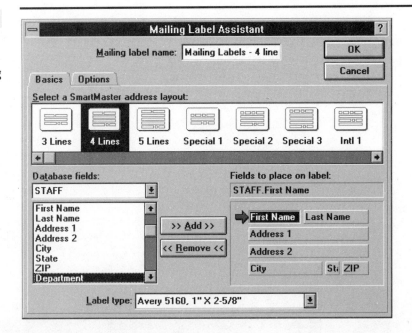

6. To remove a field from the mailing label, select it in the Fields to Place on Label box and click on <u>R</u>emove.

7. Open the <u>L</u>abel Type drop-down list box, and select an Avery label code that matches the mailing labels on which you will print.

8. Either click on OK or press ↵ when you have completed your selection. Approach closes the dialog box and displays the mailing label (Figure 14.23).

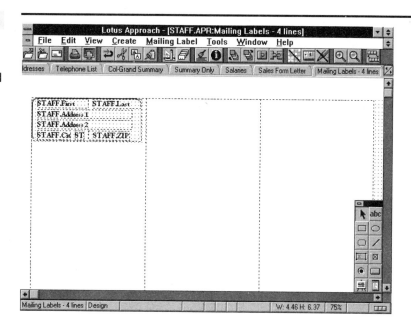

9. If needed, format the fields on the mailing label, periodically going to Browse view to check your progress. Figure 14.24 illustrates the completed mailing label in Preview. (Notice that Approach moves lines on labels to fill in empty Address 2 fields.)

**FIGURE 14.24**

The completed mailing label in Preview

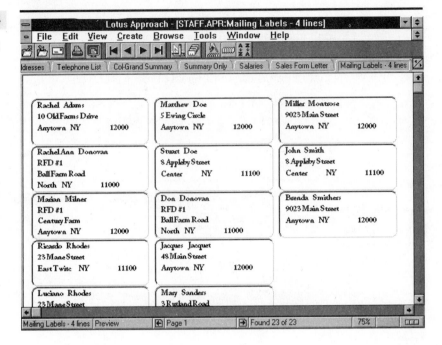

## Creating Custom Mailing Labels

To design custom mailing labels, click on the Options tab in the Mailing Label dialog box, and a new section of the dialog box opens (Figure 14.25).

These are the options in this section of the dialog box:

**Custom Label**    Type the name of the custom label that you are designing so that you can save it and use it at a later time.

**Top Margin**    Type the distance between the top border of the top row of labels and the edge of the paper on which the labels will be printed.

**Left Margin**    Type the distance between the left border of the left row of labels and the edge of the paper on which the labels will be printed.

**Width**    Type the width of the label.

**Height**    Type the height of the label.

FIGURE 14.25

The options section of
the Mailing Label
Assistant dialog box

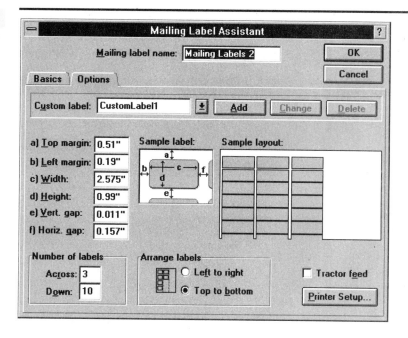

**Vert. Gap**    Type the distance between the bottom of one label and the top of the next label in a column.

**Horiz. Gap**    Type the distance between the right border of one label and the left border of the next label in a row.

**Across**    Type the number of labels in a row.

**Down**    Type the number of labels in a column.

**Left to Right**    Click on this option button to have Approach "load" the selected fields onto the labels row by row from left to right.

**Top to Bottom**    Click on this option button to have Approach "load" the selected fields onto the labels column by column from top to bottom. This is the default.

**Tractor Feed**    Check this check box if you are using continuous feed label forms. Clear this check box if you are using single sheet label forms. This is the default.

**Printer Setup**    Click on this button to open the Printer Setup dialog box in which you can define the default printer, choose a printer for this print job, and set page orientation, paper size, and the paper source.

**Add**    Click on this button to save a custom layout so that you can use it in the future.

**Change**    Click on this button to modify a custom layout that you have previously saved.

**Delete**    Click on this button to remove a custom layout that you have previously saved.

# *Presenting Information with Freelance Graphics*

Part Five introduces you to Freelance Graphics, Smart-Suite's presentation application. First, you'll learn how to create a Freelance Graphics presentation "on the fly," using SmartMaster Design Sets and filling in the blanks with your information. Then you'll find out how to customize a Freelance presentation using clip art, symbols, and special effects. You'll learn how to complete a presentation—by running a slide show, creating speaker's notes, and producing handouts.

Table V.1 illustrates and describes the Freelance Graphics SmartIcons.

# Freelance Graphics SmartIcons

| SMARTICON | DESCRIPTION |
|---|---|

**Freelance Graphics SmartIcons**

Creates a new file. [File ➤ New] *Shortcut:* Ctrl+N

Opens an existing file. [File ➤ Open] *Shortcut:* Ctrl+O

Saves the current file. [File ➤ Save] *Shortcut:* Ctrl+S

Prints the current file using the options in the Print dialog box. [File ➤ Print] *Shortcut:* Ctrl+P

Undoes the last action, if allowed. [Edit ➤ Undo] *Shortcut:* Ctrl+Z

Cuts the selection and places it in the Clipboard. [Edit ➤ Cut] *Shortcut:* Ctrl+X or Shift+Del

Copies the selection to the Clipboard. [Edit ➤ Copy] *Shortcut:* Ctrl+C or Ctrl+Ins

Pastes the contents of the Clipboard into the file at the current cursor location. [Edit ➤ Paste] *Shortcut:* Ctrl+V or Shift+Ins

Applies or removes boldface from the selection. [Text ➤ Bold] *Shortcut:* Ctrl+B

Applies or removes italics from the selection. [Text ➤ Italic] *Shortcut:* Ctrl+I

Applies or removes an underline from the selection. [Text ➤ Underline] *Shortcut:* Ctrl+U

Runs a screen show. [View ➤ Screen Show ➤ Run] *Shortcut:* Alt+F10

Runs the spell checker on the current selection or file. [Tools ➤ Spell Check] *Shortcut:* Ctrl+F2

Zooms in or zooms out the current page. [View ➤ Zoom In/View ➤ Zoom Out]

Scrolls the current page on the desktop.

Starts Lotus Media Manager, if your computer system supports multimedia. [Edit ➤ Insert Object; select Lotus Media]

Starts Lotus Sound, if your computer system supports multimedia. [Edit ➤ Insert Object; select Lotus Sound]

Starts Lotus Annotator. [Edit ➤ Insert Object; select Lotus Annotator Note]

Starts 1-2-3. [Edit ➤ Insert Object; select 1-2-3 Worksheet]

Starts Ami Pro. [Edit ➤ Insert Object; select Ami Pro Document]

Starts Lotus Notes, if it is installed.

Freelance

15

# Planning and Creating a Presentation

# Freelance
**CHAPTER 15**

In this chapter, you'll learn about creating a Freelance Graphics presentation. First, you'll learn about the elements of the Freelance Graphics window. Then you'll find out about the tools that help you create a presentation quickly and easily including SmartMaster sets. (SmartMaster sets are professionally designed page layouts, which include graphics, backgrounds, and fonts. With all the basics in hand, you'll plan, create, and edit a presentation. Remember that you can learn the fundamentals of opening and saving files by reviewing Chapter 2, and you can review editing concepts in Chapter 3.

## Introducing Freelance Graphics

Freelance Graphics is an easy-to-use presentation application that enables you to produce a professional-looking presentation almost as soon as you install the program.

Using Freelance Graphics, you can do the following:

- create a presentation from an outline. Simply write the outline and convert it into a presentation.
- build a bulleted list.
- create a *screen show*, an automated on-screen presentation.
- enhance your presentation with symbols, charts, and tables.
- draw or import pictures into your presentations.
- produce speaker notes and handouts.

## Reading and Writing Common File Formats

Freelance Graphics reads and writes Presentation (.PRE), SmartMaster Set (.MAS), Symbol Library (.SYM), and Freelance for OS/2 (.PRS) files.

Freelance Graphics imports files with the following file types: Freelance (.DRW), Adobe Illustrator (.AI), Windows/PM Bitmap (.BMP), Computer Graphics Metafile (.CGM), Harvard Graphics 2.3 Chart (.CHT), Harvard Graphics 3.0 Chart (.CH3), Micrografx Designer (.DRW), AutoCAD Drawing Interchange (.DXF), Encapsulated Postscript (.EPS), Hewlett Packard Graphics Gallery (.GAL), Digital Research (.GEM), Graphics Interchange (.GIF), Hewlett Packard Graphics Language (.HGL), OS/2 Metafile (.MET), ZSoft PC Paintbrush Bitmap (.PCX), Macintosh PICT (.PCT), PowerPoint 2.0 and 3.0 (.PPT), AutoShade Rendering (.RND), Tag Image (.TIF), Harvard Graphics 2.3 Symbol (.SYM), Harvard Graphics 3.0 Symbol (.SY3), Targa Bitmap (.TGA), WordPerfect Graphic (.WPG), Windows metafile (.WMF), 1-2-3 PIC (.PIC), Freelance Portfolio (.PFL), ASCII (.PRN), and ASCII Text (.TXT) files.

Freelance Graphics exports files with the following file types: Freelance (.DRW), Adobe Illustrator (.AI), Windows Bitmap (.BMP), Computer Graphics Metafile (.CGM), Encapsulated Postscript (.EPS), Graphics Interchange (.GIF), Hewlett Packard Graphics Language (.HGL), OS/2 Metafile (.MET), ZSoft PC Paintbrush Bitmap (.PCX), Macintosh PICT (.PCT), Targa Bitmap (.TGA), Tag Image (.TIF), WordPerfect Graphic (.WPG), Windows metafile (.WMF), and Freelance Portfolio (.PFL).

Freelance Graphics imports charts of the following file types: 1-2-3 Worksheet (.WK?), Freelance for OS/2 (.GPH), Freelance (.CH1), Graphwriter (.CHT), and Symphony Worksheet (.WR?)

# Viewing the Freelance Graphics Window

The Freelance Graphics application window (Figure 15.1) contains many of the elements that you found out about in Chapter 2. However, because you are now in a presentation application, some of the elements are focused on

helping you create a presentation. In this section, you'll get an overview of all the elements of the application window and find out about the Freelance Graphics status bar.

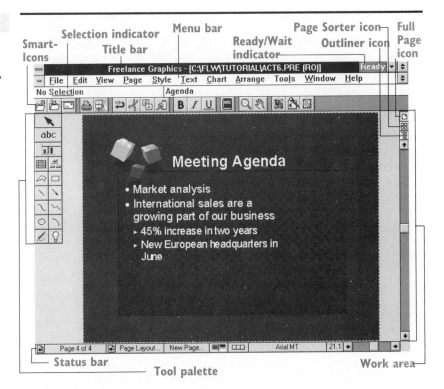

## Freelance Graphics SmartIcons

The pages starting Part Five (the beginning of the Freelance Graphics section) show all the Freelance Graphics SmartIcons. To learn how SmartIcons work, see Chapter 2.

## The Work Area

The work area displays a presentation as you work. Notice that the work area includes a vertical scroll bar. (The horizontal scroll bar appears in the status bar.) On the left side of the work area is a tool palette, described in Table 15.1.

On the right side are three buttons that allow you to view the current application in different ways.

**TABLE 15.1:** Freelance Graphics Drawing Tool Palette

| TOOL | NAME | DESCRIPTION |
|------|------|-------------|
| ▲ | Pointer tool | Selects an object in a drawing (Press Shift and click to add the next object to the selection.) |
| abc | Text Block tool | Inserts text in a drawing |
| ▯▮ | Data Chart tool | Creates a data chart |
| ▦ | Text Table tool | Creates a table |
| 品 | Organization Chart tool | Creates an organization chart |
| ⌂ | Polygon tool | Draws a polygon |
| ▭ | Rectangle tool | Draws a rectangle or, if you press and hold down the Shift key, a square |
| ╲ | Line tool | Draws a line |
| ╲ | Arrow tool | Draws an arrow |
| ∿ | Open Curve tool | Draws a curve from point to point |
| ╲ | Polyline tool | Draws a line made up of segments |
| ◯ | Circle tool | Draws an ellipse or, if you press and hold down the Shift key, a circle |

Freelance

**TABLE 15.1:** Freelance Graphics Drawing Tool Palette (continued)

| TOOL | NAME | DESCRIPTION |
|------|------|-------------|
| | Arc tool | Draws an arc, or part of a circle |
| | Freehand Drawing tool | Draws freehand |
| | Symbol tool | Adds a symbol to the current page |

Click on this button (which is the same as choosing <u>V</u>iew ➤ <u>F</u>ull Page) to view one page of your presentation at a time. Figure 15.1 (above) shows a QuickStart Tutorial presentation page in Full Page view.

Click on this button (which is the same as choosing <u>V</u>iew ➤ <u>P</u>age Sorter) to view a screenful of presentation pages. Figure 15.2 shows the QuickStart Tutorial presentation in Page Sorter view.

**FIGURE 15.2**

The QuickStart Tutorial presentation in Page Sorter view

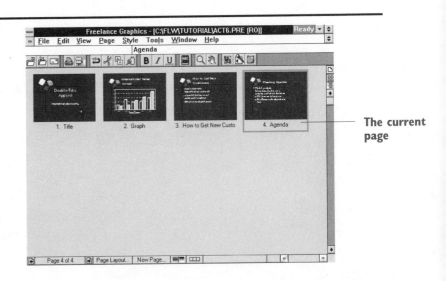

The current page

Click on this button (which is the same as choosing <u>V</u>iew ➤ Out<u>l</u>iner) to view an outline of the presentation. Figure 15.3 shows an outline of the QuickStart Tutorial presentation.

**FIGURE 15.3**

The QuickStart Tutorial Presentation in Outliner view

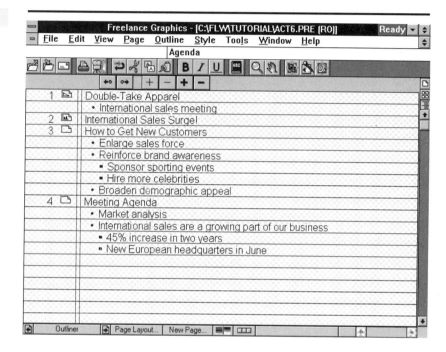

## The Freelance Graphics Status Bar

The Freelance Graphics status bar (Figure 15.4) allows you to go to a different page, open the Page Layout or New Page dialog box, view your presentation in color or black and white, display or hide Freelance Graphics' set of Smart-Icons, select a different font or point size, and scroll horizontally.

These are the buttons on the status bar:

 **Previous Page button**    Click on this button to move to the previous page, unless you are viewing the first page.

Page 6 of 13    **Page Number button**    Click on this button, which shows the current page number, to display the names of all the pages in the presentation.

# freelance
**CHAPTER 15**

**FIGURE 15.4**

The Freelance Graphics status bar consists of buttons with which you can change the look of a presentation or navigate around it.

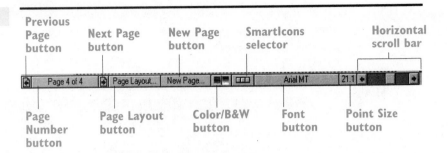

The check mark indicates the current page. If you are in Outliner view, the button displays the word *Outliner*. If you are editing a page layout, this button reads *Layout* and indicates the current page. If your presentation is greater than 20 pages, instead of listing all the pages in the presentation, Freelance Graphics opens the Go To Page dialog box.

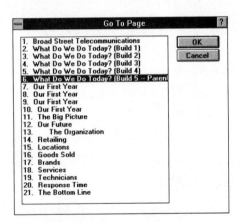

**Next Page button**    Click on this button to move to the next page, unless you are viewing the last page.

**Page Layout button**    Click on this button to open the Page Layout dialog box (Figure 15.5), from which you can select a page layout for the current page.

**New Page button**    Click on this button to open the New Page dialog box (Figure 15.6), from which you go to the next page and choose its

**520**

page layout. If you are editing a page layout, this button reads *New Layout*. When you click on this button, Freelance Graphics opens the New Layout dialog box, from which you can save a page layout as a Smart-Master set.

 **Color/B&W button**    Click on this button to switch between displaying the presentation in color or black and white.

 **SmartIcons selector**    Click on this button to display two SmartIcon items. Click on Hide to remove the SmartIcons from the desktop.

**FIGURE 15.5**

The Page Layout dialog box, from which you can select a layout for the current page

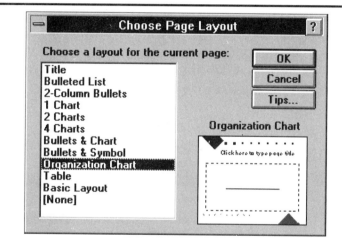

**FIGURE 15.6**

The New Page dialog box, from which you can go to the next page and choose its page layout

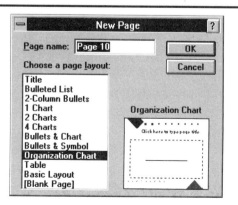

Arial MT    **Font button**    Click on this button to open the list of some of the fonts installed on your computer. To open this list, you must have selected some text. Click on More Fonts to display the More Fonts dialog box, from which you have the choice of all the fonts installed under Windows.

22.7    **Point Size button**    Click on this button to display the list of some of the point sizes for the current font. To open this list, you must have selected some text. Click on Size to display the Text Size Other dialog box, and type a point size in the Size in Points text box. If you have selected text with varying font sizes, the word *Mixed* appears in the Size in Points text box.

**Horizontal scroll bar**    Use this scroll bar to navigate between the left margin and the right margin of the window.

## Planning a Presentation

Although Freelance Graphics makes it extremely easy to write a presentation on the fly, it's best to plan it. When planning a presentation, consider these important points:

**Audience Profile and Environment**    Tailor the presentation to your audience and their surroundings. Consider such factors as the meeting time and day, the meeting location, professional and educational backgrounds of the attendees, their knowledge of the topic, and the amount of time you've been assigned.

**Your Objectives**    What do you want to happen as a result of giving the presentation? Is it purely educational? Do you want your audience to remember or have a positive feeling about certain topics? There are three basic purposes for giving a presentation: educating, informing, and selling. Although you can combine all three into a single presentation, you'll probably want to emphasize one of the three.

After determining your audience and objectives, you can get into the details of the presentation by writing an outline.

- Plan an introduction, which is an overview of the presentation and a preface to the topic of discussion. You are preparing your audience for the rest of the presentation.

- Write down the major topics, and then fill in with four or five subtopics for each. Consider ending each major topic with a short summary and an introduction to the next topic.

- Briefly summarize the presentation.

# Creating a Presentation

There are two basic ways of creating a presentation: by creating a presentation page by page in Full Page view, or by writing an outline in Outliner view and having Freelance Graphics convert it to a presentation.

- If you are creating a presentation from scratch, using the Outliner is a good choice. It is probably the fastest way to create a presentation. Once Freelance Graphics completes the pages, you'll be able to edit them on your desktop.

- If you are editing a presentation or have a little more time, using Full Page view works well. Then you can spend your time working on each page. When you start Freelance Graphics, it displays a series of dialog boxes that enable you to create a new presentation and define the Style-Master set and page on which you want to work. The opening dialog boxes enable you to open an existing presentation as well.

Typing and editing the text on a presentation page or in an outline is just about the same as creating and editing a word processing document. The main difference between working on a presentation and working on a document is the length of sentences; presentation sentences are usually short and sweet.

## Starting the Program

 When you start Freelance Graphics or when you choose File ➤ New, the application displays a series of dialog boxes. The first dialog box (Figure 15.7) welcomes you to Freelance Graphics and prompts you to either create a

**FIGURE 15.7**

The Welcome to
Freelance Graphics
dialog box

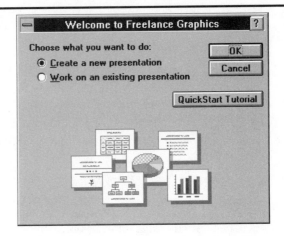

new presentation, work on an existing presentation, or start the QuickStart Tutorial.

If you wish to work on an existing presentation, Freelance Graphics displays the Choose Presentation dialog box from which you can select an existing presentation. If you choose to work on a new presentation, Freelance Graphics displays a series of screens. Click on an option button and either click on OK or press ↵.

If you click on the Create a New Presentation option button in the Welcome dialog box, Freelance Graphics displays the Choose a Look for Your Presentation dialog box (Figure 15.8). In this dialog box, you choose a SmartMaster set that provides the format and background for each page of the presentation. Freelance Graphics displays the SmartMaster set with which you worked most recently.

You can also click on the Directory button to find other SmartMaster sets. For example, if you have created your own sets and have stored them in a different directory, you can find the directory and open the desired set. Once you have chosen a SmartMaster set, click on OK.

To see the available SmartMaster sets in the Choose a Look for Your Presentation dialog box, click on a MAS file in the scroll box and look at the sample in the sample box. Keep selecting files and viewing the samples until you find a set that you like. Then click on OK to select the set and close the dialog box.

**FIGURE 15.8**

The Choose a Look
for Your Presentation
dialog box

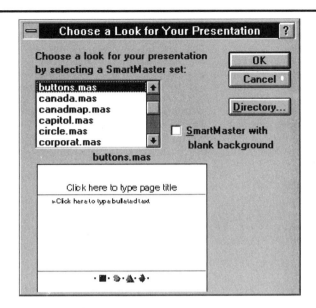

At this point, for certain printers, Freelance Graphics may display an error
message:

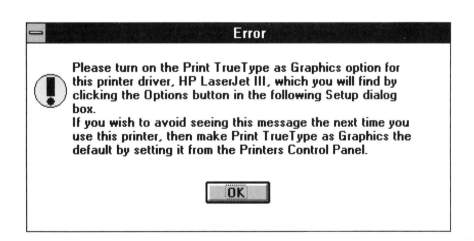

If this message appears, your printer probably supports printing TrueType fonts as graphics, but you have not selected this option in the Windows Control Panel. To correct this, follow these steps:

1. Double-click on the Control Panel icon in your Program Manager window.

2. Double-click on the Printers icon.

3. Click on the Setup button in the Printers dialog box.

4. In the next dialog box, click on the Options button.

5. In the Options dialog box, check the Print TrueType as Graphics check box.

6. Click on OK twice.

7. Click on Close.

8. Close the Control Panel window.

Selecting Print TrueType as Graphics may speed up printing and save printer memory.

## Choosing a Page Layout

Freelance Graphics displays the Choose Page Layout dialog box (Figure 15.9), with which you can select the type of page on which to work. (Click on the Tips button to open a small window that explains the dialog box and its purpose.)

 **TIP** Press down the right mouse button on an object to display a quick menu. For example, clicking the right mouse button on a text field reveals a menu with text formatting options.

When you have selected a page type, click on OK. Freelance Graphics displays the page that you have chosen (Figure 15.10). To view page layouts, click on the name of a layout in the box on the left side of the dialog box, and look at the sample on the right side.

**FIGURE 15.9**

The Choose Page
Layout dialog box

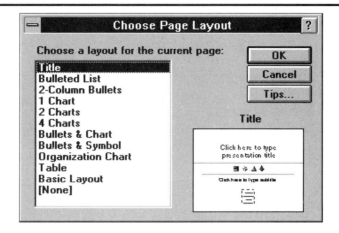

**FIGURE 15.10**

The first page of a new
Freelance Graphics
presentation—ready
for you to edit

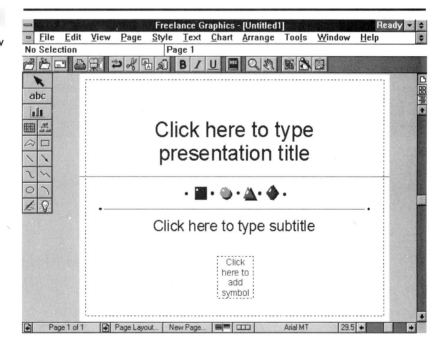

Freelance

## Creating a Presentation in Outliner View

An Outliner view outline is very similar to any document outline. You work with four different levels; Level 1, which is the highest level, is the presentation or page title line, and each of the three additional levels is indented slightly under the one above it. As you change to Level 2, 3, or 4, the bullet symbol in front of the line changes and the line moves away from the left margin. Freelance Graphics provides two shortcut keys and one key combination for use in Outliner view:

↵    Creates the next line in the outline. The level of the previous line is carried over to this line (e.g., if the previous line was at Level 2, the new line is also Level 2).

**Tab**    Demotes the current line. In other words, if the previous line was a Level 3 line, the current line becomes a Level 4 line.

**Shift+Tab**    Promotes the current line. In other words, if the previous line was a Level 3 line, the current line becomes a Level 2 line.

When you switch to Outliner view, the work area looks like a blank yellow pad (Figure 15.11). In addition, Freelance Graphics adds six icons to the window. Table 15.2 describes these icons, which help you to move from level to level in an outlin, or to collapse or expand pages or the entire presentation.

**TABLE 15.1:** Freelance Graphics Outliner Icons

| ICON | ICON NAME | MENU COMMAND AND SHORTCUT KEY | DESCRIPTION |
|---|---|---|---|
| ◄• | Promote | <u>O</u>utline ➤ <u>P</u>romote; Shift+Tab | Increases the selected line of text to the next higher level |
| •► | Demote | <u>O</u>utline ➤ <u>D</u>emote; Tab | Decreases the selected line of text to the next lower level |
| + | Expand Page | <u>O</u>utline ➤ <u>E</u>xpand; + | Displays all levels of the outline of the current page |

**TABLE 15.1:** Freelance Graphics Outliner Icons (continued)

| ICON | ICON NAME | MENU COMMAND AND SHORTCUT KEY | DESCRIPTION |
|------|-----------|-------------------------------|-------------|
| [ − ] | Collapse Page | Outline ➤ Collapse; − | Displays the highest level only in the outline of the current page |
| [ + ] | Expand Outline | Outline ➤ Expand All; N/A | Displays all levels of the outline of the entire presentation |
| [ − ] | Collapse Outline | Outline ➤ Collapse All; N/A | Displays the highest levels only in the outline of the entire presentation |

**FIGURE 15.11**

The Freelance Graphics work area in Outliner view

The first page of a presentation in Outliner

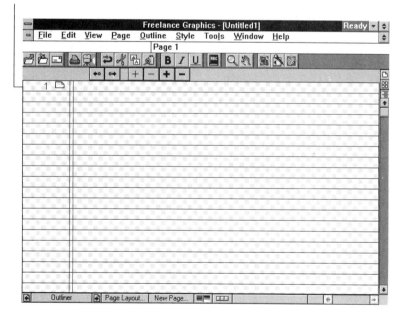

Table 15.3 shows and describes the symbols next to each page on an Outliner view page.

**TABLE 15.1:**    Freelance Graphics Outliner Symbols

| SYMBOL | THE PAGE CONTAINS |
| --- | --- |
| | Text (no graphics or symbols, charts, tables, or organization charts) |
| | Chart(s) |
| | Table |
| | Graphics or symbols |
| | Organization Chart |

To outline a Freelance Graphics presentation using Outliner view, follow these steps:

**1.** Click on the Outliner button or choose <u>V</u>iew ➤ Ou<u>t</u>liner to switch to Outliner view.

**2.** Type the presentation title (a Level 1 entry) and press ↵. Freelance Graphics adds a new line.

> 1   Broad Street Telecommunications
>     •

**3.** Type the subtitle and press ↵.

> 1   Broad Street Telecommunications
>    • The First Year and the Future Ahead
>     •

**4.** Press Shift+Tab or click on the Promote icon. Freelance Graphics promotes the new line to a new Level 1 page.

| 1 | | Broad Street Telecommunications |
|---|---|---|
| | | • The First Year and the Future Ahead |
| 2 | | |

**5.** Type the title of the second page and press ↵.

| 1 | | Broad Street Telecommunications |
|---|---|---|
| | | • The First Year and the Future Ahead |
| 2 | | What Do We Do Today? |
| | | • |

**6.** Add three bulleted items, pressing ↵ after each.

| 1 | | Broad Street Telecommunications |
|---|---|---|
| | | • The First Year and the Future Ahead |
| 2 | | What Do We Do Today? |
| | | • Selling Equipment |
| | | • Leasing Equipment |
| | | • Servicing Equipment |
| | | • |

 **7.** Press Tab or click on the Demote icon. Freelance Graphics demotes the new line to Level 3.

**8.** Add two new bulleted items, pressing ↵ after each.

| 1 | | Broad Street Telecommunications |
|---|---|---|
| | | • The First Year and the Future Ahead |
| 2 | | What Do We Do Today? |
| | | • Selling Equipment |
| | | • Leasing Equipment |
| | | • Servicing Equipment |
| | | ▪ We service what we sell. |
| | | ▪ We service other brands, too. |
| 3 | | |

 **9.** Press Shift+Tab or click on the Promote icon two times. Freelance Graphics starts a new page.

```
1 ▱   Broad Street Telecommunications
          • The First Year and the Future Ahead
2 ▱   What Do We Do Today?
          • Selling Equipment
          • Leasing Equipment
          • Servicing Equipment
              • We service what we sell
              • We service other brands, too.
3 ▱
```

**10.** Continue filling in the presentation, page by page. Save the presentation at any time. Figure 15.12 shows the first part of a presentation in Outliner view.

**FIGURE 15.12**

The first part of a presentation in Outliner view

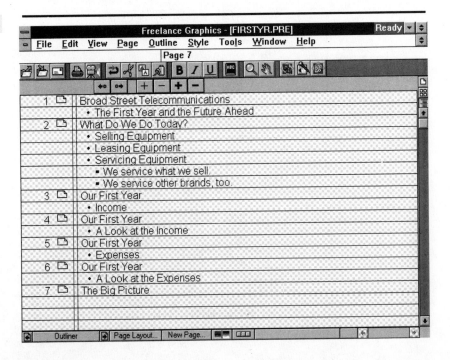

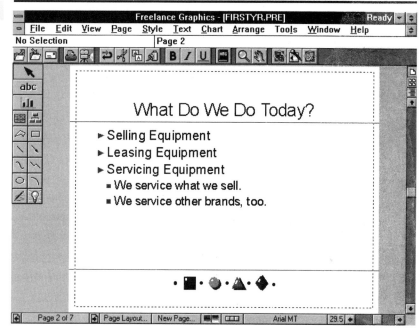 You can click on the Full Page button to view the current page of the presentation. Once in Full Page view, you can either edit or view other pages. Figure 15.13 shows the second page of the outlined pages in Full Page view.

**FIGURE 15.13**

The second page
of the sample
presentation in
Full Page view

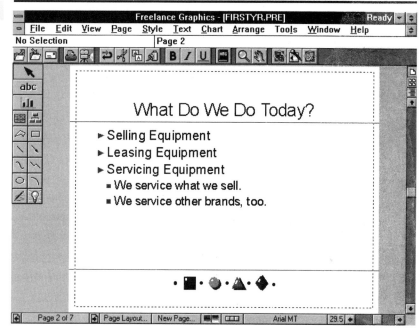 You can click on the Page Sorter button to view all the pages of the presentation, and to rearrange the pages in a presentation by dragging a page to a new location between two current pages. Figure 15.14 shows the sample presentation in Page Sorter view.

## Creating a Presentation in Full Page View

You can create or edit a presentation in Full Page view. To add more pages to the sample presentation, follow these steps:

1. Click on the Full Page button or choose View ➤ Full Page to switch to Full Page view.

**FIGURE 15.14**

All the pages of the
sample presentation in
Page Sorter view

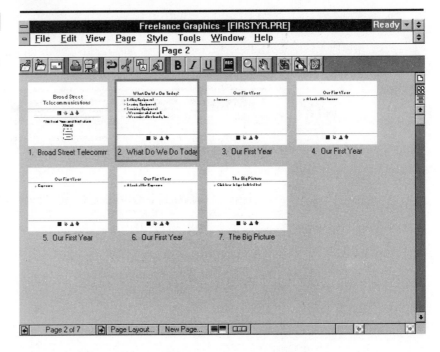

2. Click on the New Page button on the status bar, choose Page ➤ New, or
press F7. Freelance Graphics displays the New Page dialog box with the
new page number already filled in.

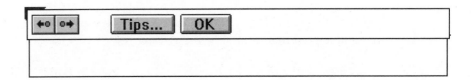

New Page...

3. Select a page layout from the Choose a Page Layout box and either click
on OK or press ↵. Freelance Graphics displays a new page on the desktop (Figure 15.15).

4. Click on Click Here to Type Page Title. Freelance Graphics opens a
box in which you can type. (To close the box without typing a title,
press Esc.)

5. Type the page title, **Our Future**, and click on OK. Freelance Graphics closes the dialog box and puts the new text in the former location of Click Here to Type Page Title. Click anywhere on the window to remove the handles from the title.

6. Click on Click Here to Type Bulleted Text. Freelance Graphics displays a box in which you can type.

7. Type **Retail Stores** and press ↵. Freelance Graphics adds a new bullet in the box.

8. Press Tab or click on the Demote button. Freelance Graphics demotes the bullet to Level 3 from Level 2.

9. Type **Selling our goods**, press ↵, type **Selling our services**, and click on OK. Freelance Graphics closes the box and displays the new bulleted items.

10. Repeat the preceding steps to add new pages. Be sure to save the presentation from time to time.

**FIGURE 15.15**

A new page in Full Page view

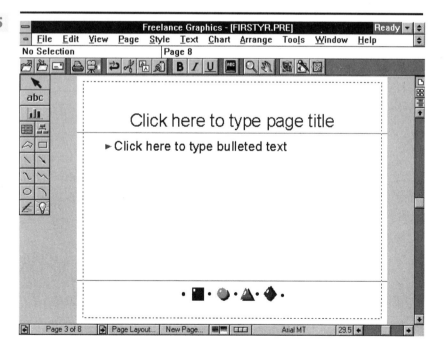

# Changing a Presentation

You can change to a new SmartMaster Set or page layout at any time without affecting your presentation.

## Changing to a New SmartMaster Set

To change to a new SmartMaster set, follow these steps:

**1.** Choose <u>S</u>tyle ➤ Choose <u>S</u>martMaster Set. Freelance Graphics displays the Choose SmartMaster Set dialog box (Figure 15.16).

**FIGURE 15.16**

From the Choose SmartMaster Set dialog box, you can select a new SmartMaster set.

**2.** Select a SmartMaster set from the scroll box.

**3.** Either click on OK or press ↵. Freelance Graphics changes the look and format of each page to that of the new set (Figure 15.17).

**FIGURE 15.17**

The sample
presentation with
a new look

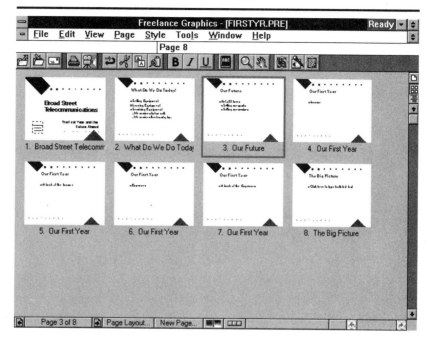

## Changing the Page Layout

You can change the layout of a page. To change the page layout for the current page in Full Page view or for a selected page in Page Sorter view, follow these steps:

| Page Layout... |

1. Either click on the Page Layout button on the status bar or choose Page ▸ Choose Page Layout. Freelance Graphics displays the Choose Page Layout dialog box.

2. Click on a new page layout and either click on OK or press ↵. Freelance Graphics applies the new page layout to the selected page (Figure 15.18).

# Adding a Table to a Presentation

You can add a table to a presentation by creating it in Freelance Graphics or by importing it (that is, copying and pasting, embedding, or linking) from its source application.

**FIGURE 15.18**

A new page layout,
ready for a table to be
inserted

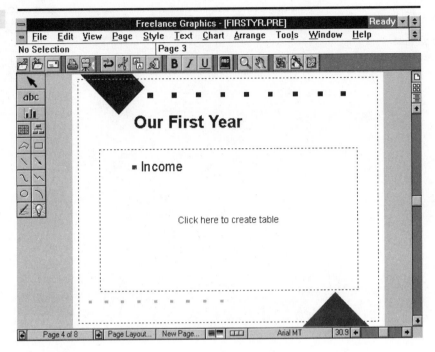

## Creating a Table

To create a table in Freelance Graphics, follow these steps:

1. Either insert a new page with the Table page layout, or change an existing page to the Table page layout.

2. If you are working on a new page, click on Click Here to Type Page Title and type a page title.

3. Click on Click Here to Create Table, or click on the Table tool. Freelance Graphics opens the Table Gallery dialog box (Figure 15.19).

4. Click on one of the Choose a Table Style buttons.

5. Choose a drop shadow from the Drop Shadow drop-down list box.

6. Choose the number of rows and columns from the Rows and Columns text/list boxes.

**FIGURE 15.19**

The Table Gallery dialog box enables you to create a table and format it.

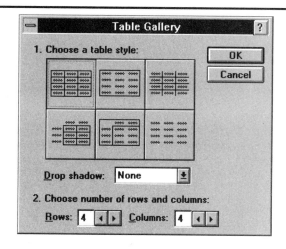

7. Either click on OK or press ↵. Freelance Graphics closes the dialog box and inserts a table on the page (Figure 15.20).

8. Click on the table and insert text or numbers. You can move from cell to cell by clicking or pressing Tab, Shift+Tab, ↓, ↑, ←, or →.

**FIGURE 15.20**

A page with an inserted table

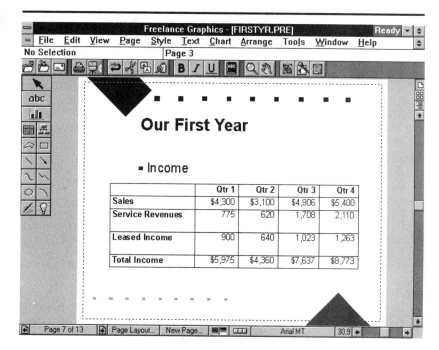

You can edit a table just as you would a spreadsheet:

- Click on a table once to select it.
- Click on a table twice to select it for editing.
- Double-click on a table (or choose Style ➤ Attributes (Table)) to open the Table Attributes dialog box. Then click on the Text Attributes option button to change the font, point size, text color, text enhancement, or text justification. Click on Cell Background & Borders and Table Background & Borders to choose background color and pattern and border color, width, and style.
- Drag a column border to the left to reduce the width, and drag a border to the right to increase the width.
- Drag corner handles to change table dimensions.
- Move a table by selecting it and dragging its border.

## Importing a Table

You can copy a table or other data into the Windows Clipboard by choosing either Edit ➤ Copy (or pressing Ctrl+C) or Edit ➤ Cut (or pressing Ctrl+X) and then choosing either Edit ➤ Paste (or pressing Ctrl+V) or Edit ➤ Paste Special to paste the table or data into the current Freelance Graphics page. You can also embed and link using DDE or OLE.

To import a table (for example, a range of 1-2-3 data) into a Freelance Graphics page using the Paste Special command, follow these steps:

1. Select a page in Full Page view.
2. Press F6. Freelance Graphics opens the Import Data dialog box (Figure 15.21).
3. Select the name of the file in which the data that you wish to copy is located. You may have to change to a different directory or drive to find the file. The data is imported into the Import Data dialog box (Figure 15.22).

**FIGURE 15.21**

In the Import Data dialog box, you can select a file from which data is imported.

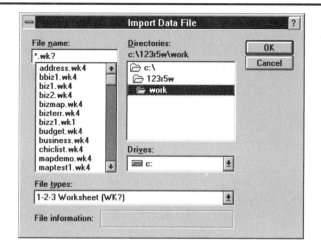

**FIGURE 15.22**

Data imported into the Import Data dialog box

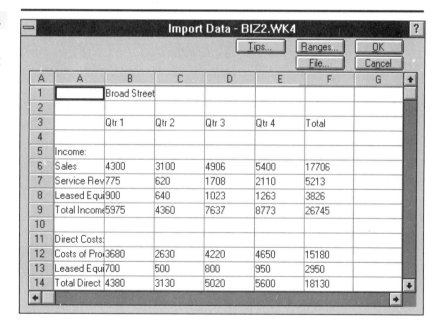

4. Select a range of data and click on OK. A message appears:

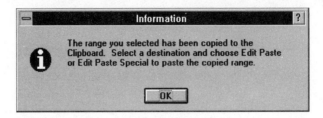

5. Click on OK.

6. Choose Edit ➤ Paste Special. Freelance Graphics opens the Paste Special dialog box (Figure 15.23). Using Paste Special allows you to select the best available format (in this case, Table (Unformatted)) for the imported data.

**FIGURE 15.23**

In the Paste Special dialog box, you can select a format for the data to be pasted.

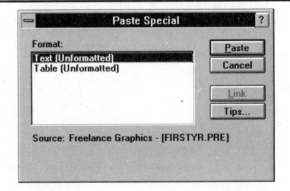

7. Click on the Paste button. Freelance Graphics pastes the selected data onto the page (Figure 15.24).

8. If needed, drag the table to the appropriate location, and edit and/or format its data (Figure 15.25).

**FIGURE 15.24**

Imported data before
formatting and moving

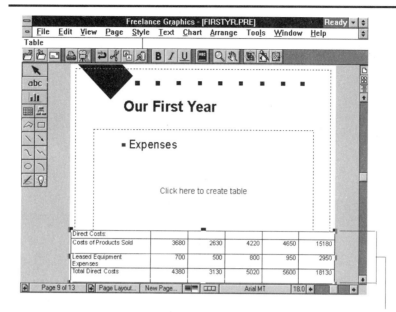

Imported
data

**FIGURE 15.25**

The final result

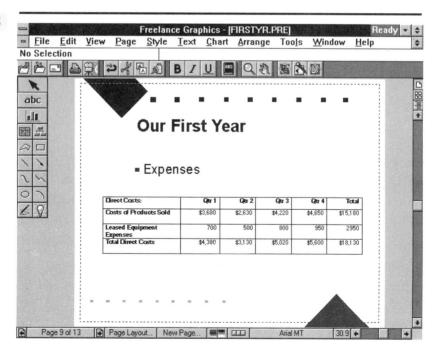

543

**WORKING TOGETHER** ▲

## Using Lotus Annotator

You can write notes for your 1-2-3 spreadsheets, Ami Pro documents, or Freelance Graphics presentations by using Lotus Annotator. To start Lotus Annotator, do one of the following:

- in 1-2-3, choose Edit ➤ Insert Object.
- in Ami Pro, choose Edit ➤ Insert ➤ New Object.
- in Freelance Graphics, choose Edit ➤ Insert Object or click on the Lotus Annotator SmartIcon.

Then, follow these steps:

1. In the Insert Object dialog box (unless you have clicked on the Lotus Annotator SmartIcon in Freelance Graphics), select Lotus Annotator Note and click on OK. The Lotus Annotator Note window appears.

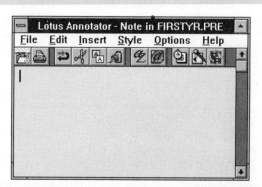

2. Type the note and either click on the Close SmartIcon or choose File ➤ Update and Exit or press F4. The Lotus Annotator Note window closes and you return to the application from which it was opened.

3. Save your file to save the note.

For more information about Lotus Annotator, open it and click on Help in the menu bar.

# Adding a Chart to a Presentation

In the same way that you can create or import a table, you can create a chart in Freelance Graphics or import it from its source application. Importing a chart allows you to maintain its original format.

## Creating a Chart

To create a chart in Freelance Graphics, follow these steps:

1. Either insert a new page with one of the Chart page layouts, or change an existing page to a Chart page layout.

2. If you are working on a new page, click on Click Here to Type Page Title and type a page title.

3. Click on Click Here to Create Chart or click on the Chart tool in the Toolbox. Freelance Graphics opens the New Chart Gallery dialog box (Figure 15.26).

4. Click on a chart type.

5. Choose a style for the selected chart type.

**FIGURE 15.26**

The New Chart Gallery dialog box, from which you select a chart type and style

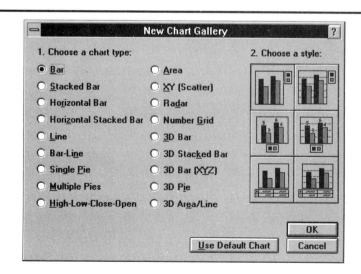

**6.** Either click on OK or press ↵. Freelance Graphics closes the dialog box and opens the Chart Data & Titles dialog box (Figure 15.27).

**7.** Click on the table and insert text or numbers. You can move from cell to cell by clicking or pressing Tab, Shift+Tab, ↓, ↑, ←, or →. Figure 15.28 shows the completed dialog box.

**8.** Click on OK. Freelance Graphics inserts the chart on the current page (Figure 15.29).

 **TIP** As you fill in the Chart Data & Titles dialog box, you can view the chart by clicking and holding down the Pre_view button. When you release the mouse button, the chart disappears from the screen.

---

**FIGURE 15.27**

In the Chart Data & Titles dialog box, you can define labels and fill in data.

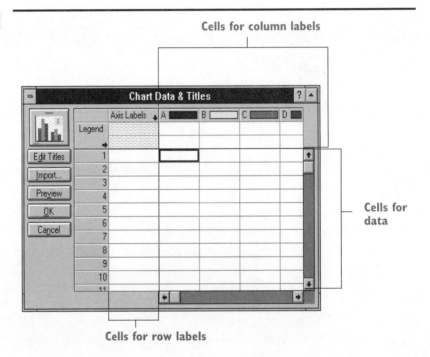

**FIGURE 15.28**

The completed Chart Data & Titles dialog box

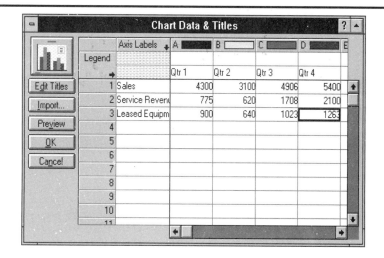

**FIGURE 15.29**

A sample chart on the current page

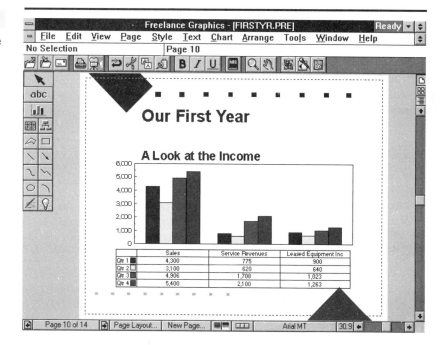

Freelance

## Importing a Chart

You can copy or import a chart using the same choice of Copy/Cut/Paste/Paste Special commands used to import a table. To import a chart from 1-2-3 into a Freelance Graphics page using the Copy and Paste Special commands, follow these steps:

1. Open 1-2-3 and click on a chart to select it.

2. Choose <u>E</u>dit ➤ <u>C</u>opy, press Ctrl+C, or click on the Copy SmartIcon to copy the chart into the Windows Clipboard.

3. Open Freelance Graphics, open a presentation, and select a page in Full Page view.

4. Choose <u>E</u>dit ➤ Paste Special. Freelance Graphics opens the Paste Special dialog box (Figure 15.30), from which you can select the best available format (in this case, 1-2-3 Graph (Formatted)) for the chart.

5. Click on <u>P</u>aste. Freelance Graphics pastes the chart into the presentation page (Figure 15.31).

6. If needed, drag the chart to the appropriate location.

 **If you import a chart (or any other object) as an OLE object, when you update the object in its source application, it is also automatically updated in Freelance Graphics.**

**FIGURE 15.30**

The Paste Special dialog box with 1-2-3 Graph (Formatted) selected

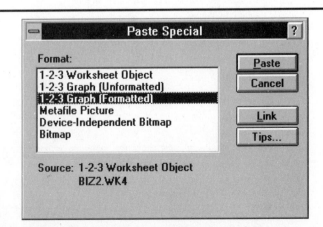

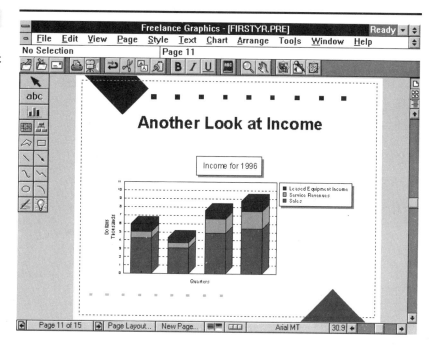

**FIGURE 15.31**

The presentation page
with an imported chart

# Creating an Organization Chart

You can create an organization chart page in a presentation. Creating an organization chart is very similar to creating an outline; organization charts have levels, and you use the same keys to promote or demote to different levels. To create an organization chart, follow these steps:

1. Either insert a new page with the Organization Chart page layout, or change an existing page to the Table page layout.

2. If you are working on a new page, click on Click Here to Type Page Title and type a page title.

3. Click on Click Here to Create Organization Chart, or click on the Organization Chart tool in the Toolbox. Freelance Graphics opens the Organization Chart Gallery dialog box (Figure 15.32).

4. Click on one of the six organization chart buttons.

**FIGURE 15.32**

The Organization Chart
Gallery dialog box

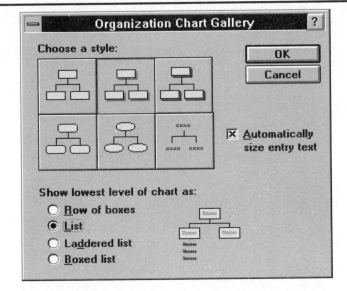

**5.** Click on an option button in the Show Lowest Level of Chart as option button.

**6.** Either click on OK or press ↵. Freelance Graphics displays the Organization Chart Entry List dialog box (Figure 15.33).

**7.** Type the first entry, the top person in the organization, that person's title, and comments, pressing ↵ after each line. (There is no need to fill in the title and comment lines.)

**8.** Fill in the next entry, a subordinate to the first entry.

**9.** Fill in the next entry. If the next entry is subordinate to the prior entry, press Tab. Freelance Graphics demotes that entry.

**10.** Continue filling in entries, pressing ↵ after the end of each line in a three-line entry. Before you type the first line in the new entry, press either Tab to demote or Shift+Tab to promote it.

**11.** To delete an entry, press Del.

**12.** When you have completed the dialog box, either click on OK or press ↵. Freelance Graphics adds the organization chart (Figure 15.34) to the presentation.

**FIGURE 15.33**

The Organization Chart
Entry List dialog box

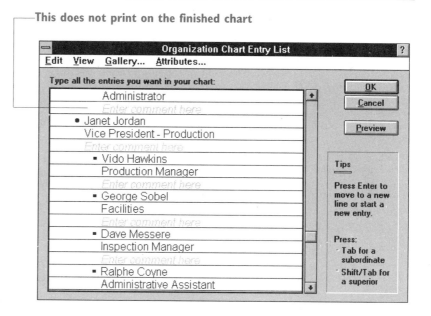

**FIGURE 15.34**

The completed organ-
ization chart added to
the presentation

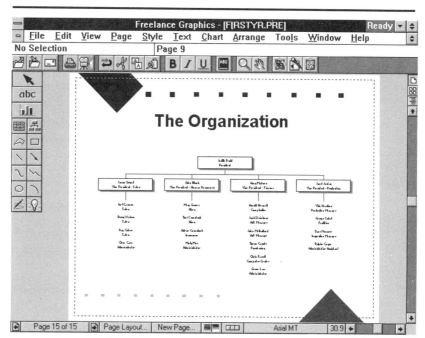

# Writing Speaker Notes

When you are giving your presentation, speaker notes serve as reminders of the topics covered on each page. To create speaker notes, follow these steps:

**1.** Select a page to make it active.

**2.** Choose Page ➤ Speaker Notes. Freelance Graphics displays the Speaker Note dialog box (Figure 15.35) for the selected page.

**FIGURE 15.35**

Type your speaker notes for a particular page into the Speaker Note dialog box.

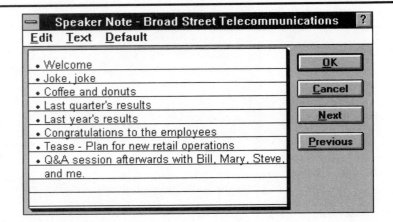

**3.** Click on OK. In Full Page view, Freelance Graphics adds an icon on the left side of the page. In Page Sorter view, the icon is in the lower-right corner of the page. Both icons indicate that there are speaker notes for this page.

# Selecting Print Options

Whether you decide to print from the Print Preview window, choose File ➤ Print, press Ctrl+P, or click on the Print SmartIcon, Freelance Graphics displays the Print File Dialog box. This section provides a brief description of each print option shown in the Print File dialog box (Figure 15.36). After selecting options in the dialog box, either click on OK or press ↵.

**NOTE** When you click on the Page Setup button, you open the Page Setup dialog box, in which you can add headers and footers, change the orientation, and adjust the margins.

**Number of Copies** Select or type the number of copies (1–999) that you wish to print. The default is 1.

**From Page *n* to *n*** Select or type a starting page number in the From Page text/scroll box; the default is 1. Select or type an ending page number in the To text/scroll box; the default is 999.

**FIGURE 15.36**

The Print dialog box allows you to select options to customize printing.

```
┌─────────────────────────────────────────────┐
│ ─            Print File              ?       │
├─────────────────────────────────────────────┤
│ HP LaserJet III on LPT1:        ┌──────────┐ │
│                                 │  Print   │ │
│ ┌─Print─────────────────────┐   ├──────────┤ │
│ │                           │   │  Cancel  │ │
│ │ Number of copies:  [1]    │   ├──────────┤ │
│ │ From page: [1] to: [999]  │   │Page Setup│ │
│ │ □ Selected pages only     │   ├──────────┤ │
│ │                           │   │ Setup... │ │
│ └───────────────────────────┘   └──────────┘ │
│ ┌─Format────────────────────────────────┐    │
│ │ ● Full page             □ 2      ▢     │    │
│ │ ○ Speaker notes                        │    │
│ │ ○ Audience notes        □ 4     ▦      │    │
│ │ ○ Handouts                             │    │
│ │ ○ Outline               □ 6     ▦      │    │
│ └────────────────────────────────────────┘   │
│  ☒ Adjust color library for color printing    │
│  □ Graduated fills as solid                   │
│  □ Print without SmartMaster background       │
└─────────────────────────────────────────────┘
```

**Current Page Only**    Check this check box to print only the current page. In Page Sorter view, this check box is Selected Pages only.

**NOTE**  To select multiple pages in Page Sorter view, press and hold down the Shift key, move the mouse pointer to the desired page, and click the left mouse button. As long as you hold down the Shift key, you can add more pages to the selection by clicking on them. To "deselect" a selection, simply click on an unselected page.

**Full Page**    Click on this option button if you wish to print each page at full size.

**Speaker Notes**    Click on this option button if you wish to print a small version of the page at the top of the paper and the speaker notes at the bottom of the page.

**Audience Notes**    Click on this option button if you wish to print a small version of the document at the top of the paper, leaving room for the audience to make notes at the bottom of the page.

**Handouts**    Click on this option button if you wish to print several presentation pages on one page. You can select 2, 4, or 6 pages per sheet of paper.

**Outline**    Click on this option button only in Outliner view to print only top levels of the outline. Collapsed text does not print.

**Adjust Color Library for Color Printing**    Check this check box to print in color using a different set of colors. If the colors in a presentation do not match the desktop colors, try checking this check box.

**Graduate Fills as Solid**    Click on this check box to print graduated colors in your presentation as solid colors. This may help if your printer does not handle color very well.

**Print without SmartMaster Background**    Click on this check box to print your presentation without the background color of the Smart-Master set. This is a way to print more quickly.

16

# Enhancing a Presentation

I n the last chapter, you learned Freelance Graphics basics. In this chapter, you'll learn how to enhance your presentation and perhaps even turn it into an automated slide show.

## Changing Presentation Formats

You can enhance a presentation by changing formats, much in the same way that you format Ami Pro documents or 1-2-3 spreadsheets. The Paragraph Styles dialog box (Figure 16.1) is the central dialog box for reformatting text boxes (which are considered paragraphs). To open this dialog box, either double-click on a selection, choose Text ➤ Paragraph Styles, or click the right mouse button in the desired text, then choose Paragraph Styles.

These are the options in the Paragraph Styles dialog box:

**All**   Click on this option button to indicate that you wish to change paragraph styles for all levels.

**1st**   Click on this option button to indicate that you wish to change paragraph styles for only Level 1 paragraphs.

**2nd**   Click on this option button to indicate that you wish to change paragraph styles for only Level 2 paragraphs.

**3rd**   Click on this option button to indicate that you wish to change paragraph styles for only Level 3 paragraphs.

## FIGURE 16.1

The Paragraph styles dialog box offers a large number of options for reformatting selected paragraphs.

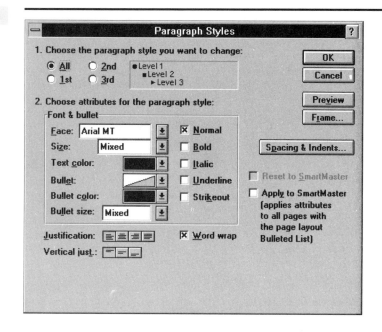

**Face**    Open this drop-down list box to change the font for the selection.

**Size**    Open this drop-down list box to change the point size for the selection.

**Text Color**    Open this drop-down list box to change the color for the selected text; click on a palette color or library color (Figure 16.2).

When you change SmartMaster sets, colors and other attributes change as well. To lock the original color for a symbol or other object, select the object, choose Style ➤ Attributes, click on a library color rather than a palette color, and click on OK.

**FIGURE 16.2**

The text and bullet
color palette

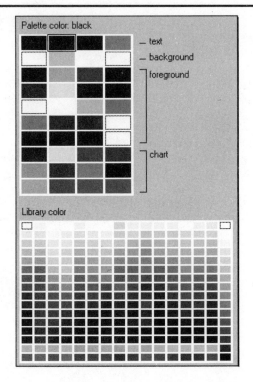

**FIGURE 16.3**

The choice of bullets
for Freelance Graphics
bulleted lists

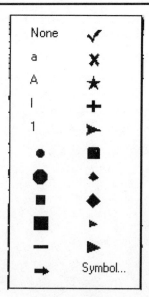

**Bullet**    Open this drop-down list box to change to a new bullet for bulleted items. Either select a displayed bullet (Figure 16.3) or click on Symbol to open the Choose Symbol for Bullet dialog box (Figure 16.4), from which you can select a symbol.

**Bullet Color**    Open this drop-down list box to change the color for bullets in the selected text; click on a palette color or library color.

**Bullet Size**    Open this drop-down list box to change the point size for bullets within the selection.

**Normal**    Check or clear this check box to apply the normal format to the selection. If you check Normal, Freelance Graphics clears all other check boxes in this group.

**Bold**    Check or clear this check box to apply boldface to or remove boldface from the selection. If you check this check box, all other check boxes in this group except Normal keep their current status.

**Italic**    Check or clear this check box to italicize or remove italics from the selection. If you check this check box, all other check boxes in this group except Normal keep their current status.

**Underline**    Check or clear this check box to underline or remove italics from the selection. If you check this check box, all other check boxes in this group except Normal keep their current status.

**Freelance**

**FIGURE 16.4**

The Choose Symbol for Bullet dialog box, from which you can select a symbol from a symbol category

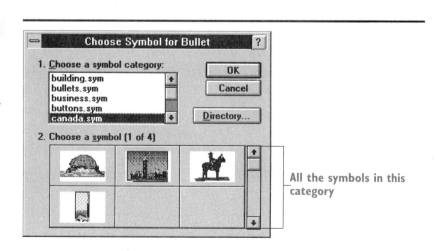

All the symbols in this category

**Strikeout**    Check or clear this check box to draw a line through the selection or remove a line drawn through the selection. If you check this check box, all other check boxes in this group except <u>N</u>ormal keep their current status.

**Justification**    Click on a button to align the selected text to the left or right margin.

**Vertical Just.**    Click on a button to vertically align the selected text.

**<u>W</u>ord Wrap**    Check or clear this check box to turn on or off word wrap.

**Pre<u>v</u>iew**    Point to this button and hold down the left mouse button to see the page as it will look with your changes.

**Frame**    Click on this button to display the Text Frame dialog box, with which you can define attributes for the invisible box that encloses the selected text.

**Spacing & Indents**    Click on this button to display the Spacing & Indents dialog box.

**Reset to <u>S</u>martMaster**    Check this check box to undo all the changes that you have made to the selection, thereby reverting to the selection's previous attributes. This check box is only available when you are editing presentation pages. (The Page Number button in the status bar will say *Layout*.)

**Appl<u>y</u> to SmartMaster**    Check this check box to apply all the attributes that you have set for this selection to all pages with the same page layout.

## Inserting a Symbol on a Page

Adding a symbol to a presentation page is easy. Table 16.1 lists the symbol categories available for Freelance Graphics.

**TABLE 16.1:** Freelance Graphics Symbol Categories

| SYMBOL CATEGORY | NUMBER OF SYMBOLS | DESCRIPTION |
|---|---|---|
| _shapes.sym | 24 | generic shapes (for example, star, cross, rectangle, arrows) |
| animals.sym | 7 | lion, rabbit, snake, turtle, owl, kangaroo, koala |
| arrows.sym | 20 | two- or three-dimensional arrows pointing in all directions |
| asia.sym | 1 | image that suggests Asia |
| asiamap.sym | 2 | map of Asia |
| backgrnd.sym | 19 | page-size backgrounds |
| benelux.sym | 3 | images that suggest Belgium, the Netherlands, or Luxembourg |
| building.sym | 7 | single buildings and skylines |
| bullets.sym | 12 | small images for use as bullets (for example, star, arrow, pointing finger, pencil, targets, light bulb) |
| business.sym | 34 | miscellaneous business images and currency symbols |
| buttons.sym | 9 | small images that you can use as bullets, including some clothing buttons |
| canada.sym | 4 | images that suggest Canada |
| canadmap.sym | 14 | maps of Canada and its provinces |
| cartoons.sym | 8 | cartoons that suggest office activities |
| commobjt.sym | 21 | common objects |
| communic.sym | 4 | envelope, satellite dish, mailbox, telephone |
| compperi.sym | 9 | computer peripherals: ports, laser printers, floppy disks, mouses, CD, computer paper |

**TABLE 16.1:**    Freelance Graphics Symbol Categories (continued)

| SYMBOL CATEGORY | NUMBER OF SYMBOLS | DESCRIPTION |
| --- | --- | --- |
| computer.sym | 15 | computer systems, fax, notebook computers |
| custom.sym | 1 | an area to which you add custom symbols |
| diagram.sym | 17 | organization charts and other symbols |
| entertai.sym | 3 | tickets, television set, theatrical masks |
| environm.sym | 5 | environment symbols: flowers, palm tree, recycling, large blue sky, large forest |
| europmap.sym | 35 | maps of European countries |
| finance.sym | 4 | pile of paper currency, safe, bag of money, piles of coins |
| flags.sym | 44 | flags of countries, the United Nations, one blank banner, and one blank flag |
| flowchrt.sym | 20 | flow chart symbols |
| food.sym | 12 | food, containers, and other food-related symbols |
| france.sym | 4 | images that suggest France |
| geoshape.sym | 12 | two- and three-dimensional geometric shapes |
| germany.sym | 2 | images that suggest Germany |
| grid.sym | 1 | large background symbol |
| hands.sym | 4 | hand holding paper, pointing hand, shaking hands, stopping hand |
| industry.sym | 8 | factories and other industrial symbols |
| italy.sym | 4 | images that suggest Italy |
| lamermap.sym | 9 | maps of Latin American countries |
| legends.sym | 10 | logo-like symbols and other common symbols |
| medical.sym | 2 | medical symbols |

**TABLE 16.1:** Freelance Graphics Symbol Categories (continued)

| SYMBOL CATEGORY | NUMBER OF SYMBOLS | DESCRIPTION |
| --- | --- | --- |
| men.sym | 15 | men in a working environment |
| offobjct.sym | 15 | office objects: envelopes, folders, binders, files, and so on |
| pacifmap.sym | 1 | a map of the Pacific Ocean and Pacific Rim countries |
| people.sym | 6 | groups of people |
| presentn.sym | 7 | easel, screen, slides, projector |
| puzzle.sym | 22 | a jigsaw puzzle and parts |
| science.sym | 3 | beaker, atomic symbol, test tube |
| spain.sym | 1 | bullfighter |
| sports.sym | 7 | sports balls |
| textbox.sym | 16 | boxes in which you insert text |
| time.sym | 3 | kitchen clock, three-minute timer, alarm clock |
| transpor.sym | 11 | modes of transportation |
| uk.sym | 4 | images that suggest the United Kingdom |
| usa.sym | 11 | images that suggest the United States |
| usamap.sym | 54 | maps of the United States and its states |
| weather.sym | 5 | moon, cloud, lightning, rain, sun |
| women.sym | 12 | women in a working environment |
| worldmap.sym | 3 | maps of the world |

If you insert a symbol on a page that includes an area reserved for a symbol (that is, the page displays *Click Here to Add Symbol*), the inserted symbol stays within the bounds of the symbol box. However, if you insert a symbol on another type of page, the symbol is in the same location and is the same size as it was when created. For example, if you create a 2 inch by 2 inch symbol in the

upper-left corner of the Paintbrush window, Freelance Graphics inserts the same 2 inch by 2 inch symbol in the upper-left corner of the presentation page.

To insert a symbol on the current presentation page, follow these steps:

**1.** With the desired presentation page in Full Page view, either click on the Symbol tool on the Toolbox, or click on Click Here to Add Symbol on Title or Bullets & Symbol pages. Freelance Graphics displays the Add Symbol to Page dialog box (Figure 16.5).

### FIGURE 16.5

The Add Symbol to Page dialog box

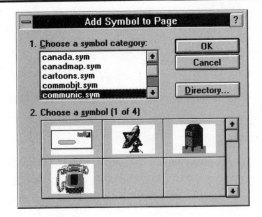

**2.** Select a symbol set from the Choose a Symbol Category scroll box. Freelance Graphics displays a set of symbols.

**3.** Double-click on the desired symbol to insert it on the presentation page (Figure 16.6).

**NOTE** The Add Symbol to Page dialog box provides custom.sym, a symbol category to which you can add your own custom symbols.

You can size and move symbols just as you would any picture. To move a symbol, drag it. To size a symbol, click on a handle and move that border or corner to the desired location. To maintain the proportions of a symbol that you

FIGURE 16.6

A symbol just inserted
on a presentation page

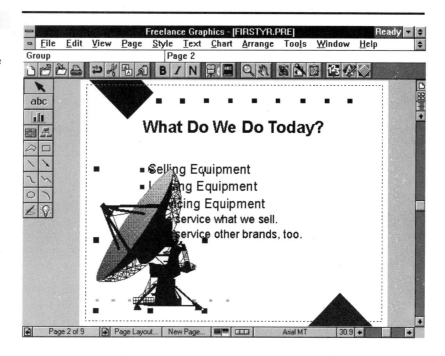

are sizing, move a corner handle. Figure 16.7 shows a sized and moved symbol
on a presentation page.

## Inserting Symbols as Bullets

You can enhance a presentation by substituting symbols for bullets in bulleted
lists. Because Freelance Graphics considers presentation text to be paragraphs,
you'll define your new bullet in the Paragraph Styles dialog box.

To use a symbol as a bullet on the current page, follow these steps:

**1.** Starting in Full Page view, double-click on the text, or select the text
and choose Text ➤ Paragraph Styles. Freelance Graphics opens the
Paragraph Styles dialog box.

**2.** Choose the paragraph style that you wish to change by clicking on All,
1st, 2nd, or 3rd.

**FIGURE 16.7**

A sized and moved symbol on a presentation page

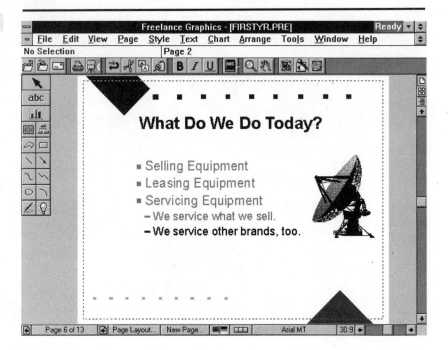

3. Click on the downward-pointing arrow on the right side of the Bullet drop-down list box. Freelance Graphics opens a box, from which you can choose a bullet or symbol to use.

4. Click on Symbol. Freelance Graphics displays the Choose Symbol for Bullet dialog box.

5. Click on a category in the Choose a Symbol Category scroll box.

6. Double-click on a symbol in the Choose a Symbol scroll box. Freelance Graphics displays the selected symbol in the Bullet drop-down list box.

7. Either click on OK or press ↵. Freelance Graphics closes the dialog box and inserts the bullet in front of the selection.

☆ **Retail Stores**

**Symbols with many lines and colors are difficult to recognize in miniature compared to one-color, two-dimensional symbols.**

## Creating and Saving Custom Symbols

You can draw your own symbols. Although Chapter 10 provides instructions on creating pictures using Ami Pro, Freelance Graphics has many of the same drawing tools. Follow these steps to create a symbol:

1. If your symbol is made up of several objects, select them by clicking on the first object, pressing Shift, and clicking on each additional object. Notice that three selected objects have many handles.

2. Choose Arrange ➤ Group. Freelance Graphics groups the objects into one object.

3. Choose Tools ➤ Add to Symbol Library. Freelance Graphics opens the Add to Symbol Library dialog box (Figure 16.8).

4. Type or select a symbol category listed in the File Name text/scroll box. To add the symbol to your own custom category, select custom.sym.

5. Click on OK. Freelance Graphics closes the dialog box, adds the symbol to the specified symbol category, and returns to the presentation.

Freelance

**FIGURE 16.8**

The Add to Symbol Library dialog box, in which you specify the file name for a custom symbol

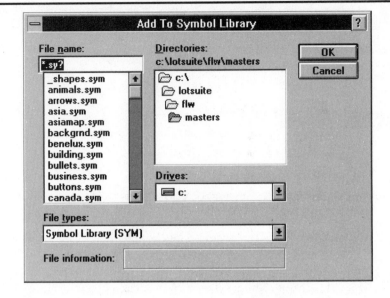

# Importing a Picture

In almost the same way that you import tables and charts into a presentation, you can import a picture. Simply follow these steps:

1. Open a presentation and, in Full Page view, display the page onto which you wish to import the picture.

2. Choose File ➤ Import. Freelance Graphics displays the Import File dialog box (Figure 16.9).

3. Double-click on the file that you wish to import. Freelance Graphics imports the picture into the current presentation page (Figure 16.10).

4. If you wish to move the imported picture into a different area of the window, drag it. (You can also size a picture by dragging its handles.) If you

**FIGURE 16.9**

The Import File
dialog box

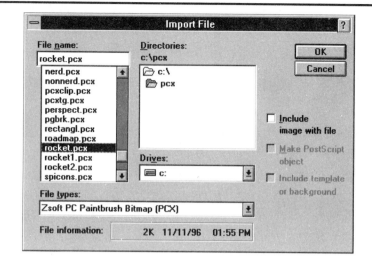

**FIGURE 16.10**

A newly imported
picture, which has not
yet been dragged to its
final location

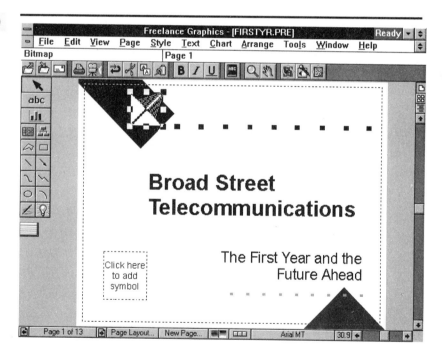

drag a picture to the Click Here to Add Symbol box, the picture takes the place of the box (Figure 16.11).

**FIGURE 16.11**

The picture in its final location on the presentation page

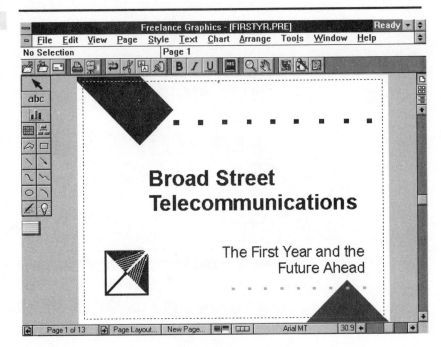

## Creating a Page Build

In a page with a bulleted list, you can add one bullet item at a time, which is called a *build*. This means that you can give a presentation that builds a page one bulleted item at a time, allowing you time to talk about each item as it appears on the page.

As you define each bulleted item, you actually create a page, called a *child page*. Each child page, which is identified within the presentation by the words *[Build n]* following the title, contains one undimmed bulleted item and one or more dimmed bulleted items. For every bulleted item, there should be one child page. The last page, with all bullets in place, is the *parent page*. Thus a build consists of one parent page and one or more child pages.

To create a build, follow these steps:

1. Select a page with a bulleted list containing two or more bulleted items.

2. Choose Page ➤ Create Build. Freelance Graphics creates the build, adds appropriate pages, and displays an information message (Figure 16.12).

3. Click on OK. Freelance Graphics closes the information message box. Figure 16.13 shows the changed presentation in Page Sorter view. Notice that Pages 2, 3, 4, and 5 are the child pages, and Page 6 is the parent.

 **NOTE** To delete a build, choose **Page ➤ Delete Build**. **Freelance Graphics deletes all the child pages. Even if you have moved the child pages out of the presentation, Freelance Graphics deletes the build.**

**FIGURE 16.12**

A message box that provides information about build pages

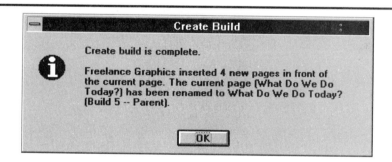

## Running a Screen Show from within Freelance Graphics

You can show your presentation on your computer monitor manually or automatically. If you run a screen show manually, you control when the next page appears; you don't have to worry about synchronizing your comments and the screen show. If you run the show automatically, you can set the speed at which pages change. You can also set the screen show to run continuously, which works very well at conferences and expositions.

**FIGURE 16.13**

A presentation with five build pages—one parent and four children, as well as some of the original presentation pages

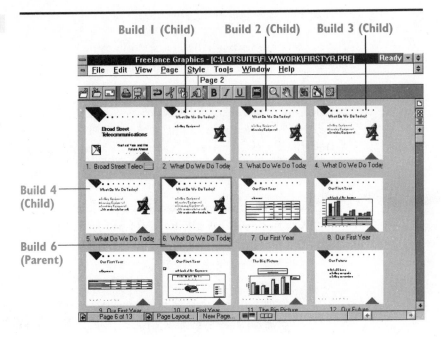

During a screen show, you can branch to a specific presentation page, start an application, draw on the screen using the mouse pointer, temporarily stop the show, or use video and sound.

 To start a screen show of the current presentation, click on the Screen Show SmartIcon, press Alt+F10, or choose <u>V</u>iew ➤ Screen Show ➤ <u>R</u>un. Freelance Graphics starts the screen show using the default screen show settings or the effects that you have specified. You can also create a screen show to run from the DOS prompt. For instructions, see the following section, "Creating a Stand-Alone Screen Show to Run under DOS."

To control the screen show, you can click a mouse button or press a key:

| TO TAKE THIS ACTION: | PRESS: | CLICK: |
|---|---|---|
| Display the next page | ↵ or PgDn | the left mouse button |
| Display the previous page | PgUp | the right mouse button |

| TO TAKE THIS ACTION: | PRESS: | CLICK: |
|---|---|---|
| Pause the screen show | Spacebar | N/A |
| Resume a paused screen show | Spacebar | N/A |
| Display the List Pages dialog box (Figure 16.14) to jump to another page in the screen show | Esc | N/A |
| Display the List Pages dialog box to stop the screen show | Esc | N/A |

**NOTE** To optimize a screen show for display on your desktop, choose File ➤ Printer Se*t*up. In the Printer Setup dialog box, click on the Optimize for Screen Show option button. This adjusts the dimensions of the pages in the show to your desktop dimensions.

**FIGURE 16.14**

The List Pages dialog box

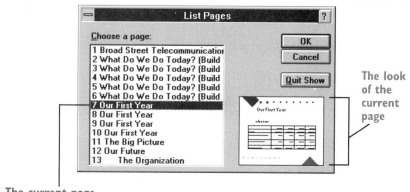

# Creating a Stand-Alone Screen Show to Run under DOS

You can create a DOS version of your screen show. This means that you can copy the show, including an executable file that runs the show, onto a disk and bring it with you on the road.

To create a standalone screen show, choose <u>V</u>iew ➤ <u>S</u>creen Show ➤ <u>P</u>repare Standalone. Freelance Graphics opens the Export Screen Show dialog box (Figure 16.15) in which you name the screen show and click on OK. Freelance Graphics exports each page to its own file, with a *.GX2 extension. As it exports each page, it displays a status box, telling you the page that is being exported and its file name.

**FIGURE 16.15**

The Export Screen Show dialog box

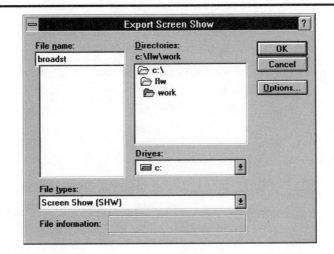

These are the files in a stand-alone screen show:

| | |
|---|---|
| *Show*.SHW | The screen show file (for example, BROADST.SHW) |
| *Page*.GX2 | One *.GX2 file per page of your presentation. If your screen show name is BROADST.SHW, Freelance Graphics takes the first six characters and appends the page number to each file (for example, BROADS1, BROADS2, and so on). |
| SHOW.EXE | The executable file with which you run the show |

To run a screen show from the DOS prompt, type **SHOW** *fname* (where *fname* is the name of the *.SHW file).

Freelance

To pause a stand-alone show, press Esc. Freelance Graphics displays the Screen Show Status screen (Figure 16.16), which indicates whether or not pages have been shown. If the show contains more pages than can be shown at once, press PgDn, PgUp, Home, End, ←, →, ↓, or ↑ to move around the list. If you press Esc again, Freelance Graphics displays another Show screen (Figure 16.17), from which you can press ↵ to start the show from a selected page, Spacebar to resume the show, or Esc to end it.

**FIGURE 16.16**

The Screen Show Status screen indicates whether or not pages have been shown.

```
Screen Show Status
 #    File                          Status
 1    BROADS1.GX2                    Ok.
 2    BROADS2.GX2                    Ok.
 3    BROADS3.GX2                    Ok.
 4    BROADS4.GX2                    Ok.
 5    BROADS5.GX2                    Ok.
 6    BROADS6.GX2                    Ok.
 7    BROADS7.GX2                    Ok.
 8    BROADS8.GX2                    Ok. Show ended here.
 9    BROADS9.GX2                    Picture not shown.
10    BROADS10.GX2                   Picture not shown.
11    BROADS11.GX2                   Picture not shown.
12    BROADS12.GX2                   Picture not shown.
13    BROADS13.GX2                   Picture not shown.



       Press PGUP, PGDN, HOME, END to see the rest of status, ESC to quit.
```

**FIGURE 16.17**

Another Show screen, from which you can start, resume, or end the screen show

```
══════════════ Freelance Graphics Show    BROADST.SHW ══════════════
Press ENTER to start show, SPACE to pause/resume show, ESC to end show

        1:BROADS1
        2:BROADS2
        3:BROADS3
        4:BROADS4
        5:BROADS5
        6:BROADS6
        7:BROADS7
        8:BROADS8
        9:BROADS9
       10:BROADS10
       11:BROADS11
       12:BROADS12
       13:BROADS13




═══ Use cursor keys, PGDN, PGUP, HOME, END to highlight starting file ═══
```

**575**

## Using Lotus Sound

You can record and/or play waveform (.WAV) sound files using Lotus Sound (if you have a sound board installed and in operating order). Just click on the Lotus Sound icon in the Lotus Applications program group and the Lotus Sound window appears:

These are the elements of the Lotus Sound window:

**Slider**     A horizontal slot that indicates the current position in the sound file. You can drag the small knob to move to a new location in the file. When you record, the Memory Gauge replaces the Slider. The Memory Gauge indicates the amount of memory that you have used to record the current sound.

**Play/Pause**     A button on which you click to play a sound or stop playing a sound. When you record, the Stop button replaces the Play/Pause button. You can press Spacebar to play or pause.

**Rew**     A button on which you click to rewind the sound file. Press the Ctrl key to replace Rew with Step, which rewinds the sound file one-tenth of a second at a time. Press the Shift key to replace Rew with Home, which rewinds the sound file to its beginning. You can press ← to move toward the beginning of the current sound file.

**WORKING TOGETHER**

**FF**     A button on which you click to quickly move toward the end of the sound file. Press the Ctrl key to replace FF with Step, which moves the sound file one-tenth of a second at a time. Press the Shift key to replace FF with End, which moves the sound file to its end. You can press → to move toward the end of the current sound file.

**Close**     A button on which you click to close Lotus Sound. You can press Alt+F4 to close Lotus Sound.

**Record**     A button on which you click to record or stop recording. You can press **R** to record or stop recording.

**Current**     A gauge that indicates the current position in the sound file.

**Total**     A gauge that indicates the total length of the sound file. When you record, the word *Max* replaces *Total*. The Max gauge indicates the maximum recording time.

**Erase**     A button on which you click to erase the current sound from your computer memory. You can press **E** or **X** to erase the current sound.

**Lev**     A gauge that indicates the sound level. When recording, adjust the volume until some of the green bars brighten and no red bars are bright.

**Vol**     A vertical slot along which you drag a lever to adjust the volume. You can press ↑ or ↓ to adjust the volume.

To record a sound file, choose File ➤ New and click on the Record button. To stop recording, click on Record again.

To play an existing sound file, choose File ➤ Open, double-click on a file name, and click on the Play button.

For more information about Lotus Sound, open it and click on Help in the menu bar.

# Editing a Screen Show

When you wish to define and change screen show attributes, use the Edit Screen Show dialog box (Figure 16.18). To open this dialog box, choose View ➤ Screen Show ➤ Edit Effects.

These are the Edit Screen Show dialog box options:

**Choose a Page**     Click on the Previous Page button, the Next Page button, or click on the Page Number button to reveal the Choose Screen Show Page dialog box (Figure 16.19) from which you can choose a page to edit.

**Start Automatically**     Check this check box to have the screen show start automatically when you open the presentation file or when you start Freelance Graphics from within a presentation file embedded in an OLE client. The show ends after all screens have been displayed; Freelance Graphics ends if you are currently using it only to run the screen show.

**FIGURE 16.18**

The Edit Screen Show dialog box

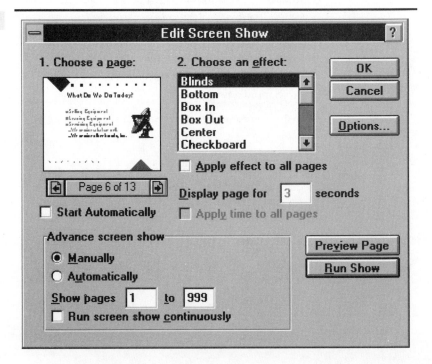

**FIGURE 16.19**

The Choose Screen
Show Page dialog box

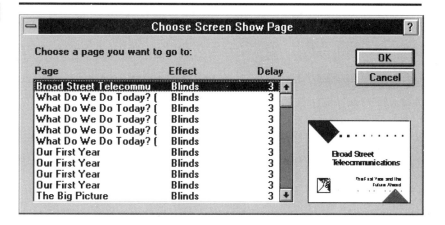

To stop a show from automatically running every time you
open it, press Esc once the show starts, and click on Quit
Show. Open the Edit Screen Show dialog box, and clear the
Start Automatically check box.

**Choose an Effect**    Click on an effect with which this page should appear on the desktop. Table 16.2 lists and describes each effect.

**Manually**    Click on this option button to give yourself control over the display of screen show pages.

**Automatically**    Click on this option button to give Freelance Graphics control over the display of screen show pages.

**Show Pages/To**    Fill in these text boxes with the range of pages to be displayed in the screen show.

**Run Screen Show Continuously**    Check this check box to run the screen show continuously until you press Esc.

**Apply Effect to All Pages**    Check this check box to apply the effect that you chose in the Choose an Effect scroll box to all the pages in the screen show.

TABLE 16.2: Freelance Graphics Page Display Effects

| EFFECT | DESCRIPTION | COMPARABLE EFFECT RUNNING UNDER DOS |
|---|---|---|
| Blinds | Displays the page with the look of opening horizontal blinds | Scroll, Up |
| Bottom | Displays the page from the bottom to the top, like raising a window shade | Wipe, Up |
| Box In | Gradually reduces the size of the black box hiding the page until it disappears into the center of the desktop | Box, In |
| Box Out | Gradually increases the size of the page from the center of the desktop until it encompasses the entire desktop | Box, Out |
| Center | Gradually displays the page spiraling from the center of the desktop block by block | Spiral, Clockwise |
| Checkboard | Displays a checkerboard made from alternate blocks of black and the page; removes the black blocks from the desktop | Fade, None |
| Curtains | Closes red curtains over a black desktop; opens the red curtains revealing the page | V-Split, In |
| Diagonal Left | From the upper-left corner, reveals the page to the lower-right corner | Weave, None |

**TABLE 16.2:** Freelance Graphics Page Display Effects (continued)

| EFFECT | DESCRIPTION | COMPARABLE EFFECT RUNNING UNDER DOS |
|---|---|---|
| Diagonal Right | From the upper-right corner, reveals the page to the lower-left corner | Weave, None |
| Draw | Displays the page without any special effects | Replace, None |
| Fade | Starting with a black desktop, reveals the page pixel by pixel | Fade, None |
| Hsplit In | Displays the page horizontally starting at the top and bottom of the desktop, until both halves meet in the center | H-Split, In |
| Hsplit Out | Displays the page horizontally starting at the center and moving toward the top and the bottom of the desktop | H-Split, Out |
| Leftside | Reveals the page vertically starting at the left side of the desktop | Wipe, Right |
| Louvers | Reveals the page as though you were opening vertical blinds | Scroll, Right |
| Paint Brush | Reveals the presentation page using an animated paintbrush, brushing from the bottom to the top in succeeding bands across the desktop from left to right | Replace, None |

Freelance

**TABLE 16.2:** Freelance Graphics Page Display Effects (continued)

| EFFECT | DESCRIPTION | COMPARABLE EFFECT RUNNING UNDER DOS |
|---|---|---|
| Pan Left | Slides the presentation page onto the desktop from the left side of the desktop | Scroll, Right |
| Pan Right | Slides the presentation page onto the desktop from the right side of the desktop | Scroll, Left |
| Rain | "Rains" vertical bands of the presentation page onto the desktop until the entire page is displayed | Replace, None |
| Replace | Displays the page quickly from the top to bottom of the desktop | Replace, None |
| Rightside | Reveals the page vertically starting at the right side of the desktop | Wipe, Left |
| Scroll Top | Slides the page onto the desktop from the top of the desktop | Scroll, Up |
| Scroll Bottom | Slides the page onto the desktop from the bottom of the desktop | Scroll, Down |
| Shade | Lowers a curtain over a black desktop; then raises the curtain, revealing the page | Scroll, Down |
| Text Top | Builds the page by moving the text onto it from the top of the desktop | Wipe, Down |
| Text Bottom | Builds the page by moving the text onto it from the bottom of the desktop | Wipe, Up |

**TABLE 16.2:**   Freelance Graphics Page Display Effects (continued)

| EFFECT | DESCRIPTION | COMPARABLE EFFECT RUNNING UNDER DOS |
| --- | --- | --- |
| Text Left | Builds the page by moving the text onto it from the left side of the desktop | Wipe, Right |
| Text Right | Builds the page by moving the text onto it from the right side of the desktop | Wipe, Left |
| Top | Displays the page from the top to the bottom of the desktop | Wipe, Down |
| Use Bitmap Colors | Enhances the colors of an imported bitmap on the selected page | N/A |
| Vsplit In | Displays the page vertically starting at the left and right sides of the desktop until both halves meet in the center | V-Split, In |
| Vsplit Out | Displays the page vertically starting at the center and moving toward the left and the right of the desktop | V-Split, Out |
| Zigzag | Reveals the page, block by block starting at the top and ending at the bottom of the desktop | Weave, None |

**Display Page for *n* Seconds**   Fill in this text box with the time (from 1 to 60 seconds) that you want this page displayed before moving to the next. This text box is available only if you clicked on the Automatically option button.

**Apply Time to All Pages**    Check this check box to apply the time that you typed in the Display Page for *n* Seconds text box to all the pages in the show.

**Options**    Click on this button to display the Screen Show Options dialog box, with which you can customize options for your show.

**Preview Page**    Click on this button to display the current page as you have edited it.

**Run Show**    Click on this button to run the screen show. When the show is over, you return to the Freelance Graphics screen from which you started. If you have selected Run Screen Show Continuously, press Esc to end the show and display the List Pages dialog box, from which you can quit the show.

## Controlling a Running Screen Show

You can control the order of pages displayed during a screen show by using the Screen Show control panel or by adding Screen Show buttons. In either case, you control the page sequence manually, but using Screen Show buttons, you can also start applications, or even incorporate multimedia effects.

### Controlling a Screen Show Using the Screen Show Control Panel

The Screen Show control panel, which is displayed on your desktop as a screen show runs, consists of four buttons with which you can go to a specific page or stop the screen show. To display the control panel, follow these steps:

1. Choose View ➤ Screen Show ➤ Edit Effects. Freelance Graphics opens the Edit Screen Show dialog box.

2. Click on the Manually option button. This gives you manual control over the display of pages.

3. Click on the Options button. Freelance Graphics displays the Screen Show Options dialog box (Figure 16.20).

4. Click OK twice. Freelance Graphics closes both dialog boxes.

**FIGURE 16.20**

The Screen Show
Options dialog box

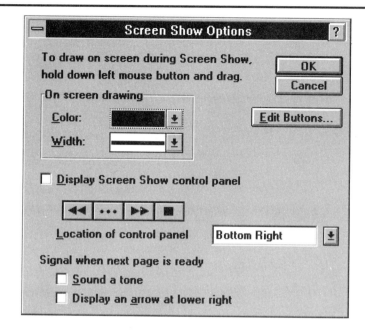

When you start the screen show, the Screen Show control panel appears in the location that you specified. Table 16.3 lists and describes the control panel buttons.

**TABLE 16.3:** Freelance Graphics Screen Show Control Panel Buttons

| BUTTON | PURPOSE |
| --- | --- |
| ◄◄ | Goes to the page before the current page |
| ••• | Displays a list of pages from which you can choose, or quit the show |
| ►► | Goes to the page after the current page |
| ■ | Quits the screen show |

## Controlling a Screen Show Using Screen Show Buttons

Defining Screen Show buttons for presentation pages allows you to control your presentation without your audience being aware if it (as with the Screen Show control panel). You can select any object on a page to serve as a Screen Show button.

To define a Screen Show button, follow these steps:

1. Select the object to be defined as a Screen Show button on the current page, which must be shown in Full Page view.

2. Choose <u>V</u>iew ➤ <u>S</u>creen Show ➤ <u>C</u>reate/Edit Button. Freelance Graphics opens the Create/Edit Screen Show Button dialog box (Figure 16.21).

**FIGURE 16.21**

In the Create/Edit Screen Show Button dialog box, you can define a button that will perform actions.

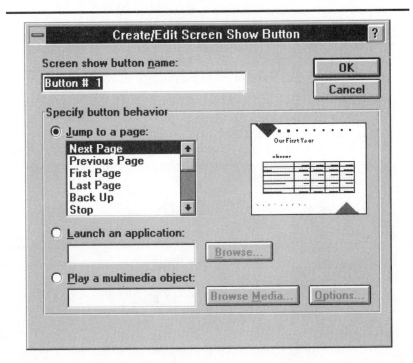

3. To define a button name, type a name in the Screen Show Button Name text box.

4. To jump to a particular page or perform an action, click on the Jump to a Page option button and select from the list.

5. To launch an application, click on the Launch an Application option button and either type the name of an executable (*.EXE), executable command (*.COM), or batch (*.BAT) file, or click on the Browse button to display the Find Application to Launch dialog box, from which you can select a file.

6. To play a multimedia object, click on the Play a Multimedia Object option button and either type the name of a wave (*.WAV), MIDI (*.MID), or movie (*.LSM, *.MMM, or *.AVI) file.

7. To select a position for a multimedia movie, click on Options. In the Multimedia Button Options dialog box, select a desktop location.

8. When you have completed the Create/Edit Screen Show Button dialog box, click on OK.

When you run the screen show, click on the object for which you defined a Screen Show button and Freelance Graphics will perform the built-in action.

# Creating Your Own SmartMaster Set

The easiest way to create your own SmartMaster set is to modify an existing set and save it with a unique name. To start, open a set; if you open the CUSTOM.MAS set, you'll be able to work with blank pages that have Click Here blocks built in. To create your own SmartMaster set, follow these steps:

1. Click on the Open File SmartIcon or choose File ➤ Open. Freelance Graphics opens the Open File dialog box (Figure 16.22).

2. Select SmartMaster Set (MAS) from the File Types drop-down list box, and go to the \flw\masters subdirectory.

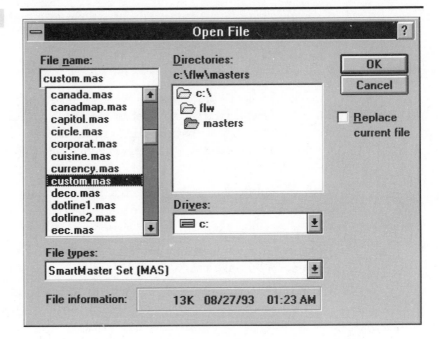

3. Click on CUSTOM.MAS, and click on OK. Freelance Graphics displays the new SmartMaster set in Page Sorter view. The diagonal lines in the Page Sorter view window (Figure 16.23) indicate that you are about to edit page layouts.

4. Either click on the Full Page icon, double-click on the first page that you wish to edit, or choose View ➤ Full Page. Freelance Graphics displays the page in Full Page view.

5. Change the page using the commands listed and described in Table 16.4.

6. Click on OK to close the dialog box and return to the Full Page view window.

7. Either click on the Page Sorter icon or choose View ➤ Page Sorter. Freelance Graphics displays the presentation pages in Page Sorter view.

8. Choose File ➤ Save As to save the new SmartMaster set.

To stop creating the custom set, click on the Return button. Then choose File ➤ Close.

**FIGURE 16.23**

The Page Sorter view window shows pages ready to edit.

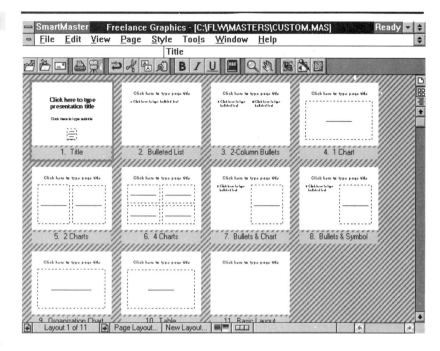

**TABLE 16.4:** Freelance Graphics SmartMaster Editing Menu Commands

| MENU COMMAND | PURPOSE |
| --- | --- |
| File ➤ Import | Imports an object, such as a bitmap, to be inserted on a page |
| File ➤ Import Chart | Imports a Freelance Graphics, Graphic writer, 1-2-3, or Symphony chart |
| File ➤ Page Setup | Changes the page orientation (that is, Landscape or Portrait); changes the margins |
| Edit ➤ Paste (or press Ctrl+V) | Pastes the contents of the Clipboard onto the page |
| Edit ➤ Paste Special | Pastes an object from the Clipboard, using a specified format, onto the page |

**TABLE 16.4:** Freelance Graphics SmartMaster Editing Menu Commands (continued)

| MENU COMMAND | PURPOSE |
| --- | --- |
| <u>E</u>dit ➤ <u>I</u>nsert Object | Inserts an object onto the page |
| <u>P</u>age ➤ <u>C</u>hoose Page Layout | Enables you to choose a page layout for the current page |
| <u>P</u>age ➤ <u>B</u>ackground | Defines a background color, mixture of two colors, or pattern for the current page. You can choose a pattern that starts with the first color and changes to the second color. |
| <u>S</u>tyle ➤ <u>D</u>efault Attributes | Changes the colors, shapes, and shadows for specified objects |
| <u>S</u>tyle ➤ Choose <u>P</u>alette | Enables you to choose a different color palette |
| <u>S</u>tyle ➤ <u>E</u>dit Palette | Enables you to customize a color palette |
| <u>T</u>ext ➤ <u>F</u>ont | Changes the font, point size, color, and/or attributes for selected text |
| <u>T</u>ext ➤ Bulle<u>t</u> | Changes the bullet style, color, and/or size for the selected text |
| <u>T</u>ext ➤ <u>N</u>ormal (or press Ctrl+N) | Applies normal text format to the selection |
| <u>T</u>ext ➤ <u>B</u>old (or press Ctrl+B) | Applies boldface to or removes boldface from the selection |
| <u>T</u>ext ➤ <u>I</u>talic (or press Ctrl+I) | Italicizes or removes italics from the selection |
| <u>T</u>ext ➤ <u>U</u>nderline (or press Ctrl+U) | Underlines or removes an underline from the selection |
| <u>T</u>ext ➤ <u>S</u>trikeout | Strikes through or removes strikethrough from the selection |
| <u>T</u>ext ➤ <u>P</u>aragraph Styles | Modifies the style of the selected paragraph |
| <u>T</u>ext ➤ Fra<u>m</u>e | Modifies the edge and area of the frame within which the selection is located |
| <u>T</u>ext ➤ Cur<u>v</u>ed Text | Curves the selected text |

To apply changes simultaneously to every page in a SmartMaster set, click on the Layout button on the status bar. From the list choose the last page, Basic Layout. Define changes to attributes or import a graphic, and Freelance Graphics modifies every page in the SmartMaster set.

Freelance

# Managing Time with Organizer

Part Six introduces you to Organizer, an easy-to-use and graphical personal information manager (PIM). In this part, you'll learn how to set up your personal calendar, schedule your future time, create to-do lists, keep a daily diary, and track your telephone calls. You'll find out how to maintain a list of anniversaries and an address book. You'll also discover how to link entries within Organizer and with other SmartSuite applications.

Table VI.1 illustrates and describes the Organizer SmartIcons.

# Organizer SmartIcons

| SMARTICON | DESCRIPTION |
|---|---|

**Organizer SmartIcons**

Opens an existing file. [File ➤ Open] *Shortcut:* Ctrl+O

Saves the current file. [File ➤ Save] *Shortcut:* Ctrl+S

Sends mail, if you have the necessary software and hardware installed. [File ➤ Send Mail]

Prints the current file using the options in the Print dialog box. [File ➤ Print] *Shortcut:* Ctrl+P

Undoes the last action, if allowed. [Edit ➤ Undo] *Shortcut:* Ctrl+Z

Cuts the selection and places it in the Clipboard. [Edit ➤ Cut] *Shortcut:* Ctrl+X or Shift+Del

Copies the selection to the Clipboard. [Edit ➤ Copy] *Shortcut:* Ctrl+C or Ctrl+Ins

Pastes the contents of the Clipboard into the file at the current cursor location. [Edit ➤ Paste] *Shortcut:* Ctrl+V or Shift+Ins

Goes back to each of the previous pages on which you worked.

Searches for text in the current file. [Edit ➤ Search] *Shortcut:* F3

Creates a link so that you can run a file. [File ➤ Reference]

**Organizer SmartIcons (continued)**

| | |
| --- | --- |
| | Displays entries from other sections in the Calendar section; displays Calendar entries in the Planner section. [Section ➤ Show Through] |
| | Adds sections from other Organizer files to this file. [Section ➤ Include] |
| | Customizes a section. [Options ➤ Customize] |
| | Displays the Help index. [Help ➤ Index] |

Organizer

17

# Scheduling
# with Organizer

# Organizer

**CHAPTER 17**

In this chapter and the next, you'll learn about Organizer, a personal information manager (PIM) that you can use in business or in your personal life. Remember that you can learn the basics of opening and saving files by reviewing Chapter 2, and you can review editing concepts in Chapter 3.

This chapter covers Organizer basics, using the Calendar section to demonstrate. At the same time you're learning about Organizer, you'll see how the Calendar works.

## Introducing Organizer

Organizer is an all-purpose personal information manager (PIM) that looks like an on-screen version of an organizer notebook.

Organizer allows you to do the following:

■ Track and control many of your activities, including keeping a daily diary, scheduling appointments, setting alarms so that you can keep your appointments and remember your anniversaries, recording incoming and outgoing telephone calls, and even starting an application at a particular time.

■ Accumulate text, graphics, and diagrams in a notebook.

■ Keep an up-to-date to-do list, and expand on to-do items in the notebook.

■ Maintain an address book—with both business and personal information—that is arranged in alphabetical or categorical order. You can import names and addresses from Approach or other database programs. You can also dial telephone numbers from your address book, if you have a modem up and running.

- Keep an anniversary list that is arranged in alphabetical, categorical, or even zodiacal order.

- Record both incoming and outgoing telephone calls with their duration; view call entries by date, name, company, status, or category.

- Maintain and view a yearly planner, which illustrates your projects and schedule day by day.

- Add new sections or customize sections to suit your own information management purposes.

- Keep multiple Organizer files so that you can separate your business and personal obligations.

- Print your Organizer information on pages that are compatible with almost any mailing label or personal organizer binder.

# Viewing the Organizer Window

The Organizer application window (Figure 17.1) contains a title bar, menu bar, and SmartIcons, as described in Chapter 2. Organizer also has its own unique work area and set of tools.

## Organizer SmartIcons

The pages starting Part Six (the beginning of the Organizer section) show the Organizer SmartIcons. To learn how SmartIcons work, see Chapter 2.

## The Work Area

On the left side of the work area is a tool palette, described in Table 17.1.

The work area displays your electronic personal organizer, with the following sections:

**Calendar**    Use the Calendar section to track your appointments and meetings, set alarms, and keep a diary, if you wish. Figure 17.2 shows the opening pages of the Calendar section.

# Organizer

**FIGURE 17.1**

The Organizer application window provides many helpful elements to help you track appointments, addresses, anniversaries, and things to do.

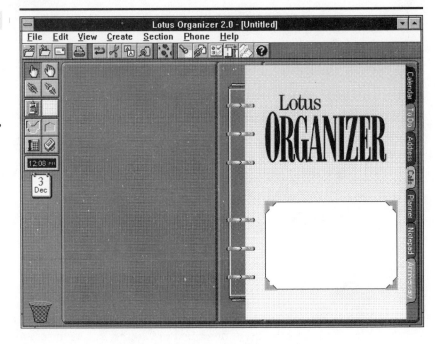

**TABLE 17.1:** Organizer Work Area Tools

| TOOL | MENU COMMAND AND SHORTCUT KEY | DESCRIPTION |
|---|---|---|
| | N/A; N/A | Selects an entry for editing or for drag and drop |
| | N/A; N/A | Picks up an entry and drops it on another page |
| | N/A; N/A | Creates a link |
| | N/A; N/A | Breaks a link |
| | Edit ➤ Cut or Edit ➤ Paste; Ctrl+X or Shift+Del to cut; Ctrl+V or Shift+Ins to paste | Copies an entry into the Clipboard; pastes the contents of the Clipboard |

TABLE 17.1:  Organizer Work Area Tools (continued)

| TOOL | MENU COMMAND AND SHORTCUT KEY | DESCRIPTION |
|---|---|---|
| | Create ➤ Appointment; Ins | Adds a new entry to the Calendar |
| | Create ➤ Task; Ins | Adds a new entry to the To Do list |
| | Create ➤ Address; Ins | Adds a new entry to the Address book |
| | Create ➤ Call: Ins | Adds a new entry to the Calls section |
| | Create ➤ Event; Ins | Adds a new entry to the Planner |
| | Create ➤ Page; Ins | Adds a new entry to the Notepad |
| | Create ➤ Anniversary; Ins | Adds a new entry to the Anniversary list |
| | Phone ➤ Dial; Ctrl+D | Dials a telephone call |
| | File ➤ Print; Ctrl+P | Prints information from a section |
| | N/A; N/A | Displays your current computer system time |
| | N/A; N/A | Displays your current computer system day and month |
| | Edit ➤ Clear; Del | Deletes dragged entries |

**FIGURE 17.2**

The opening pages of
the Calendar section

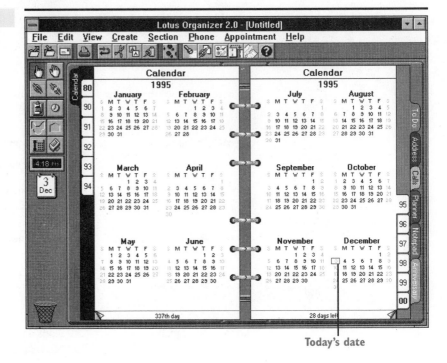

Today's date

**To Do**　Use the To Do section to document your plans, and let Organizer arrange them by date and priority. Figure 17.3 shows a page in the To Do section.

**Address**　Use the Address section to keep names and both business and home addresses and telephone numbers (which can be used in an Ami Pro mail merge). In addition, you can dial telephone numbers and keep a log of your calls. Figure 17.4 shows two pages of an Address section.

**Calls**　Use the Calls section to record both incoming and outgoing telephone calls, time calls, redial calls, and schedule future calls. Figure 17.5 shows two entries in a sample Calls section.

**Planner**　Use the Planner section to show graphically your schedule of meetings, projects, vacations, and other events. Figure 17.6 shows an unfolded Planner.

FIGURE 17.3

A page in the To Do
section, filled in with
tasks

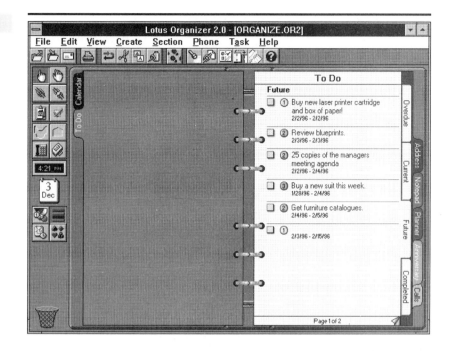

FIGURE 17.4

Two pages of an
Address section

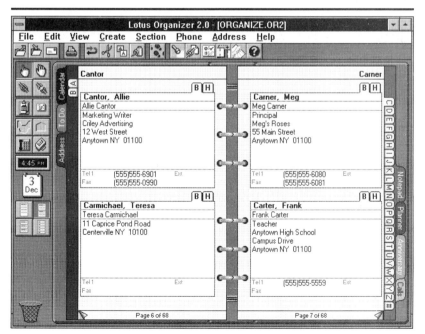

Organizer

# Organizer

**FIGURE 17.5**

Two entries in a sample Calls section

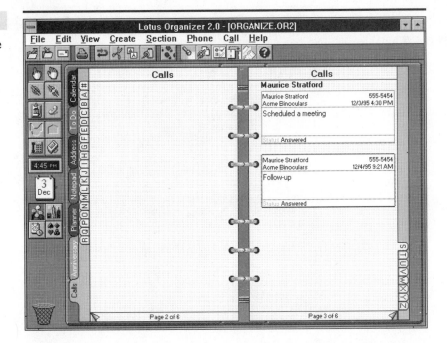

**FIGURE 17.6**

An unfolded Planner, with several events marked

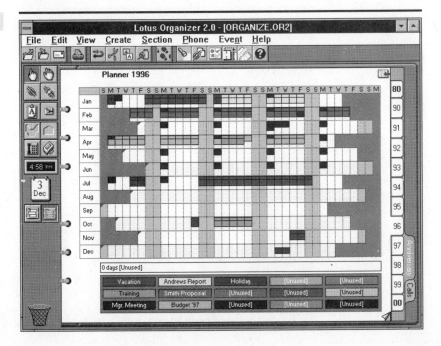

**Notepad**     Use the Notepad section to write notes and memos. You can also import text, spreadsheet data, charts, organization charts, and graphics, and export information to other applications running under Windows. Figure 17.7 shows an entry in a Notepad section.

**Anniversary**     Use the Anniversary section to register anniversaries and birthdays for this year and future years. Figure 17.8 shows the opening pages of an Anniversary section.

# Opening an Organizer File

Although you already know how to open a file, opening a new file in Organizer means that you have new, empty Calendar, To Do, Address, Calls, Planner, Notepad, and Anniversary sections with which to work. You can use multiple Organizer files to separate your business, personal, and volunteer activities, or you can keep everything in one file.

You can open a particular file automatically when you start Organizer. Choose File ➤ Organizer Preferences ➤ Organizer Setup. When Organizer opens the

**FIGURE 17.7**

An entry in a Notepad section

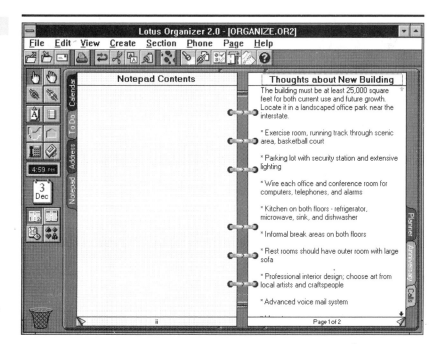

**FIGURE 17.8**

The first six months in an Anniversary section

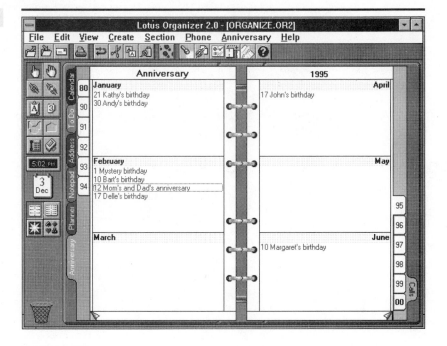

Organizer Setup dialog box (Figure 17.9), type the path and file name in the Open File text box, and click on OK.

To identify a particular Organizer file, type appropriate information in the text box on the right side of the starting work area:

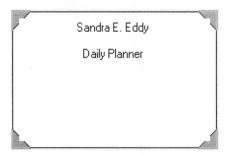

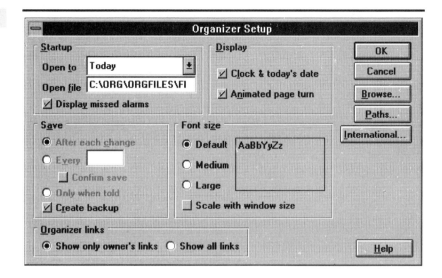

**FIGURE 17.9**

In the Organizer Setup dialog box, you can specify a file to be opened automatically when you start Windows.

When you open an .ORG file from a previous Organizer version, Organizer automatically converts them to the .OR2 format. Either choose File ➤ Open, press Ctrl+O, or click on the Open SmartIcon at the left side of the SmartIcon bar. In the Open dialog box, open the List Files of Type drop-down list box and select Organizer 1.x (*.ORG), and double-click on the .ORG file. When Organizer asks if you want to convert the file, click on OK. Organizer converts the file, showing you its progress, and then asks if you would like to always open the file when Organizer starts up. Either answer Yes or No. Organizer then opens the file.

# Opening an Organizer Section

To open an Organizer section, click on its tab:

To go to the first or last page of the Organizer, click on a nontab area of the Organizer notebook:

# Organizer Mouse and Keyboard Combination Functions

Organizer provides these special mouse/keyboard functions to navigate, select, or embed the time and/or date:

| ACTION | PURPOSE |
|---|---|
| Ctrl+Click on a tab | Return to the last page you viewed or edited |
| Click on a tab | Go to the first page of a section |
| Shift+Click on a tab | Go to the last page of a section |
| Click on the edge of the "front cover" of the notebook | Go to the front of the notebook |
| Click on the edge of the "back cover" of the notebook | Go to the back of the notebook |
| Ctrl+Click on an entry | Add the clicked-on entry to the selection |
| Shift+Click on an entry | Add all entries from the end of the previous selection to the clicked-on entry |
| Shift+Click on time to the left of the notebook | Embed the time (e.g., 10:06 PM) in text that you are editing in a *Create section-entry dialog box* |

| ACTION | PURPOSE |
|---|---|
| Shift+Click on date to the left of the notebook | Embed the date (e.g., 2/2/96) in text that you are editing in a *Create section-entry dialog box* |
| Ctrl+Shift+Click on date to the left of the notebook | Embed the date and time in text that you are editing in a *Create section-entry dialog box* |

# Working in the Calendar Section

Open the Calendar section by clicking on its tab or choosing Section ➤ Turn To ➤ Calendar. Then go to a particular date:

- Go to a date in this year's annual calendar, displayed across both opening pages, by double-clicking on it. Notice that today's date is surrounded by a red border (if you have a color monitor).

- Go to a date in another year by clicking on a year tab: 1980 (which reveals all the years in the 1980's), every year in the 1990's, and 00 (which allows you to use calendars in the 21st century). Then double-click on the date in the annual calendar.

- Go to a date on the previous or next page by clicking on the page turner, the curled page at the bottom of the left or right sides of the Calendar.

  **To open the Calendar and go to today's date, click on the date icon on the left side of the Organizer window.**

## Displaying a Calendar Format

You can display an Organizer Calendar in one of four views:

 Click on the Day per Page button (the default) to display one day per page. This is especially useful if you keep a detailed diary.

 Click on the Work Week button to display the work week on two facing pages.

**609**

  Click on the Week on Two Pages button to display one week on two facing pages.

Click on the Month on Two Pages button to display one month on two facing pages.

> **TIP** **The buttons are not displayed when you are viewing the annual calendars at the beginning of the section. To display the buttons, turn to any Calendar page.**

## Scheduling Your Activities

There are two basic ways to schedule an appointment: one for today or another day that is displayed on the current Calendar page or pages, and one for days that are not currently displayed.

### Scheduling an Activity on the Current Calendar Page

The quickest and most straightforward method to schedule an activity for a day displayed on the current Calendar page is to follow these steps:

1. Open the Calendar or choose Section ➤ Turn To ➤ Calendar.

2. Double-click on the date on which the appointment will occur. Organizer displays the page on which the date appears.

3. Click on the Calendar page. Organizer displays the times for that day in half-hour increments, starting at 8:00 AM and ending at 8:30 PM. You can move up (or down) to earlier (or later) times by clicking on the upward (or downward) pointing arrow at the top (or bottom) right of the page.

4. Double-click on the desired time. Organizer opens the Create Appointment dialog box (Figure 17.10).

**FIGURE 17.10**

A filled-in Create
Appointment dialog box

5. Type appointment information in the Description text box.

6. To set the appointment time and length, either:

   ■ click on the downward-pointing arrow at the right side of the Time drop-down list box, and drag the starting and ending times on the time tracker. For more information about the time tracker, see the section called "Setting the Time and Length of an Appointment."

   ■ type a value or click on the + or – buttons in the Duration text/option box.

7. To indicate that this appointment is tentatively scheduled at the specified date and time, check the Pencil in check box.

8. To make this appointment confidential, check the Confidential check box.

9. Click on OK. Organizer closes the dialog box and inserts the appointment on the appropriate calendar page.

## Scheduling an Activity on Any Date

To schedule an activity for any day, whether or not it's displayed on the current Calendar page, follow these steps:

1. Click on the Calendar tab or choose Section ➤ Turn To ➤ Calendar.

2. Click on the Date icon, press Ins, or choose Create ➤ Appointment. Organizer opens the Create Appointment dialog box.

3. Either type a date, or click on the downward-pointing arrow to the right side of the Date drop-down text/list box and select from the calendar that appears:

4. Type appointment information in the Description text box.

5. To find the first available free time, repeatedly click on the Find Time button until you display a suitable time. (To enable Organizer to search for time on weekends, you must change your Calendar preferences; choose View ➤ Calendar Preferences, check Include Weekends in Find Time Search in the Calendar Preferences dialog box, and click on OK.)

6. Fill in or select other options in the dialog box (see steps 6, 7, and 8 in the preceding section).

7. Click on OK. Organizer closes the dialog box and inserts the appointment on the appropriate calendar page.

## Editing an Appointment

To edit an appointment, double-click on it on the Calendar page, select it and choose Edit ➤ Edit Appointment, or press Ctrl+E. In the Edit Appointment dialog box, which looks just like the Create Appointment dialog box, select or change options using the previous steps as a guide.

You can bypass the Edit Appointment dialog box and go to the appropriate dialog box by selecting an appointment and choosing one of the following:

- To categorize an appointment, choose Appointment ➤ Categorize or press F5. Then fill in the Categorize dialog box.

- To set or change an alarm, choose Appointment ➤ Alarm or press F6. Then fill in the Alarm dialog box.

- To specify a repeating appointment, choose Appointment ➤ Repeat or press F7. Then fill in the Repeat dialog box.

- To associate a cost code with the appointment, choose Appointment ➤ Cost or press F8. Then fill in the Cost dialog box.

- To make an appointment confidential in a password-protected file, choose Appointment ➤ Confidential or press F4.

## Deleting an Appointment

To delete an appointment, drag it to the Wastebasket, select it and press Del, or choose Edit ➤ Clear.

## Setting the Time and Length of an Appointment

The time tracker enables you to set the starting time, the duration, and, implicitly, the ending time for an appointment.

When you fill in an appointment window, the starting time on the time tracker matches the time displayed in the window. The default time tracker is set to one-hour appointments. You can adjust the length of appointments in three ways:

- You can drag the top time to change the starting time and/or duration.

- You can drag the bottom time to change the ending time and/or duration.

- You can drag the time tracker by the duration time in order to change the beginning and ending appointment times but keep the same duration. When you drag the time tracker, the times change in five-minute increments and remain within the current work day.

You can press keys or use the mouse as you drag the time tracker to force certain behavior:

- Hold down the Shift key as you drag the time tracker, and it moves in 30-minute increments.

- Move the mouse pointer to the upward-pointing arrow at the upper-right corner of the time tracker, click, and hold down the left mouse button to scroll to times before 8:00 AM.

- Move the mouse pointer to the downward-pointing arrow at the lower-right corner of the time tracker, click, and hold down the left mouse button to scroll to times after 6:00 PM.

When the Create Appointment dialog box is open, and you have already scheduled appointments for the selected day, there are blue, green, and possibly red bars on the left side of the time tracker. The blue bars represent time blocks for previously scheduled appointments and the green bar represents the appointment that you are currently scheduling. If you see a red bar, you are scheduling a conflicting appointment.

**NOTE** To copy an appointment to another day that is currently displayed (remember that you can display an entire month), press and hold down Ctrl, and drag and drop the appointment. You also can drag the appointment to the Clipboard tool, display the date to which you want to move the appointment, and drag the appointment from the Clipboard to the Calendar page.

## Scheduling Conflicting Appointments

Let's say that you use Organizer to schedule a long block of time to catch up on paperwork. You also may wish to schedule a quick telephone call during that time. Organizer allows you to schedule a conflicting appointment but makes sure that you reply to a prompt and marks both appointments with a vertical red line on the Calendar page.

When you schedule a conflicting appointment, Organizer displays the Conflicting Appointment dialog box (Figure 17.11). To confirm the appointment, click on OK. To change the time of the appointment, either click on the Find Time button to have Organizer find your next free time, or select or type a new time; then click on OK. If you have moved the appointment to the next time, before clicking on OK, click on the Turn to button.

**FIGURE 17.11**

The Conflicting
Appointment dialog box

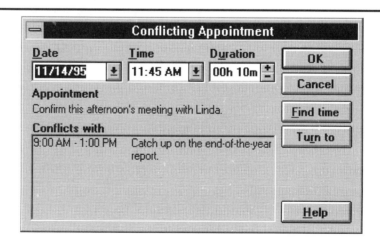

Organizer

## Setting an Alarm for an Appointment

You can set an alarm as a reminder that it's almost time for an event—in the Calendar, To Do, Calls, Planner, and Anniversary sections—to occur. To set an alarm for an appointment, follow these steps:

1. Click on the Calendar tab or choose Section ➤ Turn To ➤ Calendar.

2. Click on the Date icon, double-click on a date at the front of the Calendar, press Ins, or choose Create ➤ Appointment. Organizer opens the Create Appointment dialog box.

3. Define the appointment: Date, Time, Duration, and Description.

4. Click on the Alarm button. Organizer opens the Alarm dialog box (Figure 17.12) with the date and time of the appointment displayed.

5. Specify the number of minutes (from 0 to 23 hours and 59 minutes) before an appointment for which you want the alarm to sound. The default is 5.

6. To play an alarm tune, open the Tune drop-down list and select the tune. (If you wish to display an alarm message box without an alarm sounding, select (None).) To test the tune, click on the Play button.

**FIGURE 17.12**

In the Alarm dialog box, you can set the amount of time before an appointment that the alarm sounds.

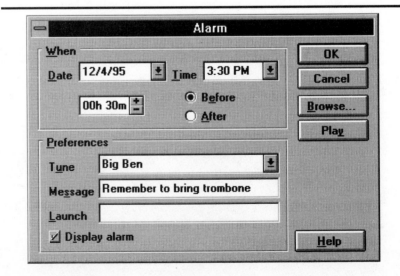

**7.** To display a message in the alarm box, type it in the Message text box.

**8.** Click on OK. Organizer closes the dialog box and returns to the Calendar.

Organizer must be running for an alarm to sound or an alarm message to display. When the alarm goes off, if you have selected a tune, Organizer plays it—whether Organizer is maximized, restored, or minimized. Whether or not you have selected a tune, Organizer displays an Alarm dialog box (Figure 17.13) when the alarm goes off.

**FIGURE 17.13**

The Alarm dialog box that appears when the alarm goes off

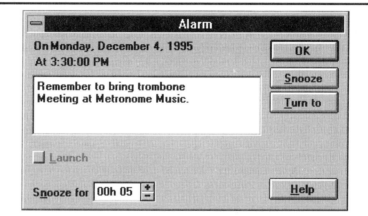

You can turn off or delay an Organizer alarm. To turn off the alarm, click on OK. To have the alarm go off again at a time that you specify, set a time in the Snooze for list box (the default is five minutes), and click on the Snooze button.

Organizer can display icons representing options for appointments: that you have made it confidential, set an alarm for it, made it a repeating appointment, pencilled it in, or assigned a category to it. To select appointment icons for display, choose View ➤ Calendar Preferences, check the appropriate check box, and click on OK. Table 17.2 illustrates the appointment icons.

## Running an Application from within the Calendar

You can run an application from within Organizer (that is, the Calendar, To Do, Calls, Planner, and Anniversary sections) at a set time. To run an

Organizer

**TABLE 17.2:** Appointment Graphics

| GRAPHIC | INDICATES |
| --- | --- |
| 🔒 | A confidential appointment |
| 🔔 | An appointment with an alarm |
| 📑 | A repeating appointment |
| ✏️ | A pencilled-in appointment |
| ♣ | A categorized appointment |

application from Calendar, follow these steps:

1. Click on the Calendar tab or choose <u>S</u>ection ➤ <u>T</u>urn To ➤ Calendar.

2. Click on the Date icon, double-click on a date at the front of the Calendar, press Ins, or choose <u>C</u>reate ➤ <u>A</u>ppointment. Organizer opens the Create Appointment dialog box.

3. Define the appointment: <u>D</u>ate, <u>T</u>ime, D<u>u</u>ration, and D<u>e</u>scription.

4. Click on the A<u>l</u>arm button. Organizer opens the Alarm dialog box.

5. If needed, adjust the date and time on which you wish to start the application.

6. In the <u>L</u>aunch text box, type the exact path and executable file name of the application to be started and go to step 9.

7. If you aren't sure about the path and name of the executable file to be started, click on the <u>B</u>rowse button. Organizer displays the Launch Application Browse dialog box (Figure 17.14).

8. Select the name of the file that you wish to execute. You may have to search through directories and subdirectories until you find it.

9. Click on OK. Organizer returns to the Alarm dialog box, and fills in the <u>L</u>aunch text box.

10. Click on OK. Organizer closes the dialog box and returns to the Calendar.

Figure 17.15 shows the Alarm dialog box with the <u>L</u>aunch text box filled in.

## Using Categories

Organizer allows you to categorize entries in every section. For example, if you use a single Organizer file for all your needs, you can separate your life into categories such as Calls, Clients, Ideas, Meetings, Personal, Travel, and Vacation; you can even assign several categories to one entry. Organizer provides

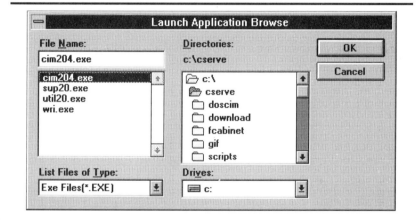

**FIGURE 17.14**

The Launch Application Browse dialog box with a directory and file selected

**FIGURE 17.15**

The Alarm dialog box showing the path and name of the file to be launched

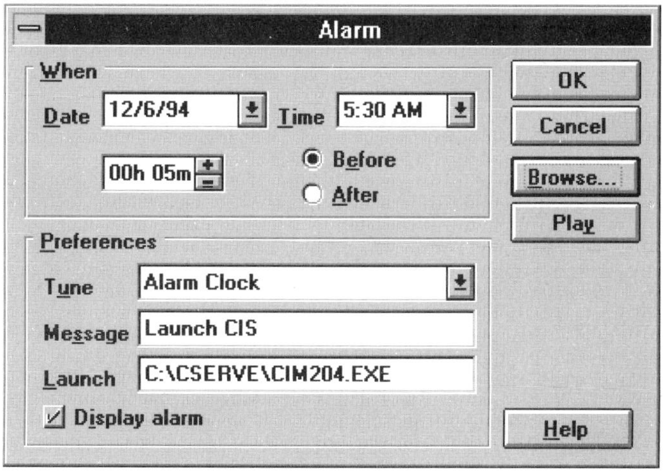

13 predefined categories; you can add, rename, or delete categories until the list matches your own requirements.

## Assigning a Category to an Appointment

To assign a category to an appointment, follow these steps:

**1.** Click on the Calendar tab or choose Section ➤ Turn To ➤ Calendar.

**2.** Click on the Date icon, double-click on a date at the front of the Calendar, press Ins, or choose Create ➤ Appointment. Organizer opens the Create Appointment dialog box.

**3.** Define the appointment: Date, Time, Duration, and Description, and so on.

**4.** Open the Categories drop-down list box.

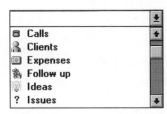

**5.** Click on a selection. Continue clicking until you have assigned all the desired categories.

**6.** To remove a category, click on it again.

**7.** When you have completed the dialog box, click on OK. Organizer closes the dialog box and returns to the Calendar page.

## Adding a Category

To add a category to the predefined list, follow these steps:

**1.** Choose Create ➤ Categories. Organizer opens the Categories dialog box (see Figure 17.16).

**2.** Type a category name in the Name text box.

**3.** Select a symbol from the Symbol drop-down list box.

**4.** If you wish to add more categories, click on Add. Organizer adds the entry to the category list.

**FIGURE 17.16**

The Categories dialog
box with a symbol
about to be selected

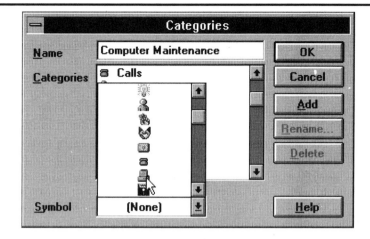

5. Repeat steps 2, 3, and 4 until you have finished.

6. Click on OK. Organizer closes the dialog box and adds the entry to the category list.

## Renaming a Category

To rename a category, follow these steps:

1. Choose Create ➤ Categories. Organizer opens the Categories dialog box.

2. Click on a category in the Categories scroll list.

3. Click on Rename. Organizer displays the Rename Category dialog box.

4. In the New Name text box, type the new category name, and click on OK.

5. Select a new or the same symbol. (If you don't do this, Organizer does not associate a symbol with the renamed category.)

6. Click on OK again. Organizer closes the dialog box.

**NOTE** You can use these same steps to change the symbol for a category.

## Deleting a Category

To delete a category, follow these steps:

1. Choose Create ➤ Categories. Organizer opens the Categories dialog box.

2. Click on a category in the Categories scroll list.

3. Click on Delete. Organizer asks you to confirm the deletion.

4. Click on Yes. Organizer returns to the Categories dialog box.

5. Click on OK. Organizer closes the dialog box.

## Specifying a Cost Code for an Appointment

You can specify a customer code and a cost code for an appointment (and for entries in the To Do, Calls, Planner, and Anniversary sections). This allows you to track the expenses associated with a particular customer and related ac-tivities. Then you can export the information in a .CSV (comma-separated values or ASCII) format to another SmartSuite or Windows application, such as a 1-2-3 spreadsheet or Ami Pro document. To identify a customer and cost code, follow these steps:

You can specify a cost code for a Calendar entry by following these steps:

1. Click on the Calendar tab or choose Section ➤ Turn To ➤ Calendar.

2. Click on the Date icon, double-click on a date at the front of the Calen-dar, press Ins, or choose Create ➤ Appointment. Organizer opens the Create Appointment dialog box.

3. Define the appointment: Date, Time, Duration, and Description.

4. Click on the Cost button. Organizer displays the Cost dialog box (Fig-ure 17.17).

5. Fill in the Customer Code text/drop-down list box with the customer name or code and the Cost Code text/drop-down list box with the price per hour or code. (If you have already defined a code, you can select it from the list.)

**FIGURE 17.17**

In the Cost dialog box, you can specify a customer code and a cost code.

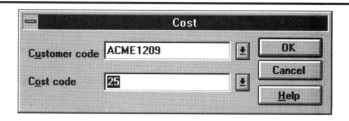

6. Click on OK. Organizer closes the dialog box.

7. Click on OK again. Organizer closes the Create Appointment dialog box.

  If cost codes don't appear with an entry, choose View ➤ Calendar Preferences, check the Cost Codes check box, and click on OK.

## Securing Organizer Files and Appointments

You can use a password to restrict the viewing and editing of an appointment. Before making an appointment confidential, protect your Organizer file with a password.

---

**WORKING TOGETHER ▲**

## Printing an Organizer Calendar from within Ami Pro

You can print an Organizer Calendar from within Ami Pro in two ways: by using the _CALORG.STY style sheet or by using the ORGCAL.SMM macro. To create a calendar, open both Ami Pro and Organizer and do one of the following:

■ Choose File ➤ New. In the New dialog box, double-click on _CALORG.STY or Calendar - Monthly, from Lotus Organizer, depending on whether the List by Description check box is cleared or checked.

**623**

**WORKING TOGETHER** ▲

■ Choose Tools ➤ Macros ➤ Playback. In the Play Macro dialog box, double-click on ORGCAL.SMM.

In the Monthly Organizer Calendar dialog box, select a Month and Year from the drop-down list box and click on OK. The macro runs and creates a calendar, which you can edit or print as you would any other Ami Pro document.

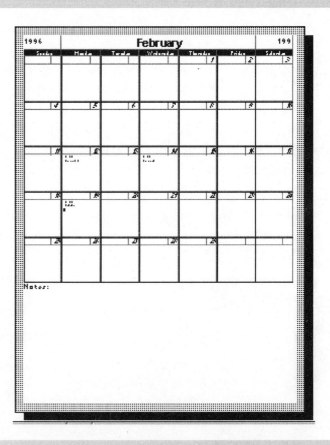

## Setting a Password for an Organizer File

You can define a password to an Organizer file in order to protect it from others.

When someone attempts to open a secured file, he or she is denied access until the defined password is typed. Organizer passwords are case-sensitive so if you type all uppercase letters for a password defined using lowercase letters, Organizer does not allow access to the file.

To define a password, follow these steps:

1. Choose File ➤ Organizer Preferences ➤ User Access, or press Ctrl+U. Organizer displays the User Access dialog box (Figure 17.18).

2. Click on Password. Organizer opens the Password dialog box (Figure 17.19).

3. Type a password in the Password text box.

**FIGURE 17.18**

The User Access
dialog box

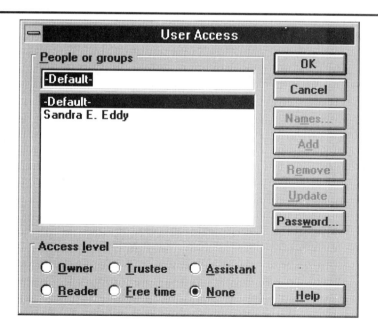

**FIGURE 17.19**

Type a password in the
Password dialog box.

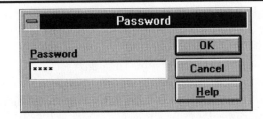

 **It is extremely important for you to write down the password and put it in a secure place. If you forget your password, you no longer have access to the protected file.**

4. Click on OK.

5. Verify the password by retyping it in the Verify Password dialog box.

6. Click on OK three times.

To delete the passwords for a secured file, open the file, and choose File ➤ Organizer Preferences ➤ User Access, or press Ctrl+U. Click on Password, and in the Password dialog box, click on OK, after leaving the Password text box empty. In the Verify Password box, also click on OK without filling in the Verify Password text box. Then click on OK two more times. This automatically removes all the assigned passwords.

To change the passwords in a secured file, open the file, and choose File ➤ Organizer Preferences ➤ User Access, or press Ctrl+U. Click on Password, and in the Password dialog box, type a new password, and click on OK. Type the same password in the Verify Password box, and click on OK. Then click on OK two more times.

## Creating Repeating Appointments

When you have an appointment or meeting that takes place on a regular basis, you can create a repeating appointment. For example, you can schedule a meeting on every Monday or on the 1st and 15th forever or for a limited period. You also can create repeating entries in Calls, To Do, Anniversary, and Planner.

The Repeat dialog box (Figure 17.20) controls repeating appointments. As you are selecting options for a repeating appointment, keep looking at the Your Selection box; you'll be able to tell if you're on the right track.

**FIGURE 17.20**

The Repeat dialog box, which controls repeating appointments

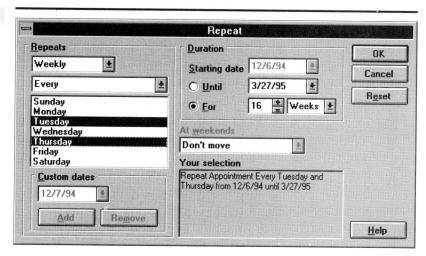

These are examples of several repeating appointments and the Repeat dialog box options used to schedule them:

| APPOINTMENT | SELECTED OPTIONS |
| --- | --- |
| Every Monday at 9:00 AM for the next year | In the Create Appointment dialog box, specify the date of the first appointment, and select the time and the duration. In the Repeat dialog box, from the Repeats group, select Weekly, Every, and Monday; and in the Duration group, select 1 and Year. |
| The 1st and 15th of every month for the next year | In the Create Appointment dialog box, specify the date of the first appointment, and select the time and the duration. In the Repeat dialog box, from the Repeats group, select Monthly (Dates) and 1st, hold down Ctrl, and select 15th; and in the Duration group, select 1 and Year. |

**APPOINTMENT**    **SELECTED OPTIONS**

| APPOINTMENT | SELECTED OPTIONS |
|---|---|
| Every Monday, Wednesday, and Friday for three months | In the Create Appointment dialog box, specify the date of the first appointment, and select the time and the duration. In the Repeat dialog box, from the Repeats group, select Weekly, Monday, hold down Ctrl, and select Wednesday and Friday; and in the Duration group, select 3 and Months. |
| Every other Thursday until June 30, 1996 | In the Create Appointment dialog box, specify the date of the first appointment, and select the time and the duration. In the Repeat dialog box, from the Repeats group, select Weekly, Every Other, and Thursday; and in the Duration group, click on Until and type 6/30/96. |
| December 4 and 5; January 11 and 30 | In the Create Appointment dialog box, specify December 4, and select the time and the duration. In the Repeat dialog box, from the Repeats group, select Custom, click on the downward-pointing arrow in the Custom Dates group, click on December 5, click on Add, click on the downward-pointing arrow in the Custom Dates group, click on the right-pointing arrow on the calendar, click on January 11, click on Add, click on the downward-pointing arrow in the Custom Dates group, click on 30, and click on Add. |

To create a repeating appointment, follow these steps:

1.  Click on the Calendar tab or choose Section ➤ Turn To ➤ Calendar.

2.  Click on the Date icon, double-click on a date at the front of the Calendar, press Ins, or choose Create ➤ Appointment. Organizer opens the Create Appointment dialog box.

3.  Define the appointment: Date, Time, Duration, and Description.

4. Click on the Repeat button. Organizer displays the Repeat dialog box.

5. Fill in or select options in the Repeat dialog box using the previous examples as your guide.

6. When you have finished selecting options, click on OK. Organizer returns to the Create Appointment dialog box.

7. Click on OK again. Organizer returns to the Calendar page.

## Moving an Appointment to Another Day

To move an appointment to a day that you can see on the open Calendar pages, drag it to its new day.

To move an appointment to a day that you cannot see, follow these steps:

1. Click on the tool at the top right of the toolbox.

2. Click on the appointment to be moved. Organizer adds an entry icon to mouse pointer.

3. Go to the page that holds the day to which you wish to move the appointment.

4. Click on the new day. Organizer drops the appointment onto the new day and de-activates the tool.

  **To copy an appointment to a new location, press Ctrl when you drag and drop the appointment. Organizer keeps the original appointment in its starting date and a copy in the new date.**

If you are networked with other computers, you can go beyond tracking your own meetings and appointments; you can schedule meetings, invite attendees, and reserve resources. For further information, see the *Exploring Organizer* manual and the Organizer Help facility.

Organizer

18

# Managing Data
# with Organizer

I n the previous chapter, you found out how to manage your time using Organizer and you learned many Calendar basics. In this chapter, you'll find out how to manage data. In the To Do, Address, Notepad, Planner, Anniversary, and Call sections, you can keep track of your ideas, plan for the days ahead, and store important names, addresses, birthdays, and anniversaries. You also can store telephone numbers and track completed and attempted telephone calls.

As you read and work through this chapter, be aware that the features covered in Chapter 17 work in most of the Organizer sections described in this chapter. For example, you can set alarms, launch applications, categorize, and create repeating entries in all but the Address section. For detailed information about using these features, please refer to Chapter 17.

# Working in the To Do Section

An Organizer To Do list allows you to put all your tasks in one place and list them according to priority, status, starting date, and category. The following sections will help you create and maintain your own To Do list.

## Displaying a To Do Format

You can display a To Do list in one of four views:

 Click on the Priority button (the default) or choose Ⅴiew ➤ 1 By Priority to display tasks by priority (1, 2, 3, and None).

 Click on the Status button or choose Ⅴiew ➤ 2 By Status to display tasks by status (Overdue, Current, Future, and Completed).

Click on the Start Date button or choose <u>V</u>iew ➤ <u>3</u> By Start Date to display tasks by starting date (one tab per month).

 Click on the Category button or choose <u>V</u>iew ➤ <u>4</u> By Category to display tasks by category (all the currently defined categories and uncategorized tasks arranged under alphabetical tabs).

## Adding a Task to the To Do List

To add a task to your To Do list, follow these steps:

**1.** Click on the To Do tab or choose <u>S</u>ection ➤ <u>T</u>urn To ➤ To Do.

 **2.** Click on the Insert icon, click on a page, press Ins, or choose <u>C</u>reate ➤ T<u>a</u>sk. Organizer opens the Create Task dialog box (Figure 18.1).

**3.** Type a description of the task in the Description text box. The text box holds thousands of characters, but it's best to type just a few lines at the most.

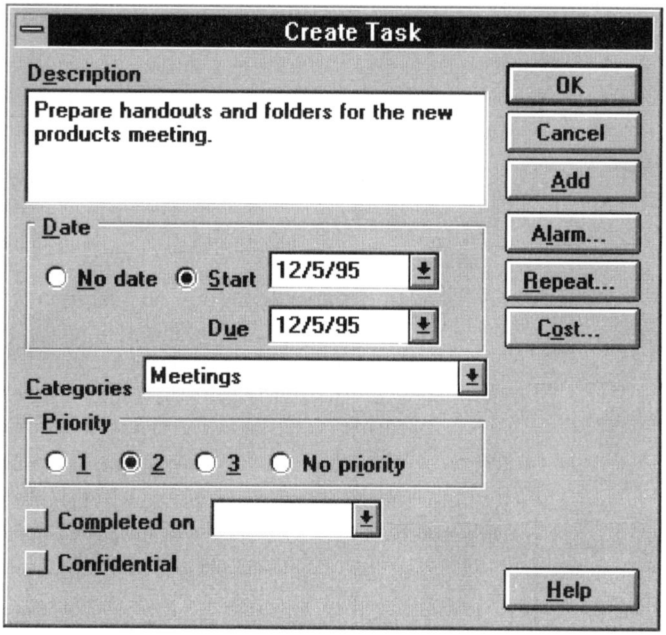

FIGURE 18.1

The filled-in Create Task dialog box

**Create Task**

Description

Prepare handouts and folders for the new products meeting.

[OK]
[Cancel]
[Add]

Date

○ No date  ◉ Start  12/5/95
Due  12/5/95

[Alarm...]
[Repeat...]
[Cost...]

Categories  Meetings

Priority

○ 1  ◉ 2  ○ 3  ○ No priority

☐ Completed on
☐ Confidential

[Help]

**Organizer**

633

**4.** Type or select a starting date (today is the default):

| ◀ **December 1995** ▶ | | | | | | |
|---|---|---|---|---|---|---|
| **Su** | **Mo** | **Tu** | **We** | **Th** | **Fr** | **Sa** |
| 26 | 27 | 28 | 29 | 30 | 1 | 2 |
| 3 | 4 | 5 | 6 | 7 | 8 | 9 |
| 10 | 11 | 12 | 13 | 14 | 15 | 16 |
| 17 | 18 | 19 | 20 | 21 | 22 | 23 |
| 24 | 25 | 26 | 27 | 28 | 29 | 30 |
| 31 | 1 | 2 | 3 | 4 | 5 | 6 |

**5.** Type or select an ending date (today is the default).

**6.** To categorize this task, select from the Categories drop-down listbox.

**7.** Set a Priority. The default is No Priority, the top priority is 1, and the lowest is 3.

**8.** Check the Confidential check box if you wish this task to be confidential (that is, read-only or not viewable by certain individuals) and if this Organizer file is password-protected. For information about securing files, see Chapter 17.

**9.** Click on OK. Organizer adds the task to the To Do list.

 **You can set alarms for entries, associate cost codes with entries, and define repeating entries in the To Do section. See Chapter 17 for information about these topics.**

Organizer To Do list tasks are color-coded:

**Red text**    indicates an entry that is overdue (beyond its due date and not checked as complete).

**Green text**    indicates a current task, which falls on today's date.

**Blue text**    indicates a task that you will start and complete at a future date.

**Black text**    indicates with a green check in the box preceding the entry is an entry that you have checked as complete.

## Editing a Task

To edit a task, double-click on it, select it and choose Edit ➤ Edit Task, or press Ctrl+E. In the Edit Task dialog box, which looks just like the Create Task dialog box, select or change options using the previous steps as a guide.

You can bypass the Edit Task dialog box and go to the appropriate dialog box by selecting a task and choosing one of the following:

- To categorize a task, choose Task ➤ Categorize or press F5. Then fill in the Categorize dialog box.

- To set or change an alarm, choose Task ➤ Alarm or press F6. Then fill in the Alarm dialog box.

- To specify a repeating task, choose Task ➤ Repeat or press F7. Then fill in the Repeat dialog box.

- To associate a cost code with the task, choose Task ➤ Cost or press F8. Then fill in the Cost dialog box.

- To make a task confidential in a password-protected file, choose Task ➤ Confidential or press F4.

## Deleting a Task

To delete a task, drag it to the Wastebasket, select it and press Del, or choose Edit ➤ Clear.

## Completing a Task

When you have completed a task, you can delete it if you don't need to keep a record, or you can mark it as complete. To mark a task as completed, click on it to open the Edit Task dialog box. Then check the Completed check box, select or type a date if you wish, and click on OK. Organizer closes the dialog box, places a check mark in the box preceding the entry, and moves the entry to the bottom of the appropriate page.

Organizer

## Displaying To Do Tasks in the Calendar

To display To Do tasks for a particular Calendar date or range of dates or in the Planner section, follow these steps:

 **1.** Click on the Show Through SmartIcon or choose Section ➤ Show Through. Organizer opens the Show Through dialog box (Figure 18.2).

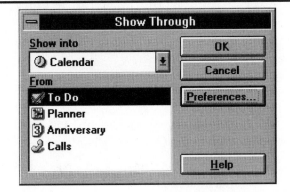

**2.** Open the Show into drop-down list box and select either Calendar or Planner.

**3.** In the From list, click on To Do, the section to be displayed.

**4.** Click on OK. Organizer closes the dialog box and displays tasks in appropriate dates in the Calendar or Planner.

### February 1996
#### Friday 2

① Buy new laser printer cartridge and box of paper!
② 25 copies of the managers meeting agenda

# Working in the Address Section

In the Address section, you can produce a list of names and addresses, search for names or addresses on a list, dial a telephone number (if you have a modem), and import and export information to other Windows applications. Figure 18.3 shows the dialog box that you fill in when adding new business and home names and address information to the Address section.

**FIGURE 18.3**

The Create Address dialog box, which you fill in with new Address information for both business and home

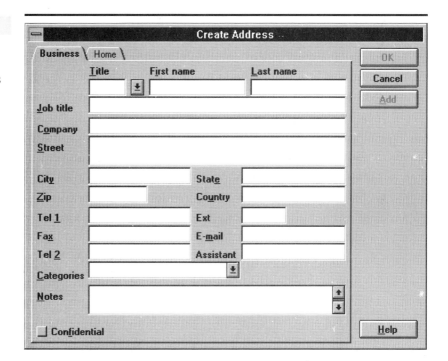

## Displaying an Address Format

You can display an Address book in one of four views:

 Click on the All button or choose <u>V</u>iew ➤ <u>1</u> All to display one complete set of business or home data on a page.

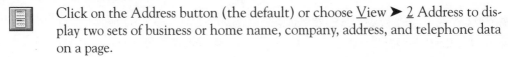

Click on the Address button (the default) or choose <u>V</u>iew ➤ <u>2</u> Address to display two sets of business or home name, company, address, and telephone data on a page.

Click on the Contact button or choose <u>V</u>iew ➤ <u>3</u> Contact to display three sets of business or home name, company, telephone, and e-mail data on a page.

Click on the Phone button or choose <u>V</u>iew ➤ <u>4</u> Phone to display 18 sets of business or home name, and primary telephone data on a page.

## Entering Names, Addresses, and Other Information

Enter names and addresses into the fields by tabbing from field to field or by clicking on a field and either typing or selecting information from a drop-down list box. (You also can add information to a drop-down list.)

This dialog box contains two sections: Business and Home, marked by tabs. The information in three fields at the top of the dialog box and the categories by which you identify this individual appear in both sections of the dialog box. Other fields, for address, telephone, fax, and e-mail appear on both Business and Home sections of the dialog box.

These are the fields in the business and home sections of the Create Address dialog box:

> **Title**    Mr., Ms., Miss, Mrs., Dr., and Prof. If a title isn't on this drop-down list/text box, you can type it. (Once you add this information, it appears in both sections of the dialog box.)
>
> **First Name, Last Name**    The individual's name. (This information also appears under both business and home tabs.)
>
> **Job Title**    The individual's position in the company.
>
> **Company**    The company with which the individual is associated.

**NOTE** After typing a company name and pressing Enter, Organizer searches through the address book for a record with the same company name in the Company field. If a duplicate is found, the Similar Address Found dialog box appears. Click on OK, and Organizer adds address and telephone information to the new record.

**Street**   Several lines for a street address, post office box, apartment, and so on. (You can enter separate addresses for business and home.)

**City**   The city in which the individual's business (Business tab) and/or home (Home tab) are located.

**State**   The state in which the individual's business (Business tab) and/or home (Home tab) are located. Either spell the entire name or use the two-letter abbreviation.

**Zip**   The business (Business tab) and/or home (Home tab) zip code.

**Country**   The country in which the business is located.

**Tel 1**   The primary telephone number (for example, 1-555-555-5555 or 555-5555) for this individual. For more information about connecting a modem and automatically dialing the telephone, see the section, "Working in the Calls Section," later in this chapter.

**Ext**   Telephone extension. You can enter one number for business and one for home.

**Fax**   The fax number. You can enter one number for business and one for home.

**E-mail**   An e-mail address for this individual. You can enter one address for business and one for home.

**Tel 2**   Another telephone number for the individual or company. You can enter one number for business and one for home.

Organizer

**Assistant**   The name of the individual's assistant or a person whom you can call instead of the individual.

**Categories**   The category or categories that best fit this individual. (This information also appears under both business and home tabs.)

**Notes**   Any user-defined information about this individual (e.g., likes, dislikes, hobbies, notes about the last order, and so on. You can enter one note for business and another for home.

**Confidential**   Check this check box to hide this record from those who don't have the appropriate password. For information about securing files, see Chapter 17.

**Spouse**   The names of the individual's spouse.

**Children**   The names of the individual's children.

To insert a record, follow these steps:

1. Click on the Address tab or choose $\underline{S}$ection ➤ $\underline{T}$urn To ➤ Address.

2. Click on the Insert icon, press Ins, choose $\underline{C}$reate ➤ $\underline{A}$ddress, or double-click on the blank part of a page.

3. When you have completed the dialog box, click on OK. Organizer adds the information to the Address book. Organizer displays the page (Figure 18.4) on which the information is stored.

**TIP**   You can choose whether to display business information, home information, or a combination. Choose $\underline{V}$iew ➤ Address $\underline{P}$references to open the Address Preferences dialog box. From the $\underline{F}$oreground Tab drop-down list box, click on Business, to display business information; Home, to display home information; or Select, to determine whether to display business or home information for a particular record. Then click on OK to close the dialog box.

**FIGURE 18.4**

Two facing pages of
filled-in name and
address information

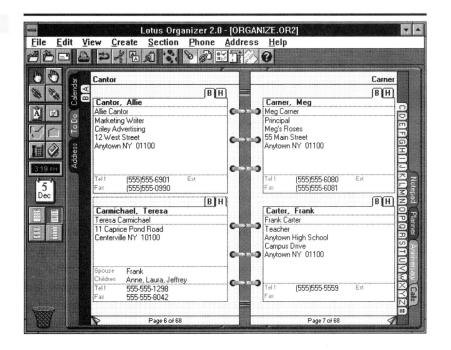

## Editing an Address

To edit an address, double-click on it, select it and choose Edit ➤ Edit Address, or press Ctrl+E. In the Edit Address dialog box, which looks just like the Create Address dialog box, select or change options using the previous steps as a guide.

You can bypass the Edit Address dialog box and go to the appropriate dialog box by selecting an address and choosing one of the following:

■ To categorize an address, choose Address ➤ Categorize or press F5. Then fill in the Categorize dialog box.

■ To make an address confidential in a password-protected file, choose Address ➤ Confidential or press F4.

## Deleting an Address

To delete an address, drag it to the Wastebasket, select it and press Del, or choose Edit ➤ Clear.

## Copying an Entry to a New Entry

To copy the active address entry to a new entry, follow these steps:

**1.** Choose Edit ➤ Copy Special ➤ All Fields. Organizer opens the Copy Special dialog box, as shown in Figure 18.5.

**FIGURE 18.5**

The Copy Special dialog box with a record displayed

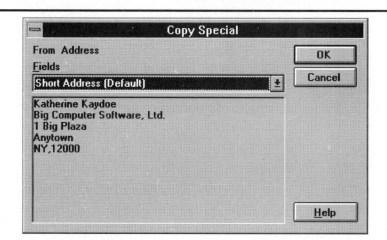

**2.** From the Fields drop-down list box, select the fields to be added. The Fields text box shows the fields to be added using the current selection.

**3.** Click on OK. Organizer copies the information to the Clipboard. Notice that the Clipboard tool contains a small address icon.

**4.** Either drag the icon from the Clipboard tool or choose Edit ➤ Paste. Organizer copies the information from the selected fields to a new record. Then you can edit the new record to make it unique.

## Finding Information in Organizer

Organizer allows you to find information easily—not only in the current section but also throughout Organizer. To search for information in Organizer, follow these steps:

1. Click on the Find SmartIcon, choose Edit ➤ Find, or press Ctrl+F. Organizer displays the Find dialog box (Figure 18.6).

2. In the Find text box, type a *search string*, the text for which you are searching. You can type a partial word, or use the wildcard * to search for the combination of characters that you specify.

3. To search for an exact match of upper- and lowercase characters, check the Case-Sensitive check box.

4. To search for an entire word, not a partial word, check the Whole Word check box.

5. To search through one section, open the Section drop-down list box, and click on a selection, or to search through every section, click on the All Sections option button.

6. To clear the list after this search, click on Clear List; to add the results of the next search to this one, click on Append to List.

**FIGURE 18.6**

The Find dialog box, in which you type and specify search specifications

7. To find the next occurrence of the search string, click on Find <u>N</u>ext.

8. To find all occurrences of the search string, click on Find <u>A</u>ll.

9. To turn to the selected entry on the Occu<u>r</u>rences scroll list, click on <u>T</u>urn to.

10. To close the dialog box, click on Close.

## Filtering Information

Another way to search within an Organizer file is by filtering your information. An Organizer *filter* uses a criteria that you specify to gather a subset of information for one or more sections. For example, you can find all the addresses located in a particular city or state in order to call only those individuals. Or you can find all Calendar entries for a certain cost code.

After creating a filter, you can save it or add it to a menu, so that you can use it again at any time.

To create a filter, follow these steps:

1. Choose <u>C</u>reate ➤ <u>F</u>ilters. Organizer opens the Filters dialog box, as shown in Figure 18.7.

**FIGURE 18.7**

The Filters dialog box

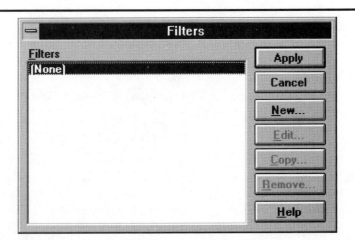

2. Click on <u>N</u>ew. Organizer displays the New Filter dialog box (Figure 18.8).

3. Type the filter name in the <u>N</u>ame text box.

4. From the Section drop-down list box, click in an empty box, and select the section for which you are creating the filter.

5. From the Field drop-down list box, click in the next box in the row and select the field in which the filtering takes place.

6. From the Test drop-down list box, click in the next box in the row and select a condition with which Organizer tests the field.

7. In the Value text box, click in the next box in the row and type the value for which the filter is searching. (If you wish Organizer to display a prompt box in which you type a value, precede the typed value with a question mark.)

8. From the And/Or drop-down list box, click in the next box in the row and select AND or OR to add another row of conditions.

9. To add other conditions to this filter, repeat steps 4 to 8.

10. To add a menu item to the View Apply filter menu, check the <u>S</u>how in View—Apply Filter Menu check box.

11. When you have completed building the filter, click on OK. If your filter is valid, Organizer closes the dialog box and saves the filter. Otherwise, Organizer displays an error message. After editing the filter, click on OK.

12. Click on Apply. Organizer runs the filter against the section or sections for which you created it. At the conclusion of a search, the affected sections only contain records and entries that match the filter. For example,

**FIGURE 18.8**

The New Filter dialog

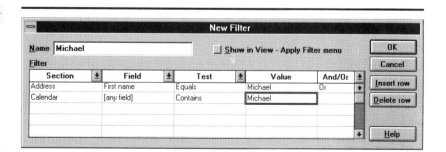

all the Calendar pages except for those that match are blank, and in the Notepad, all pages except for those that match are missing.

To clear a filter, choose Create ➤ Filters. In the Filters dialog box, select (None) and click on Apply.

To edit a filter, choose Create ➤ Filters. In the Filters dialog box, select the filter you wish to edit and click on Edit. In the Edit Filter dialog box (Figure 18.9), after changing the options and values, click on OK.

You can copy a filter and then edit it under its new name. This means that you don't have to create a slightly different filter from scratch. To copy a filter, choose Create ➤ Filters. In the Filters dialog box, select the filter you wish to copy and click on Copy. In the Copy Filter dialog box, overtype the name and edit the filter. Then click on OK.

To delete a filter, choose Create ➤ Filters. In the Filters dialog box, select the filter and click on Remove. To confirm the deletion, click on Yes. Then click on Close.

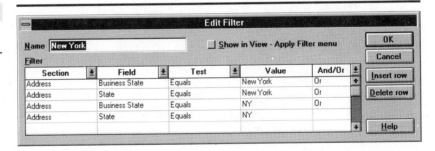

| Section | Field | Test | Value | And/Or |
|---|---|---|---|---|
| Address | Business State | Equals | New York | Or |
| Address | State | Equals | New York | Or |
| Address | Business State | Equals | NY | Or |
| Address | State | Equals | NY | |

Name: New York

Show in View - Apply Filter menu

OK · Cancel · Insert row · Delete row · Help

# Working in the Notepad Section

The Organizer Notepad allows you to keep detailed notes about ideas, projects, and so on. In fact, it's possible to have an Organizer notebook with only Notepad sections.

## Displaying a Notepad Format

You can arrange the pages in the Notepad section in four ways:

 Click on the Page Number button or choose View ➤ 1 By Page Number (the default) to arrange the pages by the current order in which you have placed them.

Click on the Title button or choose View ➤ 2 By Title to arrange the pages alphabetically by page title.

Click on the Date button or choose View ➤ 3 By Date to arrange the pages by creation date—from the oldest page to the newest.

Click on the Category button or choose View ➤ 4 By Category to arrange pages by category.

## Adding an Entry to the Notepad

To add an entry to the Notepad section, follow these steps:

**1.** Click on the Notepad tab or choose Section ➤ Turn To ➤ Notepad.

**2.** Click on the Insert icon, click on the first, second, or last page of the section, press Ins, or choose Create ➤ Page. Organizer opens the Create Page dialog box (Figure 18.10).

**3.** Type a title in the Title text box.

**4.** To import a bitmap (.BMP), metafile (.WMF), or text file (.TXT), click on File.

**5.** In the File dialog box, double-click on a file name. (You may have to select a file type or display directories and subdirectories to find the desired file.)

**6.** If you wish to select attributes for the page, click on Page.

**7.** Choose page styles:

> **Start a Chapter**    Check this check box to create a new chapter for this Notepad page.
>
> **Links Page**    Check this check box to link this page to another page or entry in the file.

Organizer

**FIGURE 18.10**

In the Notepad Page Insert dialog box, you control all aspects of a new Notepad page or pages.

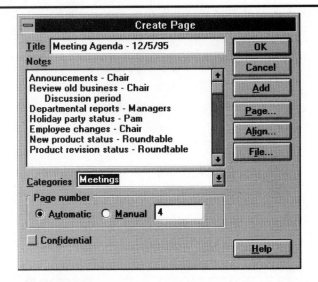

**Folded**     Check this check box to create a wide, foldable page, which includes a button with which you can unfold or fold the page.

**Color**     Click on the downward-pointing arrow to open a palette from which you can choose a background color for the page.

8. If you are importing a bitmap or metafile, select a size option:

**Original Size**     Click on this option button to keep the graphic its original size.

**Fit to Page**     Click on this option button to resize the graphic to fit the page.

**Fill Entire Page**     Click on this option button to change the size of the graphic to fill the entire page.

**Percentage**     Click on this option button and type a value in the text box to increase the size of the graphic by a certain percentage.

**Maintain Aspect Ratio**     Check this check box to keep the graphic in its original proportions.

9. Click on OK.

10. To change the alignment of the page, click on A̲lign, and click on L̲eft (the default), C̲enter, or R̲ight horizontal alignment, and/or T̲op (the default), Ce̲nter, or B̲ottom vertical alignment. Then click on OK.

11. To automatically number the pages in the Notepad, click on A̲utomatic. To manually number this page, click on M̲anual and type a value in the text box.

12. Check the Confidential check box to make this page confidential if this Organizer file is password-protected.

13. Click on OK. Organizer adds the page or pages to the Notepad section, and inserts an entry in the table of contents.

## Editing a Page

To edit a page, go to the page and double-click on it, select it and choose E̲dit ➤ E̲dit Page, or press Ctrl+E. When the Edit Page dialog box opens, edit the text or select options, and click on OK. To add, change, or delete the text on the page, click on the page and work as you would in a word processor. To leave edit mode, press F2.

You can bypass the Edit Page dialog box and go to the appropriate dialog box by selecting a page and choosing one of the following:

- To categorize a page, choose Pa̲ge ➤ C̲ategorize or press F5. Then fill in the Categorize dialog box.

- To assign page attributes, choose Pa̲ge ➤ P̲age. Then fill in the Page dialog box.

- To change alignment of text on the page, choose Pa̲ge ➤ A̲lign. Then fill in the Align dialog box.

- To import a graphic or text file, choose Pa̲ge ➤ F̲ile. Then fill in the File dialog box.

- To make a task confidential in a password-protected file, choose Pa̲ge ➤ Confi̲dential or press F4.

Organizer

## Deleting a Page

To delete a page, drag it to the Wastebasket, select it and press Del, or choose Edit ➤ Clear.

# Working in the Planner Section

The Planner is a graphical view of a year's or quarter's events. You can look at color-coded entries and see the time—up to four adjacent or eight overlapping blocks per day—that you have reserved for events.

## Displaying a Planner Format

You can look at the Planner in two ways:

 Click on the Quarter per Page button or choose View ➤ 1 Quarter per Page to display the Planner over four pages—one for each quarter of the year.

 Click on the Year per Page button or choose View ➤ 2 Year per Page (the default) to display the Planner on one page per year.

## Adding an Event

There are two ways to add an event in the Planner: you can click on the legend at the bottom of the page and then click on a date in the grid, or you can fill in a dialog box.

The easy way to add an event in the Planner is to click on its block in the legend and click near the top of one of the blocks in the morning or afternoon on the desired date. (If you click toward the bottom of a block, you inadvertently may insert an overlapping event.) You also can click on the block in the legend and drag across the dates on which you want to place the event. (If you drag across a weekend, the event is placed there as well.) You can drag across a block but not down and across other blocks on the same day or range of days; once you've added an event to a single block, you can't incorporate additional blocks. You also can drag an entire event to another block of time—perhaps to the afternoon from the morning, or to the next week.

Organizer enables you to insert as many as four events in a morning and four more in the afternoon—if you overlap the entries. To insert an overlapping event, click on the bottom of an existing event. Remember that you can drag an event into place. The best way to master inserting multiple events on a day or block of days is to practice, practice, practice.

To add an event to the Planner section using a dialog box, follow these steps:

1. Click on the Planner tab or choose <u>S</u>ection ➤ <u>T</u>urn To ➤ Planner.

2. Click on the Insert icon, press Ins, double-click on a date, or choose <u>C</u>reate ➤ Eve<u>n</u>t. Organizer opens the Create Event dialog box (Figure 18.11).

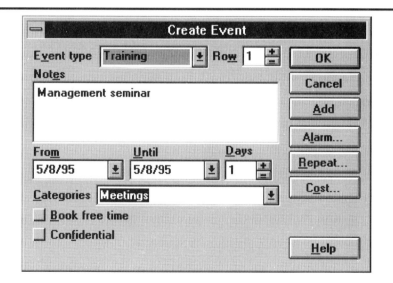

3. Choose an event from the E<u>v</u>ent Type drop-down list box.

4. Select one of the four rows from the Ro<u>w</u> list box.

5. Type anything related to the event in the Not<u>e</u>s text box.

**651**

6. Type or select a starting date from the Fro<u>m</u> on drop-down list box. To-day's computer system date is the default. If you click on the downward-pointing arrow, a calendar from which you can choose appears:

| ◀ | **May 1995** | | | ▶ | | |
|----|----|----|----|----|----|----|
| **Su** | **Mo** | **Tu** | **We** | **Th** | **Fr** | **Sa** |
| 30 | 1 | 2 | 3 | 4 | 5 | 6 |
| 7 | 8 | 9 | 10 | 11 | 12 | 13 |
| 14 | 15 | 16 | 17 | 18 | 19 | 20 |
| 21 | 22 | 23 | 24 | 25 | 26 | 27 |
| 28 | 29 | 30 | 31 | 1 | 2 | 3 |

7. Type or select an ending date from the <u>U</u>ntil drop-down list box. Today's computer system date is the default. If you click on the downward-pointing arrow, a calendar from which you can choose appears. You also can select the duration of an event by typing or selecting a value from the <u>D</u>ays list box.

8. To categorize the event, select from the <u>C</u>ategories drop-down list box.

9. Check the <u>B</u>ook Free Time check box to insert this event into the Calendar, which helps you to avoid scheduling conflicts. The default is a cleared check box.

10. Check the Con<u>f</u>idential check box to make this event confidential if this Organizer file is password-protected. The default is a cleared check box.

11. To set an alarm for the event, click on A<u>l</u>arm, fill in the Alarm dialog box, and click on OK.

12. To define this as a repeating event, click on <u>R</u>epeat, fill in the Repeat dialog box, and click on OK.

13. To associate a cost code with this event, click on C<u>o</u>st, fill in the Cost dialog box, and click on OK.

14. To insert this event without closing this dialog box (so that you can add other events), click on <u>A</u>dd.

15. To insert this event and close the dialog box, click on OK.

## Editing an Event

To change the attributes for an event, go to the event and double-click on it, select it and choose Edit ➤ Edit Event, or press Ctrl+E. When the Edit Event dialog box opens, select options or type in the text boxes, and click on OK. To leave edit mode, press F2.

You can bypass the Edit Event dialog box and go to the appropriate dialog box by selecting an event and choosing one of the following:

- To categorize an event, choose Event ➤ Categorize or press F5. Then fill in the Categorize dialog box.

- To set or change an alarm, choose Event ➤ Alarm or press F6. Then fill in the Alarm dialog box.

- To specify a repeating event, choose Event ➤ Repeat or press F7. Then fill in the Repeat dialog box.

- To associate a cost code with the event, choose Event ➤ Cost or press F8. Then fill in the Cost dialog box.

- To make an event confidential in a password-protected file, choose Event ➤ Confidential or press F4.

## Deleting an Event

To delete an event, drag it to the Wastebasket. If the Delete Repeating Event dialog box (Figure 18.12) appears, select an option, and click on OK.

FIGURE 18.12

The Delete Repeating Event dialog box with the default settings for December 6, 1995

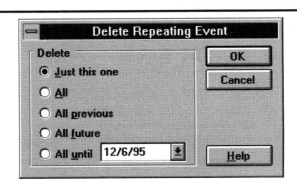

**Just This One**   Click on this option button to delete the event from this date. However, if you added two events at separate times, Organizer treats each as separate.

**All**   Click on this option button to delete the entire block of events that you added.

**All Previous**   Click on this option button to delete this event and all previous events in this range.

**All Future**   Click on this option button to delete this event and all the next events in this range.

**All Until**   Click on this option button to delete this event and all the next events in this range until the date that you type in the text box or select from the calendar that pops up.

## Naming an Event

To change or define the name of an event or (Unused) in the legend at the bottom of the Planner, either double-click on the name or choose View ➤ Planner Preferences, and click on Key. In the Planner Key dialog box (Figure 18.13), overtype the event, and then click on OK twice.

**FIGURE 18.13**

The Planner Key dialog box

# Working in the Anniversary Section

The Anniversary section allows you to keep track of important birthdays and anniversaries. Remember that you can choose to display Anniversary entries in the Calendar section, and you can set alarms so that you'll never send a belated birthday card again.

## Displaying an Anniversary Format

You can display anniversary entries in four ways:

Click on the Month button or choose <u>V</u>iew ➤ <u>1</u> By Month Number (the default) to display entries three months to a page.

Click on the Year button or choose <u>V</u>iew ➤ <u>2</u> By Year to display all the entries for an entire year on two facing pages.

Click on the Zodiac button or choose <u>V</u>iew ➤ <u>3</u> By Zodiac to display entries by their zodiacal signs.

Click on the Category button or choose <u>V</u>iew ➤ <u>4</u> By Category to arrange pages by category in the order in which they were added.

## Adding an Entry to the Anniversary List

To add an entry to your Anniversary list, follow these steps:

**1.** Click on the Anniversary tab or choose <u>S</u>ection ➤ <u>T</u>urn To ➤ Anniversary.

**2.** Click on the Insert icon, double-click on a blank part of a page in the section, press Ins, or choose <u>C</u>reate ➤ <u>A</u>nniversary. Organizer opens the Create Anniversary dialog box (Figure 18.14).

**FIGURE 18.14**

The Create Anniversary dialog box

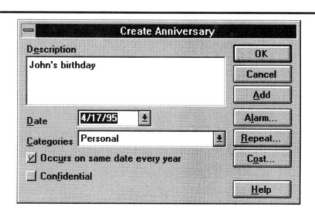

Organizer

3. Type a description of the event in the Description text box.

4. Type or select a date from the Date drop-down list box. Today's computer system date is the default. If you click on the downward-pointing arrow, a calendar from which you can choose appears:

| ◀ | April 1995 | | | | ▶ | |
|:---:|:---:|:---:|:---:|:---:|:---:|:---:|
| **Su** | **Mo** | **Tu** | **We** | **Th** | **Fr** | **Sa** |
| 26 | 27 | 28 | 29 | 30 | 31 | 1 |
| 2 | 3 | 4 | 5 | 6 | 7 | 8 |
| 9 | 10 | 11 | 12 | 13 | 14 | 15 |
| 16 | 17 | 18 | 19 | 20 | 21 | 22 |
| 23 | 24 | 25 | 26 | 27 | 28 | 29 |
| 30 | 1 | 2 | 3 | 4 | 5 | 6 |

5. To categorize the event, select from the Categories drop-down list box.

6. Check Occurs on Same Date Every Year to mark a birthday or anniversary date. If you are tracking holidays, which can occur on different dates each year, clear this check box. The default is a checked check box.

7. Check the Confidential check box to make this entry confidential if this Organizer file is password-protected. The default is a cleared check box.

8. To set an alarm for this event, click on Alarm, fill in the Alarm dialog box, and click on OK.

9. To define this as a repeating event, click on Repeat, fill in the Repeat dialog box, and click on OK.

10. To associate a cost code with this event, click on Cost, fill in the Cost dialog box, and click on OK.

11. To insert this event without closing this dialog box (so that you can add other events), click on Add.

12. To insert this event and close the dialog box, click on OK.

## Editing an Anniversary

To change the attributes for an anniversary, double-click on it, select it and choose Edit ➤ Edit Anniversary, or press Ctrl+E. When the Edit Anniversary dialog box opens, edit the text, select options, and click on OK.

You can bypass the Edit Anniversary dialog box and go to the appropriate dialog box by selecting an anniversary and choosing one of the following:

- To categorize an anniversary, choose Anniversary ➤ Categorize or press F5. Then fill in the Categorize dialog box.

- To set or change an alarm, choose Anniversary ➤ Alarm or press F6. Then fill in the Alarm dialog box.

- To specify a repeating event, choose Anniversary ➤ Repeat or press F7. Then fill in the Repeat dialog box.

- To associate a cost code with the anniversary, choose Anniversary ➤ Cost or press F8. Then fill in the Cost dialog box.

- To make an anniversary confidential in a password-protected file, choose Anniversary ➤ Confidential or press F4.

## Deleting an Anniversary

To delete an anniversary, drag it to the Wastebasket, select it and press Del, or choose Edit ➤ Clear.

# Working in the Calls Section

Making and receiving telephone calls may be the most important aspect of your working day, so it's a good idea to be very careful about keeping a record your calls—both incoming and outgoing, attempted and completed. Using the Calls section, you also can time calls, redial calls, and schedule future calls.

Open the Calls section by clicking on its tab or choosing Section ➤ Turn To ➤ Calls.

**Organizer**

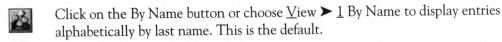

## Displaying a Calls Section Format

You can display the Calls section in one of four views:

Click on the By Name button or choose <u>V</u>iew ➤ <u>1</u> By Name to display entries alphabetically by last name. This is the default.

Click on the By Company button or choose <u>V</u>iew ➤ <u>2</u> By Company to display entries alphabetically by company name.

Click on the By Date button or choose <u>V</u>iew ➤ <u>3</u> By Date to display entries arranged by date—from oldest to newest.

Click on the By Category button or choose View ➤ <u>4</u> By Category to display entries arranged by category.

## Getting Ready to Dial

Organizer enables automatic dialing if a telephone is properly connected to your modem, which in turn must be connected correctly to your computer. Before trying to dial your telephone, check that Organizer recognizes the communications (COM) port to which the modem is attached. To check your modem settings, follow these steps:

1. Choose <u>F</u>ile ➤ Organizer Preferences ➤ <u>D</u>ialer. Organizer opens the Dialer Preferences dialog box, as shown in Figure 18.15.

2. From the Port drop-down list box, select the communications port to which your modem is connected. If you have a serial mouse, it's probably connected to COM1 (the default). If you aren't sure of the communications port for your modem, try COM2.

3. If your telephone is touchtone, click on <u>T</u>one (the default); otherwise, click on P<u>u</u>lse.

4. Select or type other options. When in doubt, use the Organizer defaults.

5. After you have completed the dialog box, click on OK.

If you have problems getting a dial tone or in hanging up, refer to "Troubleshooting Modem Settings" in the help facility. In addition, if the TECH-NOTE.OR2 file is in the \org2\orgfiles directory, open it, and look at the

**FIGURE 18.15**

The Dialer Preferences
dialog box with some
typical options selected
or changed

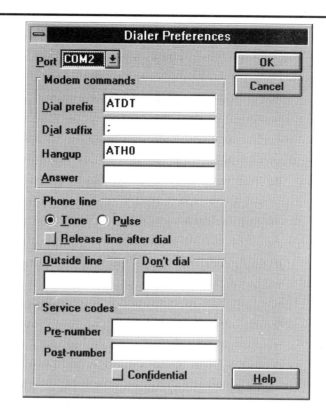

chapter, "Autodialer & Modem." Another source of help is your modem's user
documentation.

## Autodialing a Telephone Number

To dial a telephone number, follow these steps:

**1.** Click on the Telephone icon, drag an entry from any Organizer section
to the Telephone icon, choose Phone ➤ Dial, or press Ctrl+D. Organizer displays the Dial dialog box (Figure 18.16). If you dragged an entry
from the Address book to the Telephone icon, the Number is already
filled in.

**FIGURE 18.16**

Organizer's Dial dialog
box, from which you
can dial a telephone
number

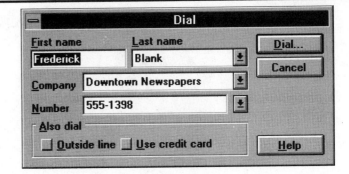

2. If the First Name, Last Name, and Company text boxes are empty, you
   can fill them in; however, it's not required. If the individual you are calling is in your address book, you can open the drop-down list boxes and
   select the last name and company.

3. If the Number text box is empty, type a telephone number (for example,
   1-555-555-5555 (long distance) or 555-5555 (local). If the individual
   you are calling is in your address book, you can open the drop-down list
   boxes and select the telephone number. You can edit the number, if
   needed.

4. To dial the number, click on Dial. The Dialing dialog box (Figure 18.17)
   displays the number and allows you to automatically enter information
   in the phone log, hang up, or redial.

**FIGURE 18.17**

The Dialing dialog box

## Quick-Dialing a Telephone Number

Organizer can dial the number of an entry in any section. Just click on the entry, and choose Phone ➤ Quick Dial or press Ctrl+Q. Organizer dials the telephone number without displaying the Dial dialog box. You also can quick-dial the last number that you dialed.

## Creating a Future Telephone Call

Before you make a telephone call, you can document it in detail. Just fill in and select options from the Create Call dialog box. To plan and optionally make and record a call, follow these steps:

1. Click on the Call tab or choose Section ➤ Turn To ➤ Call.

2. Click on the Insert icon, double-click on a blank part of a page in the section, press Ins, or choose Create ➤ Call. Organizer opens the Create Call dialog box (Figure 18.18) and starts the Stopwatch.

3. Type or select a date from the Date drop-down list box. Today's computer system date is the default. If you click on the downward-pointing arrow, a calendar from which you can choose appears.

4. Type or select a time from the Time drop-down list box. The current computer system time is the default. If you click on the downward-pointing arrow, the time tracker appears. You can select a duration from either the time tracker or the Duration list box.

5. Type or select a name, company name, and telephone number from the First Name, Last Name, Company, and Number text/drop-down list boxes, respectively. Note that the address information in the drop-down list boxes comes from the Address section.

6. Type a description of the call in the Notes text box.

7. If needed, select the call status from the Status drop-down list box. The default is Planned. If you select Follow up, Organizer inserts a follow-up call to this call.

8. To categorize the call, select from the Categories drop-down list box.

9. Check the Outside Line check box to precede the telephone number with an outside line code. The default is a cleared check box.

FIGURE 18.18

The Create Call
dialog box

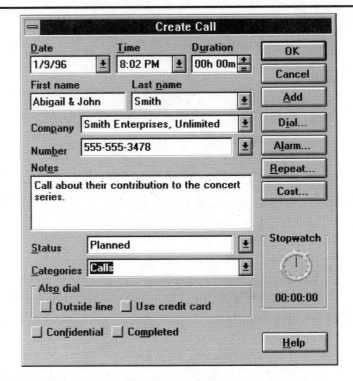

10. Check the Use Credit Card check box to precede the telephone number with a credit card number. The default is a cleared check box.

11. Check the Confidential check box to make this entry confidential if this Organizer file is password-protected. The default is a cleared check box.

12. Check the Completed check box if you have completed the call. The default is a cleared check box.

13. To set an alarm for the call, click on Alarm, fill in the Alarm dialog box, and click on OK.

14. To define this as a repeating call, click on Repeat, fill in the Repeat dialog box, and click on OK.

15. To associate a cost code with this call, click on Cost, fill in the Cost dialog box, and click on OK.

16. To stop the Stopwatch, click on or near it; to reset the Stopwatch, click again.

17. To add this call to the Calls section without closing this dialog box (so that you can add other events), click on Add.

18. To add this call to the Calls section and close the dialog box, click on OK.

## Tracking an Incoming Call

When a call comes in, you can time it and record information about it. To track an incoming call, follow these steps:

1. After you pick up the receiver, choose Phone ➤ Incoming Call. Organizer opens the Create Call dialog box.

2. Click on the Stopwatch to start timing the call.

3. At the conclusion of the call, hang up the receiver, and click on the Stopwatch.

4. Fill in the text boxes and select options as you would when creating a call.

5. Click on OK. Organizer closes the dialog box and inserts the record of the call in the Calls section.

## Defining a Follow-up Call

To define a follow-up call, choose Call ➤ Follow Up. Then fill in the Create Follow up Call dialog box. If you set an alarm, you'll get a reminder to make the follow-up call.

As you are making a telephone call, you can define it as a follow-up call by selecting the Follow up status from the Status drop-down list box.

## Editing a Call

To change the attributes for a call, double-click on it, select it and choose Edit ➤ Edit Call, or press Ctrl+E. When the Edit Call dialog box opens, edit the text, select options, and click on OK.

You can bypass the Edit Call dialog box and go to the appropriate dialog box by selecting a call and choosing one of the following:

- To categorize a call, choose Call ➤ Categorize or press F5. Then fill in the Categorize dialog box.

- To set or change an alarm, choose Call ➤ Alarm or press F6. Then fill in the Alarm dialog box.

- To specify a repeating event, choose Call ➤ Repeat or press F7. Then fill in the Repeat dialog box.

- To associate a cost code with the call, choose Call ➤ Cost or press F8. Then fill in the Cost dialog box.

- To make an anniversary confidential in a password-protected file, choose Call ➤ Confidential or press F4.

### Deleting a Call

To delete a call, drag it to the Wastebasket, select it and press Del, or choose Edit ➤ Clear.

## Selecting Print Options

Printing in Organizer is almost the same as printing in any other SmartSuite application. The main differences are the number of available paper layouts and the options in the Print dialog box.

**NOTE**  You can add a new page layout or edit an existing layout. Choose Edit ➤ Layouts or press Ctrl+Y and make your changes in the Layouts dialog box. For further information, see the Exploring Organizer manual or "Customizing Layout Styles" or "Selecting Layout Options" in the Help facility.

Whether you decide to print by choosing File ➤ Print, pressing Ctrl+P, clicking on the Print SmartIcon, or dragging an entry to the Print icon, you have a choice of options that are tailored for printing a particular Organizer section.

These pages provide a brief description of each print option shown in the Print dialog box (Figure 18.19). After selecting options in the dialog box, click on OK.

**Section**    Select the section to be printed (that is, Calendar, To Do, Address, and so on).

**Layout**    Select the layout format. To view a sample of the layout before printing, click on the Layouts button.

**Paper**    Select page dimensions or a particular planner size. To view a sample of the paper and to see the actual dimensions, click on the Layouts button and then click on the Paper button.

**Single Sided**    Click on this option button to print on a single side of each sheet. This is the default.

**Double Sided**    Click on this option button to print on both sides of each sheet. When printing double-sided, Organizer prompts you to turn the paper to the second side and insert it in the printer.

**FIGURE 18.19**

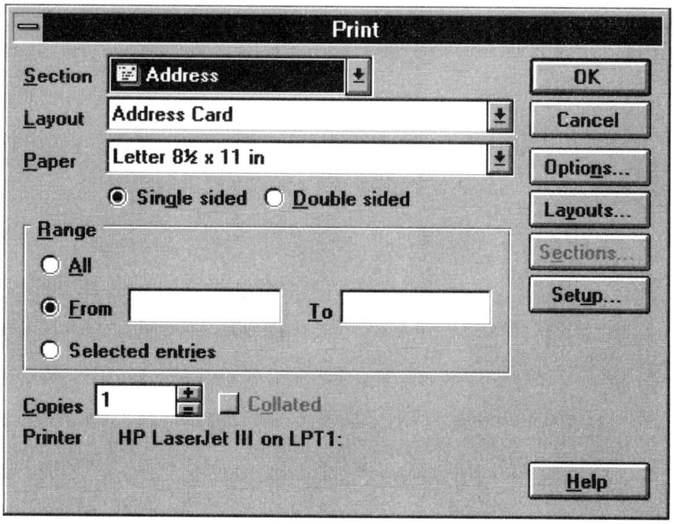

The Print dialog box allows you to select options to customize printing an Organizer section, part of a section, or all sections.

<u>R</u>ange    You have three options:

**All**    Print all the information from the selected section.

**From**    Print a range starting with a value such as the page number, starting name, or date in the first text/list box and ending with the ending value in the <u>T</u>o text/list box.

**Selected Entries**    Print entries that you selected before you chose <u>F</u>ile ➤ <u>P</u>rint.

<u>C</u>opies    Select or type the number of copies that you wish to print.

Co<u>l</u>lated    Print all the pages of a section, starting with the first page and ending with the last page before starting to print the next copy.


For more information about printing in Organizer, see the *Exploring Organizer* manual or look up "Printing" in the Help facility.

# *Appendices*

The last part of this book features four appendices. Appendix A, "Installing Lotus SmartSuite," describes hardware and software requirements, provides detailed instructions on installing SmartSuite and individual applications, and gives you a brief overview of removing an application from your computer system. Appendix B, "Overview of the Windows Environment," provides a thorough introduction for newcomers to Windows. Appendix C, "Customizing Your SmartSuite Environment," helps you customize your SmartSuite applications, and especially SmartIcons, to suit your needs. Appendix D, "SmartSuite Shortcut Keys and Key Combinations," provides a list of the shortcut keys and key combinations common to at least two of the SmartSuite applications.

# A

# Installing Lotus SmartSuite

Than appendix provides information about installing Smart-Suite. Before installing SmartSuite, you should have already installed Windows 3.1 or a more recent version, if available, and installed printers and other peripheral devices using the Windows Control Panel applications. To ensure that you can reinstall a SmartSuite application if something happens to your original installation disks, you should also make copies of the disks and store them away from your computer.

## Minimum Hardware and Software Requirements

These are the minimum requirements for installing a SmartSuite application:

- An IBM PC or 100% compatible personal computer with an 80386, 80486, or higher microprocessor.
- PC DOS, MS-DOS 3.3, or a more recent version.
- Windows 3.1 or a more recent version.
- At least 4 megabytes of RAM (*random access memory*), your computer's main memory and temporary storage area. This ensures that you can run at least one SmartSuite application. The more RAM you have, the better a SmartSuite application runs. To run multiple SmartSuite applications simultaneously, use at least 6 megabytes of RAM.
- A permanent swap file, at least 6 megabytes, if you wish to run more than one SmartSuite application simultaneously. Set up as large a swap file as Windows recommends.
- A floppy disk drive—3.5-inch high-density, for installation and backups.
- An IBM 8514, SVGA (super VGA) or VGA monitor.

■ A mouse or other pointing device compatible with Windows 3.1 or greater.

■ At least 33 megabytes of hard disk drive space for a minimum installation. The amount of space required depends on the files that you choose to install. For a complete installation, reserve at least 62 megabytes.

■ A printer compatible with Windows 3.1 or greater.

# Installing SmartSuite

Installing a SmartSuite application is easy. The installation program displays a series of dialog boxes that help you decide which options to choose. In the first dialog box, choose the type of installation:

**Full Install**     The recommended choice; the installation program installs the SmartSuite application and selects the most appropriate options for you.

**Customize Install**     For experienced users; the installation program allows you to select the SmartSuite application files that you wish to install.

**Minimum Install**     The installation program installs the minimum number of application files.

 **NOTE**     If you wish to reinstall a SmartSuite application at a later time and choose another installation type, just run the installation program again.

In the next dialog box, you can accept the suggested directory, enter another directory name, or select another drive identifier. The installation program displays the approximate amount of hard disk space SmartSuite requires.

To install SmartSuite, follow these steps:

1. After turning on your computer, at the DOS prompt (C:\>), type **win** to start Windows.

2. Insert the first installation disk into the appropriate disk drive.

**Appendices**

3. From the Program Manager window, choose File ➤ Run. Windows opens the Run dialog box.

4. In the Command Line text box, type either **a:install** or **b:install**, depending on the disk drive in which you inserted the installation disk (see step 2). Press ↵. A message box appears. The Lotus SmartSuite Installation Program Welcome and copyright window appears.

5. Type your name and company name in the appropriate text boxes and click on Next.

6. Confirm that the names you entered are correct. The Specify Lotus SmartSuite Directory dialog box appears.

7. Click on Next. If the installation program senses that a SmartSuite application is already on your computer system, you are asked whether you wish to install the new version in the same directory as the existing version.

8. Click on Next to accept the current directories. The Select Lotus Smart-Suite Applications dialog box appears with all applications—SmartCenter, 1-2-3, Ami Pro, Approach, Freelance Graphics, Organizer, and ScreenCam—selected for installation.

  **In the Select Lotus SmartSuite Applications dialog box, you can select specific applications to be installed. So if you need to reinstall an application or add a previously-uninstalled application, check or clear check boxes until only the applications you wish to install are checked.**

9. Click on Next. The installation program displays the Install Options dialog box.

10. Click on Next to select the Default Features - Automatic Install. If you have any questions about the types of installation you can select, click on the Help button. If the installation program finds existing paths for any SmartSuite applications, the Overwrite Existing Paths dialog box appears.

11. Click on Next. The installation program asks whether you wish to install the Document Sharing Application.

**12.** If Lotus Notes is *not* installed on your computer, click on <u>N</u>o. Otherwise, click on <u>Y</u>es. The Select Program Group dialog box appears.

**13.** Click on <u>N</u>ext to accept the suggested program group in which the SmartSuite icons will be displayed.

**14.** Click on <u>Y</u>es to have the installation program start copying files to your hard drive. The installation begins.

**15.** After installing the contents of one disk, the installation program prompts you to insert the next one and either click on OK or press ↵. The installation program shows you how the installation is progressing and informs you when it is complete. At the end of the installation, you are prompted to update AUTOEXEC.BAT.

**16.** Click on <u>M</u>ake Copy. The installation program creates a file named AUTOEXEC.LTS, which you can compare against AUTOEXEC.BAT and copy into AUTOEXEC.BAT.

**17.** Click on <u>D</u>one to return to Windows. Notice that the installation program sets up the Lotus Applications program group.

At the end of the installation, the installation program updates files and asks you if you wish to take the guided tour. If you decline, you return to the Main Menu dialog box. Click on E<u>x</u>it Install to return to Windows. Notice that the installation program sets up the Lotus Applications program group window.

# Removing a SmartSuite Application from Your Computer

If you ever wish to delete a SmartSuite application from your computer, it's important not only to delete the program files but also to consider whether to delete or edit these other entries to save hard disk space:

- the lotusapp directory and its subdirectories in the root directory.
- the directory and subdirectories in which the program files are located.
- initialization files (for example, 123r5.ini, amipro.ini, amipro2.ini, approach.ini, flw2.ini, organize.ini) and other associated files from the

**Appendices**

\windows directory.

■ lotus.ini and progman.ini.

■ win.ini. In particular, look in the [extensions] and [embedding] sections.

  **If you aren't sure which files to delete, don't delete them! Once removed, you will have to completely reinstall the program to get them back again, wasting much of your valuable time. Before deleting any files from your computer, back them up onto floppy disks or tape.**

B

# Overview of the Windows Environment

This appendix is devoted to the Windows novice. You'll learn several ways of starting Windows, find out about its basic elements, and get an overview of how to use the Windows File Manager application, which can help you to run your SmartSuite applications more efficiently. If you need more help or want more details about these or other Windows features, see the *Microsoft Windows User's Guide* or *Mastering Windows 3.1 Special Edition* (SYBEX, 1993).

Windows is a graphical user interface (GUI—pronounced *gooey*), which emphasizes the use of graphics rather than typed commands to get the job done. In most cases, instead of typing one or more commands, you'll select a graphical representation of those commands.

## Starting Windows

The most common way of starting Windows is to type **win** at the DOS prompt and then press ↵. Windows automatically selects the appropriate mode (Standard or 386 Enhanced) for your computer system. Since a minimum requirement for running a SmartSuite application is an 80386 or 80486 microprocessor, you should be in 386 Enhanced mode. The following list provides some of the other ways that you can start Windows:

| | |
|---|---|
| win : | Starts Windows without displaying the introductory logo |
| win/3 | Starts Windows in 386 Enhanced mode |
| win 123w | Starts Windows and then starts 1-2-3 |
| win amipro | Starts Windows and then starts Ami Pro |
| win approach | Starts Windows and then starts Approach |

| win flw | Starts Windows and then starts Freelance Graphics |
| win organize | Starts Windows and then starts Organizer |

# The Basic Components of Windows

The three basic Windows elements are the desktop, the window, and the dialog box. After starting Windows, the first window on the screen is the Program Manager (Figure B.1). The look and contents of this window depend on many factors, including the number and types of programs you have installed, the applications that you use most often, how you like to plan and organize, your favorite colors, and so on.

## Desktop

The entire glass or plastic surface of your monitor is the desktop. The desktop contains all the objects displayed electronically on the screen, including program group windows, dialog boxes, icons, buttons, title bars, scroll bars, and menus.

**FIGURE B.1**

A sample Program Manager window, which contains eight windows—two restored and six minimized.

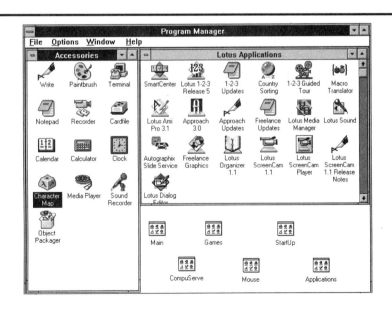

## Program Group Windows

A window is a large or small rectangular area within the desktop. You can usually change the size and location of a window. Obviously, if a window takes up the entire desktop, it's impossible to move. However, once you decrease its size, you can move it around the desktop and change its size.

Figure B.1 (above) shows windows in three sizes. The largest window, the Program Manager, is *maximized*; it can't get any bigger. The six very small windows are *minimized*; they can be no smaller. The two intermediate windows are *restored*; you can adjust their size.

Each program group window, regardless of its size, can contain one or more applications—related or not. Although the Windows Setup installation program sets up your initial program group windows, you can add, change, or delete program group windows and their contents. Applications in program group windows are represented by *icons*, which are small graphics.

  The Startup program group has one special characteristic: all the programs in this group start automatically when you start Windows. For example, if you use Organizer every day immediately after you start work, put its icon in Startup. Then after starting Windows, you'll have the Organizer application window on your desktop, ready to go. After you first install Windows, the Startup group is empty. It's up to you to add appropriate applications.

## Dialog Boxes

Windows displays a dialog box, which is a small window, when you select many commands. Dialog boxes (Figure B.2) contain some elements that are common to other windows and others that are unique to dialog boxes. You'll learn about these elements later in this appendix.

**FIGURE B.2**

The Windows International - Date Format dialog box, which shows some of the options available in a typical dialog box.

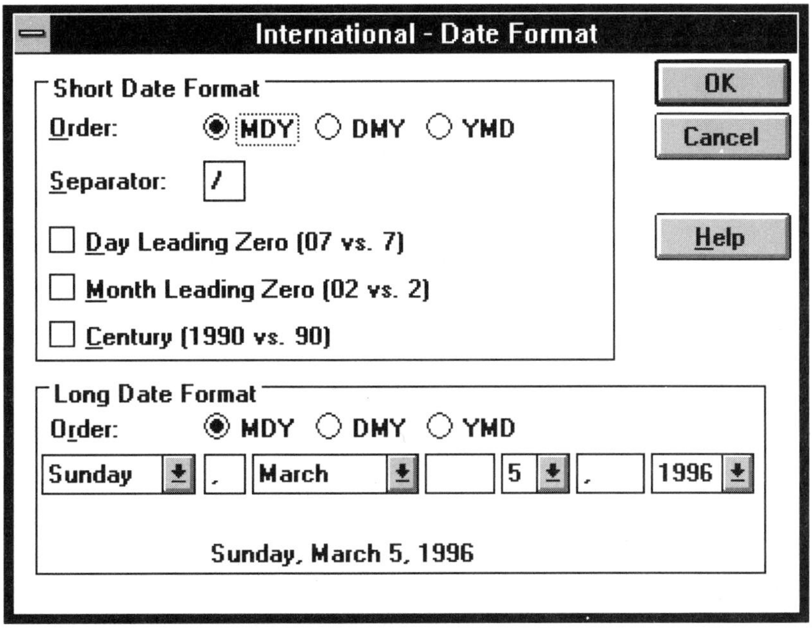

## Elements of a Window

Although at first glance, the Program Manager window seems to be cluttered with all sorts of objects, once you place them into their categories, you'll have a better idea of how Windows works.

### Title Bar

The title bar, the topmost element, displays the name of the window or dialog box and contains one or more buttons.

### Control Menu Button

On the left side of the title bar of both windows and dialog boxes is the *Control Menu button*, which controls window size and position and allows you to either close the window or application or to switch to another Windows application. Click on the Control Menu button to open a menu from which you

Appendices

can select commands. Double-click on the control menu to close the window (and therefore the application or document inside the window) or dialog box.

**NOTE** To open a menu using the keyboard, press the Alt key and then press the selection key, the underlined letter in the word (for example, the H in <u>H</u>elp)

To move a window to a new location using the keyboard, press Ctrl+M and press any combination of ←, →, ↓, and ↑. To move a window using the mouse, move the mouse pointer to the title bar, click and hold down the left mouse button, and drag the window.

To size a window using the keyboard, press Ctrl+S and press any combination of ←, →, ↓, and ↑. To size a window using the mouse, move the mouse pointer to any border or corner of the window. When the mouse pointer changes to a double-pointing arrow, click and hold down the left mouse button and drag the border or corner.

## Minimize Button

On the right side of a window title bar, the *minimize button* allows you to reduce an active application to an icon. The application still runs in its minimized state but gives you room to view one or more other open windows.

## Maximize Button

On the right side of a window title bar, the *maximize button* enables you to increase the size of a minimized or restored active window to the entire computer screen. If a window is already maximized, you'll see the restore button in place of the maximize button.

## Restore Button

On the right side of a window title bar, the *restore button* decreases a maximized window so that its dimensions are the same as its last restored size. If a window is restored, you'll see the maximize button in place of the restore button.

# Menu Bar

Immediately beneath the title bar, the menu bar displays the main Windows commands. Move the mouse pointer to a word on the menu bar and click, and Windows opens a menu of commands.

## Menu Commands

Once you open a menu, you can select a command by clicking on it. You can close the menu by clicking again at the top of the menu or anywhere on the desktop outside the list of menu commands. To select a command using the keyboard, press the underlined letter. To close a pull-down menu using the keyboard, press Esc.

Here are some additional facts about the commands in menus:

- Related commands on a menu are grouped together and separated from other groups of commands with a horizontal line.

- If a command looks dimmed, it is inactive. You'll have to perform some action before you can use the command. For example, to choose Edit ➤ Undo, you must have performed an action that can be undone.

- If a command is preceded by a check mark, this command can be turned on or off. For example, in Windows if you choose Options ➤ Save Settings on Exit, when you end this Windows session, all the changes that you have made are saved. However, if the Save Settings on Exit command is not preceded by a check mark, changes are not saved.

**TIP**
A novice Windows user can inadvertently cause some bizarre effects on the desktop. One way of quickly returning to your previous desktop settings is to choose Options ➤ Save Settings on Exit (to inactivate the command), exit Windows, and start Windows again. After you restart Windows, choose Options ➤ Save Settings on Exit to activate the command (i.e., put a check mark before the command) so that Windows will save your settings the next time you exit.

**Appendices**

■ If a command is followed by an *ellipsis* (…), selecting the command opens a dialog box in which you select choices and type text. Figure B.2 (above) shows a typical dialog box and its options.

■ If a command is followed by a right-pointing arrow, selecting the command opens a *cascading menu*, which is a submenu from which you can select another command.

■ If a command is preceded by a dot, the command function is the current selection.

## Scroll Bars

There are two types of scroll bars—the vertical bar (see Figure B.1) at the right side of some windows, lists, and work areas, and the horizontal bar at the bottom of some windows, lists, and work areas. Pressing and holding down the left mouse button on the arrows at the ends of the scroll bar, and dragging the *scroll box* or *thumb* (the small box inside the scroll bar) allow you to move around a file or window. The scroll box also indicates your current location in a document. For example, the scroll box in Figure B.1 indicates that you are viewing the top of the window. The absence of a scroll bar indicates that you are viewing the entire contents of a window, file list, or work area.

## Elements of a Dialog Box

As you have already learned, a dialog box is a small window that has many of the characteristics of other windows. For example, all dialog boxes have a title bar and most have a control menu button. Some dialog boxes even have their own menu bars from which you can open menus and select commands. Dialog boxes also have their own unique elements, as shown in Table B.1.

## Managing Files Using File Manager

You can use File Manager to manage your files more efficiently than you can from within a Windows application, such as any SmartSuite application. For example, you can delete superfluous files, create a new 1-2-3 subdirectory and

**TABLE B.1:** Dialog Box Elements

| ELEMENT | NAME | DESCRIPTION |
|---|---|---|
| `.SAM` | text box | A box into which you type information, such as a file name or option name. A text box often is combined with a list box, forming a text/list box. |
| `[-c-]` `[-a-]` `[-b-]` `[-c-]` | drop-down list box | A box, which when opened, displays a list of options from which you can choose. |
| `OK` | command button | A button, which when selected, implements a command. Common command buttons are OK, Cancel, Close, and Help. |
| ⊠ ☐ | check box | A box in which you either place an X (check) or remove the X (clear). The third setting for a check box is shaded, which indicates that a selection includes a combination of both choices or has neither choice. In a group of check boxes, you can check or clear any combination. |
| ◉ ○ | option button | Also known as a radio button, from which you can select just one option. When you select an option button, all other option buttons in the group are cleared. |
| `2` | list box | A box that contains a list of options from which you can select. Just click on the up or down arrow to move up or down through the list, respectively. A list box often is combined with a text box, forming a text/list box. |
| `Header` | dotted box | A border that indicates your current position in the dialog box. |

**Appendices**

then move a group of files to it, rename a group of files, and so on. Although you will only learn a few File Manager functions in this section, you can learn more by reading the *Microsoft Windows User's Guide* or *Mastering Windows 3.1 Special Edition* (SYBEX, 1993).

To start File Manager, double-click on its icon. Windows displays the File Manager window (Figure B.3). On the left side of the window is the Tree pane, which displays icons representing directories and subdirectories for the current drive. On the right side of the window is the Contents pane, which lists the directories and files in the currently selected directory.

## Finding Files

If you know the directory of a file, you can click on the directory icon in the Tree pane and then, in the Contents pane, look for the icon representing the file.

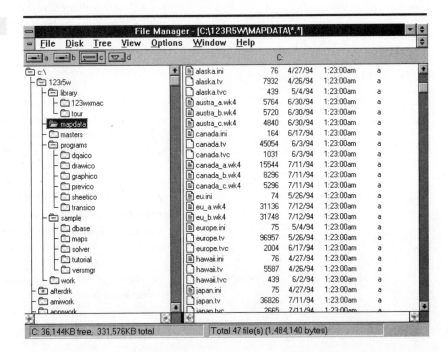

**FIGURE B.3**

The File Manager window with the Tree pane and the Contents pane

To search for a file or group of files if you don't know the directories in which they are located, File Manager provides the Searc<u>h</u> command on the <u>F</u>ile menu. To search throughout the current drive, display the top of the Tree pane and click on the root directory icon (for example, *c*: for a hard drive or *a*: for a disk drive). Then choose <u>F</u>ile ➤ Searc<u>h</u>. In the <u>S</u>earch for text box in the Search dialog box, type your search criteria. For example, type **abc\*.\*** to search for a file whose first three characters are **abc**, which ends with any number of characters, and which has any extension. For a successful search, File Manager displays a list of found files.

## Deleting Files

The quickest way to delete one or more files is to select them in the Contents pane, press Del, and confirm the deletion, if asked.

## Creating a Subdirectory

To create a subdirectory, click on the icon representing the directory under which the new subdirectory will reside. Then choose <u>F</u>ile ➤ Cr<u>e</u>ate Directory. In <u>N</u>ame text box in the Create Directory dialog box, type a directory name that is no longer than eight characters and that follows other DOS conventions. See your DOS documentation for more information.

## Moving Files

The fastest way to move files from one directory to another within the same drive is by using drag and drop. First adjust your view of the Tree pane so that you can see the icons for both the source directory (which currently holds the files) and the destination directory (to which you are moving the files). Then click on the icon for the source directory, select the files to be moved, and drag them to the target directory.

The other way to move files is to select them, choose <u>F</u>ile ➤ <u>M</u>ove or press F7, and type the destination directory in the <u>T</u>o text box in the Move dialog box. If you haven't selected one or more files to be moved, you will have to fill in the <u>F</u>rom text box as well. Then either click on OK or press ↵.

## Copying Files

The copy operation is almost identical to the move operation. However, if you are copying files within the same drive, be aware that moving files is not the same as copying them, but you can also use drag and drop to copy files from one directory in one drive to another directory on another drive. Just press and hold down Ctrl and then drag and drop. You'll drag a copy to its new location, keeping the original in its original location.

The other way to copy files is to select them, choose File ➤ Copy or press F8, and type the destination directory in the To text box in the Copy dialog box. If you haven't selected one or more files to be copied, you will have to fill in the From text box as well. Then either click on OK or press ↵.

 **TIP** Copying files is a quick way of backing up. Just copy files to a disk and store the disk in an area away from your computer.

## Renaming Files

If your company develops file naming conventions and you must rename your files, choosing File ➤ Rename is the most efficient way to rename them. To rename a file, select it in the Contents window, choose File ➤ Rename, and fill in the From (if needed) and To text boxes in the Rename dialog box.

# Customizing Your SmartSuite Environment

This appendix provides information about customizing your working environment in each of the SmartSuite applications. The first part of the appendix provides an overview of ways in which you can change your environment, application by application. The second part deals with customizing SmartIcons.

# Changing Your 1-2-3 Environment

In 1-2-3, you can determine the way in which you view the current spreadsheet and/or future spreadsheets, set worksheet default formats, and select default formats and user setup options.

## Changing View Preferences

Choose View ➤ Set View Preferences to open the Set View Preferences dialog box (Figure C.1), in which you can change your view preferences.

These are the options in this dialog box:

**Worksheet Frame**    Check this check box (the default) to change the display of the frame around the worksheet (clear it to have no display of row and column labels):

- *Standard* displays the familiar lettered column labels and numbered row labels. This is the default.

- *Characters* displays even-numbered column and row labels, beginning with 2.

- *Inches* displays numbered row and column labels every inch.(The columns and rows are by default an inch wide.)

FIGURE C.1

The 1-2-3 Set View Preferences dialog box, showing its default settings

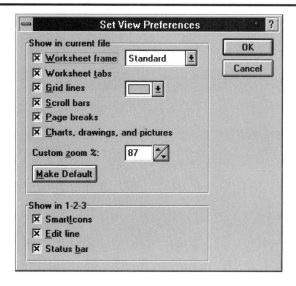

■ *Metric* displays numbered row and column labels every centimeter.

■ *Points/Picas* displays even-numbered row labels in points and column labels in picas.

**Worksheet Tabs**    Check this check box to display a tab for every spreadsheet in this file (the default); clear the check box to clear tabs from the window.

**Grid Lines**    Check this check box to display grid lines in the application window (the default). To change the color of grid lines, click on the downward-pointing arrow to open a color palette. Clear this check box to clear grid lines from the window.

**Scroll Bars**    Check this check box to display horizontal and vertical scroll bars in the application window (the default). Clear this check box to clear the scroll bars from the window.

**Page Breaks**    Check this check box to display page breaks in the application window (the default). Clear this check box to clear page breaks from the window.

**Charts, Drawings, and Pictures**    Check this check box to display charts, drawings, and pictures in the application window (the default).

Clear this check box to dim the <u>C</u>hart and <u>D</u>raw commands so that you can't even create charts, drawings, and pictures for this spreadsheet.

**Custom <u>Z</u>oom %**     Check this check box to set the custom zoom to a value from 25% to 400%. Then when you choose <u>V</u>iew ➤ <u>C</u>ustom, 1-2-3 zooms the spreadsheet to the specified value.

**<u>M</u>ake Default**     Click on this button to make the new setings the default for future spreadsheets.

**Smart<u>I</u>cons, <u>E</u>dit Line, Status <u>B</u>ar**     Check this check box to display these elements on the application window (the default). Clear this check box to remove the elements from the application window.

## Changing Default Settings

Choose <u>S</u>tyle ➤ <u>W</u>orksheet Defaults to open the Worksheet Defaults dialog box (Figure C.2), in which you can set your worksheet defaults.

These are the options in this dialog box:

**<u>F</u>ace**     Type a font name in the text box or select a font name from the scroll box. The default is Arial MT.

**<u>S</u>ize**     Type a point size in the text box or select a point size from the scroll box. The default is 12.

**<u>M</u>ake Default**     Click on this button to make the selected options the default.

**F<u>o</u>rmat**     Select a number format from the drop-down list box. The default format is Automatic.

**Display <u>Z</u>eros as**     Check this check box to display zeros as a value that you type in the text box. Clear this check box to hide zeros immediately after you type them in the spreadsheet. The default is to display zeros as 0.

**<u>P</u>arentheses**     Check this check box to display the contents of cells within parentheses, whether they are positive or negative values. Clear

**FIGURE C.2**

The 1-2-3 Worksheet
Defaults dialog box,
with its default settings

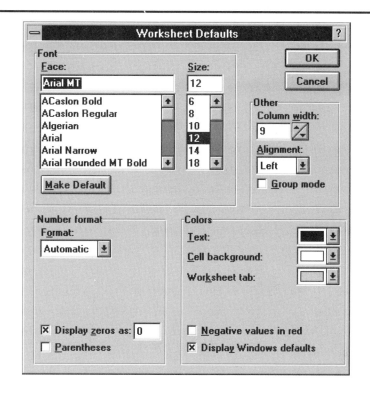

this check box (the default) to display the contents of cells without parentheses.

**Column Width**    Type or select a column width value from 1 to 240 characters. The default is 9.

**Alignment**    Select the cell alignment: Left, Right, or Center. The default is Left.

**Group Mode**    Check this check box to apply all the worksheet defaults to every worksheet in this file. Clear this check box (the default) to apply the worksheet defaults to just the current worksheet.

**Text**    Open this drop-down list box to reveal a color palette from which you can select a new default text color. The starting default color is black.

**Cell Background**     Open this drop-down list box to reveal a color palette from which you can select a new default cell background color. The starting default color is white.

**Worksheet Tab**     Open this drop-down box to reveal a color palette from which you can select worksheet colors.

**Negative Values in Red**     Check this check box to display negative values in red. Clear the check box (the default) to display negative values in the current text color.

**Display Windows Defaults**     Returns the defaults to the original settings (for example, black text on a white background).

## Changing User Setup

Choose Tools ➤ User Setup to open the User Setup dialog box (Figure C.3), in which you can specify user defaults. The 123r4.ini initialization file stores these settings.

These are the options in this dialog box:

**Skip New File and Welcome Screens**     Check this box to start 1-2-3 without a prompting checkbox. A clear screen is the default.

**Drag-and-Drop Cells**     Check this check box to be able to drag and drop cells with your mouse. This is the default.

**Confirm Drag-and-Drop**     Check this check box (the default) to have 1-2-3 warn you if drag-and-drop will overwrite data.

**Use Automatic Format**     Check this check box (the default) to set the default format to Automatic. Clear this check box to set the default format to General.

**Save Files Every n Minutes**     Check this check box and either type or select a value to have 1-2-3 automatically save the current file every 1 to 99 minutes, with a default of 10 minutes. The default is a cleared check box.

**FIGURE C.3**

The 1-2-3 User Setup
Defaults dialog box,
with its default settings

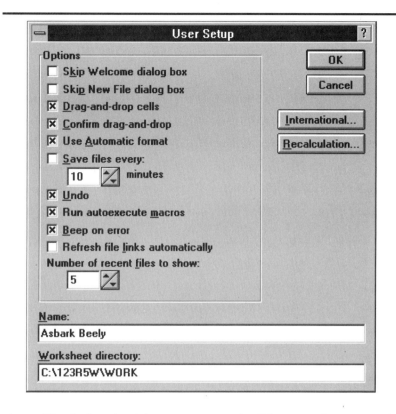

**Undo**    Check this check box to activate the Edit ➤ Undo command. This is the default.

**Run Autoexecute Macros**    Check this check box (the default) to automatically run autoexecute macros when you start 1-2-3.

**Beep on Error**    Check this check box (the default) to beep when an error occurs or when 1-2-3 encounters a {Beep} command in a macro. In order to hear a beep, you must check the Enable System Sounds check box in the Sound dialog box in the Windows Control Panel.

**Refresh File Links Automatically**    Check this box to refresh links between files when you open a 1-2-3 file. A cleared check box is the default.

**Number of Recent Files to Show**    Type or select a value from 0 to 5 to set the number of recent files to be displayed at the bottom of the File menu. The default is 4. To open one of the files on the File menu, just click on the file name or type the underlined number preceding the file name.

**Name**    Type the name of the individual who uses this copy of 1-2-3. This name is the one that is "stamped" in 1-2-3 (for example, in the Version Manager).

**Worksheet Directory**    Type the path and subdirectory in which you wish 1-2-3 files to be stored.

**International**    Click on this button to open a dialog box in which you can set date and time formats; translate .WK1 and text files; define the characters used for decimal points, thousands separators, argument separators, and negative numbers; and specify the symbol and position of the currency character.

**Recalculation**    Click on this button to open a dialog box in which you can choose to recalculate automatically or manually and set other recalculation options.

# Changing Your Ami Pro Environment

In Ami Pro, you can specify the way in which you view documents, and select default formats and user setup options.

## Changing View Preferences

Choose View ➤ View Preferences or click on the View Preferences Smart-Icon to open the View Preferences dialog box (Figure C.4), where you can specify the way in which you view documents.

These are the options in this dialog box:

**Column Guides**    Check this check box to display vertical lines that mark the borders of columns. The default is a cleared check box.

FIGURE C.4

The Ami Pro View
Preferences dialog box,
with its default settings

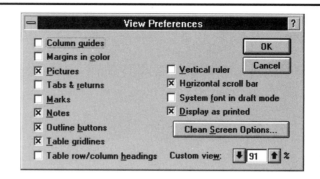

**Margins in Color**    Check this check box to display the margins in a different color or with a pattern. The default is a cleared check box.

**Pictures**    Check this check box (the default) to display pictures in frames. If you clear this check box, Ami Pro displays a frame but not the picture within.

**Tabs & Returns**    Check this check box to display tab marks and carriage returns in documents. The default is a cleared check box.

**Marks**    Check this check box to display marks (column breaks, page breaks, inserted rulers, inserted page layouts, floating headers, floating footers, and DDE links) in documents. The default is a cleared check box.

**Notes**    Check this check box (the default) to display the mark that indicates the location of a note in a document.

**Outline Buttons**    Check this check box (the default) to display the button that indicates an outline element in outline mode.

**Table Gridlines**    Check this check box (the default) to show the gridlines marking the borders of cells in a table.

**Table Row/Column Headings**    Check this check box to show row and column headings (like spreadsheet labels) in a table when you are editing it. The default is a cleared check box.

**Vertical Ruler**    Check this check box to display a vertical ruler in the application window. The default is a cleared check box.

**Horizontal Scroll Bar**    Check this check box (the default) to display a horizontal scroll bar in the application window.

**System Font in Draft Mode**    Check this check box to display text in Windows System font in Draft mode. When you clear this check box (the default), Draft mode text is either the paragraph style font or the font that you have applied.

**Display as Printed**    Check this check box (the default) to display the document as it will print (WYSIWYG). A cleared check box tailors the fit of the display to the screen rather than to the printer.

**Clean Screen Options**    Click on this button to display a dialog box in which you can indicate the elements that are displayed on a clean screen. Check or clear check boxes for the title bar, menu, SmartIcons, status bar, vertical and horizontal scroll bar, and the Return icon (on which you click to return to the standard screen display). The default condition of all the check boxes except the Return icon is a cleared check box.

**Custom View**    Select a value to set the custom view to a value from 10% to 400%. The default is 91%. Then when you choose View ➤ Custom, Ami Pro zooms the document to the specified value.

## Changing User Setup

Choose Tools ➤ User Setup to open the User Setup dialog box (Figure C.5), in which you can specify user defaults.

These are the options in this dialog box:

**Auto Backup**    Check this check box to create a backup file whenever you save a document. The default is a cleared check box.

FIGURE C.5

The Ami Pro User
Setup dialog box, with
its default settings

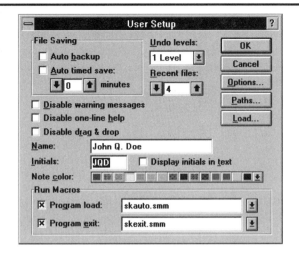

 **WARNING**

Because Ami Pro gives a backup file the same name and
extension as the original document, click on Paths and
specify a subdirectory in which Ami Pro will store backup
files. If you don't do this, every time you save a file, the
backup file will immediately overwrite the new version.

**Auto Timed Save**     Check this check box and either type or select a
value from 1 to 99 minutes in the text/list box to have Ami Pro automatically save your documents. As you work on a document, Ami Pro keeps
track of the number of minutes since the last save. When the count
reaches the minutes specified and you pause in your work, Ami Pro saves
the document. A cleared check box is the default.

**Disable Warning Messages**     Check this check box to instruct Ami
Pro to not display a message when you delete text that includes embedded markers (notes, page breaks, inserted page layouts, anchored frames,
footnotes, page tables, floating headers, floating footers, power fields,
and DDE links). The default is a cleared check box.

**Disable One-Line Help**     Check this check box to suppress the display of
command descriptions in the status bar. The default is a cleared check box.

**Appendices**

**Disable Drag & Drop**    Check this check box to disable the drag & drop feature for moving and copying a selection.

**Name**    Type the name of the individual who uses this copy of Ami Pro. This name is the one that is "stamped" in Ami Pro (for example, in Notes and in some Ami Pro templates). The default is the name entered at installation.

**Initials**    Type the initials (up to six characters) to be inserted on notes. The default is the first letter of every part (for example, first name, middle initial, and last name) of the name entered at installation.

**Display Initials in Text**    Check this check box to display the initials and a note number when you use notes in a document. The default is a cleared check box.

**Note Color**    Click on a color button or click on the downward-pointing arrow to open a color palette from which you can choose a color for notes.

**Program Load**    From the drop-down list, select a macro to run whenever you start Ami Pro.

**NOTE** To stop the SwitchKit from displaying when you start Ami Pro, either clear the check box or select a macro other then skauto.smm.

**Program Exit**    From the drop-down list, select a macro to run whenever you exit Ami Pro.

**Undo Levels**    Open this drop-down list box to specify the number of actions (from None to four levels) that Ami Pro will go back to undo. The default is 1 Level. In order to undo an action, Ami Pro must save the prior settings in a storage area (buffer). So, for every Undo Level, Ami Pro must set aside a buffer. For this reason, when you select more levels, Ami Pro's processing speed slows.

**Recent Files**    Type or select a value from 0 to 5 to set the number of recent files to be displayed at the bottom of the File menu. The default is 4.

To open one of the files on the File menu, just click on the file name or type the underlined number preceding the file name.

**Options**     Click on this button to display the User Setup Options dialog box (Figure C.6) in which you can set a hyphenation hot-zone, select window/orphan control, turn on or off pair kerning, specify hyphenation options, indicate whether printing and text flow occurs in the background, and specify graphic display speed options. For more information, see the Help topics "Setting Typographic Options" and "Setting Speed Options."

**FIGURE C.6**

The Ami Pro User Setup Options dialog box, with its default settings

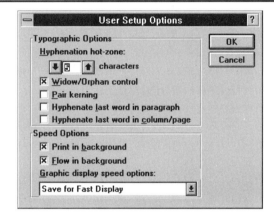

**Paths**     Click on this button to display the Default Paths dialog box (Figure C.7), which allows you to define paths for documents, style sheets, backups, macros, and SmartIcons. For more information, see the Help topic "Setting Default Paths."

**FIGURE C.7**

The Ami Pro Default Paths dialog box, with its default settings

**Appendices**

**699**

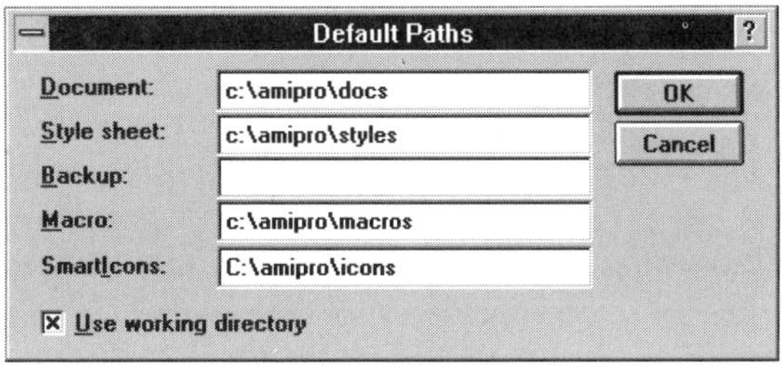

**Load**    Click on this button to display the Load Defaults dialog box (Figure C.8), which allows you to specify the starting view, mode, and style sheet when you start Ami Pro. You can start with these view options: Custom or Standard, and Clean Screen, Styles Box, and/or Maximized window. You can start in Layout, Outline, or Draft mode. You can select the default style sheet (Default is the default) and the way that the style sheets are listed in the New dialog box (check the List by Description check box, the default) or a list of style sheet file names (clear the List by Description check box). For more information, see the Help topic "Setting Load Defaults."

**FIGURE C.8**

The Ami Pro Load
Defaults dialog box,
with its default settings

# Changing Your Approach Environment

In Approach, you can change your environment using the Preferences dialog box (Figure C.9). Just choose Tools ➤ Preferences and click on one of the seven tabs: Display, Order, Password, Dialer, Database, Index, or General. Then select the desired options, click on the Save Default button if you wish to make the settings your new defaults, and click on OK.

FIGURE C.9

The Approach
Preferences dialog
box, showing the
Display options

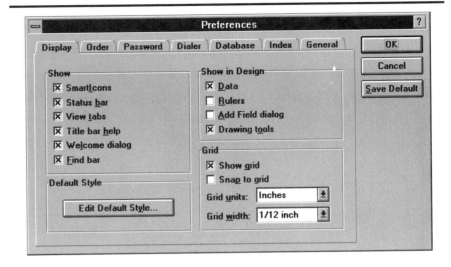

Click on the Display tab to display or hide elements on the Approach window
and in the Design environment. In addition, use this section to edit the default style. These are the options in this section of the dialog box:

**SmartIcons**    Check this check box to display the SmartIcons bar on
the Approach window. This is the default.

**Status Bar**    Check this check box to display the status bar at the bottom of the Approach window. This is the default.

**View Tabs**    Check this check box to display the view tabs right below
the SmartIcons bar on the Approach window. This is the default.

**Title Bar Help**    Check this check box to display in the title bar a
short description of the selected menu or command. This is the default.

**Welcome Dialog**    Check this check box to display a Welcome dialog
box when you first start Approach. This is the default.

**Find Bar**    Check this check box to display the Find button bar under
the Find SmartIcons in the Find environment. This is the default.

**Edit Default Style**    Click on this button to open the Define Style dialog
box in which you can change the default style, including field attributes,

lines and color for borders and fill, label attributes, picture attributes, and background color and border.

**Data**    Check this check box to show your data in the Design environment. This is the default.

**Rulers**    Check this check box to display the rulers in the Design environment. A cleared check box is the default.

**Add Field Dialog**    Check this check box to display the Add Field dialog box in the Design Environment. A cleared check box is the default.

**Drawing Tools**    Check this check box to display the drawing tools palette in the Design Environment. This is the default.

**Show Grid**    Check this check box to show the grid in the Design environment. This is the default.

**Snap to Grid**    Check this check box to have graphic elements snap to the grid when you move or create them. A cleared check box is the default.

**Grid Units**    Open this drop-down list box to select the unit of measure: inches (the default) or centimeters.

**Grid Width**    Click on this drop-down list box to choose the width of the grid (in inches): $\frac{1}{16}$, $\frac{1}{12}$ (the default), $\frac{1}{8}$, $\frac{1}{4}$, or $\frac{1}{2}$. If you choose a small width measurement, you'll be able to fine-tune the positions of elements on forms.

Click on the Order tab to display the Order section of the Preferences dialog box (Figure C.10) to specify the order in which records are sorted in the Browse environment.

These are the options in this section of the dialog box:

**Maintain Default Sort for**    Open this drop-down list box and select the database affected by changes in order.

**Database Fields**    Select a sort field from this scroll box.

**Add**    Click on this button to add the selected sort field to the Fields to Sort on box.

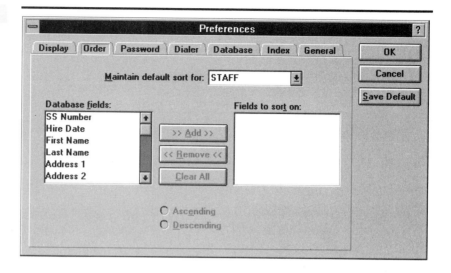

The Approach
Preferences dialog
box, showing the
Order options

**Remove**    Click on this button to remove the selected field from the
Fields to Sort on box.

**Clear All**    Click on this button to clear all the fields from the Fields
to Sort on box.

**Fields to Sort on**    A box in which selected sort fields are contained.

**Ascending**    Click on this option button to specify that fields are
sorted from A to Z. This is the default.

**Descending**    Click on this option button to specify that fields are
sorted from Z to A.

Click on the Password tab to display the Password section of the Preferences
dialog box (Figure C.11) so that you can protect the selected database.

These are the options in this section of the dialog box:

**Password for This Approach File**    To define a password for this Approach file, check the check box and type a password in the text box. Retype the password in the Confirm Password dialog box; then click on OK.

**Database Name**    Open this drop-down list box and select a database,
if needed.

**Appendices**

FIGURE C.11

The Approach
Preferences dialog box,
showing the Password
options

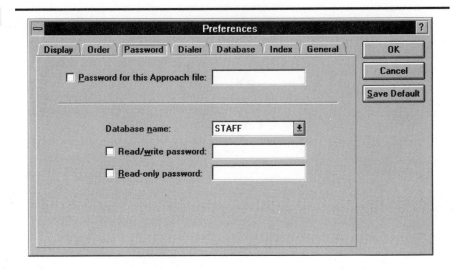

**Read/Write Password**    To define a read/write password for this database, check the check box and type a password in the text box. Retype the password in the Confirm Password dialog box; then click on OK.

**Read-Only Password**    To define a read-only password for this database, check the check box and type a password in the text box. Retype the password in the Confirm Password dialog box; then click on OK.

Click on the Dialer tab to display the Dialer section of the Preferences dialog box (Figure C.12) so that you can specify communications defaults.

These are the options in this section of the dialog box:

**Modem Port**    Open this drop-down list box and select the communications port to which your modem is connected.

**Baud Rate**    Open this drop-down list box and select your modem's baud rate.

**Dial Prefix**    In this text box, type the code for your dial prefix, or accept the default code.

FIGURE C.12

The Approach
Preferences dialog
box, showing the
Dialer options

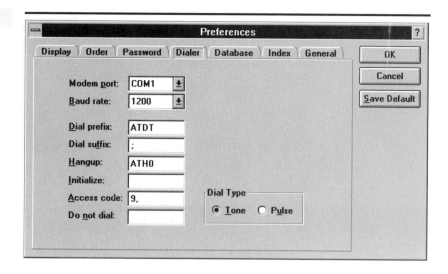

**Dial Suffix**   In this text box, type the code for your dial suffix, or accept the default code.

**Hangup**   In this text box, type the code to "hang up" the modem, or accept the default code.

**Initialize**   In this text box, type the code to initialize the modem, or accept the default code.

**Access Code**   In this text box, type the access code to dial out, or accept the default code.

**Do Not Dial**   In this text box, type the code that you wish to use to stop dialing.

**Tone**   Click on this option button if your telephone is the touch-tone type.

**Pulse**   Click on this option button if your telephone is the pulse type.

Click on the Database tab to display the Dialer section of the Preferences dialog box (Figure C.13) so that you can specify database defaults.

### FIGURE C.13

The Approach Preferences dialog box, showing the Database options

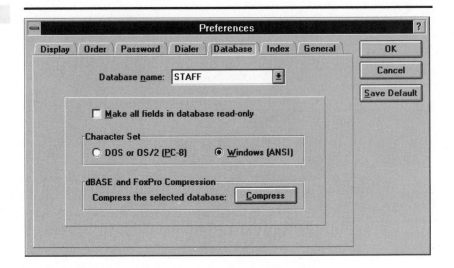

These are the options in this section of the dialog box:

**Database Name**    Open this drop-down list box and select the database to which you will apply changes to the defaults. The current database is already selected.

**Make All Fields in Database Read-Only**    Check this check box to make all the fields in the selected database read-only. This prevents others from editing your work. The default is a cleared check box.

**DOS or OS/2 (PC-8)**    Check this option to use characters from the PC-8 character set.

**Windows (ANSI)**    Check this option to use characters from the ANSI character set furnished with Windows.

**Compress**    Click on this button to compress the selected database.

**You can also set database options for a Paradox file or for SQL tables. For more information, see the User's Guide.**

Click on the Index tab to display the Index section of the Preferences dialog box (Figure C.14) to associate an index with a database or close an index.

**FIGURE C.14**

The Approach Preferences dialog box, showing the Index options

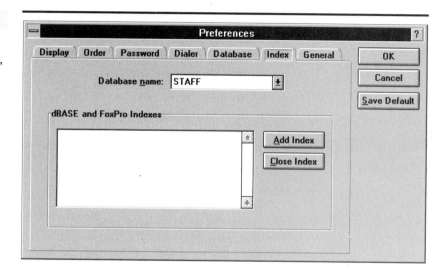

These are the options in this section of the dialog box:

**Database Name**     Open this drop-down list box and select the database to which you will apply changes to the defaults. The current database is already selected.

**Add Index**     Click on this button to add the selected index to the current database in order to maintain it for either dBASE or FoxPro.

**Close Index**     Click on this button to close the selected index and no longer maintain it for either dBASE or FoxPro.

Click on the General tab to display the General section of the Preferences dialog box (Figure C.15) to specify miscellaneous attributes.

**Appendices**

**FIGURE C.15**

The Approach
Preferences dialog
box, showing the
General options

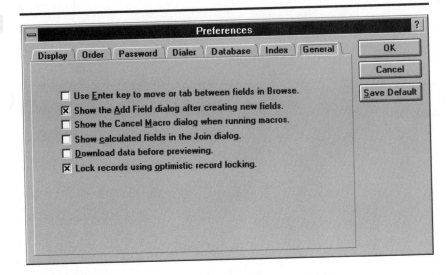

These are the options in this section of the dialog box:

**Use Enter Key to Move or Tab between Fields in Browse**   Check this check box to be able to use ↵ in the same way that you use the Tab key to move from field to field. A cleared check box is the default.

**Show the Add Field Dialog after Creating New Fields**   Check this check box to display the Add Field dialog box after you add a new field to a database. This is the default.

**Show the Cancel Macro Dialog when Running Macros**   Check this check box to display the Cancel Macro dialog box while you are running a macro. A cleared check box is the default.

**Show Calculated Fields in the Join Dialog**   Check this check box to display calculated fields in the Join dialog box when you are joining databases. A cleared check box is the default.

**Download Data before Previewing**   Check this check box to have Approach download a copy of the current database to your hard drive whenever you go to the Preview environment.

**Lock Records using Optimistic Record Locking**   Check this check box to allow simultaneous editing by individuals on a networked version of Approach. When two users work on the same record, Approach allows the first user to save and then alerts the second user that someone has just changed the record and asks whether he or she wishes to overwrite those changes.

# Changing Your Freelance Graphics Environment

In Freelance Graphics, you can determine how your application appears in the application window, specify the unit of measure, select grid options, define style defaults for objects, and select certain formats and user setup options.

## Changing View Preferences

Choose View ➤ View Preferences to open the View Preferences dialog box (Figure C.16), in which you can change your view preferences.

**FIGURE C.16**

The Freelance Graphics View Preferences dialog box, with its default settings

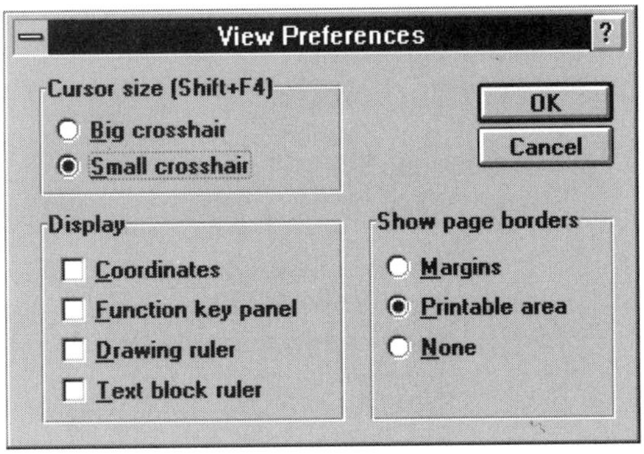

These are the options in this dialog box:

**Cursor Size**    Choose Big Crosshair or Small Crosshair (the default) for drawing on a presentation page. Press Shift+F4 to switch between big and small crosshairs.

<u>C</u>oordinates    Check this check box to display X and Y coordinates in the edit line, between the menu bar and SmartIcons. A cleared check box is the default.

<u>F</u>unction Key Panel    Check this check box to display a function key panel at the bottom of the application window. Then you can click on a function key in the panel to perform an action. A cleared check box is the default.

<u>D</u>rawing Ruler    Check this check box to display horizontal and vertical rulers using the default unit of measure (millimeters, centimeters, inches, points, or picas). A cleared check box is the default.

<u>T</u>ext Block Ruler    Check this check box to display a ruler within an open text block box. A cleared check box is the default.

Show Page Borders    Click on one of three option buttons: selecting <u>M</u>argins displays a dashed border indicating the margins; <u>P</u>rintable Area displays a dashed border indicating the area that your current printer driver can print, and <u>N</u>one does not display any border.

## Changing the Unit of Measure and Specifying Grid Options

Choose <u>V</u>iew ➤ <u>U</u>nits & Grids to open the Units & Grids dialog box (Figure C.17), in which you can change your unit of measure and specify grid options.

These are the options in this dialog box:

Units    Click on an option button to select the default unit of measure: <u>M</u>illimeters (the default), <u>C</u>entimeters, <u>I</u>nches, <u>P</u>oints, or Pic<u>a</u>s.

<u>D</u>isplay Grid    Check this check box to display the grid, which allows you to align objects on presentation pages. A cleared check box is the default.

<u>S</u>nap to Grid    Check this check box (or press Shift+F7) to place objects on the grid lines as you add them to the page. Objects already on the page do not snap to the grid after you select this option; you must move them. A cleared check box is the default.

FIGURE C.17

The Freelance
Graphics Units &
Grids dialog box, with
its default settings

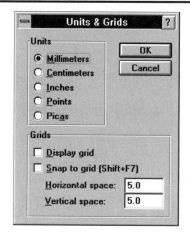

Horizontal Space    Type a value for the measurement between horizontal dots on the grid. Valid values are from 0.2 to 93.4 with only one decimal digit. The default value is 5.0 millimeters or the equivalent for your default unit of measure.

Vertical Space    Type a value for the measurement between vertical dots on the grid. Valid values are from 0.2 to 93.4 with only one decimal digit. The default value is 5.0 millimeters or the equivalent for your default unit of measure.

## Changing Style Attributes for Drawing Tools and Objects

Choose Style ➤ Default Attributes to open one of seven dialog boxes, in which you can change attributes for drawing tools, rectangles, lines and curves, paragraph styles, polygons and shapes, circles/ellipses, and bitmaps. Figure C.18 shows the Style Default Attributes Mixed dialog box. You must be in current page mode to open this dialog box.

**NOTE**

The Paragraph Styles dialog box, which is identical to the Default Paragraph Styles dialog box, is documented in Chapter 16.

Appendices

## FIGURE C.18

The Freelance Graphics Style Default Attributes Mixed dialog box, with its default settings

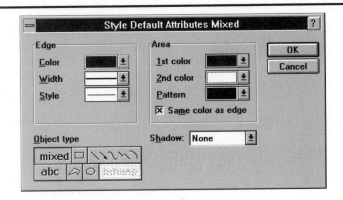

The Style Default Attributes Mixed dialog box, Style Default Attributes Rectangle dialog box, Style Default Attributes Line & Curve dialog box, Style Default Attributes Polygon & Shape dialog box, and Style Default Attributes Circle/Ellipse dialog box share many of the same options. These are the options in these dialog boxes:

**Color**    Click on this drop-down list box to display a palette from which you can choose a color for the border of an object. If some drawing tools have different Edge and Border colors, the sample in the box is split between white and gray.

**Width**    Click on this drop-down list box to display eight line widths from which you can choose.

**Style**    Click on this drop-down list box to display six line styles (including None) from which you can choose.

**Object Type**    Click on a button in this group to display a style attributes dialog box for mixed, rectangle, line and curve, default paragraph styles, polygon & shape, or circle/ellipse. You can also select a bitmap and display the Style Attributes Bitmap dialog box.

**1st Color**    Click on this drop-down list box to display a palette from which you can choose a foreground color for an object. If some drawing tools have different Edge and Border colors, the sample in the box is split between white and gray.

**2nd Color**    Click on this drop-down list box to display a palette from which you can choose a secondary color for an object. If some drawing tools have different Edge and Border colors, the sample in the box is split between white and gray.

**Pattern**    Click on this drop-down list box to display patterns from which you can select for the object.

**Same Color as Edge**    Check this check box to match the 1st Color with the edge color.

**Shadow**    Click on this drop-down list box to apply a shadow to the selected object. Your choices are None, Bottom Right, Bottom Left, Top Right, and Top Left.

**Rectangle Rounding**    Click on this drop-down list box in the Style Default Attributes Rectangle dialog box to select the amount of rounding for the corners of a rectangle. You can choose from None, Low, Med, and High.

**Marker**    Click on this drop-down list box in the Style Default Attributed Line & Curve dialog box to select a marker for the points on a line, arrow, curve, polyline, or arc. You can select from 11 marker types and None (no marker).

## Changing Style Attributes for Bitmaps

When a bitmap is the selected object and you choose Style ➤ Attributes, Freelance Graphics displays the Style Attributes Bitmap dialog box (Figure C.19).

These are the options in this dialog box:

**Contrast**    Move the scroll box along this scroll bar or type a value from −5 to 5 in the text box to adjust the *contrast*, the ratio of black to white, in a color or gray-scale bitmap.

**Brightness**    Move the scroll box along this scroll bar or type a value from −5 to 5 in the text box to adjust the brightness in a color or gray-scale bitmap.

**Appendices**

**FIGURE C.19**

The Freelance
Graphics Style
Attributes Bitmap
dialog box, with its
default settings

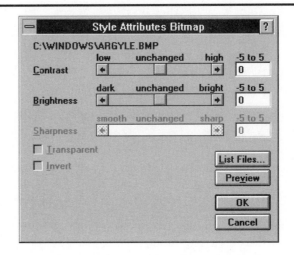

**Sharpness**    Move the scroll box along this scroll bar or type a value
from −5 to 5 in the text box to adjust the *sharpness*, the refinement of
the border and line display, in a gray-scale bitmap only.

**Transparent**    Check this check box to make all the colors in the
bitmap except black transparent so that objects underneath show.

**Invert**    Check this check box to change the black to white and the
white to black in a monochrome bitmap.

**List Files**    Click on this button to open the List Files dialog box so
that you can find a missing .BMP, .GIF, .PCX, .TGA, or .TIF file.

**Preview**    Click and hold down the mouse button to see how the
bitmap looks with the changes that you have made.

## Changing User Setup

Choose Tools ➤ User Setup to open the User Setup dialog box (Figure C.20),
in which you can specify user defaults.

**FIGURE C.20**

The Freelance
Graphics User Setup
Defaults dialog box,
with its default settings

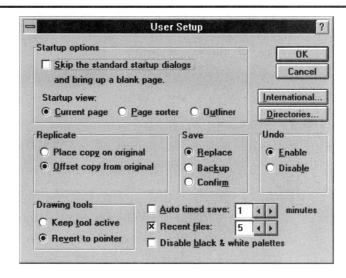

These are the options in this dialog box:

**S̲kip the Standard Startup Dialogs and Bring Up a Blank Page**
Check this check box to start Freelance Graphics without displaying the
opening dialog boxes. A cleared check box is the default.

**Startup View**     Click on an option button to open Freelance Graphics
in a particular view: C̲urrent Page (Full Page), P̲age Sorter, or Outliner.
Current Page is the default.

**Replicate**     Click on an option button to indicate the position of a
replicated object; click on Place Copy on Original to place the replicated
object exactly on top of the copied object, or click on O̲ffset Copy from
Original (the default) to place the replicated object so that you can see
both the replicated and copied objects.

**Save**     Click on an option button to indicate the way that you want to
save files. Click on R̲eplace (the default) to replace the prior version of
this file when you save. Click on Bac̲kup to save the current version and
save the prior version as a backup file in the c:\flw\backup subdirectory.
Click on Confir̲m to have Freelance Graphics prompt you to replace or
back up the file or to cancel the save process.

**Undo**    Click on the Enable (the default) or Disable option button to turn on or off Edit ➤ Undo.

**Drawing Tools**    Click on the Keep Tool Active option button to keep the drawing tool that you selected active, or click on the Revert to Pointer option button (the default) to activate the pointer tool.

**Auto Timed Save**    Check this check box and either type or select a value to have Freelance Graphics automatically save the current file every 1 to 99 minutes, with a default of 1 minute. The default is a cleared check box.

**Recent Files**    Type or select a value from 1 to 5 to set the number of recent files to be displayed at the bottom of the File menu. The default is 5. To open one of the files on the File menu, click on the file name or type the underlined number preceding the file name.

**Disable Black & White Palettes**    Check this check box to use the Microsoft Windows black and white options for printing on a black and white printer or other printing device. The default is a cleared check box, or the Freelance Graphics color options are used.

**International**    Click on this button to open a dialog box in which you can set date and time formats, define the characters used for decimal points, thousands separators, argument separators, and negative numbers, select the symbol and position of the currency character, and specify the code page.

**Directories**    Click on this button to display the User Setup Directories dialog box, which allows you to specify the directory in which Freelance Graphics stores your work; SmartMasters, palettes and symbols; and your backup files.

# Changing Your Organizer Environment

In Organizer, you can change the look of the "notebook"—the size of section tabs, the color of the notebook cover and inside tab pages—and you can select display preferences. You also can customize attributes for each Organizer section.

## Changing the Contents and Look of Your Organizer

Choose Section ➤ Customize to open the Customize dialog box (Figure C.15), in which you can define new sections, rename and delete existing sections, and include sections from other Organizer files.

These are the options in this dialog box:

**Binder**   Open the Color and Texture drop-down list boxes to select a color and texture, respectively, for the cover of the organizer.

**Size to Name**   Check this check box (the default) to adjust the size of tabs to the size of their names.

**FIGURE C.21**

The Customize dialog box, with its default settings

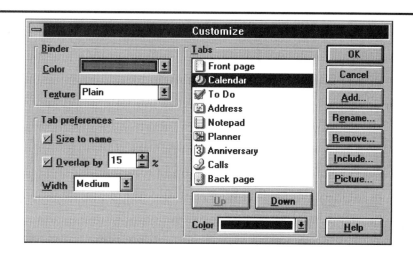

**Appendices**

**Overlap by *n*%**     Check this check box (the default) and type a value from 0 to 100 in the text box. The default is 15%.

**Width**     Open this drop-down list and select Narrow, Medium, or Wide to specify the width of the tabs. Medium is the default.

**Tabs**     Click on a tab name to perform an action on it.

- To move it above the previous tab on the list, click on Up. Up is in-active if the first section is selected.

- To move it below the next tab on the list, click on Down. Down is inactive if the last section is selected.

- To change its color, open the Color drop-down list box and make a selection.

- To add a new section, click on Add. For example, you can add a second Calendar section and use it as a diary.

- To rename a section, click on Rename, type a new name, and click on OK.

- To remove a section, click on Remove, and respond to the deletion prompt.

- To include a section from another organizer file in the organizer, click on Include.

- To insert a picture on a section tab page, click on Picture.

## Changing Organizer Preferences

Choose File ➤ Organizer Preferences and select a command from the sub-menu to change general Organizer preferences: Organizer Setup, Printer Setup (the standard Windows dialog box), Meeting Notices (if you're on a network), User Access (see "Setting a Password for an Organizer File" in Chapter 17), and Dialer (see "Getting Ready to Dial" in Chapter 18).

To open the Preferences dialog box (Figure C.16), in which you can change save and display options, choose File ➤ Organizer Preferences ➤ Organizer Setup.

FIGURE C.22

The Organizer Setup
dialog box

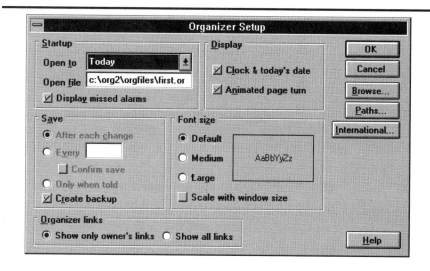

These are the options in this dialog box:

**Startup**    Select your opening file and page in this group. From the Open to drop-down list box, select a section or page to turn to when you start Organizer, and in the Open File text box, type the path and name of the Organizer file automatically opened.

**Save**    Click on an option button, and optionally a check box, to specify the way that Organizer saves your files. Click on the After Each Change option button to save after every editing change you make. Click on Every n and fill in the text box to automatically save the file every n minutes. If you check the Confirm Save check box, Organizer prompts you before an automatic save. Click on the Only When Told option button to save only when you want. Check the Create Backup check box to have Organizer save the previous saved version of the file as a backup whenever you save this version of the file.

**Organizer Links**    Check the Show Only Owner's Links option button to show just your links, or check the Show All Links option button to show both your links and those created by other users.

**Appendices**

**Display**     Check the Clock & Today's Date check box to display the time and date icons in the application window, and check the Animated Page Turn check box to animate the page turn.

**Font Size**     Select the size of the display font: Default (8 point), Medium (10 point), or Large (12 point). Check the Scale with Window Size check box to keep the text in height/width proportion. To see the effects of your selection, look at the sample.

## Changing Section Preferences

You can change preferences for each section by opening the View menu and choosing the bottom command from the menu (Calendar Preferences, To Do Preferences, Address Preferences, Notepad Preferences, Planner Preferences, Anniversary Preferences, or Calls Preferences).

In the resulting dialog box (for example, Figure C.17), select options that make Organizer easier to use.

**FIGURE C.23**

The Calendar
Preferences dialog box
with the default
settings

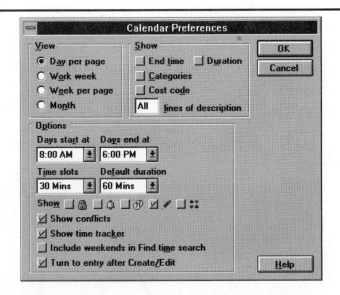

These are the options in the Calendar Preferences dialog box:

**View**    Click on an option button to select the way in which you view this section when you start Organizer. Your choices are Day per Page, Work Week, Week per Page, or Month.

**Options**    Select options or check or clear check boxes to select the look of a page. You can choose a starting and ending hour, time slots (from 5 to 60 minutes), the default duration (from 5 to 60 minutes) for an activity, and you can show icons representing activities, conflicting appointments, and the time tracker. You can include weekends in a search, and you can turn to an entry that you just created or edited.

**Show**    Select check boxes and fill in a text box to select the look of an entry. You can display the end time, duration, categories, and cost code for an entry. You can display all or some lines of a description.

These are the options in the To Do Preferences dialog box:

**View**    Click on an option button or select a date option to select the way in which you view this section when you start Organizer. Your choices are Priority, Status, Start Date, Category, or Due Date or Completion Date.

**Options**    Select options or check or clear check boxes to select the look of a page. You can choose a starting heading or priority code. You can show page tabs, icons representing the type of activity, and completed tasks. You can delete a task when it's completed, and you can turn to an entry that you just created or edited.

**Show**    Select check boxes and fill in a text box to select the look of an entry. You can display the start date, due date, completed date, categories, and cost code for an entry. You can display all or some lines of a description.

**Status Color**    Select from drop-down list boxes to change the color of a task by status: Overdue, Current, Future, and Completed.

**Appendices**

These are the options in the Address Preferences dialog box:

**View**    Click on an option button to select the way in which you view this section when you start Organizer. Your choices are <u>A</u>ll, A<u>d</u>dress, Co<u>n</u>tact, and Phon<u>e</u>.

**Options**    Select options or check or clear check boxes to select the look of a page. You can choose whether the Business, Home, or the Selected information is displayed, and you can select the location of the next heading on a page. You can show or hide address tabs, an index line, and an icon indicating that an address is locked. You can choose to turn to an entry that you just created or edited.

**Sort by**    Select an option button and fill in a text box to select the way in which the address book is sorted. You can sort by <u>L</u>ast Name, Company, <u>C</u>ategory, or a particular field.

These are the options in the Notepad Preferences dialog box:

**View**    Click on an option button to select the way in which you view this section when you start Organizer. Your choices are Pag<u>e</u> Number, <u>T</u>itle, <u>D</u>ate, and Category.

**Options**    Select options or check or clear check boxes to select the look of a page. You can choose how to start a chapter, how to display the table of contents, and how to number pages. You can show icons representing activities, and you can turn to an entry that you just created or edited.

**Show**    Select check boxes and fill in a text box to select the look of an entry. You can display the T<u>i</u>tle and <u>C</u>ategories.

These are the options in the Planner Preferences dialog box:

**View**    Click on an option button to select the way in which you view this section when you start Organizer. Your choices are <u>Q</u>uarter or <u>Y</u>ear.

**Options**    Select options or check or clear check boxes to select the look of a page. You can choose a starting and ending hour. You can show or hide the key, automatically unfold the planner, and you can turn to an entry that you just created or edited.

These are the options in the Anniversary Preferences dialog box:

**View**    Click on an option button to select the way in which you view this section when you start Organizer. Your choices are <u>M</u>onth, <u>Y</u>ear, <u>Z</u>odiac, and <u>C</u>ategory.

**Options**    Select options or check or clear check boxes to select the look of a page. You can choose the way in which you start headings and whether to show page tabs. You can show icons representing activities, you can select page color, and you can turn to an entry that you just created or edited.

**Show**    Select check boxes and fill in a text box to select the look of an entry. You can display the date, categories, and cost code for an entry. You can display all or some lines of a description.

These are the options in the Calls Preferences dialog box:

**View**    Click on an option button to select the way in which you view this section when you start Organizer. Your choices are P<u>e</u>rson, Compan<u>y</u>, <u>D</u>ate, and C<u>a</u>tegory, or Status, Number, or Incomplete.

**Options**    Select options or check or clear check boxes to select the look of a page. You can choose the way in which you display the next heading and whether to show page tabs. You can show icons representing activities, and you can turn to an entry that you just created or edited.

**Show**    Select check boxes and fill in a text/list box to select the look of an entry. You can display the name, company, status, categories, number, date and time, and cost code for an entry. You can display all or some lines of a description.

**Appendices**

# Customizing SmartIcons

In every SmartSuite application, you can change the displayed SmartIcons. You can add or remove SmartIcons, change their location on the application window, and change their size. In fact, you can even create your own SmartIcons.

Choose Tools ➤ SmartIcons in 1-2-3 and Approach; or Tools ➤ SmartIcons in Ami Pro or Freelance Graphics; or File ➤ Organizer Preferences ➤ SmartIcons in Organizer to display a dialog box in which you can customize SmartIcons. Figure C.24 shows the 1-2-3 SmartIcons dialog box. All other SmartSuite SmartIcons dialog boxes look exactly the same; only the icons differ.

## Changing SmartIcon Sets

Add SmartIcons to an existing set by selecting the set from the drop-down list box at the top center of the dialog box. Then drag an icon from the Available Icons scroll box to the scroll list in the center of the dialog box.

**FIGURE C.24**

The 1-2-3 SmartIcons dialog box, in which you can edit SmartIcons and sets

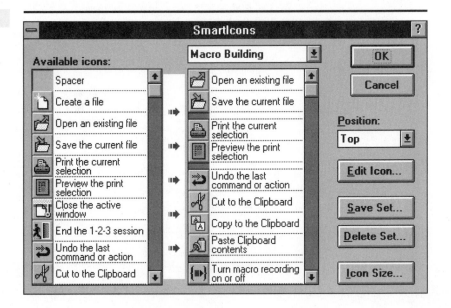

**TIP** **You can space icons by dragging a Spacer. (A Spacer looks like a plain gray button, but when you drag it to the toolbar, it puts a space between buttons. This allows you to separate unrelated buttons.)**

To remove a SmartIcon from the set, drag it off the set. (You don't need to drag it back to its original position in the Available Icons scroll box.)

To save a SmartIcons set, click on the Save Set button. In the Save Set of SmartIcons dialog box, name the set and its file name, and click on OK.

To delete a SmartIcons set, click on the Delete Set button. In the Delete Sets dialog box, select the set to be deleted, and click on OK. The SmartIcons set is deleted without any prompts or warnings.

## Changing the Size of SmartIcons

Click on the Icon Size button to select the icon size. Selecting Large provides the advantage of a display that is easier to see, but there is only room for approximately 16 SmartIcons. Selecting Medium, the default, enables the display of 26 or 27 SmartIcons. The number of SmartIcons actually displayed in the application window depends on the size of the window itself. (There is no "Small" option.)

## Changing the Position of SmartIcons

Use the Position drop-down list box to specify the location of the current SmartIcons set. You can select these positions:

- Top (the default) displays the SmartIcons set above the work area and below the menu bar.
- Left displays the SmartIcons set at the left side of the application window.
- Right displays the SmartIcons set at the right side of the application window.

**Appendices**

■ Bottom displays the SmartIcons set just above the status bar.

■ Floating displays the SmartIcons set in a sizable, moveable window, which you can move to any location in the application window—even on top of other elements, such as the menu bar or status bar.

## Creating SmartIcons

To edit or create a new SmartIcon, click on the Edit Icon button. The Edit Icon dialog box (Figure C.25) appears.

To create a new icon starting with a blank icon, click on New Icon. Give the icon a file name and click on OK. You don't have to worry about typing an extension; .BMP is added for you. Type the macro and a description, and start editing. Click on the downward-pointing button to the right of the color buttons under the icon to open a color palette from which you can choose.

When you select a color, you can click with the left or right mouse button. This means that you can select two colors at a time. To apply the colors onto the blank button, click with either the left or right mouse button to apply one

**FIGURE C.25**

The Edit Icon dialog box

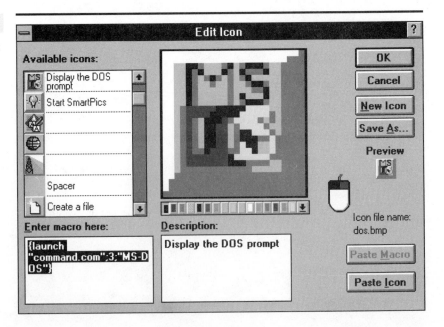

of the two colors. As you work, look at the SmartIcon in the Preview box. When you have completed the button, click on OK.

To create a SmartIcon using a bitmap, copy the bitmap into the Windows Clipboard. Then in the Edit Icon dialog box, click on Paste Icon. You can edit the SmartIcon using the color palette. When you have completed the button, click on OK.

## Editing SmartIcons

Editing a SmartIcon is very similar to creating a SmartIcon. Standard icons are protected from editing, but you can make a copy by giving it a new file name when prompted. To edit, click on a SmartIcon and click on Edit Icon. If prompted, give the icon a name and then you can edit a copy. When you have completed your editing, click on OK.

For more information about customizing SmartIcons, see one of the Smart-Suite *User's Guides* or the SmartIcons Reference in the Help facility.

**Appendices**

# D

*SmartSuite*
*Shortcut Keys and*
*Key Combinations*

P ressing a shortcut key or key combination is the fastest way to perform an action or issue a command. Table D.1 lists the most common shortcut keys and key combinations for SmartSuite applications.

**TABLE D.1:** SmartSuite Shortcut Keys and Key Combinations

| SHORTCUT KEY OR KEY COMBINATION/ APPLICATION(S) | DESCRIPTION |
|---|---|
| ↓ (all applications) | Moves down one row or line while editing |
| ← (all applications) | Moves left one column or character while editing; moves up to the previous item in a group |
| → (all applications) | Moves right one column or character while editing; moves down to the next item in a group |
| ↑ (all applications) | Moves up one row or line while editing; moves up to the previous item in a group |
| Alt+Backspace (1-2-3, Ami Pro, Organizer) | Reverses the last 1-2-3 or Ami Pro action, if supported; reverses the last deletion from the Organizer trash basket |
| Alt+F1 (1-2-3, Freelance Graphics) | Embeds a non-keyboard character at the current cursor location |
| Backspace (1-2-3, Ami Pro) | Deletes the character to the left of the current cursor location |
| Ctrl+← (1-2-3, Ami Pro, Approach, Organizer) | Moves to the left |
| Ctrl+→ (1-2-3, Ami Pro, Approach, Organizer) | Moves to the right |

| SHORTCUT KEY OR KEY COMBINATION/ APPLICATION(S) | DESCRIPTION |
| --- | --- |
| Ctrl+B *(1-2-3, Ami Pro, Freelance Graphics)* | Applies or removes boldface from selected characters |
| Ctrl+E *(1-2-3, Ami Pro, Freelance Graphics)* | Centers data within a cell or between the left and right margins |
| Ctrl+E *(Approach)* | Opens the InfoBox |
| Ctrl+End *(AmiPro, Approach, Freelance Graphics, Organizer)* | Moves to the end of the Ami Pro document; moves to the last Approach record; moves to the end of the outline or block of text in Freelance Graphics; goes to the last page of the notebook or the end of the block of text in Organizer |
| Ctrl+Home *(all applications)* | Moves to the first cell in the first spreadsheet in the 1-2-3 file; moves to the beginning of the Ami Pro document; moves to the first Approach record; moves to the beginning of the outline or block of text in Freelance Graphics; goes to the first page of the Notebook or the beginning of the block of text in other sections in Organizer |
| Ctrl+I *(1-2-3, Ami Pro, Freelance Graphics)* | Applies or removes italics from selected characters |
| Ctrl+L *(1-2-3, Ami Pro, Freelance Graphics)* | Aligns data with the left margin of a cell, document, or presentation page |
| Ctrl+L *(Approach)* | Shows drawing tools |
| Ctrl+N *(1-2-3, Ami Pro, Freelance Graphics)* | Removes character formatting from selected characters |
| Ctrl+O *(1-2-3, Ami Pro, Approach, Organizer)* | Opens an existing file |
| Ctrl+P *(all applications)* | Opens the Print dialog box so that you can print all or part of the current file |
| Ctrl+R *(1-2-3, Ami Pro, Freelance Graphics)* | Aligns data with the right margin of a cell, document, or presentation page |
| Ctrl+S *(all applications)* | Saves the current file or view file in Approach |

**Appendices**

TABLE D.1: SmartSuite Shortcut Keys and Key Combinations (continued)

| SHORTCUT KEY OR KEY COMBINATION/ APPLICATION(S) | DESCRIPTION |
| --- | --- |
| Ctrl+U *(1-2-3, Ami Pro)* | Underlines or removes the underline from selected characters |
| End *(all applications)* | Moves to the end of the entry or line in 1-2-3, Ami Pro, Approach, and Freelance Graphics; moves to the last page in the current Organizer section |
| F1 *(all applications)* | Opens a help window that may be related to the active object |
| Home *(all applications)* | Moves to the beginning of the entry or line in 1-2-3, Ami Pro, Approach, Freelance Graphics, or the Organizer Address section; moves to the first page in the current Organizer section (except for Address); goes to today's date in a pop-up calendar in an Organizer dialog box |
| PgDn *(all applications)* | Moves down the number of rows currently shown in the 1-2-3 window; moves down one screen in Ami Pro or in Outliner view in Freelance Graphics; moves to the next Approach record; moves to the next page in Current Page or Page Sorter view in Freelance Graphics; moves to the next Organizer page or month |
| PgUp *(all applications)* | Moves up the number of rows currently shown in the 1-2-3 window; moves up one screen in Ami Pro or in Outliner view in Freelance Graphics; moves to the previous Approach record; moves to the previous page in Current Page or Page Sorter view in Freelance Graphics; moves to the previous Organizer page or month |
| Shift *(Ami Pro, Approach, Freelance Graphics)* | In conjunction with other navigation keys, selects from the current cursor position to the new cursor location |
| Shift+Tab *(1-2-3, Ami Pro, Approach, Freelance Graphics)* | Moves to the previous option, from right to left and from bottom to top order; moves to the left the number of columns shown in the window |
| Tab *(1-2-3, Ami Pro, Approach, Freelance Graphics)* | Moves to the next option, from left to right and from top to bottom; moves to the right the number of columns shown in the window |

# Index

**Index**

Index

**Index**

**Index**

Index

## N

**Name dialog box**
for Lotus 1-2-3 charts, 253, *253*
for Lotus 1-2-3 named ranges, 165–
168, *167*
**named ranges in Lotus 1-2-3, 165–
170.** *See also* cells
defining, 165
deleting, 168
inserting in formulas, 169–170, *169,
170*
moving, 190
naming, 165–168, *167*
**Named Settings options,** Lotus 1-2-3
Page Setup dialog box, 214, *215*
**Named Style dialog box,** Lotus 1-2-3,
191, 192–193, *192*
**naming**
charts, 252–253, *253*
files, **64**
pages in multiple-spreadsheet files,
206
ranges of cells in Lotus 1-2-3, 165–
169, *167*
styles in Lotus 1-2-3, 192
**navigating**
Lotus 1-2-3 spreadsheets, 117,
130–131
in Organizer, 608, 609
work area
with keyboard, 55–56
with mouse, 53–55, *54*
Worksheet window in Lotus 1-2-3,
117
**navigator list,** in Lotus 1-2-3, 169, *169*
**Navy .DIF files,** 267
**networks,** Organizer on, 629
**New Chart Gallery dialog box,** Freelance Graphics, 545–547, *545*
**New dialog box**
Ami Pro, 281–282, *281*
Approach, 418–419, *418*
**New Filter dialog box,** Organizer,
645, *645*
**New Page dialog box,** Freelance
Graphics, 520, *521*

**New Record SmartIcon,** Approach,
440, 443
**newsletter style sheets,** in Ami Pro,
330–332, *332*
**non-printing characters in Ami Pro**
displaying and hiding, **312**, *313, 314*
finding and replacing, 348, 349
**normal text style,** 97–98
**#NOT# operator,** in Lotus 1-2-3 formulas, 158–159
**not equal to (<>)**
in Approach searches, 456
in Lotus 1-2-3 formulas, 158
**Notepad section of Organizer, 646–
650.** *See also* Organizer
adding pages and entries, **647–649,**
648
aligning text, 649
assigning page attributes, 649
categorizing pages, 619–620, 649
creating confidential pages, 649
customizing, **722**
deleting pages, **650**
editing pages, **649**
importing files, 647, 648, 649
Notepad display formats, **647–648**
numbering pages, 649
overview of, 605, *605,* 646
**@NOW function in Lotus 1-2-3,**
172–173
**.NS4 files,** 112, 113
**Number of Copies option,** Ami Pro
Print dialog box, 349
**Number Format dialog box.** *See also*
Lotus 1-2-3
changing data formats, 137–138, *137*
hiding data, 200–201, *200,* 441
overview of, 191
**number sign (#),** in Lotus 1-2-3 headers and footers, 213
**numbering pages**
in Ami Pro, 335, 339–340, *339, 340*
in Notepad section of Organizer, 649
**numeric fields.** *See also* Approach
data entry in, 450
defining, 419–420
finding, 461

formatting, 424–426
overview of, 414, 415
**numeric formulas,** in Lotus 1-2-3,
**157–158**

## O

**Object Linking and Embedding
(OLE).** *See also* Dynamic Data
Exchange
embedding
data and time in Organizer,
608–609
editing embedded objects, 26
movies, 20
objects, 25–26
linking
Ami Pro with Freelance Graphics, 29, 288–289, *288, 289*
objects, 23–24
overview of, 22
PicturePlus fields
data entry in, 451–452
overview of, 414, 416
**objects, 358.** *See also* graphic objects
**ODBC files,** 401
**Office Writer files,** 267
**Open File dialog box**
Freelance Graphics, 587, *588*
overview of, 41, *42*
**opening**
Approach InfoBox, 421
Clipboard Viewer, 90
files, 41–42, *42*
InfoBox, 421, 449
Organizer files, 605–607
from previous versions, 607
Organizer sections, 607–608
presentations in Freelance Graphics, 524
**operators**
in Lotus 1-2-3, 157–159, *160*
for searches in Approach, 456–458
**optimizing,** screen shows, 573
**options.** *See* commands
**Options dialog box,** Spell Check, 58–
59, *59*

**Index**

# Instant answers to your 1-2-3 questions.

Get instant answers about 1-2-3's new SmartIcon features, enhanced DOS compatibility, one-step charting, new report templates, full integration with SmartSuite and much more.  A must-have book!

*Now available wherever computer books are sold.*

280 pages.
ISBN 1583-7

**SYBEX**

**Shortcuts to Understanding.**

SYBEX, Inc.
2021 Challenger Drive
Alameda, CA 94501
1-800-227-2346
1-510-523-8233

# Clear, concise, readable, friendly.

Let Lotus Books take you through all the basic and advanced features of the world's most widely used e-mail system. Learn how to create and send messages, streamline your work, and even customize your mailbox. Covers cc:MAIL, cc:MAIL Mobile and upgrading from cc:MAIL Remote.

*Now available wherever computer books are sold.*

278 pages.
ISBN 1553-5

**SYBEX**

**Shortcuts to Understanding.**

SYBEX, Inc.
2021 Challenger Drive
Alameda, CA 94501
1-800-227-2346
1-510-523-8233

# GET A FREE CATALOG JUST FOR EXPRESSING YOUR OPINION.

Help us improve our books and get a *FREE* full-color catalog in the bargain. Please complete this form, pull out this page and send it in today. The address is on the reverse side.

Name _____     Company _____

Address _____     City _____ State ____ Zip _____

Phone ( ) _____

1. **How would you rate the overall quality of this book?**

   ❑ Excellent
   ❑ Very Good
   ❑ Good
   ❑ Fair
   ❑ Below Average
   ❑ Poor

2. **What were the things you liked most about the book? (Check all that apply)**

   ❑ Pace
   ❑ Format
   ❑ Writing Style
   ❑ Examples
   ❑ Table of Contents
   ❑ Index
   ❑ Price
   ❑ Illustrations
   ❑ Type Style
   ❑ Cover
   ❑ Depth of Coverage
   ❑ Fast Track Notes

3. **What were the things you liked *least* about the book? (Check all that apply)**

   ❑ Pace
   ❑ Format
   ❑ Writing Style
   ❑ Examples
   ❑ Table of Contents
   ❑ Index
   ❑ Price
   ❑ Illustrations
   ❑ Type Style
   ❑ Cover
   ❑ Depth of Coverage
   ❑ Fast Track Notes

4. **Where did you buy this book?**

   ❑ Bookstore chain
   ❑ Small independent bookstore
   ❑ Computer store
   ❑ Wholesale club
   ❑ College bookstore
   ❑ Technical bookstore
   ❑ Other _____

5. **How did you decide to buy this particular book?**

   ❑ Recommended by friend
   ❑ Recommended by store personnel
   ❑ Author's reputation
   ❑ Sybex's reputation
   ❑ Read book review in _____
   ❑ Other _____

6. **How did you pay for this book?**

   ❑ Used own funds
   ❑ Reimbursed by company
   ❑ Received book as a gift

7. **What is your level of experience with the subject covered in this book?**

   ❑ Beginner
   ❑ Intermediate
   ❑ Advanced

8. **How long have you been using a computer?**

   years _____
   months _____

9. **Where do you most often use your computer?**

   ❑ Home
   ❑ Work

   ❑ Both
   ❑ Other _____

10. **What kind of computer equipment do you have? (Check all that apply)**

    ❑ PC Compatible Desktop Computer
    ❑ PC Compatible Laptop Computer
    ❑ Apple/Mac Computer
    ❑ Apple/Mac Laptop Computer
    ❑ CD ROM
    ❑ Fax Modem
    ❑ Data Modem
    ❑ Scanner
    ❑ Sound Card
    ❑ Other _____

11. **What other kinds of software packages do you ordinarily use?**

    ❑ Accounting
    ❑ Databases
    ❑ Networks
    ❑ Apple/Mac
    ❑ Desktop Publishing
    ❑ Spreadsheets
    ❑ CAD
    ❑ Games
    ❑ Word Processing
    ❑ Communications
    ❑ Money Management
    ❑ Other _____

12. **What operating systems do you ordinarily use?**

    ❑ DOS
    ❑ OS/2
    ❑ Windows
    ❑ Apple/Mac
    ❑ Windows NT
    ❑ Other _____

**13.** On what computer-related subject(s) would you like to see more books?

_____

_____

_____

_____

**14.** Do you have any other comments about this book? (Please feel free to use a separate piece of paper if you need more room)

_____

_____

_____

_____

PLEASE FOLD, SEAL, AND MAIL TO SYBEX

**SYBEX INC.**
Department M
2021 Challenger Drive
Alameda, CA
94501